PC SIMULATION SOFTWARE

SIM PILOT'S GUIDE

737
-300

IXEG
VERSION FOR
X-PLANE

PUT TOGETHER BY
MIKE RAY
CAPTAIN UAL

This is an empty page that has been
inserted for production reasons.

This page is

LEFT BLANK !
... on purpose

This is an empty page that has been
inserted for production reasons.

This page is

LEFT BLANK !
... on purpose

*This is an empty page that has been
inserted for production reasons.*

This page is

LEFT BLANK !
... on purpose

PILOT HANDBOOK

SIMULATOR
AND
CHECKRIDE

PROCEDURES

PUT TOGETHER BY

MIKE RAY
CAPTAIN UAL

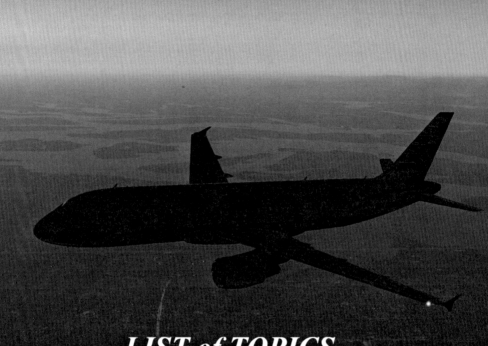

LIST of TOPICS
Alphabetically listed

High Flight

Oh! I have slipped the surly bonds of earth
And danced the skies on laughter-silvered wings;
Sunward I've climbed, and joined the tumbling mirth
Of sun-split clouds - and done a hundred things
You have not dreamed of - wheeled and soared and swung
High in the sunlit silence. Hov'ring there
I've chased the shouting wind along, and flung
My eager craft through footless halls of air.
Up, up the long delirious, burning blue,
I've topped the windswept heights with easy grace
Where never lark, or even eagle flew -
And, while with silent lifting mind I've trod
The high untresspassed sanctity of space,
Put out my hand and touched the face of God.

Pilot Officer Gillespie Magee
No 412 squadron, RCAF
Killed 11 December 1941

PILOT'S PRAYER

"Please God, don't let me screw up!"

Unnamed astronaut

ACKNOWLEDGEMENTS

...and "THANK YOU".

Initially, it was **Dr. Jack Rubino**, the head of Human Resources at the United Airlines Training Center in Denver, Colorado that contacted me and asked if I would be interested in doing an Airbus project. I had not thought about it before, but Jack's argument was compelling and certainly appealed to my ego (remember that I am a pilot).

Dr. Rubino told me that he had met the Vice President of Training at Airbus at a social event and they had discussed briefly the development of a flight manual for pilots that would be "different". After having seen the book, "747-400 Pilot Handbook", they both agreed that it represented a really good model for developing a document that provided a unique and useful format for introducing a pilot to a new airplane.

So, here is a that "different kind of manual" ... written specifically for pilots. It represents my idea about what a basic pilot handbook should look like. Maybe it could have been more or bigger, but fundamentally it is everything that it ever will be. Possibly light on deep technical detail, the book is designed to be about how to actually operate the airplane from the front seat.

Once I thought it was complete, I went over it again and again and again until I was ready to puke; then I turned that "rough" manuscript over to my proofreader, **Chief Ron Davis** (retired from the San Diego Fire Department) and who (unfortunately) doesn't know beans about either aviation or the Airbus. He gamely provided a third party (non-pilot) perspective and attempted to clear up some of the goobers and hickeys that subtly creep into any document; however, he eventually gave up because he simply couldn't understand the vernacular.

My printer, **Dave Marlow** from Whitmar Electronic Press in San Diego has worked with me in developing some of the unique features of the document. His advice and direction where the printing side is concerned has been greatly appreciated.

Fortuitously, a terrific reviewer, **Guy Reinhardt**, appeared unexpectedly and read the book. Surprisingly he found literally scores of additional typos and grammatical mistakes. Guy's ability to sift through the complex verbiage is amazing ... and all his suggested fixes were then included in the existing version.

But then, in a heroic demonstration of reckless abandon, another fearless reviewer and professional aviation expert, **Martin Papanek**, appeared and suggested that he could take this document to even higher levels of accuracy. Martin is an experienced Airbus instructor and it was truly amazing for me to see just how much more minutiae and detail there was left to discover and repair. Wheew! I owe a great deal of gratitude and unlimited appreciation to all my proofreaders. Thank you, Martin, for your patience and perseverance.

DISCLAIMERS

... disclaiming stuff about the book.

This IS NOT a book by Airbus Company.

This manual, book, or guide is an __UNOFFICIAL__ document which has absolutely nothing to do with **AIRBUS COMPANY**. I want it clearly understood that those guys neither approve or endorse this checkride manual.

"Airbus Company", "Airbus", Airbus A320" are registered trademarks of Airbus.

In the title of this book and in the text, where I have made mention of the words "Airbus" or "Airbus A320" or any similar term or terms, it is in no way intended to be an infringement of the trademark privileges of Airbus. There is NO subtle intent to imply that any of the brand identity should transfer to this manual. Any references are specifically and only for the sole purpose of identifying the subject of our discussion.

This "Unofficial Airbus A320 Manual" shall in no way be a substitute or represent the official appropriate manuals or data.

Any moron who thinks that they can simply take the material in this manual and use it in place of the official documents is confused. This stuff is **NOT** presented as a replacement or substitute for the "real" stuff; nor is it implied that it is some kind of useful summary or simplified interpretation of all those vast piles of official real documents and libraries filled with reams of almost totally indecipherable verbiage. No sir, not a bit of it.

This document and the material in it is intended for use during the checkride and NOT (under any circumstances) to be used as a source for actually flying the airplane.

There is simply **NO IMPLIED CARRY OVER** value from this material to the real airplane. I am presenting what I believe to be true, while relying only on hearsay, innuendo, and reference to the huge mountain of official training and reference materials that even I could hardly understand. I am passing it on to you as my interpretation only. I am not now and never have had a job as a certified pilot instructor. I am a just another ordinary real life airline pilot that spent over 30 years flying for a major US air carrier and just loves talking about airplanes.

INTRODUCTION

Come fly with me ... let your mind and imagination soar through the heavens as we meet and become acquainted with our beautiful new sweetheart. She is as lovely and responsive as her beauty suggests, and I know you will come to appreciate and enjoy her subtle yet demanding personality. Ever a challenge ... she will provide many hours of pure enjoyment and satisfaction as you get to know her intimately.

For the next few moments of your life, you are going to be treated to an immersion into the world of the Airbus A320. Few people on earth will know as much about this marvelous piece of aviation engineering as you hopefully will. But the experience is much, much more than a simple teaching-learning experience ... it is an all encompassing experience. You will dream about her and she will occupy most of your waking moments as you ponder her intricate details and minute characteristics. She is so complex, that a lifetime spent with her is not enough to know everything about her ... She is ALWAYS full of surprises and just when you think you know her, she will do something that is totally unexpected.

So come on and join me as we become intimately acquainted with what is arguably one of the most beautiful and functional pieces of technology ever conceived by mankind.

Abbreviations

a SHORT LIST of a few of the bewildering and strange Airbus TERMS

ACARS .... ARINC Communications and Reporting System
ACP .... Audio Control Panel
ACGW .... Aircraft Gross Weight
ADI .... Attitude Director Indicator
ADIRS .... Air Data Inertial Reference System
ADIRU .... Air Data Inertial Reference Unit
ADM .... Air Data Module
ADMIN .... Administration
ADR .... Air Data Reference
AEVC .... Avionics Equipment Ventilation Computer
AFE .... Above Field Elevation
AFDS .... Autopilot Flight Director System
AGL .... Above Ground Level
AH .... Alert Height (only on CAT III)
AIM .... Aeronautical Information Manual
AIDS .... Aircraft Integrated Data System
AIU .... Audio Interface Unit
ALL WX .... All Weather
AMU .... Audio Management Unit
ANU .... Aircraft Nose Up
AOA .... Angle of Attack (alpha)
AP .... Auto Pilot
APPU .... Asymmetry Position Pick-off Unit
APU .... Auxiliary Power Unit
ARINC .... Aeronautical Radio, Inc.
A/THR .... Auto Thrust
ATIS .... Automatic Terminal Information Service
ATOG .... Allowable Takeoff Gross Weight
ATSU .... Air Traffic Services Unit
ATT .... Attitude
ATTND .... Attendant
AVAIL .... Available
BARO .... Barometric
BCL .... Battery Charge Limiter
BCDS .... BITE Centralized Data System
BFO .... Beat Frequency Oscillator
BITE .... Built-in Test Equipment
BLD .... Bleed
BMC .... Bleed monitoring Computer
BRK .... Brake
BSCU .... Brake and Steering Control Unit
BTC .... Bus Tie Contactor
C .... Captain, Celsius, Center, course
CA .... Cabin Altitude
CAB .... Cabin
CAM .... Cabin Attendant Module
CANC .... Cancel
CAP .... Capture, Captain
CAT .... Category, Clear Air Turbulence
CAUT .... Caution
CAVOK .... Ceiling and Visibility OK
CAVU .... Ceiling and Visibility Unrestricted
CB .... Circuit, Cumulo-nimbus
CBMS .... Circuit Breaker Monitoring System
CDAP .... Constant Descent Approach Procedure
CDL .... Configuration Deviation List
CDLS .... Cockpit Door Locking System
CDU .... Control Display Unit
CF .... Centerline fix
CFDIU .... Centralized Fault Data Interface Unit
CFDS .... Centralized Fault Display System
CFIT .... Controlled Flight Into Terrain
C/L/R .... Command/Leadership/Resource management
CG .... Center of Gravity
CH .... Channel, change
CHR, CHRONO .... Chronometer
CI .... Cost index
CIDS .... Cabin Inter-communication Data System
CKPT .... Cockpit
CLNC .... Clearance or Clearance Delivery
CLR .... Clear, Clearance
CLR .... Command Leadership Resource
CONF, CONFIG .... Configuration
CPA .... Closest Point of Approach
CPCU .... Cabin Pressure Controller Unit
CQP .... AQP version of an annual checkride
CRC .... Continuous Repetitive Chime
CRS .... Course
CRM .... Crew Resource Management
CRT .... Cathode Ray Tube
CSCU .... Cargo Smoke Control Unit
CSD .... Constant Speed Drive
CSM/G .... Constant Speed Motor/Generator
CSTR .... Constraint
CTR .... Center
CVFP .... Charted Visual Flight Procedures
CVR .... Cockpit Voice recorder
CZC .... Cabin Zone Controller
DA .... Decision Altitude or Drift Angle
DC .... Direct Current
DDRMI .... Digital Distance Radio Magnetic Indicator
DEACT .... Deactivated
DECEL .... Decelerate
DEF/AB .... Definitions/abbreviations
DEP ARR .... Departure Arrival
DES .... Descend, Descent
DEST .... Destination
DFDR .... Deferred
DFDR .... Digital Flight Data Recorder
DFIDU .... Dual Function Interactive Display Unit
DH .... Decision Height
DIFF .... Differential
DIL .... Deferred and Inbound Log (maint)
DISCH .... Discharge
DMC .... Digital Management Computer
DME .... Distance Measuring Equipment
DMU .... Data Management Unit

DPWM .... Display Planned Weight Manifest
DRM .... Dispatch Release Message
DSPCH .... Dispatch
DTMF .... Dual Tone Multi-Frequency
DVRSN .... Diversion
DVRT .... Divert
EAI .... Engine Anti Ice
EAT .... Expected Approach Time
ECAM .... Electronic Centralized Aircraft Monitoring
ECB .... Electronic Control Box (APU)
ECON .... Economy
ECP .... ECAM Control Panel
EDP .... Engine Driven Pump
EEC .... Electronic Engine Control
EFC .... Expect Further Clearance
EFCS .... Electronic Flight Control System
EFIS .... Electronic Flight Instrument System
EGPWS .... Enhanced Ground Proximity Warning System
EGT .... Exhaust Gas Temperature
EIS .... Electronic Instrument System
EIU .... Engine Interface Unit
ELAC .... Elevator Aileron Computer
ELEV .... Elevator
E/O, EO .... Engine Out
EOSID .... Engine Out SID
EPR .... Engine Pressure Ratio
EPR/ATOG .... Performance Data Sheet
ETA .... Estimated Time of Arrival
EVMU .... Engine Vibration Monitoring Unit
E/WD .... Engine/Warning Display
EXPED .... Expedite
EVAC .... Evacuate
F .... Flaps, Degrees Fahrenheit
FAC .... Flight Augmentation Computer
FADEC .... Full Authority Digital Engine Control
FAF .... Final Approach Fix
FAP .... Final Approach Point
FAS .... Final Approach Segment
FBS .... Fixed Base Simulator
FCDC .... Flight Control Data Concentrator
FCOM .... Flight Crew Operating Manual
FCU .... Flight Control Unit
FD .... Flight Director
FDIU .... Flight Data Interface Unit
FDU .... Fire Detection Unit
FF .... Fuel Flow
FFS .... Full Flight Simulator
FIDS .... Fault Isolation and Detection System
FL .... Flight Level
FLX/MCT .... Flex/Maximum Continuous Thrust
FMA .... Flight Mode Annunciator
FMCS .... Flight Management Computer System
FMGC .... Flight Management Guidance Computer
FMGS .... Flight Management Guidance System
FMS .... Flight Management System
FMU .... Fuel Metering Unit
FMV .... Fuel Metering Valve
FOB .... Fuel On Board
FOM .... Flight Operations Manual
FOQA .... Flight Operations Quality Assurance
FPA .... Flight Path Angle
FPD .... Flight Path Director
FPF .... Flight Plan Forecast
FPL .... Fleet Planned Landing
F-PLAN .... Flight Plan
FPPU .... Feedback Position Pick-off Unit
FPV .... Flight Path Vector
FQI .... Fuel Quantity Indicator
FRM .... Fault Reporting Manual
FRV .... Fuel Return Valve
FTI .... Flight Technical Specialist
FWC .... Flight Warning Computer
FWS .... Flight Warning System
GA .... Go-Around
GCU .... Generator Control UNit
GPS .... Global Positioning System
GPWS .... Ground Proximity Warning System
GS, G/S .... Glide Slope or Ground Speed
HCU .... Hydraulic Control Unit
HDG .... Heading
HF .... High Frequency
Hg .... Mercury
HP .... High Pressure
hPa .... Hectopascals
HSI .... Horizontal Situation Indicator
HYD .... Hydraulic
IAF .... Initial Approach Fix
IAP .... Instrument Approach Procedure
ICAO .... International Civil Aviation Organization
IDENT .... Identifier
IDG .... Integrated Drive Generator
IFR .... Instrument Flight Rules
IGN .... Ignition
IGVA .... Inlet Guide Vane Actuator
ILS .... Instrument Landing System
IM .... Inner Marker
IMC .... Instrument Meteorological Conditions
INIT .... Initialization
INBD .... Inboard
INOP .... Inoperative
IPC .... Intermediate Pressure Check Valve
IPPU .... Instrumentation Position Pick-off Unit
IRS .... Inertial Reference System

Screenshot from Wilco A320 Series car by Feelthere

ISA	International Standard Atmosphere
KIAS	Knots Indicated Airspeed
KTS	Knots
LAF	Load Alleviation Function
LCA	Line Check Airman
LCD	Liquid Crystal Display
LDA	Localizer-type Directional Aid
LE	Leading Edge
L/G	Landing Gear
LGCIU	Landing Gear Control Interface Unit
LGPIU	Landing Gear Position Indicator Unit
LNAV	Lateral Navigation
LP	Low Pressure
LLWAS	Low Level Wind-shear Alert System
LLZ	ILS Localizer (ICAO)
LM	Line Maintenance
LRC	Long Range Cruise
M	Mach
MAP	Missed Approach Point
MAX	Maximum
MCDU	Multifunction Control Display Unit
MCT	Maximum Continuous Thrust
MDA	Minimum Descent Altitude
MDA	(in MCDU) any minimum based on barometric altimeter.
MEA	Minimum Enroute Altitude
MEL	Minimum Equipment List
METAR	Aviation Routine Weather Report (ICAO)
M/F/L	Maintenance/Fuel/Loading
MIN	Minimum
MKR	Marker
MLH	Maintenance Log History
MLW	Maximum Landing Weight
MM	Middle Marker
MMO	Mmax MACH Operating Speed
MRD	Maintenance Release Document
MRM	Maintenance Reporting Manual
MSL	Mean Sea level
MID	Middle (RVR)
MMI	Manual Magnetic Indicator
MTOG	Maximum Allowable Takeoff gross Weight
MVA	Minimum Vectoring Altitude
MX	Maintenance
N	Engine or APU RPM (%)
NAM	Nautical Air Miles
ND	Navigation Display
NM	Nautical Miles
NOTAM	Notice To Airman
N/R	Not Required
NWS	Nosewheel Steering
OAT	Outside Air Temperature
OBS	Observer
OEW	Operational Empty Weight
OM	Outer Marker
OMC	Observer Member of Crew
OPP	Opposite
OPSPEC	FAA Operational Specifications
OPT	Optimum
OVBD	Overboard
OVHT	Overheat
OVRD	Override
PASS	Passenger
P/B	Pushbutton
PBD	Place/Bearing/Distance Waypoint
PBX	Place-Bearing/Place-Bearing
PC	Proficiency Check-ride
PCT	Percent
PCU	Power Control Unit
PDC	Predeparture Clearance
PF	Pilot Flying
PHC	Probe Heat Computer
PI	Pilot Instructor or Procedural index
PFD	Primary Flight Display
PIREP	Pilot Report
PNF	Pilot Not Flying
POS	Position
POSBD	Posted Bulletins
PPOS	Present Position (Dynamic)
PPU	Position Pick-up Unit
PRED	Predictive
PRM	Precision Runway Monitoring
PROC	Procedure
PROG	Progress
PROT	Protection
PROX	Proximity
PSI	Pounds per Square Inch
PTT	Push To Talk
PTU	Power Transfer Unit (Hydraulic)
PWS	Predictive Wind Shear
QNE	Standard Pressure (at altitude)
QNH	Standard Pressure (at Field Elevation)
RA	Resolution Advisory (TCAS)
RA	Radio Altimeter
RAT	Ram Air Turbine (Blue Hyd System)
RC	Required Controlling
RCA	Reach Cruise Altitude
RDI	Remote Dial-up Interface
RDU	Redispatch Unacceptable
REV	Reverse
RMI	Radio Magnetic Indicator
RMP	Radio Management Panel
RNAV	Area Navigation
RNP	Required Navigation Performance
RWY	Runway
RO	Rollout (RVR)
RSV	Reserve
RSVR	Reservoir

RTE	Route
RTO	Rejected Takeoff (Abort)
RVR	Runway Visual Range
RVSM	Reduced Vertical Separation Minimum
RWY	Runway
SAI	Standby Attitude Indicator
SAM	System Aircraft Maintenance
SAMC	SAM Controller
SAT	Static Air Temperature
SE	Single Engine
SC	Standards Captain, Single Chime
SD	System Display, Step Descent Point
SDAC	System Data Acquisition Concentrator
SDCU	Smoke Detection Control Unit
SEC	Spoiler Elevator Computer
SELCAL	Selective Calling
SFCC	Slat Flap Control Computer
SI	Static Inverter (DC-AC)
SID	Standard Instrument Departure
SL	Sea Level
SMGCS	Surface Movement Guidance and Control System
SI	Static Inverter
SOP	Standard Operating Procedure
SPLR	Spoiler
SRS	Speed Reference System
SSD	Single Segment Dispatch
STAR	Standard Terminal Arrival Route
STRG	Steering
STS	Status
TA	Traffic Advisory (TCAS)
TAS	True Airspeed
TAT	Total Air Temperature
T/C	Top of Climb
TCAS	Traffic Collision and Avoidance System
TD	Touchdown (RVR)
T/D	Top of Descent
TE	Trailing Edge
TEMP	Temperature
TERPS	Terminal Instrumental Procedure
TERR	Terrain
TFC	Traffic
TGT	Target
THR	Thrust
THS	Trimmable Horizontal Stabilizer
TKOFF	Takeoff
TLA	Thrust Lever Angle
TLA	Three letter acronym
TMPY	Temporary
TOGA	Take-Off/Go-Around (TO/GA)
TOG	Takeoff Gross
TOGW	Takeoff Gross Weight
T-P	Turning Point
TR	Transformer Rectifier (AC-DC)
TRK	Track
TROPO	Tropopause
TRU	Transformer Rectifier Unit or True heading
TW	Tailwind
V	Volts
VA	Design Maneuvering Speed
VAPP	Approach Speed
V/DEV	Vertical Deviation
VERT	Vertical
VFE	Flaps/Slats Extended Limit Speed
VFE NEXT	Max Speed for the Next Flap
VFR	Visual Flight Rules
VHF	Very High Frequency
VLE	Extended Gear Limit Speed
VLO	Operating Gear Limit Speed
VLS	Lowest Selectable Speed
VMC	Visual Meteorological Conditions
VMCA	Minimum Control Speed Ground
VMCA	Minimum Control Airspeed Air
VMO	Maximum Operating Speed
VIA	IAF (on MCDU)
VMAX	The lower of Vmo, Mmo, VLE, and VFE
VNAV	Vertical Navigation
VOR	VHF Omnidirectional Range
VOT	VOR Test
VR	Rotation Speed
VREF	Reference Speed
VS	Stall Speed
V/S	Vertical Speed
VSI	Vertical Speed Indicator
VSW	Stall Warning Speed
V1	Takeoff Decision Speed
V2	Takeoff Safety Speed
WAG	Wild Ass Guess
WAI	Wing Anti Ice
WARN	Warning
WHC	Window Heat Computer
WPT	Waypoint
WR	Weather Radar
W/S	Windshear
WSHLD	Windshield
WTB	Wing Tip Brakes
WX	Weather
WXR	Weather Radar
X-BLEED	Cross Bleed
X-FEED	Cross Feed
XFR	Transfer
XPDR	Transponder
XTK	Crosstrack
ZFW	Zero Fuel Weight
ZFWCG	Zero Fuel Weight Center of Gravity

WHAT KINDA BOOK IS THIS, ANYWAY ?

This rather imposing collection of information about the Airbus A320 is certainly NOT intended to be a substitute for that huge pile of official documents that you have already accumulated ... you know the materials I am referring to. That vast mountain of publications and printed handouts from the Company, the Federal Aviation Agency, the Air Traffic Control administrator, Airbus airplane company, your Mother-in-law, and whoever else who may have something to say. All those sources are way more important and authoritative than what I have put in this book ... but I thought that condensing some of that material into a smaller, more compact collection may help to understand all that other really important stuff.

So I wrote down as much of the information that I thought was interesting to pilots ... and I just said it in a little different way.

LIGHTEN UP. LET'S HAVE SOME FUN !

THIS BOOK IS WRITTEN FOR PILOTS.
...not specifically for lawyers, government officials, or management types ... just the pilot in them.

The sole purpose of this manual is to help prepare the pilot-student for a training and checkride experience.

Here are some of the concepts used in writing this book:
It is assumed that the reader is ALREADY an airline-type pilot or at least a seriously interested person. That allows the assumption of a certain level of competency and familiarization with the ATC system and general aviation knowledge on your part. Therefore, that will not be a specific part of this presentation.

It is also assumed that the reader has never seen an Airbus A320 series airplane before ... in fact, it is further assumed that the student has never flown an Airbus product of any kind before. Because of that, there may be a needless "over-simplification" of some of the details.

That leads me to make this point. The book will repeat a description or detail that I think fits into the flow of the text, even though we may have already covered that item earlier. I will also try and define the abbreviations and acronyms as they appear. I will try to tell you where the specific feature is located when we talk about it ... in short, the text is written so that an entry level pilot will be able to follow along without undue reference to "other" source materials.

published by UNIVERSITY of TEMECULA PRESS, Inc.

The really serious portion of the book ... you can skip this part.

HOW DO PILOTS LEARN STUFF?

In the beginning, a bunch of guys dressed in white lab coats and calling each other "Doctor" did some experiments. They took cats and mice and wired them to complicated instruments and recording devices and made them run mazes and do stuff like that. From the data they collected they developed a complex set of criteria regarding learning. Their conclusions went something like this.

> They found that there are two separate parts to learning.
> *Cognitive understanding and*
> *Psycho -Motor skill demonstration.*

The Cognitive part of learning is the ability to understand and conceptualize the nature of the required task, and
The Psycho-Motor Skill part is actually being able to accomplish the task.

Airline Pilots could have saved them a lot of time and effort because they have known this all along. When they go for their training and check-rides at the Training Center for their airline, they continually experience the two separate parts to the evaluation:

> **ORAL EXAM** (which is the Cognitive part), and
> **SIM RIDE** (which is the PsychoMotor Skills demonstration).

THERE ARE 2 SEPARATE LEARNING DOMAINS

This Study and Information Manual will be divided into those two separate domains.
       PART 1- Information directed at systems information in preparation for articulating a proficiency level knowledge of the aircraft systems during the **ORAL EXAMINATION** and
       PART 2- Description of how to do the actual hands-on maneuvers with suggested tips and techniques in preparation for the actual manipulation of the controls during the **SIMULATOR EVALUATION**.

---

probably worthless and certainly boring
DISCUSSION:

It has been my observation that regular garden variety Airline Pilots, in preparation for their checkride, all too often concentrate about 85% of their study and preparation time concentrating on **SYSTEM REVIEW** directed at performing well during the cognitive discussion that takes place during the Oral Examination. What I propose here is a study mechanism and toolset where the "student" pilot can be exposed to both learning venues and begin to understand how the whole memory set comes together. The concept here is to help the pilot achieve a more complete knowledge base so that they are able to **BOTH ARTICULATE AND DEMONSTRATE** how the airplane flight systems operate.

The object of this book is to help you begin to "**GET IT**". This is the goal of any good instructor or teaching system ... to start the student on the road to gaining a more complete understanding of the operation of a complex system such as the Airbus A320 series airplane.

SCOPE OF THE **CONTENTS:**
HOW THIS BOOK IS LAID OUT.

In keeping with our two modality teaching/learning model, this book breaks the mountain of material down into two "*general*" sections.

- The first part is composed of setup, system description, and knowledge items. This is the cognitive part of learning referred to during the **Oral Exam**, and is followed by

- The actual manipulation of the airplane controls. This is called the Psycho-motor skills demonstration known as the **Simulator Checkride**.

THE FIRST PART
BASIC DESCRIPTION OF SYSTEMS

- SYSTEM REVIEW
- GROUND SCHOOL
- PRE-FLIGHT MATERIAL

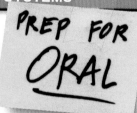

PREP FOR
ORAL

THE SECOND PART
OPERATION OF THE SYSTEMS

- SETUP FLOWS
- PUSHBACK
- ENGINE START
- TAXI-OUT
- TAKE-OFF
- CLIMB
- CRUISE
- APPROACH
- DESCENT
- LANDING
- TAXI-IN
- PARKING
- SECURE SHUTDOWN

PREP FOR
SIM-
RIDE

On our journey through this volume, there will be a huge number of additional items that will be included if they fall naturally into the flow of the material. Much of the more obvious information that should be intuitively obvious will be ignored.

published by UNIVERSITY of TEMECULA PRESS, Inc.

PART 1
THE SYSTEM REVIEW

Here is the section where a new Airbus pilot can learn about some of those strange and esoteric doodads and thingamajigs that populate the A320 cockpit. Presented here is a simple, basic system review of the cockpit parts that will help answer some of your initial questions and assist in gaining familiarity with the flight deck layout.

This is also an invitation to become acquainted with your new front office. I think you will agree with me and come to see the genius and pure craftsmanship that is inherent in the design. The beautiful and functional Airbus cockpit is absolutely cutting edge state-of-the-art aviation technology at its finest.

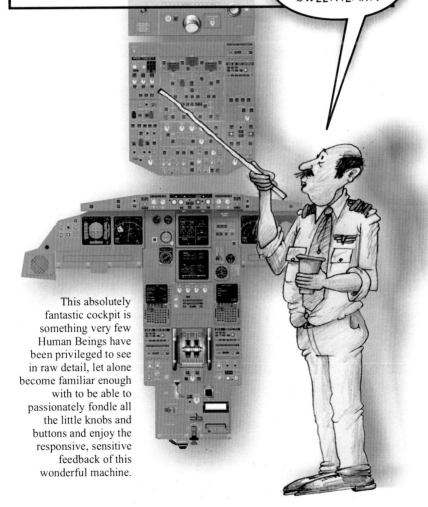

LET'S TALK ABOUT OUR NEW SWEETHEART!

This absolutely fantastic cockpit is something very few Human Beings have been privileged to see in raw detail, let alone become familiar enough with to be able to passionately fondle all the little knobs and buttons and enjoy the responsive, sensitive feedback of this wonderful machine.

CATALOG of PARTS

Here is how to find where all these
mysterious and strange sounding buttons and switches are located.

Before even the most seasoned pilot can climb into the seat of any new jet and even begin to understand the operation of the systems, there must first be a familiarization with the content and layout of the seemingly incredibly complex and unknowable cockpit. I am proposing here that you go over this catalog of parts and get a little acquainted with the dazzling array of instrumentation that populates the flight deck. A small word of caution, there "*MAY BE*" slight differences between what is presented here and your "real" cockpit. However, these differences are subtle and probably not important.

I have divided the cockpit into 15 sections to make it more easily digestible for us mere human pilots.

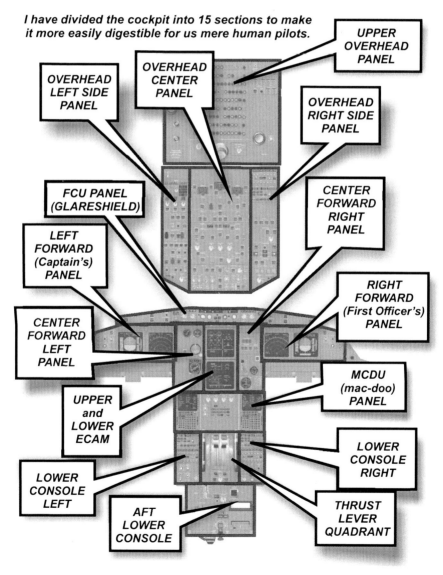

UPPER OVERHEAD PANEL

OVERHEAD CENTER PANEL

OVERHEAD LEFT SIDE PANEL

OVERHEAD RIGHT SIDE PANEL

FCU PANEL (GLARESHIELD)

CENTER FORWARD RIGHT PANEL

LEFT FORWARD (Captain's) PANEL

RIGHT FORWARD (First Officer's) PANEL

CENTER FORWARD LEFT PANEL

MCDU (mac-doo) PANEL

UPPER and LOWER ECAM

LOWER CONSOLE RIGHT

LOWER CONSOLE LEFT

AFT LOWER CONSOLE

THRUST LEVER QUADRANT

published by UNIVERSITY of TEMECULA PRESS, Inc.

BEFORE WE GET STARTED: First things first ...
just how do these funny looking light-switches work?

LIGHT SWITCH TECHNOLOGY

Many of the switches featured on the Airbus are a push-release type of design. Let me try to describe how they operate.

If you want to change the setting, you push the switch in. This actuates a **MECHANICAL** release, and when you release it, the switch operation will change to the alternate setting.

Most of the switches also incorporate a message feature that can display information regarding the nature of the operating system. Messages such as **ON, OFF, MAN, AUTO, FAULT** and so forth; may be displayed when appropriate.

POTENTIAL PILOT PROBLEM:

*These switches have to be pushed **ALL THE WAY IN** to release the mechanical switching mechanism. Sometimes, pilots will "tap" the button, or depress the switch too rapidly for the release to reposition.*

SUGGESTED TECHNIQUE

1. **DEPRESS THE BUTTON FULLY**.
2. **MOMENTARILY HOLD** switch in depressed position.
This is less than a second to allow mechanical release to actuate.
3. **RELEASE and OBSERVE** that the switch is selected to desired action.

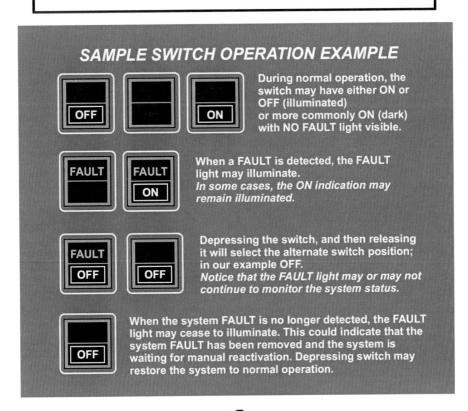

SAMPLE SWITCH OPERATION EXAMPLE

OFF | | **ON** — During normal operation, the switch may have either ON or OFF (illuminated) or more commonly ON (dark) with NO FAULT light visible.

FAULT | **FAULT ON** — When a FAULT is detected, the FAULT light may illuminate. *In some cases, the ON indication may remain illuminated.*

FAULT OFF | **OFF** — Depressing the switch, and then releasing it will select the alternate switch position; in our example OFF. *Notice that the FAULT light may or may not continue to monitor the system status.*

OFF — When the system FAULT is no longer detected, the FAULT light may cease to illuminate. This could indicate that the system FAULT has been removed and the system is waiting for manual reactivation. Depressing switch may restore the system to normal operation.

Flightdeck panel preview

UPPER OVERHEAD PANEL

NOTE

This subpanel in the upper right corner is NOT normally used by pilots. It is for maintenance and troubleshooting purposes.

Details on the next page are for information ONLY.

COCKPIT DOOR-LOCK CONTROLS

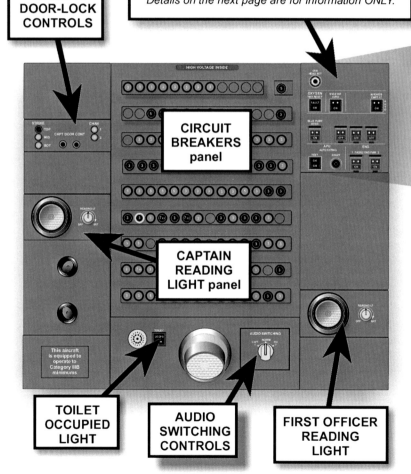

CIRCUIT BREAKERS panel

CAPTAIN READING LIGHT panel

TOILET OCCUPIED LIGHT

AUDIO SWITCHING CONTROLS

FIRST OFFICER READING LIGHT

published by UNIVERSITY of TEMECULA PRESS, Inc.

CVR
(COCKPIT VOICE RECORDER)
HEADSET RECEPTACLE

BLUE
HYDRAULIC SYSTEM
override:
This switch allows BLUE system to be energized without the engine running. Normally, the BLUE system can be pressurized after engine start by either ELECTRIC PUMP or RAT. RAT can produce up to 2500 PSI.

OXYGEN TIMER RESET
switch
There are two parts to the indicator light.
ON - resets system and shuts OFF the ON light.
FAULT- If it comes ON, door latches have remained energized longer than 30 seconds.

SERVICE
INTERPHONE
OVERRIDE

AVIONICS
COMPARTMENT
LIGHT

LEAK
MEASUREMENT
VALVES
MAINTENANCE ONLY!
BUT ...IF a LIGHT is ON,
it means part of the hydraulic system is inoperative.

ENG MAINT PANEL
not used by pilots
Switch powers **FADEC** without engine running
IF **ENG FIRE** switch not released.
NOTE:
FADEC
(FULL AUTHORITY DIGITAL ENGINE CONTROL)

APU
AUTO-EXTINGUISHING
TEST PANEL
APU TEST SWITCH
and
APU TEST
CIRCUIT RESET
NOTE:
ACTUATING
THIS TEST WILL
SHUT DOWN
THE APU

page 21

Flightdeck panel preview

OVERHEAD
left side panel

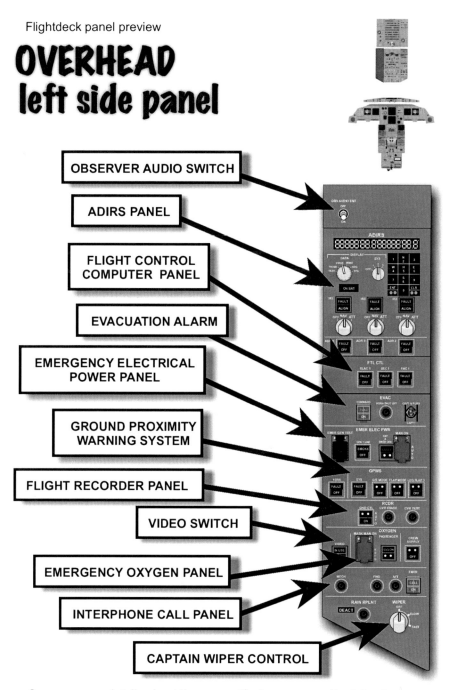

OBSERVER AUDIO SWITCH

ADIRS PANEL

FLIGHT CONTROL COMPUTER PANEL

EVACUATION ALARM

EMERGENCY ELECTRICAL POWER PANEL

GROUND PROXIMITY WARNING SYSTEM

FLIGHT RECORDER PANEL

VIDEO SWITCH

EMERGENCY OXYGEN PANEL

INTERPHONE CALL PANEL

CAPTAIN WIPER CONTROL

Some cursory details about these specific items are on the following pages:

published by UNIVERSITY of TEMECULA PRESS, Inc.

OBSERVER AUDIO ENTERTAINMENT
(OBS AUDIO ENT)

Usually, the entertainment **CHANNEL 9** is used to relay cockpit communications to the cabin for passenger monitoring.

ADIRS PANEL
(Air Data Inertial Reference System)

NOTE: *Pilots **DO NOT** normally input aircraft LAT/LONG position information into this unit except in extremely rare instances of a failure.*

OK to select **STS** (status) to provide a countdown to completion during the alignment.

THE ONLY NORMAL PILOT INPUT IS TO SELECT THE THREE POWER SWITCHES TO "NAV " TO INITIATE THE ALIGNMENT CYCLE .

 DO NOT MOVE THE JET DURING ALIGNMENT
(takes about 10 minutes).

POINT of POTENTIAL CONFUSION:
The instrument is numbered 1-3-2, instead of 1-2-3. Just a note of awareness here, that CAPT IR/ADR is #1, F/O is #2, CAPT or F/O can use #3.

"Flashing" **IR ALIGN** *light means;*
- *Present position not entered after 10 minutes*
- *Error between shutdown position and entered position.*
- *Alignment fault.*

"Steady" **IR FAULT** *light means:*
- *IRU unavailable.*

ADIRS ON BAT *light means: Normal check on startup, runs for a few seconds. Steady light indicates that unit is running on battery.*
- *IR 1 will run on battery until it fails.*
- *IR 2 and 3 will run for 5 minutes*

However, IF ATT HDG on CAPT 3, then:
- *IR 3 will run on battery until it fails, and*
- *IR 1 and 2 will run for 5 minutes.*

FLIGHT CONTROL COMPUTER PANEL

The **FLY-BY-WIRE** flight control system normally controls the flight control surfaces using **THREE** independent **ELECLTRICALLY** controlled **HYDRAULIC** systems.

> **IN AN EMERGENCY** ... The pilots can maintain control using **MECHANICAL** connections to the **STABILIZER** and **RUDDER**. There will be a **USE MAN PITCH TRIM** message on the **PFD**.

The **FLIGHT CONTROL** system consists of:
> Two sidesticks
> Two autopilots
> Two Elevator Aileron Computers (ELACs)
> Three Spoiler Elevator Computers (SECs)
> Two Flight Augmentation Computers (FACs)

The **FAC**s (*Flight Augmentation Computers*) have 3 main functions:
> Rudder and Yaw Damping inputs
> Flight Envelope and Speed computations
> Windshear Detection

EMERGENCY EVACUATION SIGNAL PANEL

Flip up the plastic cover, and depress the switch and the **EVAC** light flashes and the horn sounds in the **COCKPIT** and the **CABIN**.

Pushing the switch a second time **CANCELS** the **EVAC ALARM**.

This switch is permanently safety wired.

KNOW THIS:
Pushing the **HORN SHUTOFF** button, silences the **EVAC HORN** in the **COCKPIT**.
The horn continues to sound throughout cabin.

EMERGENCY ELECTRICAL POWER
CONTROL PANEL

 DO NOT SELECT THIS SWITCH.
THE RAT WILL FALL OUT.
Even on the ground!
THIS SWITCH IS ***ALWAYS*** HOT!

The **EMER GEN TEST**
switch is normally used only
by maintenance.

SMOKE LIGHT
This light illuminates
AMBER when smoke is
detected in the **AVIONICS
VENTILATION** system.
This switch is used during the
"AVIONICS SMOKE ECAM" procedure.

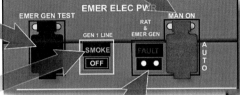

RAM AIR TURBINE (RAT) & EMERGENCY GENERATOR LIGHT

IF this **FAULT** light comes on,

 it indicates that the **RAT HAS BEEN DEPLOYED,**
BUT
RAT EMERGENCY TURBINE (RAM AIR TURBINE or RAT)
is ***NOT SUPPLYING POWER***, <u>AND</u>
(on some A320s) the nose gear is retracted!

NOTE: The **RAT** will continue to supply power down to 140 kts; however
on "older A320s" once the gear is down, **RAT** ceases to operate. *The
good news:* ***On "newer" A320s and A319s, the rollout capability is
good down to 125 knots***.

SOME QUESTIONS answered:

The **RAT** deploys automatically when:
1. Airspeed greater than 100 knots, <u>AND</u>
2. Loss of AC BUS 1and AC BUS 2
OR
The RAT can be deployed MANUALLY using the
EMER ELEC PWR MAN ON switch

HOW DOES IT WORK?
*The airstream spins a little propeller on the **RAT** that supplies **HYDRAULIC**
PRESSURE to the BLUE SYSTEM. This allows **BLUE** system to power the*
***EMERGENCY GENERATOR** using a **HYDRAULIC MOTOR**. The **RAT** also supplies*
HYDRAULIC POWER** to 2 **SPOILERS** (one in **EACH WING**) and the **RUDDER.

GROUND PROXIMITY WARNING SYSTEM
Called the **GPWS** or "**JIP-WIS**"

NOTE:
There are some differences in the installation between airplanes. This is considered the "standard" Airbus setup.

Operation of the **ON-OFF** switch is intuitive: that is **OFF** is **OFF** and **ON** is **ON**. There are reasons why a pilot might want to *MANUALLY* switch off different features during different flight operations.
Here are three common ones:

1. G/S MODE should be selected **OFF** during a **GLIDESLOPE OUT or LOCALIZER ONLY** approach.

2. FLAP MODE should be selected **OFF** when landing with other than **LANDING FLAPS 3 or FULL**. For example during a **HYDRAULIC FAILURE** or **NO FLAP** abnormality.

3. LDG FLAP 3 should be selected **OFF** when **FLAPS 3** is selected as the final flap setting.

4. RADAR NOTE: If in **AIRBUS** configuration, **EGPWS (Enhanced GPWS** which has a **TERRAIN** database) must be *MANUALLY* deselected using the **TERRAIN** switch in order to display the weather radar.

COCKPIT VOICE RECORDER (CVR) and DIGITAL FLIGHT DATA RECORDER (DFDR)

Generally, operation of the **CVR** is automatic, and while the **CVR** is programmed to stop recording 5 minutes after the last engine is shut down, any power interruption will cause the unit to revert to automatic operation.

Normal **SOP** is to select the **GND CTL** "**ON**" so that the reading of the checklists can be recorded.

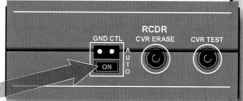

The **AUTO ON** light indicates that both the **CVR** and the **DFDR** are energized for operation.

CVR ERASE button will erase recording IF
**It is held for 2 seconds, AND
Airplane is on the ground, AND
PARK BRK handle is ON.**

CVR TEST requires PARKING BRAKE switch MUST be "ON."

OXYGEN PANEL

OXYGEN MASK MAN...ON switch.

AUTO (cover closed): The mask **_DOORS_** at the individual passenger seats open automatically when the **_CABIN ALTITUDE_** exceeds 14,000 feet.

PILOT SCREW-UP: Confuses "**_CABIN_**" altitude with the "**_AIRPLANE_**" operating altitude. The cabin altitude is displayed on both the **LOWER ECAM CRUISE** page and the **ECAM CAB PRESS**

PUSHING "MASK MAN ON" SWITCH will *OPEN ALL THE CABIN MASK DOORS.* Requires maintenance action to restore to operation.

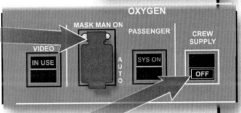

When **CREW SUPPLY** light **ON,** it indicates that low pressure OXYGEN is supplied to the Crew Masks (Desirable and NORMAL). If the switch is **OFF** (as indicated) the Oxygen Supply Valve is **CLOSED** (No Oxygen can flow). We want this to be **ON.**

CALL SELECTORS and WIPER CONTROLS

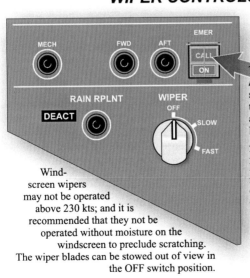

To call **ALL FLIGHT ATTENDANT** stations at the same time, use this switch. Selection is accompanied with WHITE lights, AMBER lights, RED flashing lights, and an EMERGENCY CALL message. In addition, CHIMES sound throughout the cabin.

Windscreen wipers may not be operated above 230 kts; and it is recommended that they not be operated without moisture on the windscreen to preclude scratching. The wiper blades can be stowed out of view in the OFF switch position.

Flightdeck panel preview

OVERHEAD
center panel

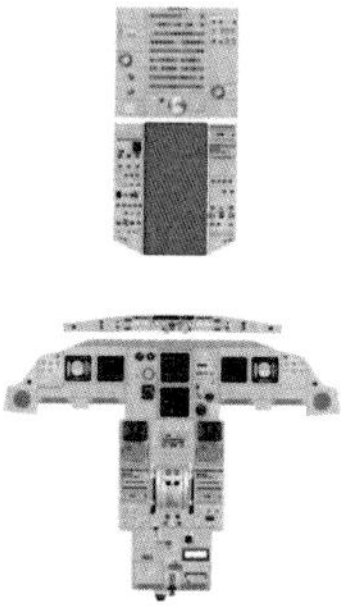

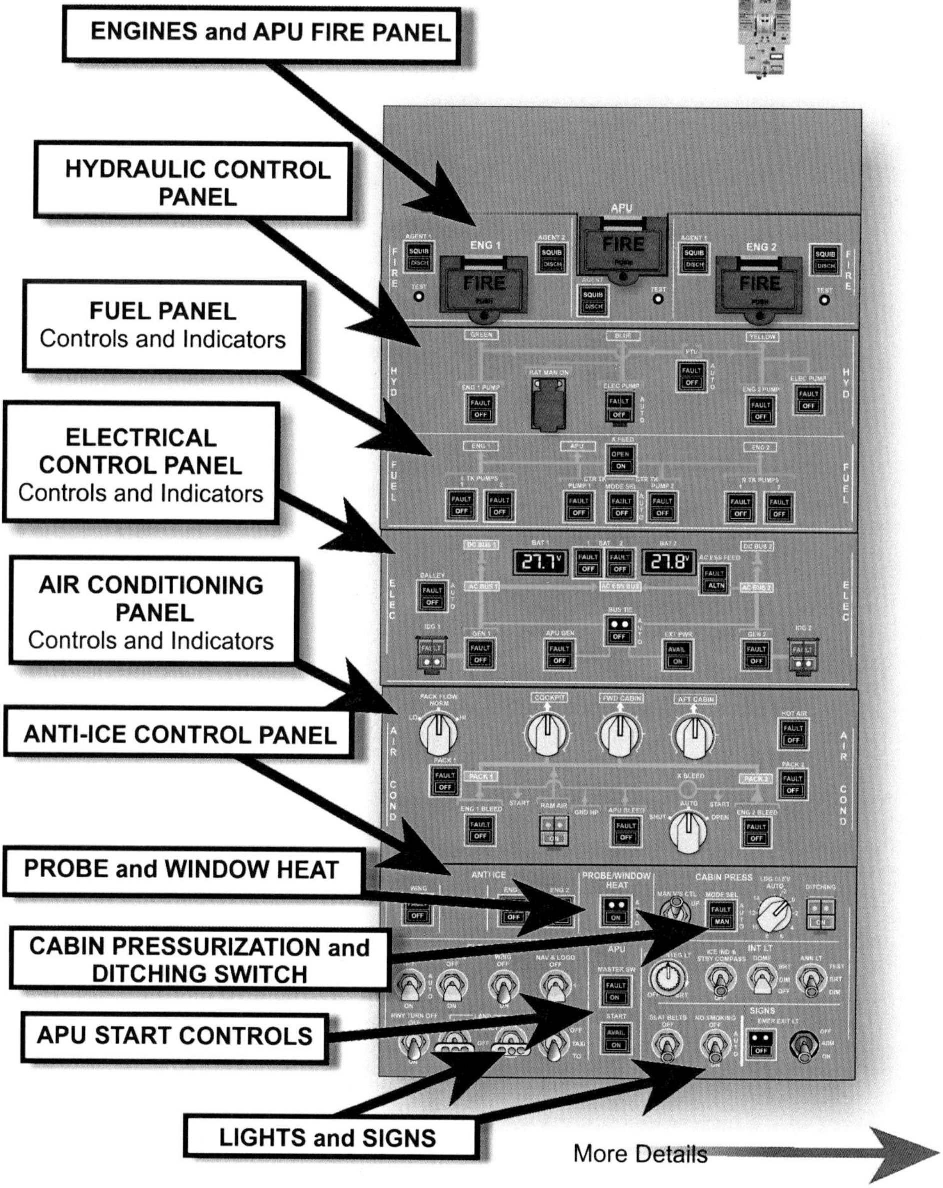

ENGINES and APU FIRE PANEL

HYDRAULIC CONTROL PANEL

FUEL PANEL
Controls and Indicators

ELECTRICAL CONTROL PANEL
Controls and Indicators

AIR CONDITIONING PANEL
Controls and Indicators

ANTI-ICE CONTROL PANEL

PROBE and WINDOW HEAT

CABIN PRESSURIZATION and DITCHING SWITCH

APU START CONTROLS

LIGHTS and SIGNS

More Details

published by UNIVERSITY of TEMECULA PRESS, Inc.

ENGINE and APU FIRE PANEL
Controls and Indicators

When FIRE WARNING detected:

▬ Continuous Repetitive Chime (CRC) sounds,
▬ appropriate FIRE light on FIRE PANEL illuminates,
▬ All MASTER WARNING LIGHTS illuminate,
▬ ECAM WARNING on the E/WD,
▬ If an ENGINE FIRE,
the appropriate FIRE LIGHT illuminates
on ENG panel just aft of the throttle console.

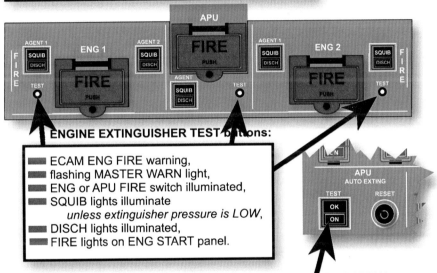

ENGINE EXTINGUISHER TEST buttons:

▬ ECAM ENG FIRE warning,
▬ flashing MASTER WARN light,
▬ ENG or APU FIRE switch illuminated,
▬ SQUIB lights illuminate
unless extinguisher pressure is LOW,
▬ DISCH lights illuminated,
▬ FIRE lights on ENG START panel.

IMPORTANT NOTE REGARDING THE APU FIRE TEST SWITCH:

Pushing the APU test switch on the FIRE panel **DOES NOT** cause the APU to shut down.

HOWEVER, pushing the APU TEST button on the **APU AUTO EXTINGUISHING** panel on the **UPPER OVERHEAD PANEL**

SHUTS DOWN THE APU!

There are **4 ENG AGENT** switches. They are armed when the corresponding **FIRE** switch is activated. The SQUIB light illuminates to indicate activation.

When armed and LIGHT/SWITCH is pushed momentarily;
▬ Fire Extinguisher Bottle is **DISCHARGED**, and
▬ **DISCH** light illuminates when pressure becomes **LOW**.

NOTE: *Each engine has 2 dedicated FIRE EXTINGUISHERS, APU has 1 extinguisher.*

ARE WE ON FIRE?

HOW DOES IT KNOW ?

There are three sets of double loops mounted in parallel.

- one set for the **Engine and Pylon on each side**, and
- one set for the **APU compartment**.

These detect heat by registering a change in resistance.
When they get **HOT** they register an *OVERHEAT*,
when they get **REALLY HOT,** they register a *FIRE*.
Normally it takes _**BOTH**_ sensor wires to detect
a fire before an alarm is given,

WHAT IF ONE OR BOTH
OF THE SENSORS IS BROKEN?

Here's what they did about that,
If there is a fault or break in one of the sensors.
it alerts the system and the system
reverts to a single sensor warning.

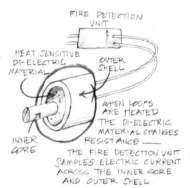

Fire warnings appear when:
- **BOTH LOOPS DETECT A FIRE.**

- **ONE LOOP DETECTS THE FIRE**
  and **THE OTHER LOOP IS FAULTY.**

- **A BREAK IN BOTH LOOPS OCCURS**
  WITHIN 5 SECONDS.

-**A FIRE TEST IS PERFORMED.**

What does the FIRE SWITCH DO when it is activated?

ENGINES	APU
Silences Aural warning	Shuts down APU
Arms Squibs (Squib light ON)	Silences Aural Warning
Deactivates Generator	Arms Squibs (Squib light ON)
FADEC power removed	Closes THESE ITEMS:
Closes THESE ITEMS:	- FUEL LP valve
- FUEL LP valve	- APU fuel pump turned OFF
- Hyd Fire Shutoff	- APU Bleed
- Engine Bleed	- CROSSFEED valve
- Pack Flow Control	- APU generator

Later in our discussion regarding engine shutdown, if the engine will not shut
down using normal techniques we will discover that an "approved" technique is
to "starve" the engine by selecting the **ENGINE FIRE SWITCH** (which closes
the **FUEL LP** valve).

NOTE: *Only selecting the **ENGINE or APU FIRE SWITCH** does not release
the fire suppression agent into the **ENGINE** or **APU** compartment.*

published by UNIVERSITY of TEMECULA PRESS, Inc.

HYDRAULIC CONTROL PANEL

DO NOT PUSH THIS SWITCH.
THE RAT WILL FALL OUT.
THIS SWITCH ALWAYS HOT!
Even on the ground!
Can only be reset by maintenance action on the ground.

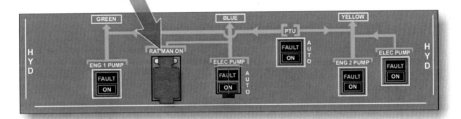

Illumination of any of the 5 FAULT light indicates:

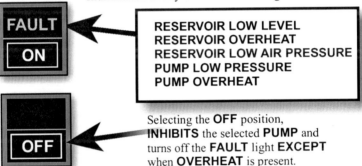

RESERVOIR LOW LEVEL
RESERVOIR OVERHEAT
RESERVOIR LOW AIR PRESSURE
PUMP LOW PRESSURE
PUMP OVERHEAT

Selecting the **OFF** position,
INHIBITS the selected **PUMP** and
turns off the **FAULT** light **EXCEPT**
when **OVERHEAT** is present.

The **LOWER ECAM** will display the
settings and indications relative to the
hydraulic system.

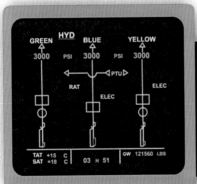

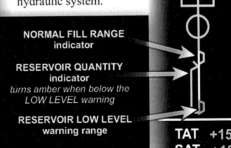

NORMAL FILL RANGE
indicator

RESERVOIR QUANTITY
indicator
turns amber when below the
LOW LEVEL warning

RESERVOIR LOW LEVEL
warning range

NOTE: *The RESERVOIR QUANTITY indicator*
moves up and down to correspond to the indication.

HYDRAULIC SYSTEM DESCRIPTION

SITUATION 1:

IF A PUMP QUITS, IT IS NOT REALLY A BIG DEAL ... BECAUSE

Every pump is backed up by an alternate hydraulic power source.

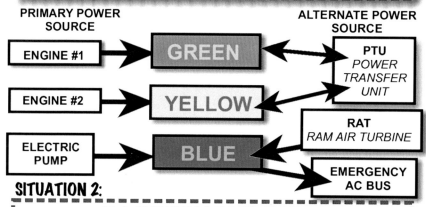

PRIMARY POWER SOURCE

ALTERNATE POWER SOURCE

ENGINE #1 → **GREEN** ← PTU *POWER TRANSFER UNIT*

ENGINE #2 → **YELLOW** ←

RAT *RAM AIR TURBINE*

ELECTRIC PUMP → **BLUE** ←

EMERGENCY AC BUS

SITUATION 2:

IF A SYSTEM LOSES FLUID

IT IS NOT POSSIBLE TO TRANSFER HYDRAULIC FLUID BETWEEN SYSTEMS. THEREFORE, ... SOME SYSTEMS CAN NO LONGER BE OPERATED.

Here is a list of the items that would no longer operate if their system lost all hydraulic fluid.

GREEN

-REVERSER #1
-GEAR RETRACTION
-NOSE WHEEL STEERING
(if gear extended manually)

BLUE

-The EMERGENCY GENERATOR or RAT

YELLOW

-REVERSER #2
-PARKING BRAKE ACCUMULATOR RECHARGING
-CARGO DOOR

RAT stuff

The **RAT** extends automatically when:
    1. AC busses 1 and 2 are not electrically powered, **AND**
    2. Speed is above 100 knots.
The **RAT** can be extended manually by pressing **EMER ELEC PWR MAN ON** switch on overhead **ELEC** panel.
Here's what the **RAT** does:
    Pressurizes the **BLUE SYSTEM** to 2,500 psi ... **ONLY**! There is an **EMERGENCY GENERATOR** that is then powered by a **HYDRAULIC MOTOR**. This system requires 140 Knots airspeed to operate.
NOTE: *Some differences exist between the early A320s and later versions that cause the system to stop operating when the NOSE GEAR is in transit.*
THE RAT DOES NOT PROVIDE HYDRAULIC PRESSURE DIRECTLY TO ANY FLIGHT CONTROL SURFACES.

published by UNIVERSITY of TEMECULA PRESS, Inc.

a BRAKE SYSTEM discussion

Probably the most difficult and complex issue regarding the hydraulic system is the relationship between:

- **YELLOW SYSTEM**
- **PARKING BRAKE**
- **STEERING**
- **HYDRAULIC PRESSURE GAUGE**
- **GREEN SYSTEM**
- **BSCU**

I can almost guarantee that the Check Captain will **DEMAND** an explanation of this relationship from the pilot candidate.

Here is a pilot's explanation of the details of this system.

If you look at the pressure gauge located near the gear handle you are looking at the pressure in the **PARKING BRAKE** and **ALTERNATE BRAKING** system supplied by the **YELLOW SYSTEM.**

The **NORMAL** brake system uses **GREEN SYSTEM** pressure. That gauge **DOES NOT** reflect **GREEN SYSTEM** or **NORMAL BRAKING** pressure. Here is where pilots get confused.

When you depress the **RUDDER BRAKES** or **"TOE" BRAKES** then you are selecting **GREEN SYSTEM** and the pressure gauge should indicate **"ZERO"**.

Further confusion, when you depress the rudder toe brakes, the system shifts to **GREEN** system. **IF** you see **ANY** pressure indicating on the gauge, that means that **YELLOW** system pressure is available to the alternate brakes ... then you have a **PROBLEM**!

That problem is a failure of either the **BSCU** (Braking and Steering Control Unit) or **BDDV** (Brake Dual Distribution Valve) and renders the airplane a potential unguided and unstoppable rolling disaster without **IMMEDIATE** and **PROPER** action.

The situation is further exacerbated because the proper action by the pilot involves a totally nonintuitive response. The Captain **MUST** remove pressure from the brakes before turning OFF the **BRK & STRG** switch in order the actuate the alternate system.

> If the Captain has pressure on the **TOE BRAKES** when the
> **BRK & STRG** switch is turned off, the airplane will
>
> # HIT A BRICK WALL.

We will be constantly referring to this situation many more times during the course of our discussion about this airplane.

FUEL PANEL
Controls and Indicators

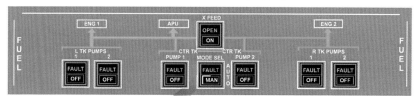

MODE SELECTOR SWITCH

If MODE SEL SWITCH is *DARK*

This means **AUTO** operations allowed. Here are three **AUTO** situations:

1	If fuel in **CENTER TANK**; then **CENTER TANK PUMPS RUN** (except when SLATS are extended.)
2	Turns off any **PUMP** 5 minutes after **LOW LEVEL** indication.
3	**BOTH ENGINE PUMPS** run for 2 minutes after engine **START** (if fuel present and regardless of slats position).

If MODE SEL *FAULT* LIGHT ON .. means

CENTER TANK *contains more then* **550 pounds** *and* **LEFT or RIGHT WING TANK** *less than* **11,000 pounds**.

If MODE SEL *MAN* light on ...

ALLOWS MANUAL CONTROL *of the* **CENTER TANK PUMPS** *using* **CTR TK PUMP** *switches.*

TK PUMP SWITCH

If TK PUMP *FAULT* LIGHT ON .. means

Pump pressure is **LOW**. Light inhibited when switch **OFF**.

RECIRCULATION SYSTEM:

Fuel is used to cool the **IDG** (**I**ntegrated **D**rive **G**enerators that produce electricity). Fuel goes to the engine, but a small amount is diverted to cool the **IDG**. Then the heated fuel is sent by a return line to the **WING TANK OUTER FUEL compartment**.

If the **CENTER TANK** is supplying fuel, the **WING TANK** can overflow

...SO here is what they did:

When the **INNER WING TANK** is full, the **CENTER TANK PUMPS** shut off. This causes the wing tank to supply fuel to the engine, and when it has used approximately **1100#**, the **CENTER TANK PUMP** resumes operation.

---

published by UNIVERSITY of TEMECULA PRESS, Inc.

FUEL SYSTEM
IMPORTANT FUEL NOTES:

There are **3 FUEL TANKS.**
In all, however, there are **7 FUEL COMPARTMENTS**.

The **WING TANK PUMPS** are designed to operate continuously.

The **ORDER** for fuel usage is for the **CENTER TANK** to be used **FIRST**, then **WING TANKS**.
*In order to do that, the **WING TANK** pumps are fitted with **PRESSURE RELIEF VALVES** so the **CENTER TANK PUMPS** supply greater pressure.*

FUEL CANNOT BE TRANSFERRED BETWEEN THE 3 TANKS
(except during normal fueling operations, of course. Refer to QRH.)

THERE IS NO FUEL JETTISON SYSTEM.

ENGINES WILL SUCTION FEED, BUT FROM WING TANKS ONLY.

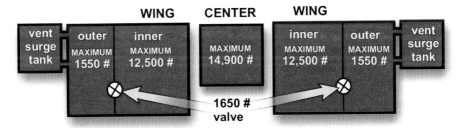

WING   CENTER   WING

| vent surge tank | outer MAXIMUM 1550 # | inner MAXIMUM 12,500 # | MAXIMUM 14,900 # | inner MAXIMUM 12,500 # | outer MAXIMUM 1550 # | vent surge tank |

1650 #
valve

The 1650 VALVE discussion:

When
***EITHER* WING INNER FUEL COMPARTMENT**
decreases to 1650 # fuel, then
***BOTH* LEFT AND RIGHT SIDE 1650 Valves OPEN.**
*They cannot be reset **UNTIL** next Fueling cycle on the ground.*

FUELING NOTES:

Requires **ELECTRICAL POWER** supplied from **EITHER**
- **EXTERNAL SOURCE**
- **APU**
- **AIRPLANE BATTERY**

NOTE: If the **BATTERY** is used to supply the electrical power for fueling:
- the **TANK MAY NOT** fill to full capacity, and
- the **TRANSFER VALVES** may not fully close.
  (However, they will close when normal power is resumed).

AIR CONDITIONING PANEL
Controls and Indicators

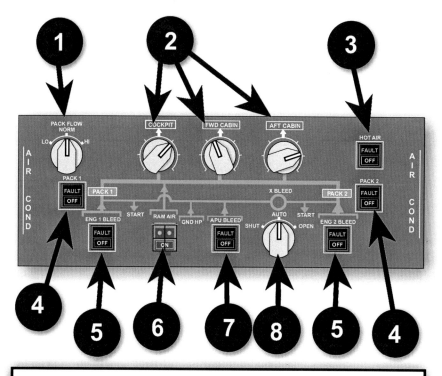

PACK FLOW selector

If **APU** is supplying air, or one pack fails, goes to **HIGH FLOW**.
In **LOW**, if **PACK** wants more air, it reverts to **NORMAL**.

The **PACK FLOW** is set manually in accordance with **PASSENGER** comfort using the 3 Zone Temperature Selectors.

ZONE TEMPERATURE selectors

The selectors may be set in accordance with the loading or with the desires of the Cabin crew depending on loading density of passengers, and ambient conditions.

HOT AIR SWITCH:

FAULT LIGHT ON: This means **DUCT OVERHEAD**.
Once the switch is turned off,
when the temperature drops to a preset normal
temperature, the **LIGHT WILL GO OUT.**

4

PACK switch:
FAULT means:
■ **PACK FLOW CONTROL** valve disagrees with commanded position, or
■ Compressor/Pack outlet **OVERHEATS**.

FAULT

5

ENGINE BLEED switch:

ON: Opens valve if:
- Upstream pressure greater than 8 psi,
- APU bleed valve closed,
- No Leak detected,
- No Overpressure detected,
- No Over temperature detected,
- ENG FIRE switch not released out,
- ENG START valve is closed.

OFF: Closes **BLEED** valve and **HP** valve.

6

RAM AIR switch (guarded**):**

OFF: (switch dark) This is the normal situation.

ON: When selected on, Ram Air may or may not flow into MIXING unit depending on the differential pressure.

NOTE: *If ditching switch is selected, switch is over-ridden and* **RAM AIR INLET is CLOSED**.

7

APU BLEED switch

ON: Valve opens IF there is **NO** leak in the **APU** or **LEFT SIDE BLEED**.
OFF: Closes the **APU** valve.

APU BLEED FAULT LIGHT: Illuminates when **LEAK** detected.

8

CROSSBLEED selector:

AUTO:
Opens crossbleed valve **IF APU BLEED VALVE OPEN**.
Closes crossbleed valve **IF APU** valve closed or **LEAK** detected.

OPEN: Opens crossbleed valve.
SHUT: Closes crossbleed valve.

ELECTRICAL CONTROL PANEL
Controls and Indicators

Three generators (one from each **ENGINE** and **APU**) provide **AC** power. Two batteries provide **DC** power for **APU** start and for **EMERGENCY** power. There is an emergency air driven **RAT** (Ram Air Turbine) that can be deployed to provide some emergency **AC** power in case all three of the main generators fail.

The Electrical system is normally **AUTOMATIC**;
and the systems normally operate **ISOLATED** from one another.

NOTE: *The APU can supply electrical power for the entire airplane on the ground.*

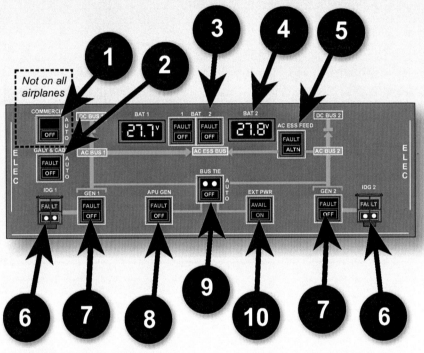

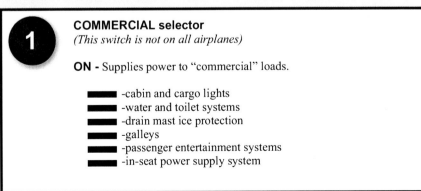

COMMERCIAL selector
(This switch is not on all airplanes)

ON - Supplies power to "commercial" loads.

- -cabin and cargo lights
- -water and toilet systems
- -drain mast ice protection
- -galleys
- -passenger entertainment systems
- -in-seat power supply system

published by UNIVERSITY of TEMECULA PRESS, Inc.

2

GALY (galley) **& CAB** (cabin) Switch

AUTO - The MAIN GALLEY bus, In-seat power, and Passenger entertainment AUTOMATICALLY SHED when:
Only ONE GENERATOR is operating,
except on ground when the APU or EXTERNAL is ON.

OFF - All that stuff is shut OFF.

FAULT LIGHT - **ON** when associated generator is above 100% its rated output. The Associated **ECAM** annunciates.

3

BAT (battery) Switch - Controls operation of the corresponding **BATTERY CHARGE LIMITER**.

AUTO - Batteries connected to DC BAT bus during:
▬ APU starting Batteries NOT connected
▬ BATTERY charging
▬ Below 100 kts on ground with **AC BUSSES 1 AND 2** unpowered.

OFF - Battery charger NOT operating and Battery line contactor open.
The OFF light will illuminate white if DC BAT bus powered.
The **HOT BAT BUSSES** remain powered.

FAULT - illuminates when **CHARGING CURRENT** outside limits ...the Battery contactor opens automatically.

4

BAT Indicator - Displays ***BATTERY VOLTAGE***.

5

AC ESS (essential) **FEED** Switch.

ALTN (alternate) - Allows **AC ESS BUS** to be powered from AC BUS 2 (*normally power comes from AC BUS 1*).

FAULT - means **AC ESS BUS** is NOT powered.

6 **IDG** Switch - Guarded with a plastic cover and normally spring loaded to the extended outward position. When pushed momentarily, it will cause the IDG to become disconnected and ***CANNOT BE RECONNECTED IN FLIGHT!***

CAUTION
1. ***DO NOT PUSH SWITCH FOR MORE THAN 3 SECONDS***.
    (*the drive disconnect coupling can be damaged*)
2. Do not disconnect the IDG when the engine is NOT running (or windmilling). *The engine must be turning.*
TIP! *If you have a "seized" engine abnormality (N1 "ZERO"), DO NOT DISCONNECT the IDG.*

FAULT - indicates:
▬▬▬ IDG oil outlet overheat,
▬▬ IDG low oil pressure. *Inhibited below 14% N2.*

---

7 **ENGINE GEN** (generator) Switch -

ON - Generator FIELD energized and Line contactor is closed **IF** electrical parameters are normal.

OFF - Opens contactor, de-energizes the generator field, and ***RESETS FAULT CIRCUITRY***.

FAULT - has only two possible indications, it means either:

1. Protection trip is initiated by GCU (Generator Control Unit), or
2. Contactor OPENS with GEN Switch still ***ON***.

---

8 **APU GEN** (generator) Switch -

ON - Generator FIELD energized and Line contactor is closed **IF** electrical parameters are normal, AND EXT PWR line contactor is OPEN.

OFF - Generator field is turned off and line contactor OPENS. illuminates only if airplane powered by AC power.

FAULT - has only two possible indications, it means either:

1. Protection trip is initiated by GCU (Generator Control Unit), or
2. Contactor OPENS with GEN Switch ON.

NOTE: The APU GEN FAULT light is inhibited from coming on during low APU speed power transfers.

9

BUS TIE Switch -

AUTO - The BUS TIE contactors open and close automatically. They keep power on AC BUSSES 1 and 2.

During ENGINE shutdown, AUTO attempts to keep AC BUS TIE powered.

OFF - Both BUS TIE contactors are OPEN.

10

EXT PWR (External Power) Switch -

Situation 1: **AVAIL LIGHT ON,** When PUSHED:

-External power contactor closes,
-AVAIL light goes OUT,
-ON light comes ON
(and remains ON until the engine generators start supplying electrical power).

Situation 2: **EXT PWR** (External Power) **ON** light illuminated:

-External power contactor OPENS,
-**ON** light goes out,
-AVAIL light illuminates.

The **NORMAL PRIORITY** is:

- **ENGINE GENERATORS,**
- **EXTERNAL POWER** *(when EXT PWR switch is ON),*
- **APU.**

After the second engine has been started, the **ENG GENERATORS** will automatically be powering the **AC busses.** The **APU** or **EXTERNAL PWR** is automatically disconnected from the **AC busses**; however, it remains connected to and continues to power the **AC BUS TIE** and the **EXT PWR ON** light remains illuminated. The **EXT PWR ON** light remains illuminated until the **EXT PWR** switch is selected **OFF**.

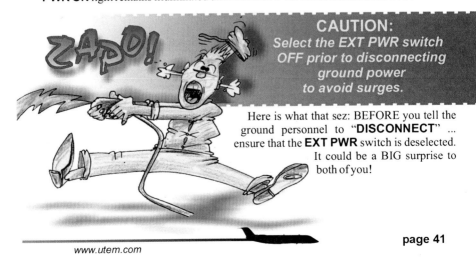

CAUTION:
Select the EXT PWR switch OFF prior to disconnecting ground power to avoid surges.

Here is what that sez: BEFORE you tell the ground personnel to "**DISCONNECT**" ... ensure that the **EXT PWR** switch is deselected. It could be a BIG surprise to both of you!

POTPOURRI PANEL

(Anti-ice, Probe and Window heat, Cabin Pressurization,
Ditching Switch, APU control, Lights and Signs.

ANTI-ICE CONTROL PANEL	**PROBE/WINDOW HEAT**	**CABIN PRESSURIZATION PANEL**

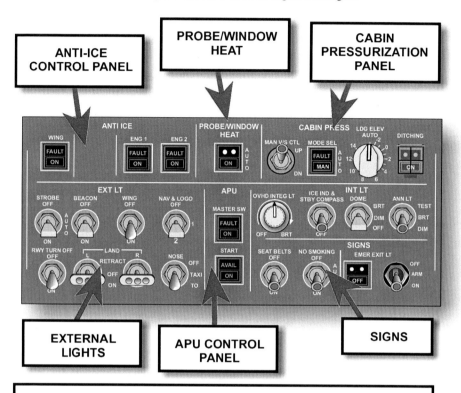

EXTERNAL LIGHTS	**APU CONTROL PANEL**	**SIGNS**

PROBE/WINDOW HEAT CONTROL SWITCH

Three independent probe heater computers *AUTOMATICALLY* control the ground/flight modes and overheat and fault indications. **The TAT probe is NOT heated on the ground.** The PROBE HEAT operates at LOW HEAT on the ground and automatically switches to HIGH in the air.

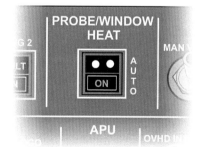

AUTO - Once one engine has started, then the automatic heating feature activates.
ON - overrides the requirement for having an engine running.

published by UNIVERSITY of TEMECULA PRESS, Inc.

ANTI-ICE CONTROL PANEL

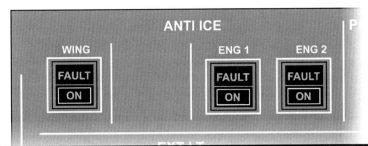

WING anti-icing operates inflight *ONLY*. Hot **BLEED AIR** is used for anti-icing **THREE OUTBOARD SLATS** on each **WING**. When either valve open:
- **EPR LIMIT** is reduced,
- **MINIMUM IDLE RPM** is increased.

ON - Anti-ice supplied to *BOTH* wings at the same time.
- **ON** light illuminates (blue)
- **WING A.** message on **ECAM MEMO**.

Wing anti-ice valves open *ONLY* IF Pneumatic Air Supply available.

NOTE:
When selected on the ground,
valve opens for 30 seconds ONLY (for test purposes).

FAULT LIGHT means:
- Wing anti-ice valve position disagrees with switch position.
- LOW PRESSURE detected.
- Flickers momentarily when valve in transit.

Hot **BLEED AIR** is used for anti-icing **ENGINE NACELLE** . Engine must be running for valve to open. When operating:
- **MAX N1 LIMITED**,
- **CONTINUOUS IGNITION** supplied,
- **MAX IDLE RPM** increased.

ON - Anti-ice supplied to SELECTED engine.

> **ON** light illuminates (blue)
> **ENG A. ICE** message on ECAM MEMO.
> Engine anti-ice valve open IF ENGINE BLEED available.

OFF - Shuts ENGINE ANTI-ICE valve off, ON light goes out.

If there is a loss of electrical power, the valves open.

FAULT LIGHT means:
- Engine anti-ice valve position disagrees with the selected position, or
- flickers momentarily when valve in transit.

CABIN PRESSURIZATION PANEL

CABIN PRESSURIZATION panel
Operates *FULLY AUTOMATIC*.
Two Identical independent Cabin Pressure Controllers (CPC) use a single
outflow valve that is powered by one of three available DC motors. Each
computer has its own DC motor and a third one is used for manual operation.
The manual operation is initiated by depressing the MODE SEL switch, and
using the MAN V/S CTL lever to toggle the outflow valve.
Only one unit will operate at a time; until the other is automatically selected after
landing or in case of failure.

QNH information comes from FMGC.
PRESSURE ALTITUDE comes from ADIRS.
REFERENCE DATA from ADIRS set by captain's barometric altimeter.
LANDING ELEVATION comes from the FMGC database.
also used are thrust lever position and ground/flight logic.
Zone controllers provide Air Conditioning and airflow information.

FAULT LIGHT - ONLY comes on when a fault is detected in **BOTH** systems.
MAN LIGHT - Pushing the MODE SEL light/switch changes to MANUAL
operation and the **MAN V/S CTL** control switch is activated.

AUTO - Outflow valve is controlled by one system at a time automatically.
Other system selected on landing.
MAN - actuates the MAN V/S CTL switch.

MAN V/S CTL (Manual vertical speed control) - To operate, HOLD the toggle
switch in position until TARGET VERTICAL SPEED (displayed on
ECAM/CAB PRESS page) is reached. Operation in this mode is s-l-o-w.

POTENTIAL BIG PROBLEM:
If you are operating the pressurization in the MANUAL MODE; the cabin
WILL NOT automatically depressurize on landing; therefore, in this case
DIFFERENTIAL PRESSURE MUST BE MANUALLY SET TO
ZERO BEFORE OPENING ANY EXIT DOOR.

---

published by UNIVERSITY of TEMECULA PRESS, Inc.

THIS IS SERIOUS!

 IF CABIN PRESSURIZATION EXCEEDS
about **10,000 feet**
THERE IS A LEVEL 3 WARNING.

A LEVEL THREE WARNING IS:
- CRC (Continuous Repetitive Chime)
- MASTER WARN flashing light
- WARNING MESSAGE on EWD (ECAM)

**MAXIMUM ALLOWED
CABIN DIFFERENTIAL**
-1.0 PSI differential
+8.6 PSI differential
NOTE:
*Safety relief valve opens
at +8.6 PSI differential*

DO NOT exceed *CABIN ALTITUDE*
of 10,000 feet **EXCEPT**:
to maintain MEA or
in an EMERGENCY

**RAM AIR INLET
*LIMIT***
Open the Ram Air Inlet
ONLY
if pressure differential is
LESS THAN 1 PSI !

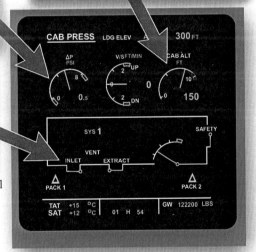

The (guarded) RAM AIR control switch is on the Air Conditioning panel.
If you should select it, the Ram Air Inlet will open. However, if there is a diff press greater than 1 psi, the control will remain normal and NO RAM AIR will flow into the mixing unit.

DITCHING SWITCH WARNING:

On the GROUND with all the doors closed; IF ANY ground conditioned air or pneumatic system air to the packs pressurizes the airplane, everybody onboard is subjected to a serious ear-banging experience.

 **IF CABIN PRESSURIZATION EXCEEDS
14,000 feet**
PASSENGER OXYGEN MASKS DEPLOY.

APU START PANEL

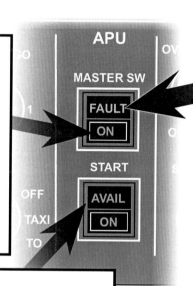

MASTER SWITCH

ON -
- ON light illuminates
- ECB power-up test initiated
- APU air inlet flap opens
- APU fuel isolation valve opens
- APU fuel pumps runs if needed
- ECAM APU page displayed

OFF -
- ON light goes out
- APU shuts down
- AVAIL light goes out

START SWITCH

ON -
- ON light illuminates

  as soon as the air inlet flap is fully open:
- APU starter is energized
- IGNITION occurs
- At a preset (unknown to pilots)
  N1, starter, and ignition shut off.

AVAIL LIGHT -
- Comes on when N1 is above 95%
- Goes out when APU shuts down.

APU START WARNING
*DO NOT start APU during fueling operations
following an APU automatic shutdown or failed start.*

published by UNIVERSITY of TEMECULA PRESS, Inc.

MASTER SWITCH FAULT LIGHT
Comes **ON** when
AUTOMATIC shutdown occurs.

APU SHUTS DOWN WHEN:
- *APU FIRE on the ground*
- *APU air inlet flap didn't open*
- *APU overspeed*
- *APU underspeed*
- *Abnormal start*
- *Over temperature*
- *Low oil temperature*
- *High oil temperature*
- *DC power failure*
- *ECB failure*
- *Loss of overspeed protection*
- *Reverse airflow.*

some APU TECH stuff

APU MAXIMUM ALTITUDES

APU start using airplane BATTERY	25,000 feet
APU start using normal electrics	39,000* feet
Two-pack operation	15,000 feet
One-pack operation	20,000 feet
For engine start	20,000 feet

***NOTE**: APU start capability is improved below 31,000 feet*

APU OIL QUANTITY

If you get an APU ECAM page LOW OIL LEVEL message: Don't panic ... the remaining oil quantity allows for normal operation for approximately 10 hours.

APU STARTER DUTY CYCLE

Start attempts	Cooling Time Limit
Between each start cycle	1 minute
After first 3 start attempts	60 minutes

Flightdeck panel preview

OVERHEAD
right side panel

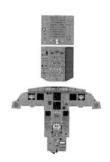

AUDIO CONTROL PANEL

RADIO MANAGEMENT PANEL

FLIGHT CONTROL PANEL

CARGO HEAT PANEL

CARGO SMOKE PANEL

VENTILATION PANEL

ENGINE MANUAL START and N1 MODE PANEL

WINDSHIELD WIPER CONTROL

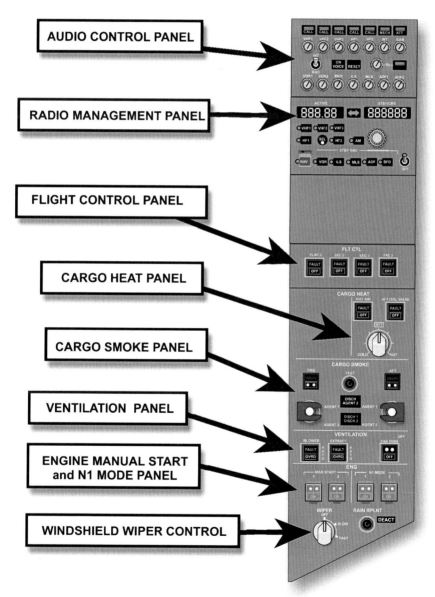

published by UNIVERSITY of TEMECULA PRESS, Inc.

COMMUNICATIONS PANELS
ACP (Audio Control Panel)

RECEPTION
volume knobs
*Adjusting volume
allows any or all
stations to be
monitored.*

TRANSMISSION
selector knobs
Only one can be selected at a time

INT/RAD
PRESS-TO-TALK
switch
*Hold this toggle switch to
broadcast on the selected
"radio," or allow HOT-MIC
on intercom (INT).*

NAV RADIO
volume
*These navigation
radios are for
monitoring only and
have no broadcast
capability. Use this
switch when
identifying the NAV
radios signal.*

ON VOICE
*Inhibits the ADF
and VOR
IDENT signals.*

RESET button
*Turns off the
CALL, MECH,
and ATT lights.*

PA
selector
*Allows PA
broadcast to be
made and
monitored using
the headset.*

HOW TO USE THE RADIOS

The radio panel is set up so that you can only broadcast with one radio at a time. Across the top of the Audio Control Panel are the selections. They are labeled appropriately and indicate with a light : VHF1, VHF2, VHF3, HF1, HF2, INT (Flight interphone or MECH light indicates a call from external interphone), and CAB (cabin/service interphone). ATT light indicate a call from a flight attendant station.

Simply depress the button with the illuminated CALL light, and all other radios will be disconnected from the broadcast even though you will still be monitoring the incoming signal.
Then, to actuate the radio transmitter, toggle the INT/RAD key or the activate the transmit trigger on the sidestick.

YOU CANNOT TRANSMIT AND LISTEN AT THE SAME TIME.
*In order to hear the incoming calls, you will have to release the transmit
button after you have made your transmission.*

COMMUNICATIONS PANELS
RMP (Radio Management Panel)

TRANSFER BUTTON
Depressing this switch will place the STANDBY frequency in the ACTIVE display; thereby tuning the selected radio to the new frequency.

STANDBY FREQUENCY (or COURSE)
This display responds to the selector knob. It shows what frequency/course we are tuning.

ACTIVE FREQUENCY
This display indicates which frequency is in use.

RADIO SELECTORS
These buttons allow us to select the radio in order to observe or change the frequency/course.

TUNING KNOB
*This knob will change the settings in the STANDBY/COURSE window **ONLY**!*

ON/OFF switch
When this switch is turned OFF or the unit fails, then RMP3 is connected directly to the associated ACP.
NOTE:
RMP3 is located on the upper overhead panel.

NOTE:
Using VHF1 radio to tune the higher frequencies (such as 135.97) an increase in background noise may occur. This is due to electrical interference. If this occurs, use the VHF2 radio instead. No logbook write-up required.

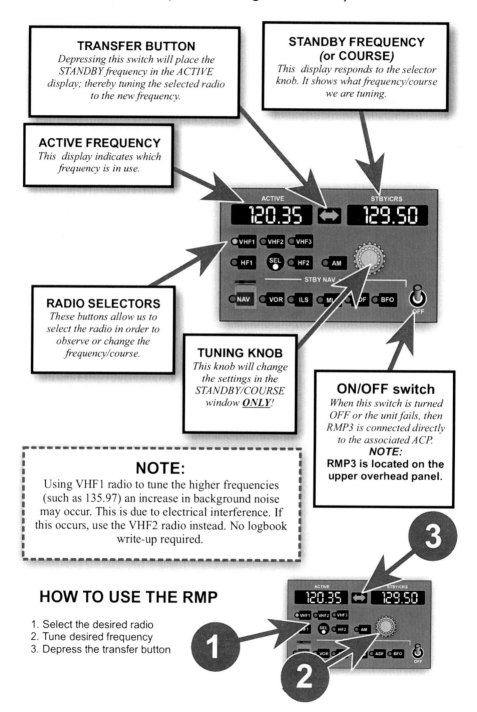

HOW TO USE THE RMP

1. Select the desired radio
2. Tune desired frequency
3. Depress the transfer button

published by UNIVERSITY of TEMECULA PRESS, Inc.

FLIGHT CONTROL (FLT CTL) PANEL

There are two of these panels on the overhead, one on the left side, and this one on the right side. They monitor and control the flight control computers. Failure of these systems results in degraded operational capability. These levels of capability are referred to as LAWS.

ELAC is the **ELEVATOR and AILERON** computer
SEC is the **SPOILER and ELEVATOR** computer
FAC is the **FLIGHT AUGMENTATION** computer

WHAT IF THEY FAIL?

THE LAWS
A short introduction.

You have certainly heard about the highly touted "**FLY-BY-WIRE**" flight control system on this airplane. Flight control computers interpret the pilot's command and move the flight control surfaces so as to achieve flight ... enhanced for safety and operational considerations, of course. This system is designed to keep the pilot from hurting the airplane or flying outside of the safe envelope box. These are the little computers that operate the flight controls and make it all happen.

As a result, when everything is going normally ... the airplane is as close to foolproof as the engineers could make it. Life is good.

There are backups to the backups and ordinarily these things work pretty well. But, when these little guys screw up or go offline ... then things get interesting.

They refer to these types of failures as **LAWS**. For example, when you are on the ground, you are operating in **NORMAL LAW - GROUND MODE**. Once the airplane gets airborne, at lift off, the controls transfers to **NORMAL LAW - FLIGHT MODE**. and remains there until the **FLARE MODE** engages during landing at **50 feet RA**.

In that envelope, should any of the control computers malfunction or fail, the airplane is said to be operating in a **DEGRADED LAW**. There are about **FIVE** basic levels of Degraded Law:
- **ALTERNATE LAW,**
- **ALTERNATE LAW WITHOUT SPEED STABILITY,**
- **DIRECT LAW,**
- **ABNORMAL ATTITUDE LAW,** and the ever popular

AFT CARGO HEAT PANEL (A320)

There are two cargo compartments. The temperature in the **FORWARD** one is controlled by routing cabin air around the enclosure.

The **AFT** cargo compartment has an automated system involving a fan and inlet and outlet valves. The temperature is controlled by the rheostat switch in the cockpit.

If smoke is detected by an "aft cargo compartment smoke detector" the system will:
- shut off the fan,
- close the valves and
- illuminate a FAULT light
 on the cockpit panel.

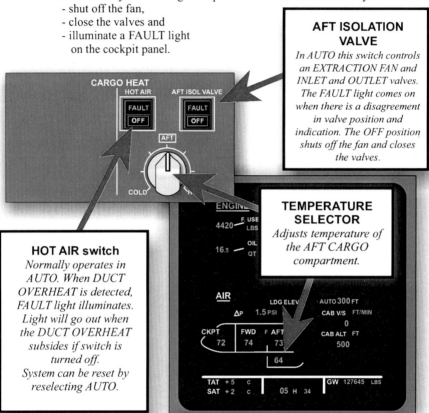

AFT ISOLATION VALVE

In AUTO this switch controls an EXTRACTION FAN and INLET and OUTLET valves. The FAULT light comes on when there is a disagreement in valve position and indication. The OFF position shuts off the fan and closes the valves.

HOT AIR switch

Normally operates in AUTO. When DUCT OVERHEAT is detected, FAULT light illuminates. Light will go out when the DUCT OVERHEAT subsides if switch is turned off.
System can be reset by reselecting AUTO.

TEMPERATURE SELECTOR

Adjusts temperature of the AFT CARGO compartment.

FWD CARGO (A320)
and FWD/AFT CARGO (A319)

Ventilation and heat are NOT available ... however, cabin air is routed around the compartments to maintain a suitable temperature inside the compartment.

NOTE:
It is OK to carry animals in either cargo compartment, although the AFT compartment is preferred.

published by UNIVERSITY of TEMECULA PRESS, Inc.

CARGO SMOKE panel

> **IF YOU GET A "SMOKE" WARNING,**
> **YOU ARE EXPECTED TO TREAT THIS AS A SERIOUS SITUATION.**

The FORWARD and REAR cargo compartments have a dual loop smoke detector system. If one system is disabled, the other still provides detection.

WHEN SMOKE IS DETECTED:

CRC (Continuous Repetitive Chime) sounds,
SMOKE light illuminate on SMOKE panel,
MASTER WARNING lights illuminate,
ECAM warning on the E/WD.

THIS IS A
BIG DEAL
...prepare to
LAND ASAP!

SMOKE indication light
Illuminates RED when SMOKE is detected. In the case of the AFT light/switch, if you push it you will
CLOSE the AFT INLET and
OUTLET ISOLATION VALVES, and
SHUT OFF the EXTRACTION FAN.

TEST button
Pressing the button tests:
-SMOKE detectors in sequence,
-SMOKE lights twice with
associated ECAM,
-DISCHARGE lights.

AGENT DISCHARGE switch.
(Has a red guard over the switch)

Intuitive arrangement allows discharge of either agent 1 or 2 in either compartment.

DISCH AGENT 2
Comes on 60 minutes after AGENT 1 discharged.
Goes OUT when AGENT 2 is discharged.

NOTE 1:
The first bottle discharges in approximately 60 seconds.
The second bottle discharges in approximately 40 minutes and is vented through a flow control system.

NOTE 2:
Expect the SMOKE warning to remain after the agent is discharged, even if the smoke source is extinguished. Here is the problem, the smoke detectors are "OPTICAL SENSORS" and the dispersed fire fighting agent itself looks like smoke to the detector.

VENTILATION panel
BLOWER FAN, EXTRACT FAN, and RECIRCULATION FANS

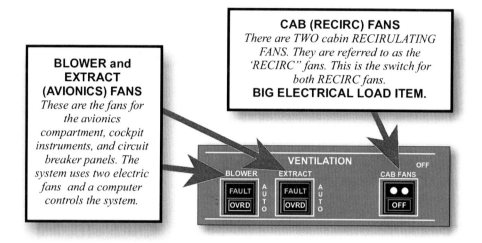

CAB (RECIRC) FANS
There are TWO cabin RECIRULATING FANS. They are referred to as the 'RECIRC" fans. This is the switch for both RECIRC fans.
BIG ELECTRICAL LOAD ITEM.

BLOWER and EXTRACT (AVIONICS) FANS
These are the fans for the avionics compartment, cockpit instruments, and circuit breaker panels. The system uses two electric fans and a computer controls the system.

BLOWER and EXTRACT (AVIONICS) FANS
Operating Modes:
There are FIVE different modes of operation for these fans.
THREE NORMAL and 2 ABNORMAL MODES:

NORMAL MODES:

1. **OPEN** *(on ground). Outside air used to cool the equipment.*

2. **CLOSED** *(in-flight and on ground with COLD air). Cooling air is circulated through a "skin heat exchanger" and exits under cargo compartment.*

3. **INTERMEDIATE** *(Inflight with warm temperature). Air is circulated through the "skin heat exchanger" and exits under the cargo compartment AND through the EXIT VALVE.*

ABNORMAL MODES:

4. **ABNORMAL** *(Either BLOWER or EXTRACT fan selected to OVRD). System reverts to CLOSED system but air is supplied from Air Conditioning system and there is NO CARGO HEATING.*

5. **SMOKE CONFIGURATION** *(When **BOTH BLOWER** and **EXTRACT** fans are selected to **OVRD**). Blower fan stops and extract fan continues to operate. Air conditioning air is used to cool the avionics and it is extracted overboard.*

published by UNIVERSITY of TEMECULA PRESS, Inc.

ENGINE MANUAL START
and N1 MODE panel

The **MAN START** panel is *NOT* normally used to start the engines. It is used by pilots during a **TAILPIPE TORCHING** situation (See **QRH** procedure).

These guarded switches will OPEN the START VALVE IF:
- *ENG MODE selector is in either CRANK or IGN/START, and*
- *N2 is less than 15%.*

When the start valve is open, the **ON** light will illuminate blue.

N1 MODE SWITCHES
(Not used during NORMAL operations)

When selected, the THRUST control reverts from the normal (EPR) control mode to the alternate (N1) control mode.

When a reversion to N1 rated or unrated mode occurs automatically, selecting the N1 MODE switch will **CONFIRM** the mode by illuminating the ON light in blue.

YIPE! - HEADS UP:
The reversion to the N1 mode is recognized by the FMGC as an engine out condition.
THEREFORE: the EO (engine out) prompt on the MCDU should be pressed to recover flight management capabilities for 2 engines.

RANDOM NOTES:

1. Recovery of the **EPR MODE** on both engines may be attempted by switching off both **ENG N1 MODE** switches.

2. When N1 is confirmed on the affected engine, the other engine **MUST BE** reverted to the rated N1 mode to ease thrust setting.

3. You will have to revert to **MAN THR** and **MANUALLY ADJUST** the thrust levers. This may result in the engines being unaligned.

4. In **unrated N1 mode**, the engine **IS NOT protected from OVERBOOST**.

DO NOT EXCEED THE N1 LIMIT.

What is the **N1** limit for your engine?
The N1 limit for the IAE engine is 100%.
Place the **N1** limit recommended by your company here:

WINDSHIELD WIPER control

Each windshield has a two-speed electric wiper that is controlled by their individual WIPER selector,

**LIMIT:
DO NOT OPERATE**
windshield wipers above
230 KIAS

Operational comment:

Operating the windshield wipers on a 'DRY" windshield is not recommended.

TECHNIQUE: *During light precipitation, the rain particles will mostly be "blown" off the windscreen surface. It is only during periods of heavy rain that the wipers are really effective.*
As far as freezing precipitation that manifests itself as Ice and snow; it is a combination of windshield heat and wipers that is most effective.

RAIN REPELLENT

"DEACTIVATED"

published by UNIVERSITY of TEMECULA PRESS, Inc.

Flightdeck panel preview

GLARE SHIELD and FLIGHT CONTROL UNIT (FCU)

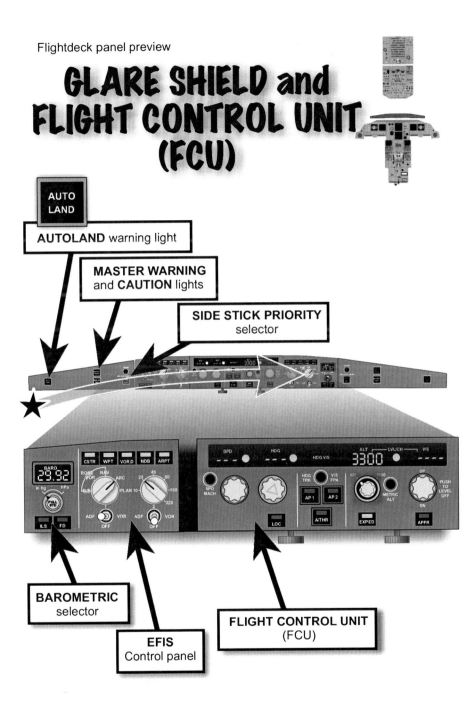

AUTO LAND

AUTOLAND warning light

MASTER WARNING and **CAUTION** lights

SIDE STICK PRIORITY selector

BAROMETRIC selector

EFIS Control panel

FLIGHT CONTROL UNIT (FCU)

AUTO LAND AUTOLAND warning light

ARMS below 200 feet RA in the LAND mode.

Light comes on when:
- Both AUTOPILOTs disengage, or
- LOCALIZER deviation is excessive, or
- LOSS of LOCALIZER signal above 15 feet RA, or
- LOSS of GLIDESLOPE signal above 100 feet RA
  (**LAND** *mode does not disengage), or*
- RADAR ALTIMETERS differ > 15 feet RA.

CHRONO switch: This switch activates an elapsed time clock on the ND. The elapsed time is displayed in the lower left corner of the ND.

MASTER WARNING light
Flashes RED for LEVEL 3 warning. With an aural (CRC - Continuous Repetitive Chime) warning.

CAUTION light
Illuminates for LEVEL 2 warnings by a single chime.

SIDE STICK PRIORITY indicator

The **RED ARROW** comes on in front of the pilot **LOSING AUTHORITY!**

GREEN light indicates that associated sidestick has **TAKEN PRIORITY.**
NOTE: On some airplanes,
"GREEN lights FLASH" if both sticks are moved simultaneously.

IT IS NEVER APPROPRIATE FOR BOTH PILOTS TO MAKE SIDESTICK INPUTS AT THE SAME TIME !!!

published by UNIVERSITY of TEMECULA PRESS, Inc.

Even though it is referred to as the:

ELECTRONIC FLIGHT INSTRUMENT SYSTEM (EFIS) CONTROL PANEL (ECP):

This panel actually controls the information on the **NAVIGATION DISPLAY (ND)**.

BAROMETRIC SELECTOR
Pull the knob and it sets Standard Barometric setting **QNE** (**29.92 in Hg/1013 hPa**); Push the knob and you can set the **QNH** (Altimeter setting).

DATA DISPLAY
push buttons

MODE
selector

DISPLAY RANGE
selector

VOR/ADF selectors
Places the indicators and pointers on the respective **ND**. Displays frequency and identifier when **VOR/ADF** selected on the **RAD NAV** page is identified.

FLIGHT DIRECTOR (FD)
Selects **FD** Command bars or Flight Path director on the **PFD**.

NOTE:
At least **ONE FD** (Flight Director) **MUST** be selected **ON** for the **A/THR** (Autothrust) to engage.

ILS or LS button
Places **ILS** information on the **PFD** including **RADIO** and **FLIGHT PATH** information (radio cluster). Labeled **LS** on some airplanes.

more EFIS CONTROL PANEL details

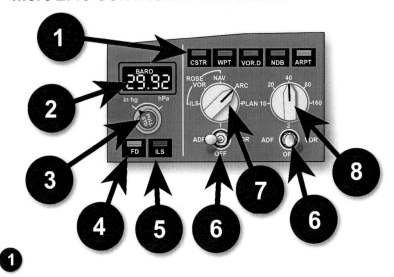

①

DATA DISPLAY on ND: Depressing these buttons will display on the ND the location and name of 5 specific navigation related ground based items. Frequently, use of these selectors is the cause of "clutter" on the ND screen and therefore it is suggested they be used singly and sparingly, particularly at higher range settings.

> **CSTR- CONSTRAINTS**
> **WPT- WAYPOINTS**
> **VOR-** location of **VORs**
> **NDB- location of** NDBs
> **ARPT- AIRPORTS.** Some airlines preset the database to display **ONLY** airports with the criteria they have set. For example, only airports with more than 6,000 feet of runway. Each airline may configure the **FMGC** to display its own set of criteria.

Place the criteria used by your airline here.

② *Let's take a moment and review this barometric stuff. Some of you new guys are going to be exposed to International flying for the first time.*
This is CRITICAL INFORMATION.

BARO window: Displays barometric pressure reference. There are two choices: Either Inches of Mercury (in Hg) or Hectopascals (hPa). Notice that they are different numerically when representing the same value. For example; the "**STANDARD**" barometric pressure is 29.92 in Hg or 1013.25 Hpa. They both represent the same pressure, but have different numerical values. Different parts of the world use either one setting or the other, there is no consensus on which should be used.

 Why does a pilot care: Because if you get confused, and place the improper reading in the window, the airplane **WILL NOT** indicate the proper altitude ... and you could _**CRASH and DIE**_!!!

page 60

③ BAROMETRIC selector: Turning this knob selects the barometric reference for all the relevant systems of the airplane/sim. If it is **PULLED**, it will display the standard reference used in the **QNE** (29.92 In Hg or 1013 hPa). If you **PUSH** the knob, you can manually select the desired barometric pressure (**QNH**) using the **OUTER SELECTOR**.
There is an **INNER** selector which allows you to select either In Hg or hPa.

④ FD: This is the FLIGHT DIRECTOR selector button. It is important to have this selected. At least one FD must be selected for the A/THR to operate.

⑤ ILS: The **ILS/IL** button will cause to be displayed on the **PFD**:
- the **LOCALIZER AND GLIDESLOPE** indicators, and
- the **ILS IDENTIFIER, FREQUENCY**, and **DME**, and
- the **COURSE BAR** on the heading scale, and
- **DEVIATION SYMBOLS** are displayed when a valid **ILS** signal received.

⑥ VOR/ADF switches: This is where you select the VOR or ADF needle to display on the ND. These needles won't display if using the PLAN mode. IDs and appropriate navaid data is also displayed.

Tuning the frequencies may be either manually or automatically done on the **RAD NAV** page of the **MCDU**. However, note that the **ADF/NDB** may not auto-tune until the **FAF**, so it is good technique to **ALWAYS** manually tune the **ADF/NDB** radios during the **ADF/NDB** approach.

---

⑦ MODE SELECTOR: There are 5 modes indicated on the selector. Most of the time, you will be using the **ARC** mode. It gives the best forward coverage; however, the **NAV (ROSE)** mode is also excellent when desiring to view features aft of the wings.
The **ILS** and **VOR** mode are used during those approaches for reference.
The **PLAN** mode is useful during flight planning and when evaluating a route. It is coupled with the **F-PLN** page of the **MCDU**. When you use the **SCROLL ARROW KEYS**, the **PLAN** display will move the selected waypoints to the center of the display, allowing you to "*walk your way through the flight plan.*"

When using the **PLAN MODE**, note that the display will be oriented to the **NORTH**.

⑧ RANGE SELECTOR: There are 6 ranges available. Pilots will be constantly twiddling this knob during a flight in order to keep the "best" picture displayed on the **ND**.
TECHNIQUE: Keep the next waypoint at the top of the ND.

The range must be 80 NM or less to display **SID** and **STAR** waypoints.

In the event of a mode or range data failure, The **ND** defaults to a **ROSE NAV** mode with an 80 NM range.

FLIGHT CONTROL UNIT (FCU)

SPEED **HEADING** **ALTITUDE**

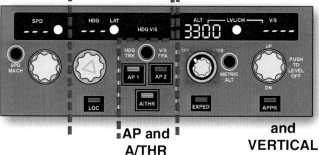

AP and A/THR

and VERTICAL SPEEDS

There are two basic modes of operation:

- **MANAGED**: This is the *AUTOMATIC* mode. The airplane is guided along the path as entered in the **MCDU**. The **FMGC** computer is "flying" that mode of operation.

- **SELECTED**: This is the **MANUAL** mode. Airplane will fly the values selected by the pilot.

GOUGE:

PUSH towards the instrument for the computer to fly,
PULL towards the pilot to take manual control.

NOTE:

Except during certain instances, such as **TAKEOFF** *or inflight with* **LOC**, **LOC*, APCH NAV**; *when you select a heading, speed, altitude, or vertical speed, the selector knob* **MUST BE PULLED within 45 seconds** *after the selection is made, or the indicator will revert to dashes and to the managed mode.*

The pilot can **ONLY** select the following **LATERAL** modes:
- **HDG** (Heading)
- **TRK** (Track)

ALL other **LATERAL** modes are **MANAGED** modes:

The pilot can **ONLY** select the following **VERTICAL** modes:
- **OP CLB, OP DES** (Open Climb, Open Descent)
- **V/S-300** (Vertical Speed greater than 300 FPM)
- **FPA-3.3** (Flight path angle greater than 3.3 degrees)
- **EXP CLB, EXP DES** (Expedited climb, Expedited Descent)
- **ALT and ALT*** (Altitude and Altitude preset)

ALL other **VERTICAL** modes are **MANAGED** modes:

---

published by UNIVERSITY of TEMECULA PRESS, Inc.

FCU *details continued*

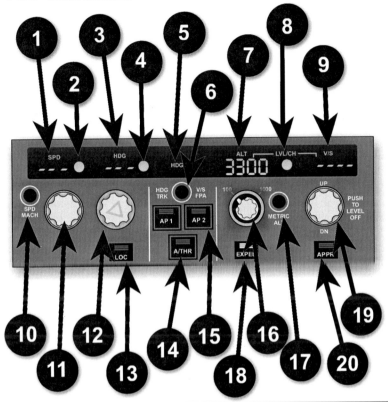

1

SPEED/MACH (SPD/MACH) window:

Displays **DASHES** when speed is operating in the Managed speed Mode (**FMGC** controlling speed).
Displays the selected **SPEED/MACH** numerically when operating in the selected mode (Pilot controlling the speed).

2

MANAGED SPEED/MACH (SPD/MACH) light:
Illuminates when a managed speed is being provided by the **FMGC**. When this light is **ON**, it indicates **SPEED** is managed and coincides with dashed lines for the **SPEED/MACH** indication.

3

HEADING/TRACK (HDG/TRK) window:
This windows displays either **HDG** or **TRK**. The selection can be toggled using the button labeled 6 on our drawing. When the **MANAGED LATERAL MODE** is engaged, then **DASHES** are displayed. Pushing the button (12) will allow a speed to be manually selected.

MANAGED HEADING/TRACK light

When this light is **ON**, it indicates HEADING/TRACK is managed and the dashed lines indicate that the FMGC is controlling the HEADING/TRACK.

FLIGHT DIRECTOR DISPLAY mode indicator light.

Displays Either HDG-V/S or TRK-FPA in response to the mode of operation selected by button 6..

HDG-V/S / TRK-FPA button

Selects either HDG-V/S or TRK-FPA for the PFD display. This is useful during the CDAP approach, for example.

ALTITUDE (ALT) window

Displays altitude selected. The window NEVER displays dashes, even when CLB or DES is engaged. This is the TARGET altitude for the FMGC.

LVL/CH light

Indicates that MANAGED VERTICAL SPEED is either armed or engaged.

VERTICAL SPEED (V/S) / FLIGHT PATH ANGLE (FPA)

Displays either the V/S or the FPA. When not in either of those modes ... displays DASHES.

SPEED/MACH button

When pushed, toggles indication between MACH and AIRSPEED.

SPEED/MACH selector: If airspeed visible in the window, rotating the knob will change the value.
If dashes visible, turning the knob has no effect.

PULL ... selected speed displays current airspeed and engages knob to allow manual changes.
PUSH ... FMGS managed airspeed engaged, managed SPD light comes on, and dashes displayed.

published by UNIVERSITY of TEMECULA PRESS, Inc.

HEADING/TRACK selector

12

PULL: Heading may be selected and jet will turn to that heading.
PUSH: **NAV** arms or engages and **LAT** light comes on.

If heading is visible in the window, rotating the knob will change that value.

PULL ... The displayed **HDG/TRK** in the display is engaged and the heading selector knob is engaged.

> IF heading is selected by the FMGC **PRIOR TO** pulling the knob: *Then the airplane turns in the shortest direction to the selected heading.*
>
> IF knob pulled **DURING** a turn (heading not visible): *Then the airplane will roll out on the existing heading.*
>
> IF heading selected **AFTER** pulling the knob: *Then the airplane will turn to the selected heading in the direction that the selector is turned.*

NOTE: *Except during TAKEOFF or inflight with LOC, LOC*, APCH NAV; when you select a heading, the selector knob* **MUST BE PULLED within 45 seconds** *or the indicator will revert to dashes.*

PUSH ... When the knob is pushed,
NAV engages and the **LAT** light illuminates.

TECHNIQUE MEMORY GOUGE

PUSH towards airplane to engage managed values,
PULL towards pilot (selected) for pilot control.

LOC button

13

Arms, Engages or Disengages **LOC** mode.

It actually "toggles" the **LOC** mode.
When the **LOC** or **LOC*** engages the selected localizer course:
- **MANAGED LAT** light comes ON, and
- Dashes appear in the **HDG/TRK** window

NOTE: *It takes a minimum of 3 seconds after arming for the LOC to arm.*

14 AUTOTHRUST (A/THR) button

Arms or disengages autothrust system (**A/THR**).

A/THR (Autothrust) button: Toggles the **AUTOTHRUST** system from engaged to off..

NOTE: *If **TOGA/LOCK** occurs, you can reset the system by toggling the **A/THR** button **OFF** and then back **ON**.*

15 AUTOPILOT (AP) button

Engages or disengages the selected autopilot.

AP (Autopilot) buttons: Toggles the selected autopilot.

NOTE: *It is necessary to engage **BOTH** autopilots to fly a coupled **ILS**.*

16 ALTITUDE (ALT) selector.

Changes altitude displays in the ALT window.
INNER SELECTOR: Changes altitude value
OUTER SELECTOR: Selects 100 or 1,000 foot increments.

PULL: **OP CLB** or **OP DES** engages.
PUSH: **CLB** or **DES** engage, and **LVL/CH** light comes on.

PULL: OP CLB or OP DES engages.

PUSH: CLB or DES engages and LVL/CH light illuminates.

17 METRIC button.

Displays **FCU (FLIGHT CONTROL UNIT)** altitude in meters.

METRIC ALT button: displays the **FCU** altitude in meters on the bottom of the lower **ECAM (SD System Display)**.

EXPED button (not used in NORMAL OPERATIONS)
When engaged, the airplane will attempt to climb/descend to the selected altitude set in the ALT window.
Sets "**GREEN DOT**" airspeed during climb and **.80M/340 kts** during descent.
It will automatically engage the managed airspeed mode.

NOTE:
EXP CLB **NOT** recommended above FL 250.

SPECIFICALLY USED ONLY FOR EMERGENCY DESCENT.

EXPED: Engages the **EXPED** mode to reach the altitude set in the altitude window with **MAXIMUM** speed gradient.
Pushing the button automatically engages managed speed.
To disengage **EXPED**, select a new vertical mode or selected speed.

CAUTION:
EXP CLB is not recommended above FL250, since the MACH NUMBER for the GREEN DOT airspeed is too low.

What is a "**GREEN DOT**" airspeed?
Green dot refers to the little circle on the airspeed indicator that is visible whenever the flaps are "0"..
It represents the BEST LIFT/DRAG speed. This gives us
- *Best angle of climb speed,*
- *Max endurance speed,*
- *Single engine driftdown speed.*

However, when using the **MACH** numbers at higher altitude above FL 250, the green dot can actually get the airplane too slow and all sorts of bad things can happen.
The angle of attack can get to the point where it triggers

"ALPHA PROT".

*Review: **ALPHA PROT** or "Alpha protection" is an automated system which prevents the angle of attack from getting too high. ... When a* **high pitch** *situation is detected, the software lowers the nose of the plane to maintain a high but still safe angle of attack. It also commands* **FULL THRUST TO ALL ENGINES.**

19

VERTICAL SPEED / FLIGHT PATH ANGLE selector.

ROTATE: This pre-selects a value.
PULL: **V/S** or **FPA** engages that value.
Rotate knob to change **V/S** in window.
PUSH: Airplane **LEVELS OFF**.

APPR (APPROACH) button

CAUTION:

Beware there is an unfortunate terminology similarity and this switch is **NOT THE APPROACH PHASE** selector. The **APPR PHASE** is manually selected using the display on the **PERF/APPR PAGE** of the **MCDU**.

- If an **ILS** approach is loaded on the **MCDU**, then selecting the **APPR** switch Arms, Engages, or Disengages the following modes:

LOC and G/S modes.

- If any" **LINE SELECTABLE**" non-**ILS** approach (such as **RNAV, VOR** or **NDB**) is loaded on the **MCDU**, then selecting the **APPR** switch Arms, Engages, or Disengages the following modes:

APP NAV, FINAL, and FINAL APP modes.

Here are some ways a pilot can screw up using the APPR button!

SCREW UP 1: _If you ARM the ILS APPR mode above 8000 feet AGL,_
  the autopilot disengages at glideslope capture
  and the Flight Directors revert to **HDG-V/S**.

SCREW UP 2: _If flying the **APPROACH-NAV** approach,_
  DO NOT SELECT ILS.

SCREW UP 3: _If flying any non-ILS approach,_
  the second autopilot **WILL NOT ARM**.

SCREW UP 4: _If flying a VOR or NDB approach,_
  the LOC and APPR buttons **WILL NOT ARM for LOC or G/S**,
  even if ILS is manually tuned.

SCREW UP 5: _An ILS approach **MUST BE selected**_
  via the F-PLAN page _of the MCDU._

SCREW UP 6: _If an ILS approach is loaded and_
  the **LOC or APPR button is depressed PRIOR TO**
  SELECTING the ILS or LS switch,
  then an AMBER ILS will flash on the PFD.

SCREW UP 7: _If a non-ILS is loaded on the F-PLAN and_
  the ILS/LS and APPR buttons are selected,
  V/DEV flashes on the PFD.

These are the ones I came up with ... I am certain, however, that there is some brain surgeon pilot out there that can come up with some additional creative screwups.

published by UNIVERSITY of TEMECULA PRESS, Inc.

Flightdeck panel preview

LEFT FORWARD "CAPTAIN'S" panel

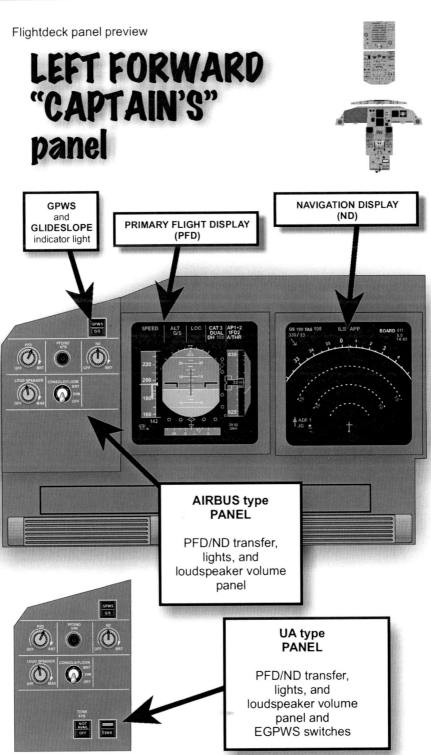

GPWS and **GLIDESLOPE** indicator light

PRIMARY FLIGHT DISPLAY (PFD)

NAVIGATION DISPLAY (ND)

AIRBUS type PANEL

PFD/ND transfer, lights, and loudspeaker volume panel

UA type PANEL

PFD/ND transfer, lights, and loudspeaker volume panel and EGPWS switches

PRIMARY FLIGHT DISPLAY

The simply fantastic and gorgeous Primary Flight Display will be the focus of most of your attention during a flight. This truly amazing instrument can tell us virtually everything we need to know about *"what the airplane is doing"* at any given moment ... and what it is going to do next. We are going to spend some time tearing the **PFD** apart and examining its parts.

*I can guarantee that one of the main items of interest to the checkpilot will be the depth of your knowledge of the **PFD** (Primary Flight Display).*

...and it is of major interest to us as pilots to know as much about this instrument as we can. We should be familiar enough with the indications on the instrument to be able to give an identity and some kind of meaning to even the most obscure detail. That will be the focus of this section, later we will actually demonstrate the unit in operation during the tutorial flight.

If we look at it carefully, we can see that the **PFD** (Primary Flight Display) has **FIVE BASIC AND SEPARATE PARTS** to it, and I think it would be easier to understand if we break the instrument into these five parts and examine each piece in isolation.

5 EASY PIECES

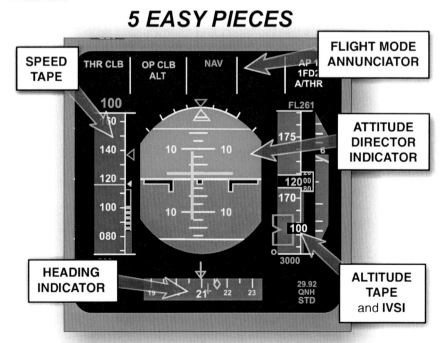

OH WOW!! Eye candy. It is a piece of aviation jewelry. Simply beautiful.

published by UNIVERSITY of TEMECULA PRESS, Inc.

TWO PRIMARY FLIGHT DISPLAY MODES
TRACK-FPA and HDG-V/S

The **PFD** has two separate modes of displaying the **ATTITUDE INDICATIONS** that affect the way the pilot receives information about the relative position and attitude of the airplane relative to the horizon and the specific relationship with the **APPROACH PATH** indications. The pilot can select either using this toggle switch on the **FCU**.

It seems to me, and this may be just a personal preference, but I advocate using the **HDG-V/S** (**HEADING/VERTICAL SPEED**) mode. It seems to be more basic in its application and simple to use.

The **TRACK-FPA** (**TRACK-FLIGHT PATH ANGLE**) display can appears to be most useful when using the "Constant Descent Approach Profile" or Non-Ils approaches. However, unless the pilot is familiar with using the display elements, the resulting orientation of the airplane can be compromised.

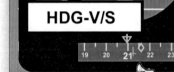

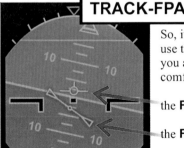

So, it is my recommendation, use the **HDG-V/S** mode unless you are already completely comfortable and familiar with using

the **FPV (Flight Path Vector)** and

the **FPD (Flight path Director)**

IMPORTANT NOTE:
Restricted use of the TRK-FPA mode
TRK-FPA is **NOT AUTHORIZED** for **TAKE-OFF** and
MUST BE DESELECTED during **GO-AROUND**.

ATTITUDE INDICATOR

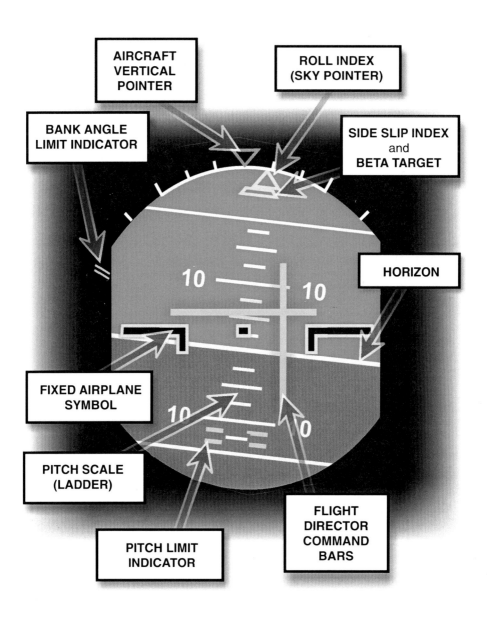

published by UNIVERSITY of TEMECULA PRESS, Inc.

ROLL INDEX: The triangular indicator points to the number of degrees scale and indicates the angle of bank on the airplane.

The airplane autoflight system is constructed so that the angle of bank should NEVER exceed the "**BANK ANGLE LIMIT INDICATOR**" (The two little green hash marks on the side of the instrument.) Those marks are set at 67 degrees on the roll scale.

SIDE SLIP indicator: When you push the rudder on the ground, this indicator will show the lateral acceleration.
Inflight; displacement indicates side slip as provided by ADIRS. When the pilot pushes the rudder on the same side as the indicator movement, this tends to center the roll index, then side slip is considered to be zero.

BETA TARGET: *If there is a difference in power output between the engines (more than .25 EPR)* then the indicator will turn "**BLUE**". Pushing the rudder to center the **BETA** index will set up the side slip for optimum airplane performance.

I should point out that operating the rudder by either the trim knob or with your feet, will *NOT* cause the autopilot to disconnect. However, any **ROLL** or **PITCH** stick pressure *WILL CAUSE AUTOPILOT TO DISCONNECT!*

FLIGHT DIRECTOR COMMAND BARS: Depressing the Flight Director selector button will arm the Flight Director bars.

When we begin the take-off roll, the **FD** bars are **NOT** displayed. This could be confusing because I have observed both of these events on different airplanes. The **FD** bars appear on the Attitude Director Indicator (**ADI**) when either:

- **SRS** is selected (Thrust levers moved to the **FLX** or **TOGA** position). or
- **GEAR STRUTS** extend after take-off.

FLIGHT DIRECTOR COMMAND BAR limits:

Bars bias out of sight when:
- **BANK** angle exceeds 45°.
- **PITCH** exceeds +25° (nose up) or -13° (nose down)
- Touchdown in the **ROLL OUT** mode

Bars "**FLASH**" when:
- a **REVERSION** occurs
- loss of **LOC** or **G/S** signal in "**LAND**" mode.

NOTE: *A "REVERSION" is an event that causes the autoflight system to automatically change mode. Here are some examples, but by no means all the possibilities.*
- *If the* **FCU** *altitude is reset when* **ALT*** *is engaged, or*
- *If* **FCU** *reset below actual airplane altitude during climb, or*
- *If* **FCU** *reset above actual altitude during a descent, or*
- *Loss of* **NAV** *mode if* **VNAV** *engaged, or*
- *Excessive vertical speed, and so forth.*

SPEED TAPE (PFD)

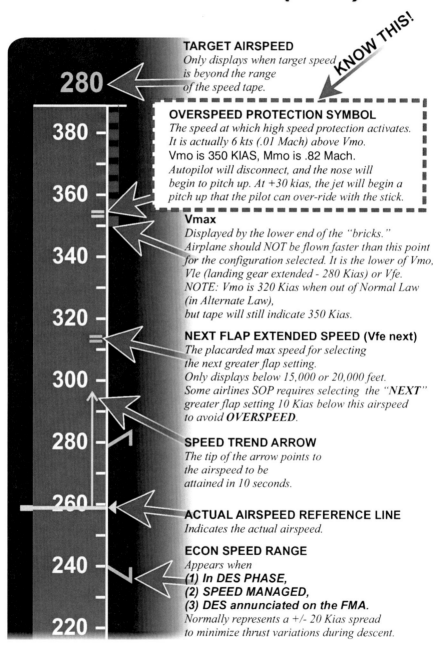

TARGET AIRSPEED
Only displays when target speed
is beyond the range
of the speed tape.

KNOW THIS!

OVERSPEED PROTECTION SYMBOL
The speed at which high speed protection activates.
It is actually 6 kts (.01 Mach) above Vmo.
Vmo is 350 KIAS, Mmo is .82 Mach.
Autopilot will disconnect, and the nose will
begin to pitch up. At +30 kias, the jet will begin a
pitch up that the pilot can over-ride with the stick.

Vmax
Displayed by the lower end of the "bricks."
Airplane should NOT be flown faster than this point
for the configuration selected. It is the lower of Vmo,
Vle (landing gear extended - 280 Kias) or Vfe.
NOTE: Vmo is 320 Kias when out of Normal Law
(in Alternate Law),
but tape will still indicate 350 Kias.

NEXT FLAP EXTENDED SPEED (Vfe next)
The placarded max speed for selecting
the next greater flap setting.
Only displays below 15,000 or 20,000 feet.
Some airlines SOP requires selecting the "NEXT"
greater flap setting 10 Kias below this airspeed
to avoid OVERSPEED.

SPEED TREND ARROW
The tip of the arrow points to
the airspeed to be
attained in 10 seconds.

ACTUAL AIRSPEED REFERENCE LINE
Indicates the actual airspeed.

ECON SPEED RANGE
Appears when
(1) In DES PHASE,
(2) SPEED MANAGED,
(3) DES annunciated on the FMA.
Normally represents a +/- 20 Kias spread
to minimize thrust variations during descent.

published by UNIVERSITY of TEMECULA PRESS, Inc.

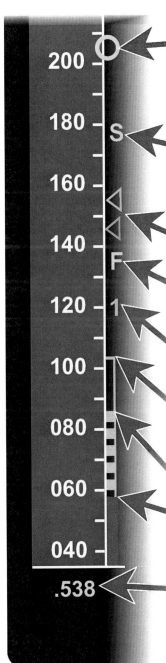

GREEN DOT SPEED

Displayed when flap handle in "0".
Represents the BEST L/D (LIFT/DRAG) speed.
This gives:
(1) Best angle in climb speed,
(2) Max endurance,
(3) Single Engine driftdown speed,
(4) Single Engine climbout speed,
(5) Holding airspeed

MINIMUM SLAT RETRACTION SPEED

Displayed when Flap handle in position 1.
Minimum speed for retraction of flaps from
position "1" to "0".
Airplane will slow to this speed during approach
when managed and Flaps 1.

TARGET AIRSPEED POINTER

SELECTED = cyan (blue)
MANAGED = magenta (purple)

MINIMUM FLAP RETRACTION SPEED

Displayed when Flap handle in position 2 or 3.
F is the min speed to retract flaps to position 1.
Airplane will slow to this speed during approach
when managed and with Flaps 2 or 3.

TAKEOFF DECISION SPEED (V1)

Because it was "selected" on
the PERF/TAKE-OFF page, it is blue.

LOWEST SELECTABLE SPEED (VLS)

The minimum speed that
provides an adequate margin
above stall. Slowest speed that
the AUTOFLIGHT will fly.

ALPHA PROTECTION SPEED

$\propto prot$
Alpha floor protection activates.

ALPHA MAXIMUM SPEED

Maximum angle of attack speed.
Holding the stick full aft, this is the slowest
speed that the airplane will allow you to fly.

MACH NUMBER

Displays when
the MACH is greater than .5 and
ILS button NOT selected.

SLOW SPEED AERODYNAMICS!!!
WHAT DOES IT ALL MEAN?

VLS

LOWEST SELECTABLE AIRSPEED. This is the slowest airspeed the autoflight and autothrust will fly.

- **VLS** in the **MCDU/FMGC** (on the **PERF APPR** page) is a database calculation predicated on **LANDING WEIGHT** and **SELECTED LANDING FLAP**.

- **VLS** on the **PFD** is a dynamic number computed by the **FAC**s.

ALPHA PROT

ALPHA PROTECTION: This is the speed corresponding to the **ANGLE OF ATTACK** at which **ALPHA PROT** activates. It is computed by the **FAC**s.

ALPHA MAX

ALPHA MAX: This is the speed corresponding to the **MAXIMUM ANGLE OF ATTACK** as computed by the **FAC**s.

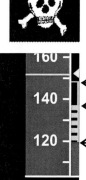

NEVER FLY BELOW THE TINY YELLOW CROSS BAR!

NEVER LET AIRSPEED GET LESS THAN THE VLS!

published by UNIVERSITY of TEMECULA PRESS, Inc.

HEADING/TRACK DISPLAY (PFD)

1 **ILS INFORMATION**

*When the **ILS** button is pressed and an **ILS** is being received, it will annunciate and display the*
- *ILS IDENTIFICATION*
- *ILS FREQUENCY*
- *ILS/DME distance IF a DME is collocated.*

2 **HEADING SCALE**

in 10 degree increments

3 **SELECTED HEADING or TRACK INDEX**

Displays when a heading is preselected while in NAV mode. Indicates the selected heading or track.

4 **HEADING SCALE REFERENCE LINE**

A fixed yellow line that indexes the moving heading scale. It displays **MAGNETIC** information. If, however, it reverts to true, then a "**TRU**" will appear over the top right corner of the heading tape.

5 **ILS FRONT COURSE POINTER**

*Appears when an **ILS** frequency and course are tuned and the **ILS** button is pushed.*

6 **ACTUAL TRACK DIAMOND**

*Indicates actual track of the airplane. If displayed, the **FPV** (Flight Path Vector) indicator appears directly above the diamond on the **PFD ADI** (Attitude Director Indicator).*

7 **TRU**

Displays when true heading/track is displayed.

8 **ALTITUDE BARO SETTING** *Indicator*

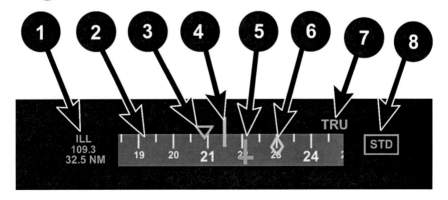

ALTITUDE TAPE (PFD)
and INSTANTANEOUS VERTICAL SPEED INDICATOR

GLIDESLOPE INDEX
Displays ONLY if the ILS/LS button is selected AND a valid ILS signal is being received.

ALTITUDE INDICATION
*Displays current barometric altitude. The window will flash "'**YELLOW**" when airplane approaches altitude target.*

*Flashes "**AMBER**" when airplane deviates from the target altitude.*

*Readout turns "**AMBER**" if airplane descends below MDA (if defined in MCDU).*

VNAV DESCENT PATH INDICATOR
Displays automatically during managed descent and approach phases. Indicates deviation from the **VNAV** *path and will move when aircraft is within* **+- 500 feet of a computed descent path.**
Numerical information available on the **PROG** *page of the* **MCDU.**

V/DEV *is something else and only appears when a Non-precision approach is selected in the* **MCDU** *and the* **APPR** *button* **ON.**

MARKER INDICATORS
Color Indicates marker passage.
Outer Marker (OM *is* **BLUE).**
Middle Marker (MM *is* **AMBER),** *and*
INNER MARKER (AWY *is* **WHITE).**

ILS INDICATOR
If an ILS is selected in the MCDU, but the ILS/LS button is not pushed, then this light will be flashing .

TARGET ALTITUDE INDICATOR
Indicates the altitude selected on the FCU.

VERTICAL SPEED INDICATOR
(IVSI) Instantaneous
Indicates rate of climb in feet per minute. Example: in our display, we are showing a descent of 600 fpm.

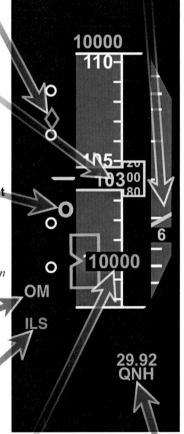

BAROMETRIC REFERENCE

published by UNIVERSITY of TEMECULA PRESS, Inc.

VERTICAL DEVIATION INDICATOR (VDI)
"THE DONUT"

Let's take a moment to discuss that little magenta "donut" that magically appears along the side of the **ALTITUDE TAPE** during the descent. The **VNAV** donut is displayed during the **DESCENT** and **APPROACH PHASES** of flight and indicates the jet's relationship to an **FMGC** computed **VNAV** path.

Suggested technique

If you start your descent about **5 NM** (Nautical miles) from the **T/D** (top of descent) point, the airplane will assume a **1,000 FPM** rate of descent and will intercept the programmed descent profile and then increase descent rate to accommodate the descent profile.

When established on the **FMGC** programmed descent profile, the **DONUT** will be centered as long as the airplane descends on profile.

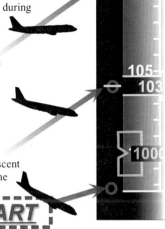

★ *HIGH or LATE START*

If you wait until you are "past" the top of descent indicator, and start a "**LATE**" descent, you will get a "you're **HIGH**" **DONUT** (indicator at the bottom of the scale).

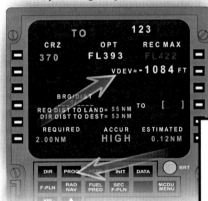

The **PFD** will usually display a **DRAG REQUIRED** message prompting you to begin your descent. Remember that the airplane

REQUIRES:

1. Manually set lower altitude, and
2. Manually select a descent mode (**PUSH** the **FCU ALT** knob).

Deviation (**VDEV**) from planned descent profile may be monitored by selecting the **PROG** key on the **MCDU**. That will display flight data for the current phase of flight on the **TO** page on **LS2** key.

NOTE 1: The **VERTICAL DEVIATION / FLIGHT PATH ANGLE (V/DEV)** indicator is used during a Non-precision approach. The effect of selecting a **FLIGHT PATH ANGLE** will be reflected in the position of the **VDEV**. Some pilots call this the "**SHOEBOX**".

NOTE 2: The **FMS LANDING SYSTEM** indicator looks like this. It is a "pseudo" glide path that has the same characteristics as an **ILS/MLS** approach. Can be used to fly straight in non-**ILS** approaches to reduced minima. Some plots call it "flying the **DIAMOND**".

FLIGHT MODE ANNUNCIATOR (FMA)

> **NOTE:**
> *The* **FMA**s *are the* **ONLY VALID** *indication of the status of the* **AUTOFLIGHT SYSTEM**.

Pilots will frequently look to the position of the position of the actuating lever or switch in order to determine if an action has occurred; however, it is possible that the positioning lever or switch may be actuated, but the appropriate action did not occur.

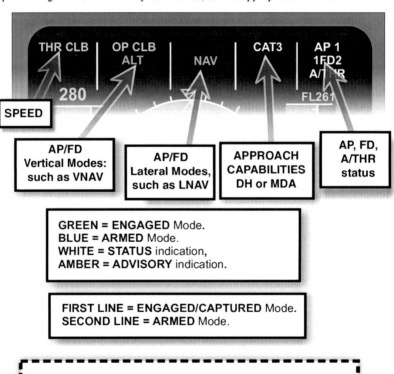

SPEED

AP/FD Vertical Modes: such as VNAV

AP/FD Lateral Modes, such as LNAV

APPROACH CAPABILITIES DH or MDA

AP, FD, A/THR status

GREEN = ENGAGED Mode.
BLUE = ARMED Mode.
WHITE = STATUS indication,
AMBER = ADVISORY indication.

FIRST LINE = ENGAGED/CAPTURED Mode.
SECOND LINE = ARMED Mode.

> When the **AUTOTHRUST** system is in an **ARMED MODE**, the **FMA** automatically engages when the **THRUST LEVERS** are placed in the "**ENGAGEMENT RANGE**".

published by UNIVERSITY of TEMECULA PRESS, Inc.

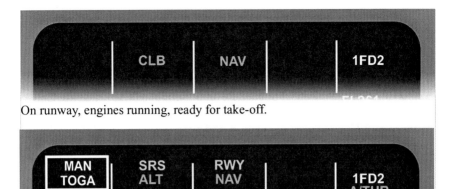

On runway, engines running, ready for take-off.

Thrust levers placed in **TOGA** (or **FLX**). **SRS** (**SPEED REFERENCE SYSTEM**) becomes active, and this places the airplane in the "**TAKE-OFF PHASE**".

Once the airplane has started to climb and the landing gear oleo extends, the Flight Directors will be displayed, and the engaged heading mode is **NAV**.

Once the airplane has passed the **ACCEL** altitude, The **LVR CLB** starts flashing to prompt the pilot to **_MANUALLY_** retard the thrust levers to the **CL** detent. If you select the **HEADING**, and the **AUTOPILOT**, they will annunciate. The airplane is now in "**CLIMB PHASE**"

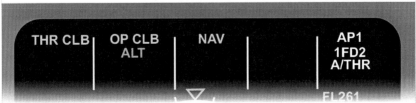

Once the airplane is operating in "managed mode" the indications during climb look like this.

After reaching the cruise altitude selected on the **MCDU** (can be checked or changed on the **PERF** page), the airplane is now operating in **CRUISE PHASE**.

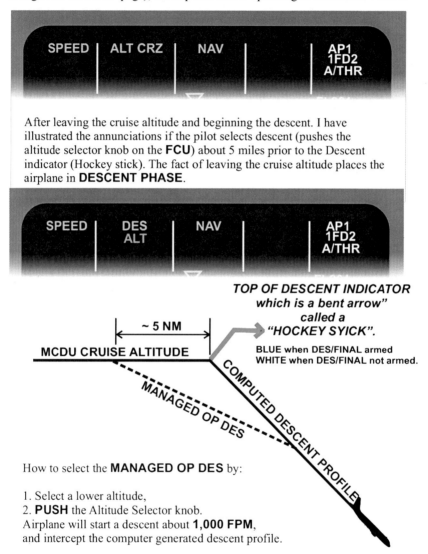

| SPEED | ALT CRZ | NAV | | AP1 1FD2 A/THR |

After leaving the cruise altitude and beginning the descent. I have illustrated the annunciations if the pilot selects descent (pushes the altitude selector knob on the **FCU**) about 5 miles prior to the Descent indicator (Hockey stick). The fact of leaving the cruise altitude places the airplane in **DESCENT PHASE**.

| SPEED | DES ALT | NAV | | AP1 1FD2 A/THR |

TOP OF DESCENT INDICATOR
which is a bent arrow"
called a
"HOCKEY SYICK".

~ 5 NM

MCDU CRUISE ALTITUDE

BLUE when DES/FINAL armed
WHITE when DES/FINAL not armed.

MANAGED OP DES

COMPUTED DESCENT PROFILE

How to select the **MANAGED OP DES** by:

1. Select a lower altitude,
2. **PUSH** the Altitude Selector knob.
Airplane will start a descent about **1,000 FPM**,
and intercept the computer generated descent profile.

The airplane will descend to the altitude selected on the **FCU** and level off.

Once inbound to the landing runway, selecting ILS on the **FCU**, and the **IDENTIFIER, FREQUENCY,** and **DME** for the runway will be displayed on the lower left corner of the **PFD**.

Then, we may select the **APPR** (or **LOC** mode if outside of 10 degrees from the localizer) mode and then select the second **AUTOPILOT**. The airplane should now be set up to intercept and fly the CAT III ILS. Here are the indications on the **FMA**.

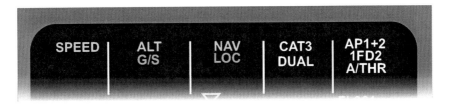

At about 400 feet **AGL**, the **AUTOPILOT** mode changes to the **AUTOLAND** coupler. There is an audible voice on the **FMA** announcing the change.

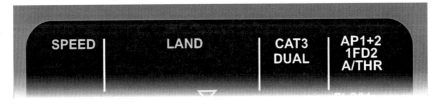

Selecting TOGA will activate the GO-AROUND PHASE. The airplane will select SRS and automatically increase thrust to TOGA, raise the nose to maintain go-around airspeed, and select current aircraft heading as Go-around track.

These are just a few of what I consider to be the most important **FMA** (Flight Mode Annunciations) on the **PFD**. I suggest that you take a moment and review them for your Oral examination on your checkride.

This is the companion piece to the **PFD**, called the
NAVIGATION DISPLAY and is referred to by
pilots as the "**ND**" (pronounced EN-DEE).

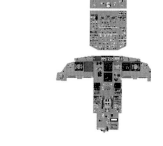

NAVIGATION DISPLAY

The Navigation Display provides information
in beautiful color for:
- ROUTE,
- TRAFFIC,
- WEATHER,
- GROUND PROXIMITY.

There are 5 modes of operation:
- ARC mode,
- ROSE NAV mode,
- ROSE VOR mode,
- ROSE ILS mode,
- PLAN mode.

ADF and **VOR** display components,
display scales, and 5 different
data display elements may also
be added to the display.

ECP
EFIS CONTROL PANEL

The controls that operate the
ND are located a smaller unit
that sits perched on the glare
shield is for some reason called
the **EFIS CONTROL PANEL**.
If I were king, I would have
labeled this piece of hardware
the **ND CONTROL PANEL**.

COMMENTS
concerning the ND:

This is the magic part of the
"**GLASS COCKPIT**" concept.
It is also referred to as the
"**MOVING MAP DISPLAY**". It
is very precise and is constantly updated during operation using the three **ADIRU**
onboard inertial navigation computers, ground based navigation aids such as
VORs, and **GPS** satellites. This is the defining technology for this **EFIS**
(Electronic Flight Instrument System) and what sets it apart from its predecessors.

NAVIGATION DISPLAY MODES

ARC MODE

The pilot has the option to select from different display options. The most commonly used display is the **ARC MODE.**

The **NAV, VOR**, and **ILS** display modes are referred to as the:
ROSE MODE

The **PLAN MODE** is useful for planning or reviewing the route. This mode gives you the ability to look ahead to details that are too distant to view using the other modes.

NOTE: *The orientation of the* **PLAN** *display is always* **NORTH**. *This can be a distracting feature.*

You "step through" the fixes along the route by using the "**UP ARROW**" on the **F-PLAN** page on the **MCDU**.

NAVIGATION DISPLAY
(ND ARC MODE)

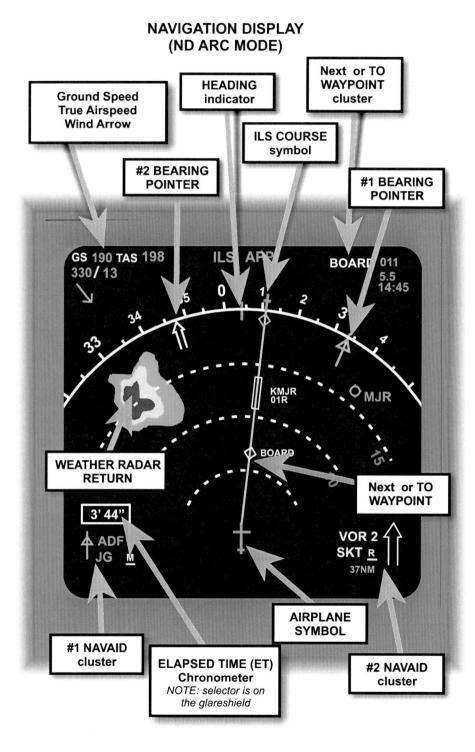

Ground Speed
True Airspeed
Wind Arrow

HEADING
indicator

Next or TO
WAYPOINT
cluster

ILS COURSE
symbol

#2 BEARING
POINTER

#1 BEARING
POINTER

WEATHER RADAR
RETURN

Next or TO
WAYPOINT

AIRPLANE
SYMBOL

#1 NAVAID
cluster

ELAPSED TIME (ET)
Chronometer
*NOTE: selector is on
the glareshield*

#2 NAVAID
cluster

published by UNIVERSITY of TEMECULA PRESS, Inc.

A little bit of
ND SYMBOLOGY

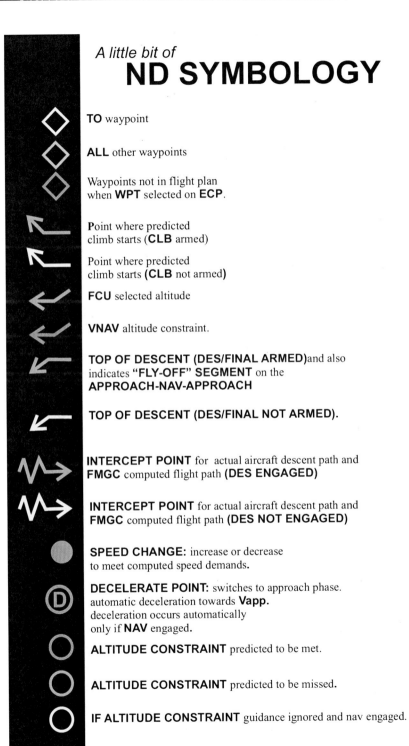

TO waypoint

ALL other waypoints

Waypoints not in flight plan
when **WPT** selected on **ECP**.

Point where predicted
climb starts (**CLB** armed)

Point where predicted
climb starts (**CLB** not armed**)**

FCU selected altitude

VNAV altitude constraint.

TOP OF DESCENT (DES/FINAL ARMED)and also
indicates **"FLY-OFF" SEGMENT** on the
APPROACH-NAV-APPROACH

TOP OF DESCENT (DES/FINAL NOT ARMED).

INTERCEPT POINT for actual aircraft descent path and
FMGC computed flight path **(DES ENGAGED)**

INTERCEPT POINT for actual aircraft descent path and
FMGC computed flight path **(DES NOT ENGAGED)**

SPEED CHANGE: increase or decrease
to meet computed speed demands**.**

DECELERATE POINT: switches to approach phase.
automatic deceleration towards **Vapp.**
deceleration occurs automatically
only if **NAV** engaged.

ALTITUDE CONSTRAINT predicted to be met.

ALTITUDE CONSTRAINT predicted to be missed**.**

IF ALTITUDE CONSTRAINT guidance ignored and nav engaged.

Flightdeck panel preview

CENTER FORWARD LEFT panel

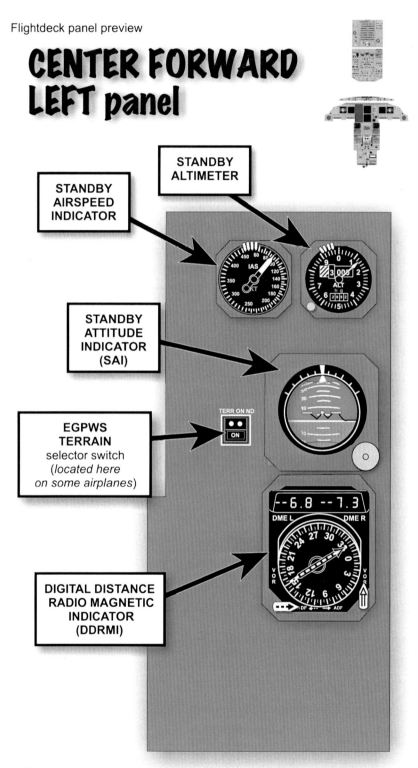

STANDBY
ALTIMETER

STANDBY
AIRSPEED
INDICATOR

STANDBY
ATTITUDE
INDICATOR
(SAI)

TERR ON ND

EGPWS
TERRAIN
selector switch
(*located here
on some airplanes*)

DIGITAL DISTANCE
RADIO MAGNETIC
INDICATOR
(DDRMI)

published by UNIVERSITY of TEMECULA PRESS, Inc.

Flightdeck panel preview

CENTER FORWARD RIGHT panel

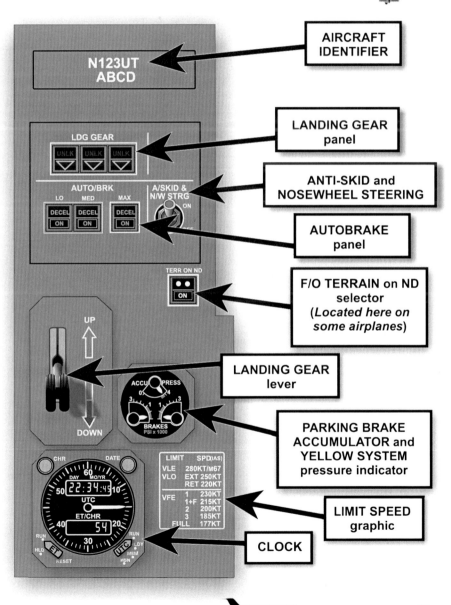

AIRCRAFT IDENTIFIER

LANDING GEAR panel

ANTI-SKID and NOSEWHEEL STEERING

AUTOBRAKE panel

F/O TERRAIN on ND selector (*Located here on some airplanes*)

LANDING GEAR lever

PARKING BRAKE ACCUMULATOR and YELLOW SYSTEM pressure indicator

LIMIT SPEED graphic

CLOCK

Flightdeck panel preview

ECAM panel (ECP)

(Electronic Centralized Aircraft Monitoring)
Control Panel

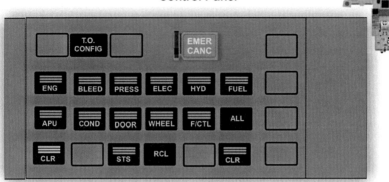

■ **T.O. CONFIG** button. When pushed it simulates **TAKEOFF** power in order to check if the airplane is properly configured. If everything is **OK**, the message **T.O. CONFIG NORMAL** is displayed in green on the **ECAM MEMO (UPPER DU,EWD)**.

■ **CLR** button. Comes on when an **ECAM** warning, caution, or status message is displayed. When illuminated, if pushed, the **ECAM** display changes

■ **EMER CANC** button.
> **WARNINGS**: Aural warning cancelled. **MASTER WARN** switches extinguish. **ECAM** not affected.
> **CAUTIONS**: cancels that specific caution for the **REST OF THE FLIGHT**! Status page automatically displays and the words **CANCELLED CAUTION** appear. Can be manually recalled by pushing the **RCL** button for more than 3 seconds.

■ **SYSTEM PAGE** buttons: Systems displayed on the lower **ECAM DU (SD)**.

■ **ALL** button: Push and hold and the pages cycle in 1 second intervals. If only one ECAM page available, tap the key to cycle the pages.

■ **RCL** button: Push to recall warning and caution messages that have been removed with the CLR button. If no messages, **NORMAL** will display for 5 seconds. Hold key for more than 3 seconds to display the **EMER CANC** messages.

■ **STS** button: Illuminates when **ECAM STATUS** page is displayed. If status page desired, pushing the button displays the **STATUS PAGE** on the lower **ECAM**.

ECAM SWITCHING PANEL

There are 4 situations addressed by this panel:

1- Loss of information to screen by DMC
(Display Management Computer), and

2- Failure of IR (Inertial Reference), and

3- Failure of Air Data (ADR), and

4- Failure of the display unit.

NOTE:

Normally systems labeled
"1" supply the Captain's side, and
"2" supply the First Officer's (F/O) side.

SITUATION 1

EIS DMC FAILURE

(Electronic Instrument System-
Display Management Computer)

This switch is used when the screen loses the ability to generate symbols and a diagonal line is displayed on the screen.

IR
(Inertial reference)

AIR DATA REFERENCE (ADR)

SWITCHING

ATT HDG | AIR DATA | EIS DMC | ECAM / ND XFR
NORM | NORM | NORM | NORM
CAPT 3 — F/O 3 | CAPT 3 — F/O 3 | CAPT 3 — F/O 3 | CAPT — F/O

ECAM
UPPER DISPLAY
OFF — BRT
LOWER DISPLAY
OFF — BRT

SITUATION 2

ECAM / ND XFR selector

Electronic Centralized Aircraft Monitoring/
Navigation Display
XFR = Transfer

This switch is used when the **LOWER ECAM** **SD** *(System Display) goes* **BLACK**.

CAPT: Transfers SD to CAPT ND.
F/O: Transfers SD to First Officer's ND

In case BOTH E/WD (upper display) and SD (lower display) go BLACK; then the selector transfers the E/WD to either ND.

ECAM
lighting controls panel

The ECAM CONTROL PANEL (ECP)

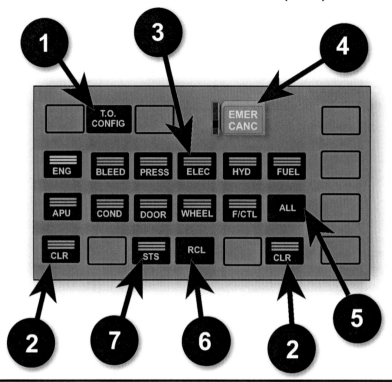

T.O. CONFIG button:

Push to see if jet configured for takeoff. If everything OK in EWD take-off menu;
then **TO CONFIG NORMAL** displayed in the takeoff memo.

CLR button:

Illuminates when an ECAM warning, caution, or status message displayed. Depressing CLR button changes the display.

SYSTEM PAGE buttons:
Pushing causes the **ECAM** to display the selected system on the **LOWER ECAM** screen.
Pushed button will illuminate when depressed or when associated system **ADVISORY** is detected.

*If the button is pushed while illuminated,
the SYSTEM PAGE or CURRENT WARNING is displayed.*

EMER CANC button:

When pushed:

WARNINGS:
Aural warning cancelled,
MASTER WARN switches extinguish,
ECAM message NOT affected.

CAUTIONS:
Currently displayed **CAUTION** cancelled for remainder of the flight.
CANCELLED CAUTION message and title of inhibited failure appear.
Can be manually recalled by pushing **RCL** button for more than 3 seconds.

NOTE: ONLY spurious MASTER CAUTIONS should be cancelled.
(For example: Excess V/S during emergency descent)

ALL button:
When depressed and held, all the systems pages display by
flipping in 1 second intervals.

IF ECAM FAILS: Push and hold the **ALL** button until the desired
page displays, then release button to keep that screen displayed.

IF ONE ECAM SCREEN INOPERATIVE: Push the ALL button
repeatedly to cycle the pages.

RCL button: Pushing recalls previously inhibited warnings.
NORMAL appears for 5 seconds if **NO** warnings.
Push button for more than 3 seconds, **CAUTION** messages
removed by the use of the **EMER CANC** button can be recalled.

STS (status) button: When you push this button, the STATUS
page is displayed on the **ECAM LOWER DISPLAY (DU)**.

The **STATUS** page can be cleared by pushing the **STS** button a
second time,
or by pushing the **CLR** button.

Flightdeck panel preview

E/WD
Engine/Warning Display
upper ECAM display

ENGINE CONTROL PARAMETERS

FUEL INDICATION

FLAPS/SLATS

MEMO/FAILURE INFORMATION

1. During normal **OPS**, displays **MEMO**s.
2. If **SYSTEM FAILURE** detected, displays failure and required action.
3. (Most) actions clear the messages as the action is completed.
4. When **ECAM CLR** button is pushed, previous **MEMO** reappears.

published by UNIVERSITY of TEMECULA PRESS, Inc.

Flightdeck panel preview

SD
System Display
Lower ECAM display

The **SD** (System Display) has 12 different system pages that can be selected using the **ECAM** Control Panel, **OR** are displayed **AUTOMATICALLY** when
- signaled by the **FLIGHT PHASE** (provided the pilot hasn't manually selected a different page).
- **SYSTEM FAILURE,** or
- Automatic **ADVISORY**.

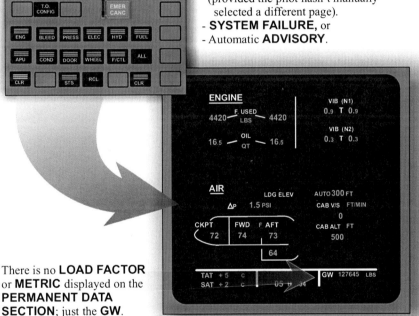

There is no **LOAD FACTOR** or **METRIC** displayed on the **PERMANENT DATA SECTION**; just the **GW**.

There is also a **STATUS PAGE** that provides an operational summary of the airplane's system status.
The **STATUS PAGE** is displayed **AUTOMATICALL**Y when
- the pilots have **CLEARED ALL THE PAGES** corresponding to any current failure, and
- when **FLAPS** lever is moved to the **UP** position.
The **STATUS** page can be selected **MANUALLY** by pushing the **STS** selector on the **ECAM** control panel.

Flightdeck panel preview

THRUST LEVER
control pedestal

THRUST LEVERS CAN ONLY BE MOVED MANUALLY.
They do not move automatically

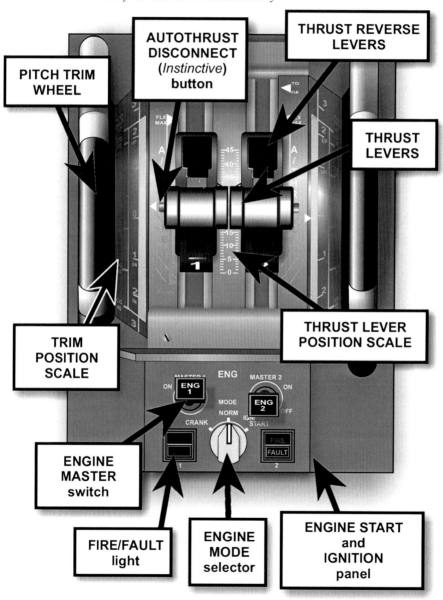

PITCH TRIM
WHEEL

AUTOTHRUST
DISCONNECT
(*Instinctive*)
button

THRUST REVERSE
LEVERS

THRUST
LEVERS

TRIM
POSITION
SCALE

THRUST LEVER
POSITION SCALE

ENGINE
MASTER
switch

FIRE/FAULT
light

ENGINE
MODE
selector

ENGINE START
and
IGNITION
panel

page 96

Let's take a moment and try to clear up an important (but apparently unclear) feature of the Airbus:

THRUST LEVER ENGAGEMENT ZONES

There are two engagement zones on the Thrust Lever quadrant:

- **CL** (Climb) engagement zone, and
- **FLX** (Flex) to **MCT** engagement zone.

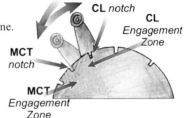

The quick and dirty of this is that you have to engage **CL** and **MCT** from forward to back, that is to say that you cannot engage **MCT** or **CL** from a lower thrust lever setting, but you must select a higher setting and then pull the thrust lever back into the notch. Ordinarily, this is not a problem and we don't even think about it, but there are three instances that need some clarification.

SITUATION ONE: *ENGINE FAILURE*

This occurs during the engine failure during take-off or **V1** cut maneuver. If the pilot elected to use **FLX** for take-off, and has a subsequent engine failure, and elects **NOT TO** push the thrust levers to the full **TOGA** setting (all legal and OK technique) ... then when it is time to select **MCT** (Max Continuous Thrust), the "good" thrust lever **MUST** be pushed lever forward and then pulled back into the **MCT** notch.

SITUATION TWO: *TOGA LK*

If you are flying and allow the airspeed to get too slow, the airspeed indicator will indicate in the "bricks" (red boxes at the bottom of the airspeed tape on the **PFD**, called **Vmin**);

A.FLOOR will annunciate on the ND and a flashing **A .FLOOR** will flash on the **PFD**, followed quickly by **TOGA LK** annunciated on the **PFD**. The thrust will go to TOGA (full take-off thrust) and be locked there.

UH-OH ... NOW WHAT DO YOU DO???

FIRST PRIORITY: *FLY THE AIRPLANE!!!*

If you are "hand-flying" be aware that the airplane is **EXTREMELY** sensitive at this point and is at stall threshold. To put this in perspective: "*YOU ARE ABOUT TO DIE*." You must v-e-r-y carefully "fly" the airplane out of the situation. Altitude permitting, allow the nose to come down as the airspeed increases, do not try to climb until you have some margin from the **Vmin** (bricks) indication. Let the airspeed build towards the **GREEN DOT**.

Once under control, the airspeed will continue to increase because the thrust levers are **LOCKED in TOGA**."
YIPE!! NOW WHAT DO I DO ???
In order to unlock the thrust levers, and reset the **A/THR**, you must cycle the **A/THR** button. This will place the autothrottles in "**SPEED**" mode and the airplane airspeed will stabilize at the blue triangle (selected airspeed).
This does **NOT**, however, reset the **CLB** mode. Even though the thrust lever is physically still in the **CLB** detent, it must be reset so that you will have the proper annunciation on the **ND**. You have to physically move the thrust levers forward of the **CL** detent and back into the notch. Confirm that **A/THR** button is illuminated and **CLB** is annunciated on the **ND**.

NOTE: *Technique is to* "**MATCH THE THRUST LEVERS TO THE THRUST INDICATED** ... *in this case, when in* **TOGALK**, *move the thrust levers to the forward "***TOGA***" position and this will satisfy the need to reset the thrust levers.*

SITUATION THREE: *NORMAL TAKE-OFF*

 If you level off and fail to select **CLB** after take-off (ignoring the flashing "**LVR CLB** warning on the **PFD**), then while the thrust levers are still in **TOGA** or **FLX**, the airspeed will increase to the point where an "overspeed" condition exists. This could place the airplane in a situation of exceeding the maximum allowable airspeed (**Vmax**). This is **NOT GOOD**!
GEE, WHAT'S THAT DINGING SOUND ?

Here is the typical confused pilot response; they will manually retard the thrust levers past the **CL** detent into **IDLE** position. The thrust will reduce, and the airplane will slow down. The **A/THR**, however, will disconnect (light on **FCU** goes out) and the airspeed will simply continue to slow until **A.FLOOR** is annunciated on the **PFD** and the **ND**; followed by a flashing **TOGA LK** on the **PFD**.
Then the typical pilot will place the throttles into the **CLB** detent . **CLB** will annunciate of the **ND**, but **WILL NOT** select the **A/THR**, and the **A/THR** button light will remain"**OFF**". The airspeed will continue to decrease until the airplane goes to **A.FLOOR** and **TOGA LK** again.

Suggested technique is to move the thrust lever to a position beyond **CLB** (**TOGA**) and then pull the thrust lever "back"(or select) to the **CLB** position. This will arm the **A/THR** and place the airplane in **CL** mode ... which is desired.

OMIGOSH !!!
Here is the technique stated another way: The thrust levers **MUST** be pushed past the **CLB** detent and then pulled "**BACK**" into the **CLB** detent to automatically reset the thrust lever automation. The **A/THR** button will once more illuminate, and the thrust will be set at **CLB**. Everything will be normal. Wheeeew!

Another technique is to simply select **CLB** and then depress the **A/THR** button to rearm the system.

Flightdeck panel preview

MCDU
(MULTIPURPOSE CONTROL & DISPLAY UNIT)
really cool pilots call it the
"MAC-DOO"

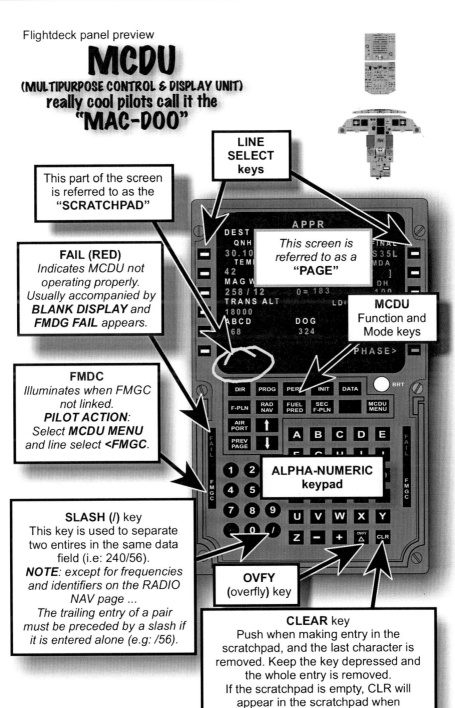

LINE SELECT keys

This part of the screen is referred to as the **"SCRATCHPAD"**

FAIL (RED)
*Indicates MCDU not operating properly. Usually accompanied by **BLANK DISPLAY** and **FMDG FAIL** appears.*

This screen is referred to as a **"PAGE"**

MCDU Function and Mode keys

FMDC
Illuminates when FMGC not linked.
PILOT ACTION:
*Select **MCDU MENU** and line select <FMGC.*

ALPHA-NUMERIC keypad

SLASH (/) key
This key is used to separate two entires in the same data field (i.e: 240/56).
NOTE: *except for frequencies and identifiers on the RADIO NAV page ...*
The trailing entry of a pair must be preceded by a slash if it is entered alone (e.g: /56).

OVFY (overfly) key

CLEAR key
Push when making entry in the scratchpad, and the last character is removed. Keep the key depressed and the whole entry is removed.
If the scratchpad is empty, CLR will appear in the scratchpad when selected, and when line selected asidw an entry, it will remove that entry.

Flightdeck panel preview

RIGHT FORWARD "FIRST OFFICER'S" panel

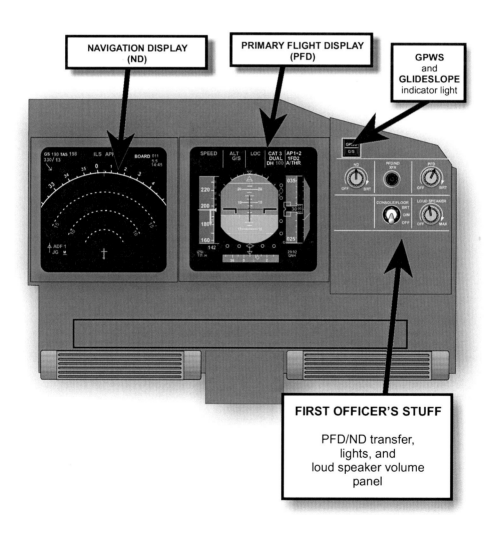

NAVIGATION DISPLAY
(ND)

PRIMARY FLIGHT DISPLAY
(PFD)

GPWS
and
GLIDESLOPE
indicator light

FIRST OFFICER'S STUFF

PFD/ND transfer,
lights, and
loud speaker volume
panel

published by UNIVERSITY of TEMECULA PRESS, Inc.

Flightdeck panel preview

LOWER CONSOLE
left side panel

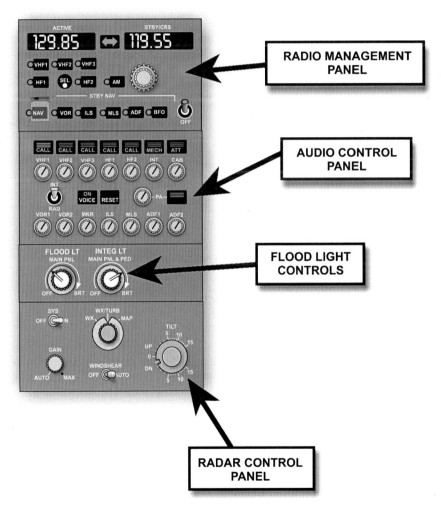

RADIO MANAGEMENT PANEL

AUDIO CONTROL PANEL

FLOOD LIGHT CONTROLS

RADAR CONTROL PANEL

Flightdeck panel preview

LOWER
CONSOLE
right side panel

RADIO MANAGEMENT PANEL

AUDIO CONTROL PANEL

TCAS PANEL

TRANSPONDER and TCAS PANEL

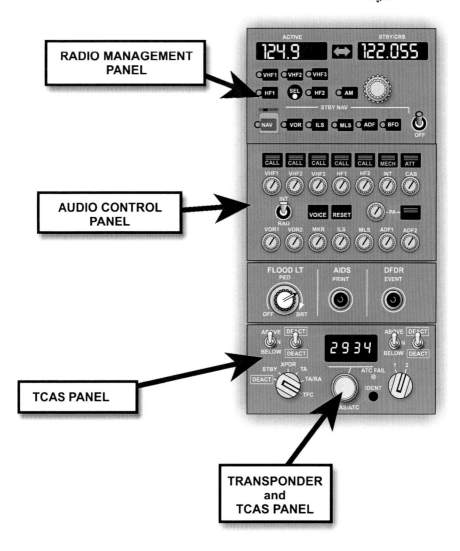

published by UNIVERSITY of TEMECULA PRESS, Inc.

Flightdeck panel preview

AFT
LOWER CONSOLE

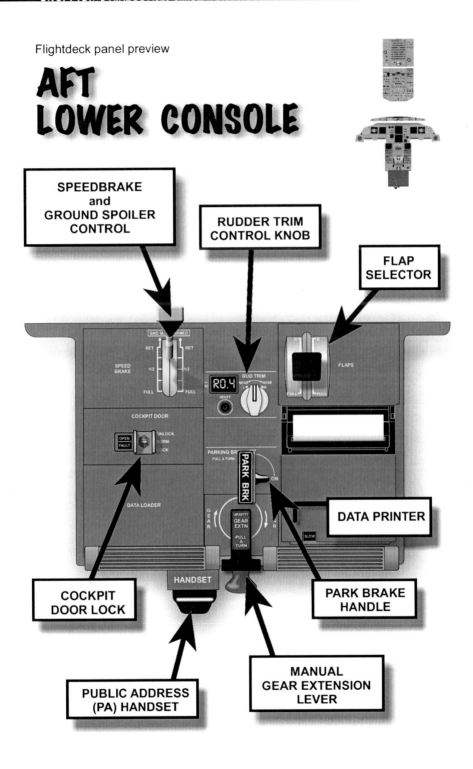

SPEEDBRAKE
and
GROUND SPOILER
CONTROL

RUDDER TRIM
CONTROL KNOB

FLAP
SELECTOR

COCKPIT
DOOR LOCK

DATA PRINTER

PARK BRAKE
HANDLE

PUBLIC ADDRESS
(PA) HANDSET

MANUAL
GEAR EXTENSION
LEVER

PILOTS ARE ONLY HUMAN ...

At the beginning of a training cycle, when initially exposed to the incredible amount of detail involved in learning a new airplane, it is difficult to imagine remembering all this pilot stuff. It makes the upgrading process a daunting task, sometimes pilots will bypass a possible change of airplane assignment simply in order to avoid the extreme pressure required to reach a passable standard of performance and knowledge.

A long time ago, a really intelligent pilot devised a really useful training method. He took the flight evolution, and divided it into appropriate sections and then listed each grouping in the order as they occurred in a typical flight process. That way, the pilot could learn each separate part in isolation. Then, accomplishing each part in order, the whole process results in a complete flight. This was known as "chaining" and I refer to this whole process as the "**FLOWS**."

YOU GUYS ARE GOING TO HAVE TO REMEMBER AND PERFORM ALL THIS STUFF FROM MEMORY

FLOWS

Once you grasp the idea of the flows, it becomes an intuitive and obvious leap to see that each flow module is part of a chain, and once one unique identifiable "**FLOW**" has been completed, we can proceed naturally and logically to the next. This is referred to as **CHAINING**, and the whole process can be viewed as a line of dominoes falling one into the other.

We can visualize the process as if they are the "**FLOW DOMINOES**."

If we take each flow module, identify it, understand it, and complete it fully ... and then, once it is complete, go logically to the next flow ... the complexity of the task is eliminated and the process of learning is vastly simplified.

FLOW DOMINOES

published by UNIVERSITY of TEMECULA PRESS, Inc.

introducing the concept of

FLOW DOMINOES

The Airbus engineers thought logically about the whole flight paradigm. They viewed it as an evolving process, a distinct line of separate events. They called these flight events "**PHASES.**"

In that same sense, we are going to enlarge on that concept and develop a much greater view of the flight evolution that will incorporate the Airbus idea. We will break the whole, complete operation of the airplane from the moment we enter the cockpit until we exit after landing into small modules called "**FLOWS.**"

While I don't want to confuse you at this point, I want you to see that there is a logical FLOW to this whole learning process. As each FLOW is completed, it leads logically into the next, like so many "**FLOW DOMINOES.**"

Simply treat each separate, small part of the flight as an individual piece of the overall picture. Learn to complete that part, and then move on to the next part. As each individual piece is completed and we move on to the next part, we will eventually complete the whole trip.

> If we take each flow module, identify it, understand it, and complete it fully ... and then once it is complete go logically to the next flow ... the complexity of the task is eliminated and the process is vastly simplified.

On the following pages, I will be acting as your guide and telling you as much as I think you need to know in order to pass your checkride with flying colors and with a minimum of stress on your part. My intent is to repeat information as many times as possible in order to have it made a part of your memory. While I don't want to simplify the importance of the material, I do intend to bypass stuff I don't think is important enough to include and to emphasis the items I think you will have to demonstrate during both the oral examination as well as the simulator ride (also called the **PSYCHO-MOTOR SKILL DEMONSTRATION**).

HERE THEN ARE THE
FLOWS

The flows start like this. The Captain may do the walk-around (not likely) ; however, it is almost traditional that the F/O does this. BUT, don't be fooled, on the checkride the First Officer will be required to know the Initial Cockpit Preparation flows and the Captain will have to be able to cogently describe a walk-around in detail.

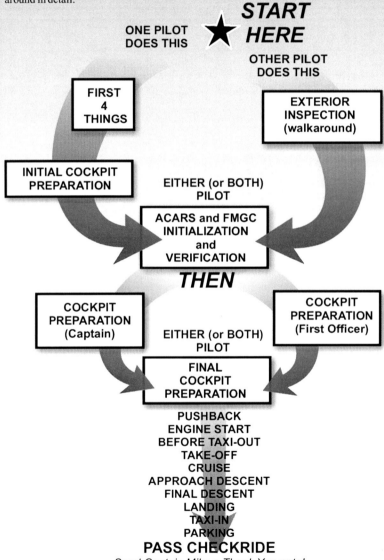

ONE PILOT
DOES THIS

★ START HERE

OTHER PILOT
DOES THIS

FIRST
4
THINGS

EXTERIOR
INSPECTION
(walkaround)

INITIAL COCKPIT
PREPARATION

EITHER (or BOTH)
PILOT

ACARS and FMGC
INITIALIZATION
and
VERIFICATION

THEN

COCKPIT
PREPARATION
(Captain)

EITHER (or BOTH)
PILOT

COCKPIT
PREPARATION
(First Officer)

FINAL
COCKPIT
PREPARATION

PUSHBACK
ENGINE START
BEFORE TAXI-OUT
TAKE-OFF
CRUISE
APPROACH DESCENT
FINAL DESCENT
LANDING
TAXI-IN
PARKING
PASS CHECKRIDE
Send Captain Mike a Thank You note!

published by UNIVERSITY of TEMECULA PRESS, Inc.

CAPTAIN to CAPTAIN
some random thoughts before we start ...

Generally speaking, your checkride Check Captain will be seeking to determine if you are capable of taking a cold dark airplane that has been sitting for an indeterminate length of time in some remote part of the earth and get it to fly safely to its destination. This determination begins even before you are actually in the cockpit.

As you approach the aircraft, there are some things you will want to know BEFORE you mount your fabulous magic carpet. These comments are NOT intended to substitute for the exterior walk-around ... but just to satisfy your professional curiosity. Here are some of those things:

 Are the wheels chocked or is the airplane attached to the tow tractor? We want to make certain that the airplane doesn't start moving until we are ready.

 Check the areas around the engine's inlet and outlet for obstructions and debris. Is there clutter such as snow piles or equipment that will be affected by the jet blast at engine start?

 Is the fuel truck or fuel station hose plugged into the airplane and the fueling in progress? If so, it might be useful to check with the person doing the fueling and determine if he is placing the latest fuel load into the airplane and that he has the correct fuel load requested for your flight.

 Is the airplane using external power? Even if the power supply is plugged in and the power source is operating, that does not mean that the airplane is operating on external power?
NOTE: The fueling may be done using battery power.

 Is the APU running? Again, even if it *IS* already running, that does not mean that the airplane is operating on APU power. Once it is selected as the power source, the APU can provide electrical power and pneumatic air for the entire airplane on the ground.

 Is unanticipated maintenance activity going on? Unless you are expecting such an event and have been briefed on it, it might be useful to go over and determine what is going on. Are there going to be unexpected delays?

 Is the main door open and a ladder or jet-way attached? Is there a way to get into and out of the airplane? Depending on the remoteness of the location, access to the airplane may be a problem.

And so on.

If this is your first trip of your Airbus career, it is likely that you will be a bit intimidated at the awesome responsibility at first, particularly if you are carrying passengers. That is a typical response and you are not alone. Take it one piece at a time, be thorough and complete each separate task before going on to the next piece of the puzzle.
There will "always" be a rush to get everything done and get the flight dispatched. Push-push-push. It is up to you as the Captain to set the tempo of the operation.

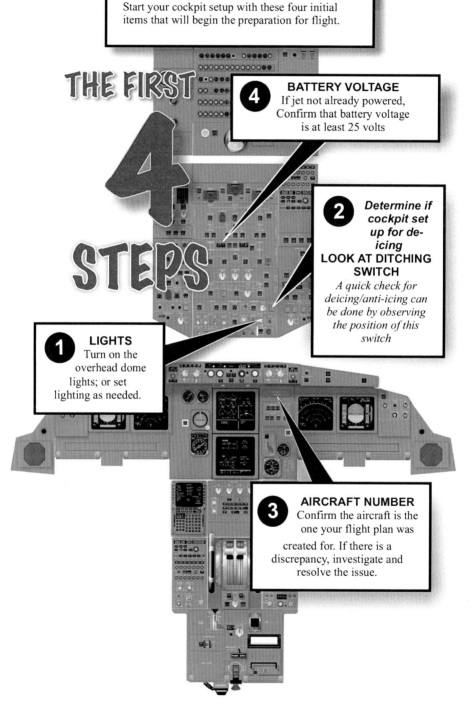

Start your cockpit setup with these four initial items that will begin the preparation for flight.

THE FIRST

4

STEPS

4 BATTERY VOLTAGE
If jet not already powered, Confirm that battery voltage is at least 25 volts

2 *Determine if cockpit set up for de-icing*
LOOK AT DITCHING SWITCH
A quick check for deicing/anti-icing can be done by observing the position of this switch

1 LIGHTS
Turn on the overhead dome lights; or set lighting as needed.

3 AIRCRAFT NUMBER
Confirm the aircraft is the one your flight plan was created for. If there is a discrepancy, investigate and resolve the issue.

published by UNIVERSITY of TEMECULA PRESS, Inc.

STEP 1

TURN ON THE LIGHTS

GOLLY, YOU DIDN'T TELL ME IT WAS GOING TO BE DARK.

It may seem that I am exaggerating, but the first time you will encounter a "real" cockpit on your own ...it will probably be on some dark rainy night and the cockpit will be pitch black.

(2) Integral instrument lighting is a good second choice, although without external power plugged in and with only battery power, the Captain's Instrument Panel lighting would be the only selected source of illumination.

TIP ! *When you flip the DOME LIGHT switch, if only the **RIGHT DOME LIGHT**(and some other essential lighting) comes ON, this is a good way to determine that there is NO AC power to the airplane.*

(1) One of the BEST choices for AIRPLANE LIGHTING is the DOME LIGHT switch. Ceiling mounted **DOME LIGHTS** provide general illumination. Since there may be NO AC AIRPLANE power source available; the **RIGHT DOME LIGHT**(and some other essential lighting) is still available with only the battery powering the system.

FLIP SWITCH TOWARDS YOU.

STEP 2

DETERMINE IF JET PREPARED FOR DEICING

NOTE: *In general, during normal airline operations, the flight crew will be notified of the status of the cockpit regarding deicing. However, for the sake of our exercise, we will assume that you do not know.*

HERE'S WHAT TO LOOK FOR ...

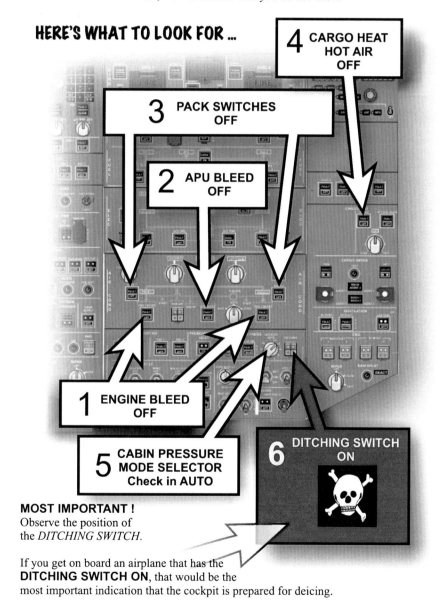

4 CARGO HEAT
HOT AIR
OFF

3 PACK SWITCHES
OFF

2 APU BLEED
OFF

1 ENGINE BLEED
OFF

5 CABIN PRESSURE
MODE SELECTOR
Check in AUTO

6 DITCHING SWITCH
ON

MOST IMPORTANT !
Observe the position of
the *DITCHING SWITCH*.

If you get on board an airplane that has the
DITCHING SWITCH ON, that would be the
most important indication that the cockpit is prepared for deicing.

STOP !

Let's take a moment and discuss the operation of the

DITCHING SWITCH

and why it is important to be aware of its position.

When the **DITCHING SWITCH** is placed **ON**, it closes up the airplane and shuts all the holes. Here are the items it **CLOSES**:

- **OUTFLOW VALVE** (main pressurization opening)
- **EMERGENCY RAM AIR INLET**
- **AVIONICS INLET and EXTRACT VALVES**
- **PACK FLOW CONTROL VALVES**

And this works really great if we are going to ditch at sea because it means that the airplane may actually float.

AND ...

Since we are at the gate prior to pushback, it is likely that we would like to have some air conditioning, and it makes good sense to get some air from the **APU** or from some outside air source introduced into the cabin.

BUT ...

YIPE! NEVER

NEVER ALLOW GROUND PERSONNEL TO INTRODUCE LOW or HIGH PRESSURE AIR INTO AN AIRPLANE THAT HAS THE DOORS CLOSED

IF THE DITCHING SWITCH is ON

It is possible to **OVERPRESSURIZE** *the cabin.*

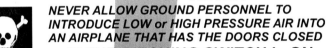

O°OO ...My EARS !

PILOT ACTION

The first thing you want to check once you have some lighting on in the cockpit is;

THE DITCHING SWITCH!

If the protective guard is dangling down, SUSPECT that the cockpit is setup for deicing/anti-icing.

If on pushback or if cabin doors closed;
DO NOT OPEN THE BLEEDS with the DITCHING SWITCH ON!

Once GATE DEICING is complete

Record the Deicing data and

DITCHING SWITCH .... OFF

STOP!

DO NOT TURN ON
ENG BLEED or APU BLEED
Until you first **VERIFY** that
the **OUTFLOW VALVE** is **OPEN**.

IMPORTANT STEP !
Verify that the
OUTFLOW VALVE is OPEN

HOW TO VERIFY

Select the **ECAM CAB PRESS**
(cabin pressurization) page.
Verify the **OUTFLOW VALVE** graphic is **OPEN** on the **LOWER ECAM SD** display.

When you have verified that the Outflow valve is indicating **OPEN**,
go ahead and turn the;
ENGINE BLEED SWITCHES .... ON

DO NOT TURN ON APU BLEED until
...... **60 seconds AFTER APU start**, or
...... Completion of deicing.

DO NOT USE APU BLEED FOR PACKS
...... until **15 minutes AFTER** deicing is complete.

APU bleed .... as required
CARGO HEAT HOT AIR switch .... as required

CARGO HEAT HOT AIR switch
may be returned to **AUTO**
...... after the **APU BLEED** switch is **OFF** or
...... **15 minutes after deicing** is complete.

published by UNIVERSITY of TEMECULA PRESS, Inc.

STEP 3

ARE WE ON THE RIGHT AIRPLANE ?

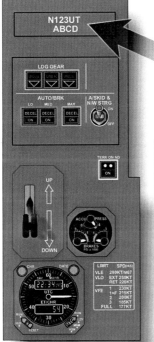

Determine if you are on the right airplane.

Compare the Airplane number on the flight papers with the ACTUAL airplane number. On most airplanes, that number is on the INSTRUMENT PANEL just above the landing gear lever.

CHECK THE AIRPLANE NUMBER !

UH-OH, WHERE IS EVERYBODY?

Every day, at airports around the world, perfectly good airline pilots get on the wrong airplane. You probably wonder how I know about such things? **IT CAN HAPPEN TO YOU!**

Some crews have even managed to actually get airborne in a fully loaded airplane with a full load of passengers and it was the wrong airplane. I am telling you this because I don't want you to be a geek.

DO THIS: *CHECK THE AIRPLANE NUMBER*
...and match it with the number on the Fight Planning Documents and "Papers"...

EVERY FLIGHT SEGMENT!

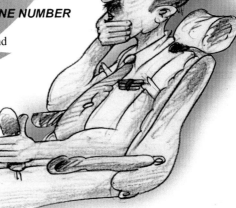

STEP 4 IF AIRPLANE NOT POWERED ...

CHECK BATTERY VOLTAGE

If the airplane is not powered by the **APU**, or
not powered by **EXTERNAL POWER**, and
The batteries have been "at rest" for at least **6 hours**.
Then we have to ensure that the batteries have at least **25 volts**.

Here is how we do that:

STEP 1	STEP 3
BATTERY 1 and 2	**BATTERY 1 and 2**
switches OFF	**switches AUTO**

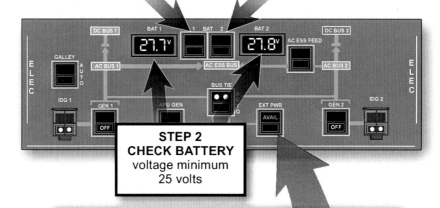

STEP 2
CHECK BATTERY
voltage minimum
25 volts

NOTE:
If the BATTERY voltage is less than 25 volts, contact
maintenance. Dispatch may or may not be allowed and
the pilot is not expected to make that assessment.

After the battery check,
ESTABLISH ELECTRICAL POWER
IF NOT YET DONE.

It is **MOST** desirable to use **EXTERNAL POWER**
instead of the **APU** because of fuel savings and cost
of operating the **APU**. So, if the **AVAIL** light is
illuminated, push the switch to establish **AC power**
to the airplane.

But if the **AVAIL** light is **NOT** illuminated, of
course, consider starting the **APU**.

published by UNIVERSITY of TEMECULA PRESS, Inc.

THE AVAIL/ON light
(external power)

If **AVAIL** is visible, that means that the external power is connected and electrical parameters are normal. The external power is AVAILABLE for use.

Pushing the switch with the **AVAIL** light illuminated,
   CLOSES the External Power Contactor
   AVAIL goes out,
   ON light illuminates.

Pushing the switch with the **ON** light illuminated,
   OPENS the External Power Contactor
   ON light goes out,
   AVAIL light illuminates.

If switch is **DARK**, that means
EXTERNAL POWER NOT AVAILABLE.

THE APU GEN lights
(Auxiliary Power Unit)

If switch is **DARK**, that means
APU POWER NOT AVAILABLE.

ON light means that the **APU** is running and automatically takes the bus **IF** the **EXTERNAL POWER NOT** connected.

APU generator field shuts **OFF**, and line contactor **OPENS**.
*The **OFF** light illuminates*
ONLY if the airplane is powered by AC.

APU FAULT light indicates that the protection circuit OPENED, or CONTACTOR opened without being selected.

... IF EXTERNAL POWER IN NOT AVAILABLE;
THEN START THE APU.

It is considered SOP(Standard Operating Procedure) to wait on starting the APU until about 10 minutes before departure. However, use your judgement to decide if it is required for air conditioning, electrical power, or powering the coffee maker.

HOW TO START THE APU.
First, do the APU FIRE TEST.

HOW TO DO THE APU FIRE TEST

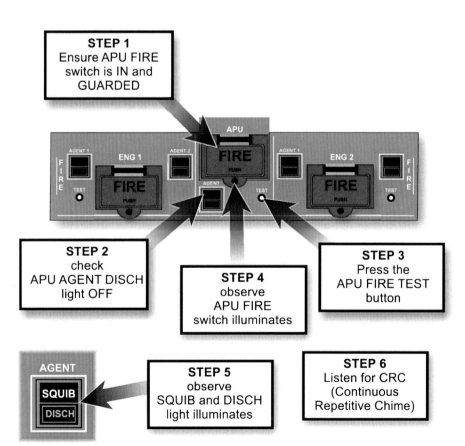

STEP 1
Ensure APU FIRE switch is IN and GUARDED

STEP 2
check
APU AGENT DISCH
light OFF

STEP 4
observe
APU FIRE
switch illuminates

STEP 3
Press the
APU FIRE TEST
button

STEP 5
observe
SQUIB and DISCH
light illuminates

STEP 6
Listen for CRC
(Continuous
Repetitive Chime)

published by UNIVERSITY of TEMECULA PRESS, Inc.

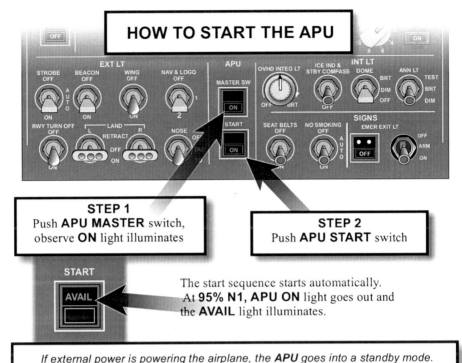

HOW TO START THE APU

STEP 1
Push **APU MASTER** switch, observe **ON** light illuminates

STEP 2
Push **APU START** switch

The start sequence starts automatically. At **95% N1, APU ON** light goes out and the **AVAIL** light illuminates.

---

*If external power is powering the airplane, the **APU** goes into a standby mode. When external power is removed, the **APU** automatically takes the **AC TIE BUS** and powers the airplane. When the engines are started and the **IDGs** start producing electricity, they will automatically take over and return the **APU** to a standby status.*

The **APU** provides electrical power as well as bleed air for:
- **AIR CONDITIONING** and
- **ENGINE START**.

Fuel for the **APU** is normally supplied from the left fuel feed line using boost pumps in the left wing tank or the left center tank.

There is a special fuel pump that guarantees adequate fuel pressure if the line pressure drops for any reason.

SPECIAL GROUND SAFETY NOTE
The **APU** can run on the ground without supervision.
If an **APU** fire occurs:
- **APU** warning goes off in cockpit,
- **HOUR** sounds in nose wheel well,
- **APU** automatically shuts down,
- **APU** fire extinguisher is discharged.

WORTHLESS DETAIL
*If the **ECAM** is powered, **AVAIL** is indicated on the **APU** display page for about 15 seconds and then is replaced with the **DOOR** display.*

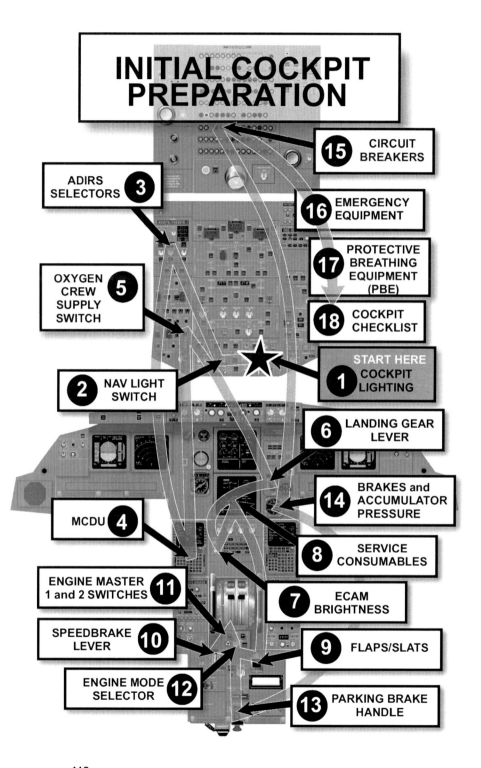

INITIAL COCKPIT PREPARATION

15 CIRCUIT BREAKERS

3 ADIRS SELECTORS

16 EMERGENCY EQUIPMENT

17 PROTECTIVE BREATHING EQUIPMENT (PBE)

5 OXYGEN CREW SUPPLY SWITCH

18 COCKPIT CHECKLIST

1 START HERE COCKPIT LIGHTING

2 NAV LIGHT SWITCH

6 LANDING GEAR LEVER

14 BRAKES and ACCUMULATOR PRESSURE

4 MCDU

8 SERVICE CONSUMABLES

11 ENGINE MASTER 1 and 2 SWITCHES

7 ECAM BRIGHTNESS

10 SPEEDBRAKE LEVER

9 FLAPS/SLATS

12 ENGINE MODE SELECTOR

13 PARKING BRAKE HANDLE

published by UNIVERSITY of TEMECULA PRESS, Inc.

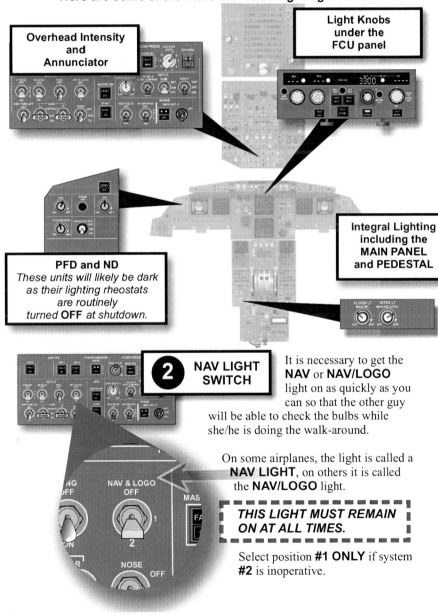

① COCKPIT LIGHTING

At this point in the cockpit setup, I wouldn't get all involved in setting up the lighting for every little dial and indicator. The idea here is to get adequate lighting so we can see what we are doing. Since we generally quickly get some light when we first enter the cockpit, when we sit down, we can tweak all the light levels to suit our needs.

Here are some of the more OBVIOUS lighting choices.

Overhead Intensity and Annunciator

Light Knobs under the FCU panel

PFD and ND
These units will likely be dark as their lighting rheostats are routinely turned OFF at shutdown.

Integral Lighting including the MAIN PANEL and PEDESTAL

② NAV LIGHT SWITCH

It is necessary to get the **NAV** or **NAV/LOGO** light on as quickly as you can so that the other guy will be able to check the bulbs while she/he is doing the walk-around.

On some airplanes, the light is called a **NAV LIGHT**, on others it is called the **NAV/LOGO** light.

> **THIS LIGHT MUST REMAIN ON AT ALL TIMES.**

Select position **#1 ONLY** if system **#2** is inoperative.

3 **ADIRS (IR) SELECTORS**

Turn **ALL THREE IR** switches to **NAV**.
DO NOT
go to ATT.
If you accidentally go to **ATT***, go back to* **OFF** *and start over.*

It is desirable to get the **ADIRS** alignment process started as soon as possible.

FULL ALIGNMENT takes about
10 minutes.

The **ALIGN** lights illuminate during the process.

ASAP
after initiating alignment:
ENTER PRESENT POSITION in MCDU

The **FMGC/ADIRS'** *MUST HAVE* a position input as soon as possible after they are turned on in order to minimize drift accumulated during the alignment cycle.
We INPUT THE PRESENT POSITION using the MCDU.

DISCUSSION:
While it is acceptable to position the **DATA** selector to **STS** to monitor the warm-up and countdown for the **ADIRS'**, it is not part of the cockpit setup flows. A lot of the pilots like to know the progress of the alignment and this would be how to do that.
We DO NOT NORMALLY input the aircraft's present position into the FMGC using the ADIRS unit on the overhead panel. The ONLY action we normally do on the unit itself is to select the units to "ON".

The airplane MUST NOT BE MOVED until the alignment is complete.

DISCUSSION:

➡️ The flight manual says:*"Enter Present Position IMMEDIATELY after placing the IR selectors in NAV."*

➡️ It also says:*"The full alignment process takes approximately 10 minutes."*

➡️ Then it says:*"The FLIGHT NUMBER must first be entered on the MCDU INIT A page in order to retrieve ACARS*

SO ... We MUST input some preliminary information into the MCDU

Since power is supplied to the **MCDU** and **FMGC** when the aircraft is powered, and because there are several **SELF TESTS** that the **MCDU/FMGC** must complete ...

☠️ **ALLOW 3 MINUTES WARM-UP BEFORE PUSHING ANY KEYS !!**

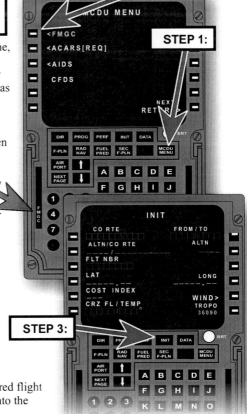

STEP 2:

STEP 1:

4 *prepping the*
MCDU

When you first "turn on" the airplane, the **MCDU** may connect to the **FMGC** or it may reflect whatever mode it was operating on when it was shut down (such as **ACARS**).

NEW GUY STUFF:
If you find the **FMGC** light **ON,** then you know that the **MCDU** is not connected to the **FMGC**, and you may even see an unexpected display on the screen. You will have to reconnect the **MCDU** to the **FMGC.** Here's how you do that:

STEP 1: Depress **MCDU MENU** key.

STEP 2: Select the **<FMGC** entry with the line select key 1 Left (**LS1L**).

STEP 3: Select the **INIT** key. This gives you the **INIT A** page.

You are now ready to input the desired flight number and position information into the **MCDU/FMGC**.

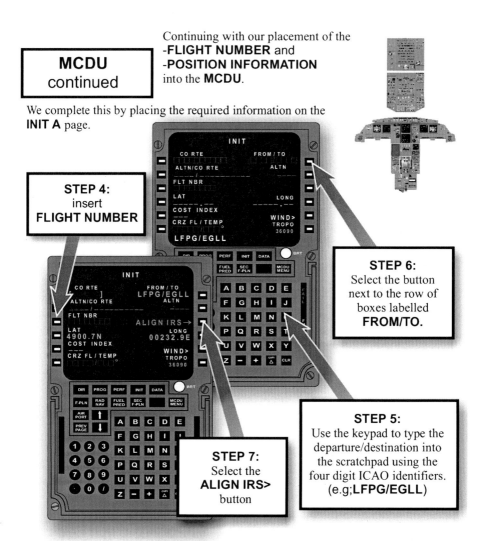

Continuing with our placement of the
-**FLIGHT NUMBER** and
-**POSITION INFORMATION**
into the **MCDU**.

MCDU
continued

We complete this by placing the required information on the
INIT A page.

STEP 4:
insert
FLIGHT NUMBER

STEP 6:
Select the button
next to the row of
boxes labelled
FROM/TO.

STEP 5:
Use the keypad to type the
departure/destination into
the scratchpad using the
four digit ICAO identifiers.
(e.g;**LFPG/EGLL**)

STEP 7:
Select the
ALIGN IRS>
button

ATTENTION NEW GUYS:

I have observed some seasoned Airbus pilots directly deviating from the Flight
Manual procedure and while "head down" in this part of the "**INITIAL COCKPIT
PREPARATION**" flow, have completed the "**ACARS and FMGC
INITIALIZATION and VERIFICATION**" steps out of sequence.

STOP WORKING WITH THE MCDU

at this point. Return to the flows as presented;
we will get back to the **MCDU** later.

I suggest that once you have selected the '**ALIGN TO**" button on the **MCDU**, that
you return to the next step in the "Initial Prep" steps as suggested in the text.

published by UNIVERSITY of TEMECULA PRESS, Inc.

OXYGEN CREW SUPPLY SWITCH ⑤

PUSH OXYGEN CREW SUPPLY SWITCH .... ON

When **CREW SUPPLY** light **ON,** it indicates that the Oxygen supply valve is open and low pressure OXYGEN is supplied to the Crew Masks.

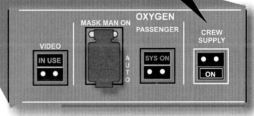

LANDING GEAR HANDLE ⑥

Confirm that the landing gear handle is .... **DOWN.**

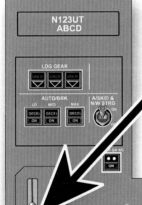

Even if the handle is in the down detent, IF the "**RED ARROW**" under the lever is illuminated:

The associated **ECAM L/G GEAR is _NOT DOWN_, and the GEAR MAY NOT ACTUALLY BE DOWN.**

Get MAINTENANCE involved. DO NOT take-off with the red arrow illuminated.

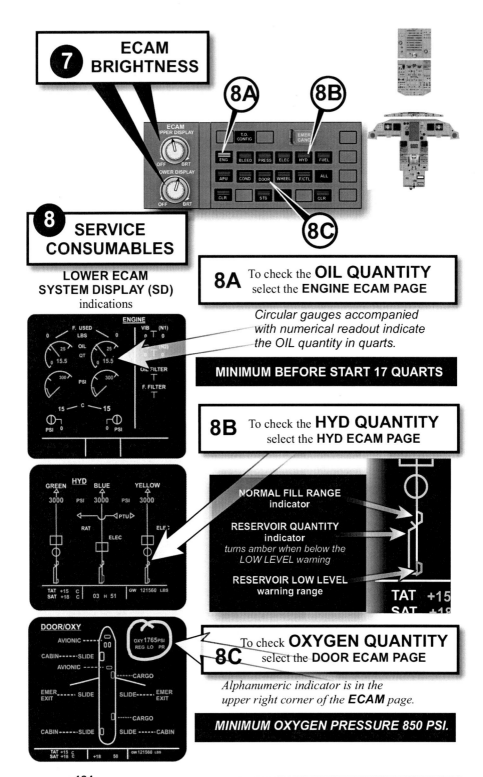

7 ECAM BRIGHTNESS

8 SERVICE CONSUMABLES

LOWER ECAM SYSTEM DISPLAY (SD) indications

8A To check the **OIL QUANTITY** select the **ENGINE ECAM PAGE**

Circular gauges accompanied with numerical readout indicate the OIL quantity in quarts.

MINIMUM BEFORE START 17 QUARTS

8B To check the **HYD QUANTITY** select the **HYD ECAM PAGE**

NORMAL FILL RANGE indicator

RESERVOIR QUANTITY indicator
turns amber when below the LOW LEVEL warning

RESERVOIR LOW LEVEL warning range

To check **OXYGEN QUANTITY**
8C select the **DOOR ECAM PAGE**

Alphanumeric indicator is in the upper right corner of the ECAM page.

MINIMUM OXYGEN PRESSURE 850 PSI.

page 124

published by UNIVERSITY of TEMECULA PRESS, Inc.

At this point, we simply want to verify the position of the Flaps and Slats.
DO NOT MOVE THE FLAP SELECTOR LEVER!

**DO NOT
MOVE FLAPS, SLATS,
or SPEED BRAKES
WITHOUT OBTAINING GROUND CLEARANCE !**

⑨ FLAPS/SLATS .... CHECK

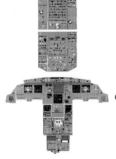

Verify that the position of the **FLAPS** lever corresponds to the **FLAP** and **SLAT** positions displayed on the **ECAM**.

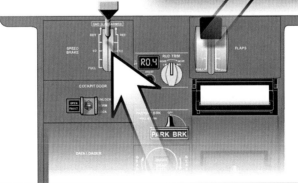

⑩ SPEED BRAKE LEVER ... RETRACT, DISARM

Verify that the **SPEED BRAKE** lever is in the **RET** (retract) position and **DOWN**.

ENGINE MASTER 1 and 2 switches ..... OFF

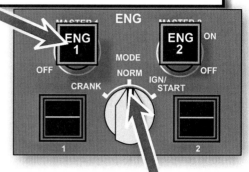

Verify that the position of the
MASTER SWITCH is **FULL AFT**,
which is the **OFF** position.

Placing the switch **OFF** does the
following things:
  -Closes the **HP** valve, and
  -Closes the **LP** valve, and
  -Turns **OFF** the **IGNITION**, and
  -RESETS BOTH CHANNELS
  OF THE FADEC.

  The **FADEC** (*F*ull *A*uthority *D*igital *E*ngine *C*ontrol) is the computer that
  controls the thrust of the engines. Pilots refer to it as the "*FAY-DECK*".

  PILOT AWARENESS NOTE: *During the "ENGINE*
  ***DUAL FAILURE**" procedure, if no relight for 30*
  seconds, the procedures recommend cycling the
  ***ENGINE MASTER** switch. "Cycling" means all the way*
  *off and back on again. This will **RESET** the **FADEC**.*

 ENGINE MODE selector..... NORM (normal).

IGN/START position: **THREE OPERATING MODES**.
  DURING GROUND START:
          - Displays **ENG** page on lower **ECAM**
          (unless another page has been manually selected).
          - **ARMS** the **ENG MASTER** switch.
          - **CLOSES PACK VALVES**.
  INFLIGHT START:
          - **ARMS** the **ENG MASTER** switch.
  WITH ENGINE ALREADY RUNNING:
          - **CONTINUOUS IGNITION** using **BOTH IGNITERS**.

CRANK:
      START VALVE OPENS if **ENG MAN START** switch **ON** and
      N2 less than 10%.
IGNITION *NOT* supplied.

NORM: If engine running, Continuous ignition supplied when either:
          - **FLX** or **TO/GA** selected on the ground, or
          - **TO/GA** selected in flight, or
          - **ENG ANTI-ICE** switch is **ON,** or
          - **ENGINE SURGE OR STALL** occurs in flight, or
          - **FLAPS** selected while in **APPROACH IDLE**.

"If **FAULT LIGHT** is illuminated, cycle **ENG MODE SELECTOR** to reset **FADEC**."

SIDEBAR *discussion about the feared and dreaded*

BSCU *AND* BDDV

The **BRAKE AND STEERING CONTROL UNIT(BSCU).**

The **BRAKE DUAL DISTRIBUTION VALVE (BDDV)**

Since it is an important part of operating this airplane from the pilot's point of view, we need to understand how the BSCU or BDDV can ruin an otherwise great afternoon.

EVERYTIME (and I mean everytime) you set the parking brakes or release the parking brakes on the ground, you will be required to check the **BSCU** and/or **BDDV** ... *and be prepared on your checkride because the Check Captain WILL fail the* **BSCU** *or* **BDDV** ... you will be required to **IMMEDIATELY** do the appropriate procedure exactly and properly to regain control of the airplane.

RECOGNIZING A BSCU or BDDV FAILURE.

You have a **BSCU** problem if:

-When the parking brake lever (switch) is placed to **OFF**,
   there is *still some pressure indicated* on the gauge.
Especially at take-off ... *this is a NO-GO situation*.
- If you turn the parking brake switch to **ON** and there is **NO pressure**.
- If you depress the toe brakes and you **see pressure** on the gauge.
- If you are cruising along and look down at the gauge and **see some pressure**.
- If you lower the landing gear and **you see pressure**.
- If you **lose nosewheel steering**.
- If you are taxiing and your **brakes fail**.

If you are taxiing or moving the airplane and you lose **NOSEWHEEL STEERING** or **BRAKES**. Here is the procedure for stopping the airplane:

STEP 1: RELEASE the **RUDDER TOE BRAKES.**
YIPE!! What could be more counter intuitive.
STEP 2: A/SKID and N/W STRG switch .... **OFF**
STEP 3. THEN Use RUDDER TOE BRAKES to stop and steer airplane using differential pressure. **DO NOT EXCEED 1,000 psi indicated on the "gauge"**.
STEP 4. When airplane has stopped, **Set the PARKING BRAKE.**
STEP 5. Get outside assistance. Use the radio, get maintenance and tower involved. It may be possible to reset the system (using outside guidance and authority) but generally using the Captain's emergency authority to reset the system is not encouraged. Continuing the trip without maintenance release and appropriate logbook entries is against Federal guidelines. This is a serious problem.

WHAT PILOTS SCREW UP.

They turn off the **A/SKID & N/W STRG** switch
with the Captain **STILL** pushing on the toe brakes!
NOTE: *Captain MUST release brakes <u>BEFORE</u> turning OFF the A/SKID & N/W STRG switch.*
OR ... *one whopping BIG stop that feels like the airplane has hit a brick wall.*

SET PARKING BRAKE .... ON
Unless brakes have been deliberately released for brake cooling.
DO NOT DEPRESS THE TOE BRAKES TO SET BRAKES.
The PARKING BRAKE switch is actually ONLY an electric switch !

Is PARKING BRAKE SET ...or NOT?

EVEN IF PARKING BRAKE HANDLE IS ON
we still have to **_CONFIRM_** that the brake is set.

CAUTION:
*The ONLY confirmation that the **PARKING BRAKES** are set is an indication of **PARKING BRAKE PRESSURE** on the **PARKING BRAKES PRESS** indicators.*

Checking the BRAKE PRESS is the _ONLY_ way to determine if the PARKING BRAKES are set.

PARKING BRAKES ARE SET

PARKING BRAKES ARE *NOT* SET

IF PARKING BRAKE HANDLE IS OFF
consider the cause. It could have been left **OFF** to allow for brake cooling.
ADDITIONAL NOTE:
If the brakes are OFF (released) then the BRAKE WEAR indicators will not be accurate when observed during the exterior inspection.

 YOU MUST REMEMBER
If the parking brakes have been left un-set for brake cooling ...
to confirm that the parking brake is set **ON** prior to
accomplishing the **BEFORE START CHECKLIST.**

published by UNIVERSITY of TEMECULA PRESS, Inc.

(14) BRAKE and ACCUMULATOR .... CHECK

CAUTION:
IF the ACCUMULATOR PRESSURE is LOW
WARNING
DO NOT pressurize the
***GREEN** (#1 engine) or **YELLOW** (#2 engine)*
system prior to engine start
WITHOUT GROUND PERSONNEL PERMISSION.

IF the accumulator pressure is LOW ...

OPERATIONAL NOTE: If you notice that the accumulator pressure is low, don't panic. The pressure usually comes back up when the cargo doors are opened or closed.

***AFTER**...you have advised appropriate ground personnel*
Here is how to recharge the accumulator.

STEP 1:
PTU (POWER TRANSFER UNIT) .... OFF
This prevents pressurizing the GREEN system.
STEP 2:
YELLOW ELECTRIC PUMP switch ..... ON
This recharges the accumulator.

STEP 3:
YELLOW ELECTRIC PUMP switch ..... OFF
STEP 4:
PTU switch .... AUTO

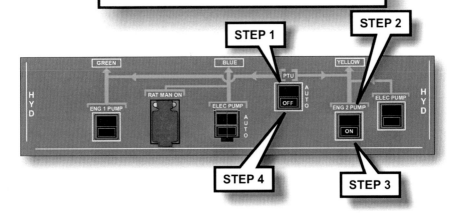

⑮ CIRCUIT BREAKERS .... CHECK

There are 6 different panels to check.

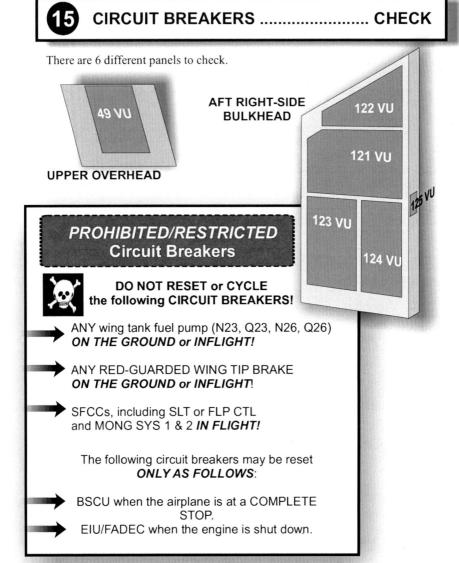

AFT RIGHT-SIDE BULKHEAD

49 VU

122 VU

121 VU

125 VU

123 VU

124 VU

UPPER OVERHEAD

PROHIBITED/RESTRICTED
Circuit Breakers

☠️ **DO NOT RESET or CYCLE
the following CIRCUIT BREAKERS!**

➤ ANY wing tank fuel pump (N23, Q23, N26, Q26)
ON THE GROUND or INFLIGHT!

➤ ANY RED-GUARDED WING TIP BRAKE
ON THE GROUND or INFLIGHT!

➤ SFCCs, including SLT or FLP CTL
and MONG SYS 1 & 2 *IN FLIGHT!*

The following circuit breakers may be reset
ONLY AS FOLLOWS:

➤ BSCU when the airplane is at a COMPLETE
STOP.
➤ EIU/FADEC when the engine is shut down.

Circuit breakers are extremely reliable and any tripped circuit breaker
should be considered an indication of a *SIGNIFICANT* system
malfunction.

BEWARE: Some circuit breakers are linked to multiple systems
and resetting or cycling may result in the loss of systems not
associated with the faulty system.

published by UNIVERSITY of TEMECULA PRESS, Inc.

CIRCUIT BREAKER RULES

1. Do not cycle more than **ONE** circuit breaker at a time.
(exceptions include authorization by a Flight Manual procedure).

2. When **CYCLING** a circuit breaker, wait at least 5 seconds before closing.

3. In flight, **ONLY** Flight Manual authority may be used to restore a system.

DEFINITIONS:

RESETTING = **PUSHING IN a CIRCUIT BREAKER** that has become unseated.
CYCLING = **PULLING and RESETTING a CIRCUIT BREAKER**.

ON THE GROUND:

THE CIRCUIT BREAKER RULE
WARNING:
RESETTING A TRIPPED CIRCUIT BREAKER
ON THE GROUND IS NOT AUTHORIZED

*The airplane MUST BE STOPPED with the
PARKING BRAKE SET prior to cycling
ANY CIRCUIT BREAKER !*

IN FLIGHT:

RESETTING a circuit breaker may be accomplished ONLY if the Captain using his
EMERGENCY AUTHORITY deems it **NECESSARY** for the **SAFETY OF FLIGHT**.

CYCLING a circuit breaker may be accomplished **ONLY** if it is a specifically directed
part of a **FLIGHT MANUAL** procedure.

*HOWEVER, THE CAPTAIN MAY USE
EMERGENCY AUTHORITY IF NECESSARY.*

A major airline has this **CAPTAIN'S NOTICE**:
Whether in the air or on the ground, **CYCLING** *a circuit breaker*
REQUIRES *an* **MRM code 996** *to be entered in the* **ACARS**.
*Enter the cycled circuit breaker(s) grid location (e.g.; D9), name (e.g.;
LGC1U), and the reason for cycling in the comments field .... and send.
This complies with current FAA directives regarding logbook currency.*

⑯ EMERGENCY EQUIPMENT .... CHECK

Verify these 7 things are **INSTALLED** and **PROPERLY STOWED**:

FIRE EXTINGUISHER (HALON)

Check pressure in the NORMAL band, seal intact.

OXYGEN MASKS

There are FOUR to check: Captain, First Officer, Observer (2).

AXE (CRASH AXE)

Check on board and stowed properly.

MEDICAL KIT, SECONDARY

Two green seals REQUIRED;
if yellow, broken, or missing ... report to maintenance.

ESCAPE ROPES

There are two rope enclosures to check.

LIFE VESTS

There are FOUR to check: Captain, First Officer, Observer (2).

FLASHLIGHT

⑰ (PBE)PROTECTIVE BREATHING EQUIPMENT .... CHECK

Observe the VISUAL INDICATOR:
BLUE indicates it is OK,
PINK "may" indicate that it needs to be replaced, if there is any question, ask maintenance to make an independent evaluation. It has been my experience that even when it looks "pink" to me, it is generally OK. The maintenance people have their own set of criteria for dispatch purposes.

⑱ Cockpit CHECKLIST CARD .... CHECK

Check for unserviceable damage, out-of-date, or missing.
There are specific guidelines in the Flight Operations Manual regarding the acceptability of checklists with damage.

INTRODUCING
THE NEXT *intimidating* FLOW SECTION

LOADING THE MCDU

We are going to divide the **MCDU** loading task into two separate domains.
First, we will initialize the **ACARS** and
Second, we will load the **FMGC**.
There may be some confusion at the start, but if we do this step by step it will
come together at the end.

Note that we have previously completed the "**ALIGN**" and
FLIGHT NUMBER entry requirements.

THERE ARE
TWO PARTS
TO THE MCDU
INITIALIZATION
AND
VERIFICATION
PROCESS. THE
ACARS AND
FMGC.

As you become more familiar and proficient with the
MCDU you will be able to develop your own flow
pattern that allows you to complete both domains
more expeditiously. In the real world, the pilot
(usually the First Officer) will be accessing
and operating in both domains
virtually simultaneously.

But right now, while
you are a newbie,
stay with the
program and be
methodical in your
application of the
required steps.
Proficiency develops
rather quickly and
the learning curve is
not that demanding,
especially if you
have worked with
the "glass" before.

Here are some GENERAL

MCDU INFORMATION

MCDU/FMGC initialization would normally be completed prior to the Captain and First Officer's cockpit preparation flows. If, however, all the necessary data is not available (flight plan, **ATC** clearance, **ATIS**, fueling data, etc) then the **MCDU/FMGC** initialization may be done at any point in the Cockpit Preparation flow. However, here is my recommendation for your checkride and until you become familiar with the flows ...
stay with the flows as they are presented here.

definition of term:

Just what do they mean by
INDEPENDENT VERIFICATION?

*One pilot loads the data without assistance or influence from the other pilot; **THEN***
*the other pilot **INDEPENDENTLY VERIFIES** all entries are correct. Discrepancies must be discussed, verified, and corrected.*

Both the **MCDU/FMGC**s and the **FCU** conducts internal testing when electrical power is first applied; so

WAIT 3 MINUTES
after the initial power application
before pushing any **MCDU** keys.

If the **PLEASE WAIT** message appears
in the scratchpad,
DO NOT PUSH ANY MCDU KEY
until the message disappears.

If the

OPP FMGC IN PROGRESS
message appears; that means
only the opposite **FMGC** is working.
*If that occurs, the **POSITION MONITOR** in the **DATA**
page displays a position for the working **FMGC** only.*

Note for First Officers:
*If you receive the **FINAL WEIGHTS** before engine start, you may enter the final **ZFW** on **INIT page B**. After engine start, **INIT page B** is automatically replaced with the **FUEL PRED** page. Use the **FUEL PRED** page to make changes.*

First, we will complete the **ACARS** initialization:

Pilots call it "AY-KARZ."

ACARS stands for
"AIRCRAFT COMMUNICATION
ADDRESSING and REPORTING
SYSTEM."

This is a system that provides high speed two-way data link communication between Pilots and ATC (for example, a PDC), Dispatchers, Load confirmation and Maintenance coordinators. The no. 3 radio is normally dedicated solely for the use of **ACARS**. The radio is not normally tuned manually, but has a sophisticated automatic system that selects frequencies that "relieve congestion" in high-traffic areas.

> *Some airplanes are equipped with an even more complex system called* **ATSU** *(***AIR TRAFFIC SERVICE UNIT***). Fortunately, however,* **ATSU** *integrates seamlessly with the* **ARINC** *system so that operations are very similar to the standard* **ARINC** *unit. Wheeew!*

Data is usually entered automatically, but information may be entered manually. Here are some places where automatic transmission of data routinely occurs:

- **OUT REPORT** is sent after **PARKING BRAKE**
  is FIRST released with all entry doors closed.
- **OFF REPORT** is sent after **LIFTOFF**.
- **ON REPORT** is sent after **TOUCHDOWN**.
- **IN REPORT** is sent after *PARKING BRAKE IS SET* AND
  an **ENTRY DOOR OPENED**.
- **ENGINE** and **AIR DATA REPORTS** sent **ENROUTE**.

How to access THE ACARS/ATSU

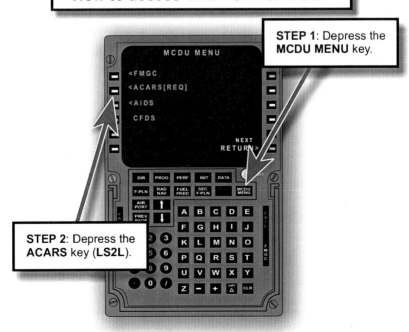

STEP 1: Depress the
MCDU MENU key.

STEP 2: Depress the
ACARS key (**LS2L**).

then INITIALIZE THE ACARS/ATSU

MAIN INDEX

<PREFLIGHT	ATC (ATS)>
<ENROUTE	COMM>
<POSTFLIGHT	REPORTS>
<MESSAGE LOG	REQUESTS>
<LINK MANAGER	FLT DATA>

STEP 3: Depress the PREFLIGHT key (LS1L).

STEP 4: Depress the INITIALIZE key (LS1L).

STEP 5: Fill in the appropriate boxes.

PREFLIGHT INDEX

<INITIALIZE	ATC (ATS)>
<FLT PAPERS	COMM>
<ATIS	REPORTS>
<PERFORMANCE	REQUESTS>
<LINK MANAGER	FLT DATA>
<MAIN	

INITIALIZE 1 / 2

FLT NO   DEPT DATE
DEPT   DEST
FPT   ALTN
FOB   FUEL / GAL
            AUTO INIT*
<RETURN

FLT NO: *Use radio call sign number or A/C registration number without alphabetical identifiers if flying military charter or ferry.*
DEPT: *Departure airport (3 digit identifier; e.g. DEN)*
FPT: *Flight Plan Time (Example: use 123 for 1 hour and 23 minutes)*
FOB: *Fuel On Board. By weight, (e.g. 62.3 thousands of pounds)*
NOTE: If the brakes are released BEFORE the final boarded fuel is entered, some flashing cursors (ACARS MSG)appear on memo section of the UPPER ECAM. If the data is not entered within 2 minutes, the report is sent anyway ... and the FUEL DATA must be sent by voice.
DEPT DATE: *Use two digit month from Flight Plan (may differ from local month).*
DEST: *Destination airport (3 digit identifier; e.g. LAX)*
ALTN: *Enter selected airports (if desired)*
FUEL/GAL: *Actual GALLONS boarded (TTL FROM TRUCKS); e.g. 1453.*

STEP 6: Select RETURN to go back to the PREFLIGHT INDEX.

go to:
PAGE 2/2 *...and enter CAPT NAME and FILE NUMBER and other pertinent requested information.*

published by UNIVERSITY of TEMECULA PRESS, Inc.

After completing the **ACARS INITIALIZATION** *and selecting the* **RETURN**
key, the **MCDU** *display should be on* **PREFLIGHT INDEX** *page.*
We can use the **ACARS** *to obtain information to complete the* **FMGC** *setup.*

OBTAIN ACARS FLIGHT INFORMATION

Here is some of the information needed from the **ACARS** in order to complete
the **FMGC** initialization:

1- ATIS
2- Weight Manifest
3- Runway Data
4- PDC (Pre-Departure Clearance)
5- Release Verify
6- Gate Connections

NOTE: At a minimum:
- *ATIS*
- *Runway Data*
are needed to complete the **FMGC**
initialization.

*Here is a chart I made up that
has a suggested sequence of
keystrokes that will help you
get the desired information.*

```
12:45 PREFLIGHT INDEX
<INITIALIZE        ATC (ATS)>
<FLT PAPERS           COMM>
<ATIS               REPORTS>
<PERFORMANCE       REQUESTS>
<LINK MANAGER     FLT DATA>
<MAIN
```

TO GET THIS	SELECT	then SELECT	then SELECT	
1- ATIS	ATC	ATIS	SEND	
2- WEIGHT MANIFEST	REQUESTS	PERFORMANCE	WEIGHT MANIFEST	SEND
3- RUNWAY DATA	REQUESTS	PERFORMANCE	SEND	
4- PDC	ATC	PDC		
5- RELEASE VERIFY	REQUESTS	DISPATCH	RELEASE VERIFY	
6- GATE CONNECTIONS	REQUESTS	GATE CONNECTIONS		

It is assumed that you can "fill in the appropriate" blanks on the selected pages using
your intuition. I won't waste your time on detailing the steps precisely.

Once we have completed the **ACARS**, we are ready to initialize the **MCDU/FMGC**

NOTE:
You cannot retrieve **ACARS** *information*
UNTIL
The **FLIGHT NUMBER** *has been entered
on the* **FMGC INIT A** *page.*

In order to continue with the FMGC initialization, we have to place the MCDU into the FMGC mode.

LINKING the MCDU to the FMGC

STEP 1:
Depress the **MCDU MENU** key.

STEP 2:
LSK 1L .... <FMGC.
This will ensure a connection from the FMGC to the MCDU.

SHORT DISCUSSION:
The MCDU can actually function as the operator control interface for many modalities other than Flight Management. That means that this unit may be used to access other databases than simply pilot stuff. Here are some potential choices you might see displayed. There are others, of course, and these are shown as examples only.

NOTE:
If the FMGC annunciator is illuminated, then the FMGC is *NOT* linked to the MCDU.

FMGC = Flight Management and Guidance Computer
ACARS = Aircraft Communication, Adressing and Reporting System
ATSU = Air Traffic Service Unit (*used in lieu of ACARS when installed*)
AIDS = Aircraft Integrated Data System (*normally Maintenance only*)
CFDS = Centralized Fault Display System (*normally Maintenance only*)

PROTOCOL NOTE:
In this presentation we will use the following notation to identify the Line Selector Keys alongside the MCDU display this way:
LSK 1L (Line Select Key 1 left).
or for another example;
LSK 2R (Line Select Key 2 Right)

---

published by UNIVERSITY of TEMECULA PRESS, Inc.

TIME-OUT
I FEEL YOUR PAIN ...

This is an almost impossible task when you first start, I know how you feel. So, since the **MCDU** is a little complex when you are first starting to use it, and we want to ensure that we get every little detail completed ...here is what has evolved in airlines around the world. It is the ubiquitous "gouge" or acronym that will help even the most memory challenged pilot to get everything done.

Before I reveal my "secret" formula for remembering the **MCDU** loading steps, let me say that there are a whole bunch of these little memory joggers out there; and different airlines favor different ones. For example, one major airline uses this scheme:

D = DATA
I = INIT page A, INIT page B
F = F-PLAN page A, F-PLAN page B
R = RAD NAV page
S = SEC F-PLAN
F = FUEL PRED page
P = PERF page

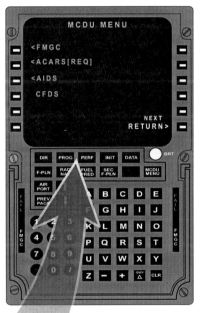

It seems to work for them. However, we will use a slightly different order to our set of pages. I tell you this to point out that when you get a little more experienced, there is nothing that says you can't do anything you want and in any order ...as long as everything gets done.

However, here is the acronym we will be using for this tutorial.

D-I-F-R-I-P+P-S
D = DATA page
I = INIT A page
F = F-PLAN page
R = RAD NAV page
I = INIT B page
P = PERF page
P = PROG page
S = SEC F-PLAN page

WHAT IS DIFRIP+PS???

D-I-F-R-I-P₁+P₂-S

DISCUSSION: Pilots have a hard time remembering stuff ...so there is a tendency to group the more obscure items into clusters and give them names ...these are referred to as "gouges" (pronounced GOW-JEZ).

The **DIFRIPPS** gouge is simply a pilot way of prompting the memory of the key sequence to press when initializing the MCDU. I have heard others, such as: **DIFRS FP.** You will have to make up your own to suit your needs.

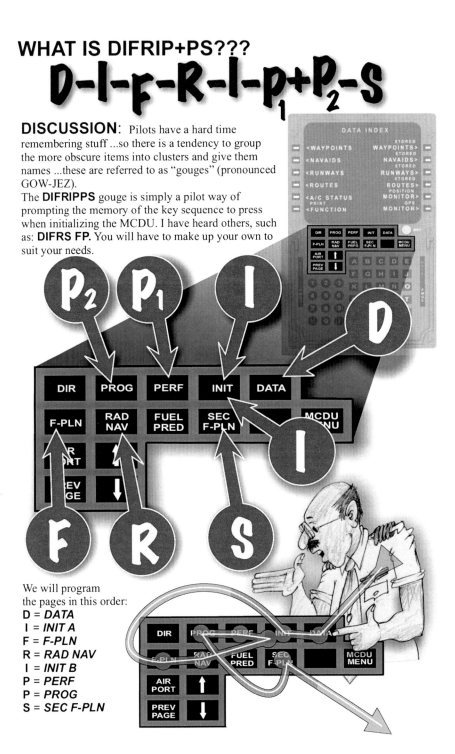

We will program
the pages in this order:
D = *DATA*
I = *INIT A*
F = *F-PLN*
R = *RAD NAV*
I = *INIT B*
P = *PERF*
P = *PROG*
S = *SEC F-PLN*

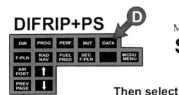

DIFRIP+PS

MCDU:Data Key

SELECT **DATA** KEY

Then select

This will reveal the **DATA INDEX** page

AC STATUS KEY (LSK 5L)

This will reveal the STATUS page
(this page is titled using the aircraft model #)

Here is where you verify that the airplane and the computer are referencing the same database.
Check and see if the following are correct:
- **AIRPLANE TYPE**
- **ENGINE TYPE**
- **CURRENT DATABASE**

The database changeover time is 0901 UTC on the first day of the database effective date.

If the database effective date does not match the airplane clock date, then a scratchpad message will appear:
CHECK DATA BASE CYCLE

If that happens or the database is out of date, here is what you do.

Line select **SECOND DATABASE** to scratchpad **(LSK 3L)**, then
Line select **ACTIVE DATABASE** entry **(LSK 2L)**.

This will move the "new" database into the active database line and update the system.

Enter the **PERFORMANCE FACTOR** if indicated on the Flight Planning documents.

DO NOT CHANGE DATABASE IN FLIGHT
If you do some bad stuff will happen:
- **the flight plan will be deleted**
- **speed predictions will go away**
- **ND will go blank**
- **green dot will be the managed speed**

WHAT CAN PILOTS SCREW UP?
*After getting airborne, they decide that the database is going to be out of date or actually get a **CHECK DATA BASE** message, then they try to change the database "IN THE AIR."*

DIFRIP+PS

SELECT INIT KEY

ENTERING THE AIRPLANE POSITION

Here is where we place the airplane **LAT/LONG** position into the **MCDU/FMGC**. When you do this step, the airplane actually knows what the **LAT/LONG** of the departure airplane is, so you don't actually put in all those numbers. Simply entering the four digit **ICAO** identifier for the destination is all that it needs.

This is a very important step, it is the **FIRST** thing we do. We have to place the **DEPART/DESTINATION** as a **FROM/TO** entry.

Since we have decided to go
FROM: **LFPG**
(Charles de Gaulle airport in Paris)
TO: **EGLL** (Heathrow Airport in London);

STEP 1: We type that in the scratchpad using the keypad of the MCDU: **LFPG/EGLL**.
NOTE: *You MUST include the " / " between the two city IDs.*

STEP 2: **LINE SELECT** the top right selector key **(LSK 1R)**

> **STEP 2: LINE SELECT**
> Top right selector
> key **(LSK 1R)**

> **STEP 3. LINE SELECT**
> the "**ALIGN NOW**"
> selection at **LSK 3R**.

STEP 3: This will cause "**ALIGN IRS**" to be automatically displayed at **LSK 3R**.
Depress the Line Select key. This will send the **LAT / LONG** of the departure airport to the **ADIRU** for the alignment process.

INIT PAGE CONTINUED

CO RTE: If your flight plan says **FMCS YES**, then you enter the flight plan using the nine-digit route designator. For example, if you are going from **CDG** to **LHR** using the route **05K**, you would enter **CDGLHR05K**.

If your flight plan says **FMCS NO**, then you enter the flight plan using the **ICAO** four letter identifiers in the **FROM/TO** boxes.
Example: **LFPG/EGLL** Notice that the same destinations are now using the ICAO four letter designators.

We will cover manually entering the flight plan when we get to the **F-PLAN** page.

FLT NBR. Note that without this flight number entered, you CANNOT retrieve the information you previously requested on the ACARS.

LAT - LONG: Confirm the values (if displayed) are consistent with the airport reference point **LAT-LONG** (for example: airport chart).

COST INDEX (CI): This is the command to the **MCDU/FMGC** to adjust the speed so as to affect fuel usage. Smaller numbers generally indicate better fuel economy but slower airspeed, higher numbers call for higher airspeeds.
Normally the numbers indicated on the flight plan are in the 35 to 50 range.

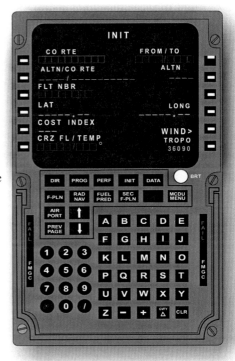

CRZ FL/TEMP: Enter the first planned cruise flight level.
TEMP: The data defaults to the **ISA**. If the flight plan provides a deviation, ...**ADD** that to the displayed and enter the new value.

TROPO: Defaults to **36,090** feet. Enter the **RCA** (Reach Cruise Altitude) **TROPO** from the flight plan or **39000** whichever is lower.
Use a **FIVE DIGIT** number.
ALTITUDE OF TROP MUST BE ENTERED IN FEET and not as a flight level or in meters.

WIND: Select the prompt and the wind pages will appear. You can insert history winds or use the forecast winds from the flight plan.

DIFRIP+PS

SELECT **F-PLN** KEY

This will reveal the FLIGHT PLAN page

When we first select the **F-PLAN** or on some airplanes, the **F-PLN** key, we will be greeted with this display. Let us take a moment and try and understand what we are looking at and what the dazzling display of entries on this page mean.

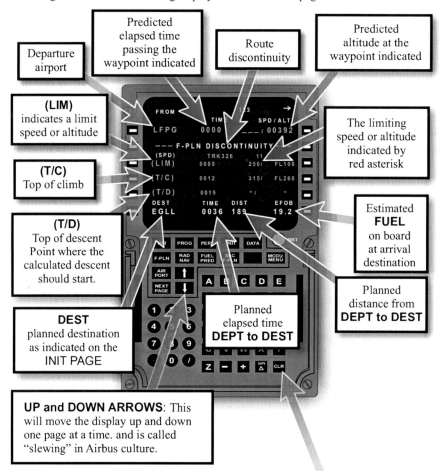

Predicted elapsed time passing the waypoint indicated

Route discontinuity

Predicted altitude at the waypoint indicated

Departure airport

(LIM) indicates a limit speed or altitude

The limiting speed or altitude indicated by red asterisk

(T/C) Top of climb

(T/D) Top of descent Point where the calculated descent should start.

Estimated **FUEL** on board at arrival destination

DEST planned destination as indicated on the INIT PAGE

Planned elapsed time **DEPT to DEST**

Planned distance from **DEPT to DEST**

UP and DOWN ARROWS: This will move the display up and down one page at a time. and is called "slewing" in Airbus culture.

The CLR key: The **CLR** key will put "**CLR**" into the scratchpad. Selecting **CLR** next to a line on the **MCDU** "erases" that line. For example: We will want to remove the "**F-PLN DISCONTINUITY**" so we would press the **CLR** key, placing the word "**CLR**" in the scratchpad. Then if you **LSK 2L**, that line would be removed and the discontinuity would disappear from the computed flight plan routing.

What is a ..
"LATERAL REVISION"

The flight manual simply states "**Perform a lateral revision** ...".
And you would probably be happy to do that if you knew what it was. Well, let
me show you how to do a lateral revision.

While this may seem to be a fairly
exhaustive exercise; it is intended to
include detail so as to cover most
questions by illustrative example.

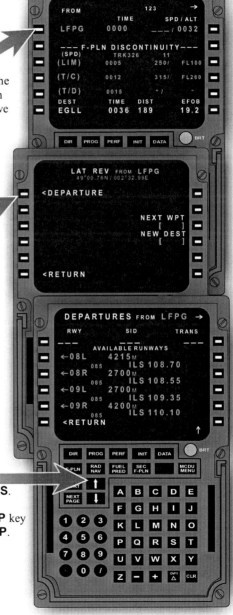

STEP 1: LEFT LINE SELECT the
appropriate **WAYPOINT** from which
the revision will occur. In our case, we
will use the **DEPARTURE**
waypoint.

STEP 2: LINE SELECT the
<DEPARTURE.
This action will cause the
available **DEPARTURE**
RUNWAYS to be displayed.

STEP 3: We can see that the
display page for the runway list
DOES NOT display the runway
we have pre-selected or have
been indicated from the **ATIS**,
Runway **27L**.
In order to get that runway
displayed, we will have to use
the scroll function;
that is, the **SLEW (ARROW) KEYS**.

When you do this, notice that the **UP** key
causes the list of choices to scroll **UP**.

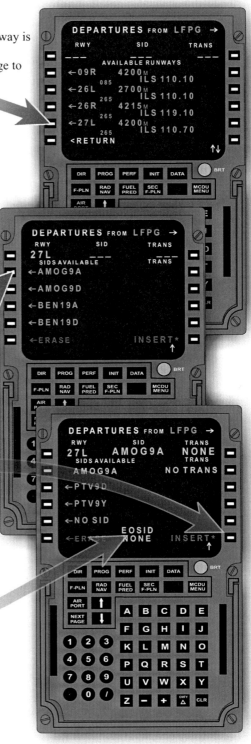

STEP 4: When your desired runway is displayed, select it.
This will cause the display to change to the **SID/TRANS** selection page.

Line select the **27L** key.

STEP 5: For training purposes, let's assume that we are assigned the **AMOG9A SID** (Standard Instrument Departure) by **ATC** as a part of our clearance.
While it is essential in real life to have a paper copy or **EFB** display of the **SID** available for review, in the sim we will find that if the **SID** is in the database, we can rely on the **MCDU** to place the waypoint/speed/altitude targets right on the **F-PLAN** page.

For our example, we will Line select the **AMOG9A** key.

STEP 6: Since there is no **TRANS** available, we now can insert the selected routing into the flight plan.
If there are changes we wish to make to the routing, we will do that **AFTER** we have activated the routing

Select the **INSERT** key.

NOTE: EOSID means "**ENGINE OUT STANDARD INSTRUMENT DEPARTURE**"
... if available, it will appear at the end of the **SID** list.
The **EOSID** can be accessed by using the slew arrow key.

published by UNIVERSITY of TEMECULA PRESS, Inc.

LOADING THE ROUTE MANUALLY

STEP 7: After we have selected and inserted the SID, we can then place the flight plan routing into the **MCDU**.

Use the arrow key to **SCROLL TO THE END OF THE SID ROUTING**. This will usually be indicated by a **F-PLN DISCONTINUITY**.

NOTE: For now, ignore the discontinuity, we will eliminate it after we have placed the complete routing in the **MCDU**.

STEP 8: From our flight planning, we have decided to fly the following routing. We obtained it from the flight papers or **MSFX/MSFS** flight planner.

LFPG.DPE.UM605.SFD.EGLL

By looking at the planned routing that we have, we can see that the **FIRST** fix after our departure airport is **DPE**. Now follow me through on this because there could be a little bit of confusion possible. We have already placed a **SID** in our routing that wasn't included in this flight plan. This is normal and desirable.

We **"HAVE TO ASSUME"** that the **SID** routing was automatically placed **"AFTER"** the departure runway by the **FMGC** and goes **"BEFORE"** the first fix in our flight plan route. Look at how the routing is depicted on the **MCDU**. In other words, the next fix after **AMOGA** will be **DPE**.

If **DPE** was not part of the departure **SID**, we can assume that the routing from the last point of the **SID** will be a direct routing to the first fix of our enroute clearance.

Generally speaking, and there are exceptions, the place where that first route fix goes will be occupied by an **F-PLN DISCONTINUITY**.

STEP 8A: TYPE "DPE" into the scratchpad.

STEP 8B: Line select the line after **AMOGA**, displacing the **"DISCONTINUITY"** with **DPE** .

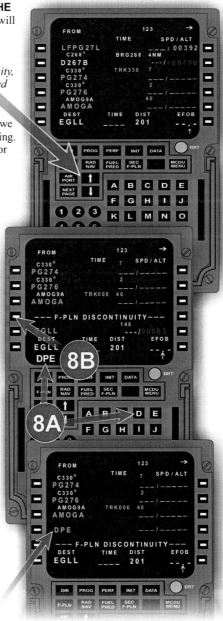

STEP 9: Once we have placed the waypoint into the **MCDU**, line selecting the waypoint will allow us to perform a **LATERAL REVISION**.

Select **DPE**, and the menu will appear. This example will be a demonstration of use of the "**VIA/GO TO**" page.

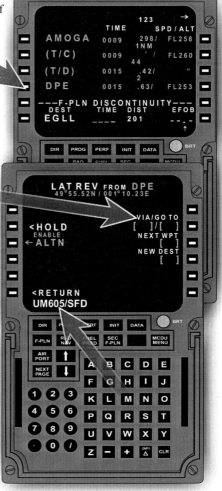

STEP 10: Since our flight plan shows a routing of **DPE.UM605.SFD**, we will enter

UM605/SFD

into the scratchpad, and then line select that entry into the **VIA/GO TO** Line (**LSK 2R**).

DISCUSSION:
Lets look at what we just did. It is called a **LATERAL REVISION**. It allows us to select from a range of interesting options:

- HOLD
- (enable) ALTERNATE
- VIA/GO TO
- NEXT WAYPOINT
- NEW DESTINATION

This is the way we can establish a re-route destination, designate a hold, enter a flight plan change, and "enable" an alternate.

Here's a couple of tricks: To hold at present position, perform the lateral revision on the **FROM** waypoint.

To enter a **NEW** waypoint, type **HELP** in the scratchpad and then line select it to the point in the flight plan where you want the new waypoint to be placed. You will then be shown the 4 different formats with which to designate the waypoint.
- **LAT/LONG** (eg; 1234.5N/67890.1W (dot-slash-dot)
- **P/B/D** (place/bearing/distance) eg; ABC/123/45 (slash-slash)
- **P/BP/B** (place-bearing/place-bearing)
  ABC-123/DEF-321 (dash-slash-dash)
- **PD** (Along track waypoint)
  eg; ABCDE/10 or ABCDE/-10 (waypoint/ plus, minus)

published by UNIVERSITY of TEMECULA PRESS, Inc.

STEP 11: This will display the **TMPY** (**TEMPORARY**) selected flight plan.

NOTE: If for some reason, you don't like this displayed flight plan, you can delete it *WHILE IT IS IN YELLOW* by simply pressing the **ERASE** key,

Or (as we are going to do) you can select it and make it a part of the **MCDU** flight plan display.

Select the **INSERT** key.

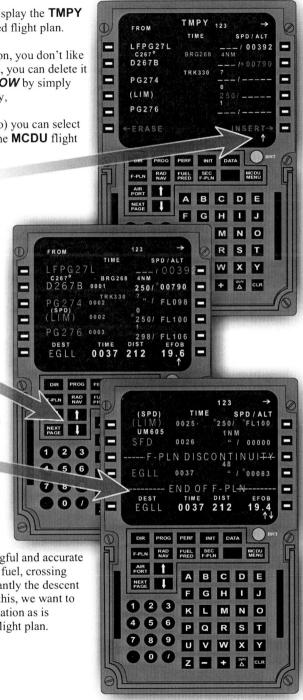

STEP 12: Use the **UP ARROW** to scroll to the bottom of the flight plan display.

If you scroll down far enough, there should be a line **"END OF F-PLAN"** visible on the display. What we want to do is have a completed flight plan on the **MCDU** (from Departure airport to Destination) so the MCDU/FMGC can provide us with meaningful and accurate data and projections on fuel, crossing times, and most importantly the descent profile. To accomplish this, we want to include as much information as is available in our initial flight plan.

Let's take a moment to look at an **APPROACH CHART** for the arrival runway. As pilots, we can make a general assessment of the situation and decide what would work for us while continuing to be compliant with the structure of the **ATC** designated approach requirements.

In our case, we are coming into Heathrow airspace from a South-East direction. The exact information will, of course, be given by ATC or available on the ATIS. Since we are planning a landing on Runway 27L (typical for arrivals into Heathrow) we will likely be using **BIG** (Biggin Hill) for our **IAF** (Initial Approach Fix).

A note on the chart indicates that **AIRSPEED** is restricted to 210 kts so we should be planning to be *AT* 210 kts or less after passing **BIG** inbound.

According to the approach chart depicted (may be outdated, but useful for this example), the inbound "**FEEDER**" route indicates we can descend to no lower than **2,500** feet immediately after departing **BIG** outbound on the **035** degree radial on **BIG**.

Since the **GSIA** (Glideslope intercept altitude) is **2,500 feet MSL** (That is designated by the little underlined **2,500** at the crotch of the "feather. You **CANNOT** descend below 2500 feet unless you are receiving the glideslope signal and descending using it for information. It also represents the beginning of the **FAS** (**Final Approach Segment**) of the approach.

So ... predicated on this meager information and the lack of any MEA guidance **into BIG, I propose that we plan to go from SFD to** BIG and cross **BIG** at or above **2,500 feet MSL** and **210** kts or less (or "**GREEN DOT**"), departing **BIG** to the runway intercept point on the **BIG 035** radial.

---

page 150

If we do not know what the arrival runway is going to be, or there is simply not enough information available to do a lateral revision, the **MCDU/FMGC** will accept the **EGLL** as a end point for the flight plan and will make its calculations accordingly. Some pilots are wary of selecting an anticipated landing runway because it can cause inaccuracies in the ETA/EFOB indications.

If we do not elect to select a landing runway, we simply must remove the "**F-PLN DISCONTINUITY**" and that would complete the flight plan entry. We would then enter a more complete lateral revision as we were approaching the destination, but for a short flight like we are planning today, we will assume that we are going to be landing on Runway **27L** at **EGLL** and perform a lateral revision reflecting that information during this pre-flight plan..
Here is how we do that.

At this point we will need to do a lateral revision of the destination airport.

Select **EITHER** the **GREEN EGLL** just under the "**END OF F-PLN**" line ... or the **WHITE EGLL** that is on the bottom line of the **MCDU** display.

For this exercise, we will select the **WHITE EGLL**.

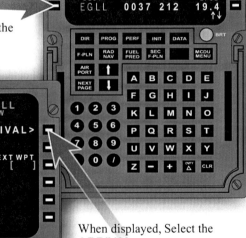

When displayed, Select the **ARRIVAL** prompt.

This page will reveal the available approaches;
Line select runway **27L** when it is revealed.

NOTE: we may have to use the **ARROW KEYS** to scroll the selections until the desired runway (in our case 27L) is revealed.

This will reveal the next page which includes a list of the available **STAR**s
(Standard Terminal Arrival Route)

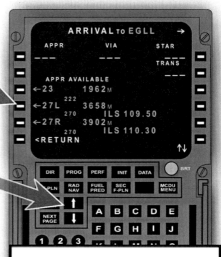

I will tell you ahead of time, that none of the available **STAR** routings will link up with the last point on our flight path. I am going to suggest that we **DO NOT** select a **STAR** at this time, but rather:
Select the **INSERT** key.

Remove the **F-PLAN DISCONTINUITY.**

Remember how to do that:
*Select **CLR** to the scratchpad, then Line select the **F-PLN DISCONTINUITY.***

published by UNIVERSITY of TEMECULA PRESS, Inc.

Since we have decided that we will make **BIG** (Biggin Hill) our **IAF** (Initial Approach Fix) we need to enter that into our flight plan.

Type **BIG** into the **SCRATCHPAD** and then

LINE SELECT the line just below **SFD**.

This will cause the **MCDU/FMGC** to automatically reveal the

DUPLICATE NAMES page.

I want to spend a few moments in discussing the "duplicate names" page.
The controlling agencies for the world **(ICAO** to name just one) got together and created a standard for naming places. There are literally hundreds of thousands of these nametags on places all over the world ... and sometimes, in spite of their best efforts, the names are duplicated.
It really wasn't very important when the criteria was developed and names beyond a certain distance from each other were tolerated... but nowdays, we have this fabulous capability that can locate anyplace anywhere on earth.

So, when there is a duplicate name, the **FMGC** will tell the **MCDU** to go "ask the pilot."

Generally, the names are easy to differentiate because, for example, on a trip of about 200 NM it is doubtful that one of the waypoints would be 3,857 NM from the starting point. So we can simply look at the list and see that the second from the top is the one we want because it is 169 NM from the airplane's starting point ... it is the "logical" choice.

But, on long trips it may be necessary to use the **LAT/LONG** solution.

Since we have decided that the second **BIG** on the list is the one we want, we could
LINE SELECT (LSK 2L).

Once we make the selection of the appropriate "**BIG**", the **MCDU** display will place **BIG** in place of the **F-PLN DISCONTINUITY**.

Use the **ARROW KEYS** to slew the display so that the next **F-PLN DISCONTINUITY** is displayed.

At this point we need to scroll through the flight plan and see if there are any "**F-PLN DISCONTINUITY**" messages. There are "rare" situations where you might want to keep a **DISCONTINUITY** in the flight plan routing, but for our tutorial, we will assume that we are going to eliminate **ALL** the discontinuities, and this is the most common situation you will encounter.

Scroll the complete flight plan entries using the "**UP ARROW**".

MCDU: Checking Loading Plan

☑ CHECKING
THE LOADED PLAN :

The recommended way to determine if there are any improper or undesirable way-points in the routing we have inserted is to look at the final total **DIST** figure and compare it with the **PLANNED DIST** figure.

Our flight planned figure was 189.8 NM. Our **FMGC** calculated distance figure is 219 NM. When we compare the two figures, they are "similar enough" to confirm that the routing is "probably" correctly inserted and we have not placed a ridiculously improper waypoint into the route structure.

DIFRIP+PS

SELECT
RAD NAV KEY

MCDU: RAD NAV key

This will reveal the
SELECTED NAVAIDS page

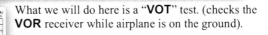

What we will do here is a "**VOT**" test. (checks the **VOR** receiver while airplane is on the ground).

Get the **VOT** frequency. That is found on the 10-9 page in the top radio frequency briefing strip.

Tune **FREQUENCY/HEADING** on the **RAD NAV** page of the **MCDU**, and Select **VOR ROSE** and the **VOR** switch on the **EFIS CONTROL** panel.

Both **VOR**s must be within 4 degrees when 180° is selected.

If no **VOT** is available, tune both **VOR**s to the same **VOR** frequency. **VOR**s must be within 4 degrees of each other when the **CDI**s (Course Deviation Indicators) are centered.

DIFRIP+PS

SELECT INIT KEY

We get to the **INIT B** page by selecting the "**NEXT PAGE**" on the **MCDU** keypad.

INIT B page

It is recommended that the best way to fill in this page is in a "**REVERSE HORSESHOE**" direction, starting with the upper right hand entry.

ZFW: Enter the **ZFW** plus the **BLOCK** fuel in the boxes.

> **NOTE**: *Sometimes you may get a* **FORMAT ERROR**. *If you do, then include a " / " (slash) before the entry.*
> (*DO NOT CHANGE the ZFW CG*) .

Once you **LSK 1R** the **ZFW** boxes, the display automatically changes to display boxes labeled "**BLOCK**." This is a request for the fuel and we find that fuel figure on the upper **ECAM** labeled **FUEL TOTAL**.

TAXI: Defaults to .4 (400 lbs). Use judgement as to requirement. Technique is to push the **LSPB** (Line Select pushbutton) to make it a "**BIG FONT**" even if you don't make a change.

RTE RSV (ROUTE RESERVE): Enter the fuel desired remaining at destination if everything went alright ... It is "recommended" that you use a "0".

FINAL QUANTITY: Leave at zero.
TIME: Check this at **45**. This is consistent with the **45** minute FAR minimums we have entered.

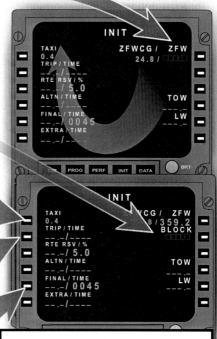

NOTE:

If "forecast" winds are NOT inserted into the INIT A page; an inaccurate or even a negative fuel number may be displayed in the EXTRA/TIME entry.

WHAT CAN THE PILOT SCREW-UP:

*The **F-PLAN** page should be completed **BEFORE** completing the INIT B page. Leaving the **FOB** entry blank will avoid the computer having to constantly re-calculate each page entry, which takes extra time and turns the computer into a slug. This could lead to the pilot getting all upset and wondering why the computer is so slow.*
*That's the reason we complete the **F-PLAN BEFORE** the INIT B.*

published by UNIVERSITY of TEMECULA PRESS, Inc.

FUEL PRED page

WHOOPS!! After the second engine has been started, the **INIT B** page can no longer be referenced and subsequent changes to the flight plan and the weights will be made using the **FUEL PRED** page.

During taxi-out, you will normally receive changes and updates to the weights and need to place those changes into the **MCDU**. Use the **FUEL PRED** page.

Enter the airplane's actual **GROSS WEIGHT** on the **FUEL PRED** page by adding the
- **FINAL ZFW** (Zero Fuel Weight) to the
- **ACTUAL FOB** (Fuel On Board).

Always enter the **FINAL CG**.

If the CG is FORWARD of 25% (that is 24.9% or LESS), use the forward **CG CHARTS** in the **TAKEOFF PERFORMANCE** section of the pilot's handbook to determine the "**FORWARD CG RUNWAY LIMIT WEIGHT**". It is kinda complicated. If you have a question, contact the dispatcher.

SERMON:

Here is a sermon from experience. If there is some anomaly or any question about the aircraft being "legal" to operate in the runway and weather environment ... coordinate with the tower and get a suitable location and **STOP THE JET AND SET THE PARKING BRAKE**.

I recommend that if both pilots are unable to satisfactorily resolve the situation that you contact the Dispatcher and involve her/him and the resources available to them to come up with the solution.

CONTACT THE DISPATCHER

While it is incumbent on the pilots to be conversant with managing the weight and balance, clutter assessment, wind-shear evaluation, and all that esoteric stuff ... there are tremendous resources available for your use. The Check Captain will be observing and evaluating your awareness in utilizing all the information sources necessary. I personally would not be reluctant to involve the Dispatcher at the very beginning of a potential problem.

The **FAR**s clearly state that the Dispatchers bear a legal shared responsibility with the Captain for the safe operation of the flight and are eager and willing to have you communicate your concerns to them. They are your ally and want to be used.

DIFRIP+PS

SELECT **PERF** KEY

This will reveal the TAKEOFF page.
There are 4 pages to this entry

Check to see that the proper departure runway is displayed. If it is not, return to the F-PLAN page and do another **LATERAL REVISION** on the **DEP** airport and insert the proper runway.

COMMENT: *If there is a runway change during the pre-takeoff phase, you would "update" the FMGC using the F-PLAN page.*

- **T/O SHIFT**: If required because runway length limited. Be sure you use ***UNUSABLE DISTANCE, NOT RUNWAY REMAINING!***

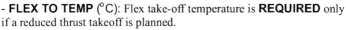
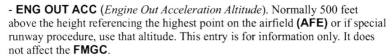

- **FLAPS**: This entry "has no effect on FMGC computations" and is for display only.

- **FLEX TO TEMP** (°C): Flex take-off temperature is **REQUIRED** only if a reduced thrust takeoff is planned.
(**NOTE**: *Flex temperature **MUST** be greater than the **OAT***).

- **ENG OUT ACC** (*Engine Out Acceleration Altitude*). Normally 500 feet above the height referencing the highest point on the airfield **(AFE)** or if special runway procedure, use that altitude. This entry is for information only. It does not affect the **FMGC**.

- **THR RED/ACC** (*Thrust Reduction / Acceleration Altitude*).

> **ACCEL ALT IS THE "PHASE TRIGGER"**
> **FOR THE CLIMB MODE.**
> *These are important numbers because at **ACCEL ALT** the airspeed indicator will slew to the climb speed, and the Flight Director will pitch radically to accommodate that change. I **STRONGLY** suggest that you **DO NOT** try to chase the flight director until **AFTER** passing **ACCEL ALT**.*

- **TRANS ALT** (*transition altitude, 18,000 feet in US, but is indicated on appropriate **ICAO** departure and airport charts*). This is the altitude which causes the **QNH** to flash yellow to remind the pilot to re-select the barometric pressure.

POTENTIAL PILOT SCREW-UP:
When planning a reduced thrust takeoff using engine anti-ice,
SUBTRACT 5°C from the FLEX temperature
BEFORE entering it into the FMGC.
*This ensures that the **FADEC** calculates the correct reduced **EPR**.*
THEN *to calculate the adjusted V speeds*
USE THE UNADJUSTED FLEX TEMPERATURE
(the temp before the 5 degree correction).

---

published by UNIVERSITY of TEMECULA PRESS, Inc.

PERF page continued

Place the calculated V speeds or those provided by the flight planning documents using the scratchpad technique in the appropriate boxes.

It is worth noting that placing an entry into the V2 box is what **ARMS the SRS**.

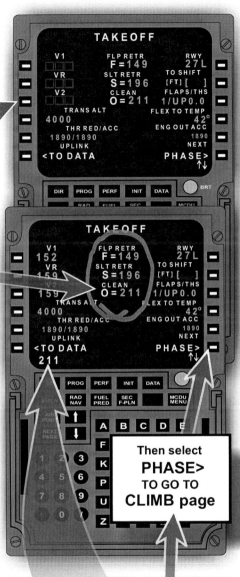

Discussion about the three values: **F**, **S**, and **O**.

These are Minimum airspeed limits.
"F" is **FLAP RETRACT** speed,
"S" is **SLAT RETRACT** speed,
"0" is **ZERO FLAP** speed.

These speeds will be indicated on the speed tape on the **PFD**.

NOTE: *In the US, the MAXIMUM speed allowed in the "Class B" airspace is 200 kts; which means we will not be able to maintain the 200 knot speed "limit" after take-off without using some flaps until outside of the "B" class boundary. In ICAO places, the maximum airspeed in the airport area is usually listed on the approach plate.*
WHOOPS! *Most jets cannot fly that slow without some flaps ... so regulations were altered to allow jets to use their "0" flap speed as the exemption airspeed. For us, that is the "GREEN DOT" airspeed.*

Then select
PHASE>
TO GO TO
CLIMB page

GOOD PILOT TECHNIQUE:
Type the "**O**" flap speed into the scratchpad. This represents the "GREEN DOT" airspeed that is the ATC mandated airspeed for operating in the "B" CLASS airspace. *We're gonna enter it on the CLIMB page.*

PROGRAMMING THE CLIMB PAGE

ENTER or **MODIFY** the following entries:

- SPD / MACH: Enter the **GREEN DOT** speed as the initial climb speed.

```
          C L B
ACT MODE
ECON
  C1
  50
    ECON
  298/.44
  SPD/MACH
 *[    ]

 PREV                    NEXT
 <PHASE                  PHASE>
 211
```

Let's go over this step with a little more clarity. The **FMGC** (and therefore the airplane) is pre-programmed to fly at 250 kts when below 10,000 feet **MSL**. And during the **CLIMB PHASE** when the airplane climbs to an altitude higher than 10,000 feet **MSL**, it will slew the airspeed to the figure displayed in the **ECON** line. However, If we want the airplane to start the climb at a different airspeed, we would enter that in the brackets on the **PERF/CLIMB** page of the **MCDU**;

```
          C L B
ACT MODE
 SPD 211
  C1
  50
    ECON
 *298/.44
  SPD/MACH
  211/.31

 PREV                    NEXT
 <PHASE                  PHASE>
```

then, once in **CLIMB PHASE**, the jet will automatically select that "bracket" airspeed as the default airspeed target.

Then select **PHASE>** to select the page.

FAR "B CLASS" RESTRICTION

When operating within about 10 nm of a major airport, we are restricted from exceeding 200 knots in US (note: other international airports have other restrictions, usually 210 kts) when flying in Class "B" airspace (that is the restricted airspace around major airports in the US). **ATC** (Air Traffic Control regulations) allow airliners to exceed that speed and use instead their "**0**" flap or "**Clean Maneuvering Speed (CMS)**" as their limitation. On Airbus airplanes, that figure is called the "**GREEN DOT**" airspeed.

Once the airplane is outside the "B" Class airspace and cleared to resume normal airspeed (some airlines use 3,000 feet) all the pilot has to do is **PUSH** the **SPD** selector on the **FCU** panel and the airspeed selector indicator of the **PFD** will slew to the appropriate pre-selected enroute climb airspeed.

PROGRAMMING THE CRUISE PAGE

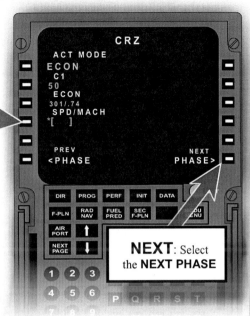

- **SPD / MACH**: Enter the desired airspeed if different from the "**ECON**" airspeed.

DISCUSSION:

We have told the airplane that we want it to cruise at a fixed airspeed or one that reflects the restrictions imposed by the **COST INDEX** we have assigned. Remember that a different **CRUISE** airspeed **CANNOT** be entered once we are airborne and the **CRZ** is the active phase. If other airspeed restrictions are imposed by **ATC** or navigational requirements, the pilot may either:

1. Change the **CI** (Cost Index) ... Setting the cost index to a "high" value will cause the airplane to "speed up." in fact, it can increase airspeed all the way to the bottom of the "red bricks" (**Vmo** or maximum allowed airspeed) on the **PFD AIRSPEED TAPE**.; but the autoflight system will **NOT** allow the airplane to exceed that maximum. This is useful in an abnormality or emergency where maximum airspeed is required or desired.

NEXT: Select the **NEXT PHASE**

> If a very high **CI** (say 200) is selected; the airplane wll fly at thie maximum allowable airspeed.

2. If a specific airspeed is desired (before the jet enters the cruise phase), enter that figure in the "**[brackets]**" on the cruise page.

3. Leaving the entry blank will result in the airplane flying **ECON** airspeed. If the flight plan requests a varying speed (.776 then .786), leave the entry blank.

4. There is always the manual (selected) option: If you get a specific request from **ATC** after you are in **CRUISE** phrase, **PULL** the airspeed selector on the **FCU** and set the requested mach number.

WARNING:

Using the **EXPED** selector commands the following airspeed:
DESCENT: managed .80/340 **KIAS** (Knots Indicated Airspeed).
CLIMB: managed "**GREEN DOT**".

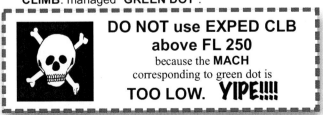

DO NOT use EXPED CLB above FL 250
because the **MACH** corresponding to green dot is
TOO LOW. YIPE!!!!

PROGRAMMING THE DESCENT PAGE

ENTER or **MODIFY** the following entries:

- SPD / MACH: Enter the desired airspeed if different from the "ECON" airspeed.

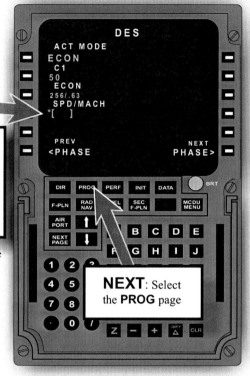

```
              DES
  ACT MODE
  ECON
   C1
  50
   ECON
  256/.63
  SPD/MACH
  *[  ]

  PREV                    NEXT
 <PHASE                  PHASE>
```

NEXT: Select the **PROG** page

DISCUSSION:
Once the airplane leaves the CRUISE altitude as set in the **PROG** page **CRZ** entry, the **DESCENT PHASE** is triggered and *descent DATA cannot be changed.*

If you wished to make a change in the descent parameters, you could switch to the 'Selected" (manual) mode, but here is a work-around for continuing "managed" mode operation.

If you wish to change the **MCDU/FMGC** descent speed after you have initiated the descent (departed cruise altitude); do this;

1. Enter a new "lower" **CRZ** altitude on the **PROG** page. This will force the **FMGC** back into the cruise phase until it crosses this " new" altitude.

2. During this time, you may make the desired changes to the **DESCENT** page.

BE AWARE:

If you should start a descent **PRIOR** to reaching your cruise altitude; during that period of time when you are descending in "cruise phase" or operating in "selected" (manual) mode, the **FMGC** no longer obeys the restrictions and crossing constraints set in the **F-PLAN** page of the **MCDU/FMGC**; but rather simply descends at a fixed rate of descent.

MORE COMPLICATING DISCUSSION:

Another point to make regarding *ANY* descent and climb operations: A managed descent (or climb) is *NOT* available if you are operating the airplane in the **HEADING** mode. You must be in **NAV** to use managed climb/descent.

DIFRIP+PS

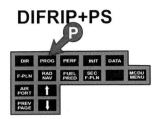

SELECT **PROG** KEY

This will reveal the TO (Take-0ff) page

- **COMPARE**:
Look at the values for:
- *CRUISE ALTITUDE and*
- *OPTIMUM ALTITUDE and*
- *MAXIMUM ALTITUDES.*

The planned cruise altitude should be lower than the **REC MAX** (Recommended Maximum) altitude and will usually be equal to or lower than the **OPT** (Optimum) altitude.

WHAT PILOTS SCREW UP:

They try to fly an airplane at an altitude for which it is too heavy or "outside the V_n (Flight Envelope)". This can result in some interesting situations; such as wing buffet and high speed stall. The **REC MAX** altitude should be taken into consideration when making an altitude selection.

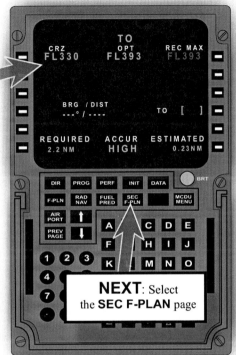

NEXT: Select the **SEC F-PLAN** page

another boring DISCUSSION:

The place where a pilot can get in trouble is trying to reach a cruise altitude for which the airplane is too heavy to fly. Sometimes during long flights, **ATC** will give you the alternative to either descend to a lower altitude (cost more fuel) or to climb to an altitude above your recommended maximum. It is a judgement call, but I would be very wary of trying to fly the jet above the maximum recommended altitude.

ENGINE FAILURE at ALTITUDE:

To further extend on this argument, if you should **LOSE** an engine while at or near the **REC MAX**, it should be of primary concern to get to a lower altitude **ASAP**. Trying to keep the jet at an altitude that it cannot maintain is the root cause of some "**UpSEt**" situations.

DIFRIP+PS

SELECT **SEC F-PLN** KEY
This will reveal the SEC INDEX page

<COPY ACTIVE: Push the
COPY ACTIVE prompt
(LSK 1L).

Why would we want to make a
"copy" of the flight plan. The
flight manual suggests that it is
because we might want to do a
"what if" scenario. Here is my
take on the subject, we make a
copy of the **F-PLAN** because
we might screw up the original
F-PLAN and be stuck trying to
reconstruct the whole thing
because the **FMGC** dumped all
the data. I have found that when
operating the **MCDU/FMGC**, it
sometimes enters my data and
dumps a lot of other interim
fixes and stuff without me
intending that to happen.
This is especially important

Some pilots will select the
FUEL PRED
page at this point in
preparation for the engine start.

when using the **DIR** function. When you drop the waypoint in the box ...
everything between here and there is now history.

YIPE!!!

GOOD PILOT TECHNIQUE:

When the second engine has been started, it is no longer possible to access
the **INIT B** page to install changes in fuel and take-off gross weight. This
chore switches to the **FUEL PRED** page and it is useful, I think, to leave
the **MCDU** on the **FUEL PRED** page at this time to facilitate making those
last minute changes from the load planner.

This is the end of the FLOW:
ACARS and FMGC INITIALIZATION
and
VERIFICATION

published by UNIVERSITY of TEMECULA PRESS, Inc.

CAPTAIN'S COCKPIT SETUP

OMIGOSH !

There are 57 steps to the Captain's Cockpit setup, and they have to be done entirely from memory. How can a mere human airline pilot ever hope to get a handle on all this stuff ... it seems simply overpowering.

But there is a way to break out the information and present it in a way that it is ...well, almost palatable. On the following pages are the 57 steps.

DO THIS FROM MEMORY ??? YOU GOTTA BE KIDDING !

I feel your pain ....

LET'S MAKE A PLAN.

START HERE

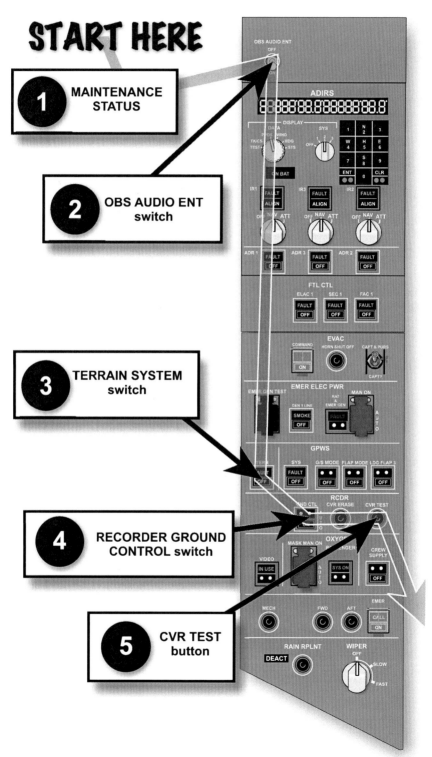

1 MAINTENANCE STATUS

2 OBS AUDIO ENT switch

3 TERRAIN SYSTEM switch

4 RECORDER GROUND CONTROL switch

5 CVR TEST button

MAINTENANCE STATUS .... CONFIRM

The **CAPTAIN MUST** do these things.
This status check **CANNOT** be delegated!

1. Confirm the correct Maintenance Documents are on board
and reviewed in accordance with directives and Federal mandates.

2. Develop a thorough understanding of
the maintenance status of the airplane.

3. Understand the potential effects of any **DF** or **CF** items
on the operation of the airplane.

4. Ensure that the crew is briefed.

OBS AUDIO ENT switch .... ON

The Observer Audio Entertainment switch will enable the
passengers to monitor the cockpit communications. It is
usually company policy to have this switch **ON**.
It is my understanding that if any negative result occurs as a result of
passengers interpreting the information they may hear, will **NOT**
result in punitive action to the flight crew..

TERRAIN SYSTEM switch .... verify ON

When **ON** is selected, this activates ALL modes of the **EGPWS**
terrain modes including POP-UP.

RECORDER GROUND CONTROL switch .. ON

This switch is turned **ON** in order to comply with **FAA**
requirement to record the reading of the Checklists.

The reason is that the CVR automatically turns off 5 minutes
after turn on, so in order to keep the CVR running, it is
necessary to manually turn it on to keep it running..

CVR TEST button .... PUSH and HOLD

The TEST PROCEDURE IS:

1. Place the RCDR GND CTL switch ON.
2. PUSH and HOLD the CVR TEST button
3. LOW FREQUENCY SIGNAL sounds over the loudspeakers.

NOTE: Loudspeakers **DO NOT** have to be turned **ON**
to hear this signal.
NOTE 2: The **PARKING BRAKE** must be **ON**.

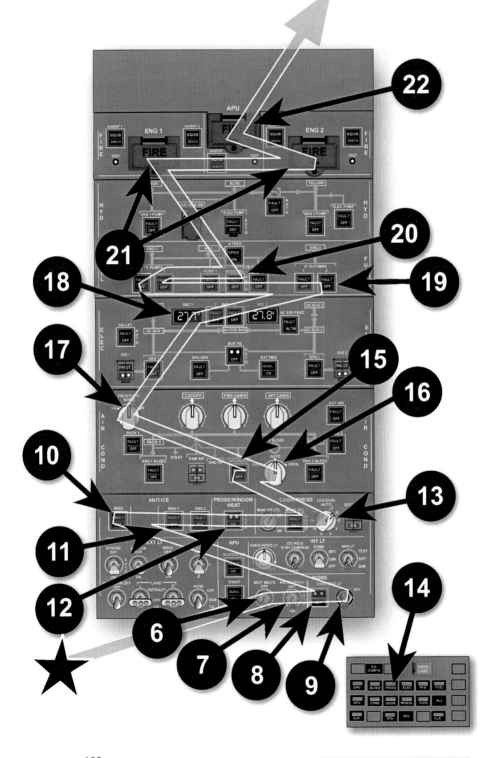

published by UNIVERSITY of TEMECULA PRESS, Inc.

6   SEAT BELT SWITCH .... OFF

OFF is selected for the period during boarding so as to avoid ambiguity being associated with the activation of the message.

7   NO SMOKING SIGN selector .... ON

Most airlines do not allow smoking and leave the sign on for the duration of the flight. In some instances, such as a charter to Havana for the Cigar smokers international convention, it may be allowed if company directives dictate.

8   EMERGENCY EXIT LIGHT selector ..... ARM

This arms the **EMERGENCY LIGHTING** system, which includes the escape path lighting, overhead emergency lights, and the **EXIT** signs.

9   ANNUNCIATOR LIGHT selector .... TEST

1. Place the **ANN LT** selector to **TEST**.
2. Visually verify **ALL** cockpit lights illuminate.
NOTE: Include **CKPT DOOR CONT** lights on the **AFT OVERHEAD** panel.
3. Confirm that all Liquid Crystal Displays (**LCD**) displays "8"s.

10   WING ANTI-ICE switch .... OFF

11   ENGINE ANTI-ICE switch .... OFF

12   PROBE/WINDOW HEAT switch .... AUTO

13   CABIN PRESSURE LANDING ELEVATION selector .... AUTO

14 ECAM PRESS page .... CHECK

VERIFY LDG ELEV
AUTO is displayed.

NOTE: *Destination field elevation MAY NOT be correctly displayed until after take-off is started.*
NOTE 2: *VENT INLET and EXTRACT VALVE may appear amber but there actually be NO malfunction. This might occur when the temperature is close to the preset valve opening or closing threshold; BUT if there is any question, notify maintenance.*

15 APU BLEED switch .... AS REQUIRED

NOTE: If **DITCHING** switch is closed, do not **OPEN** the **APU BLEED** switch.

NOTE 2: If external conditioned ground air is connected (and potable water pressure is desired), turn **BOTH** pack switches **OFF** before turning the **APU BLEED** switch **ON**.

16 CROSSBLEED selector .... AUTO

17 PACK FLOW selector .... AS REQUIRED

LO .... *If less than 115 passengers expected.*
HI .... *If Hot or Humid.*
NORM ...... *All other conditions..*

published by UNIVERSITY of TEMECULA PRESS, Inc.

18 BATTERY CHARGE CURRENT .... CHECK

HOW TO DO "THE CHECK"

1. Select the **LOWER ECAM ELEC** page.

2. Select **BAT 1** and **BAT 2** switches to **OFF**.

3. Select **BAT 1** and **BAT 2** switches back to **AUTO**.

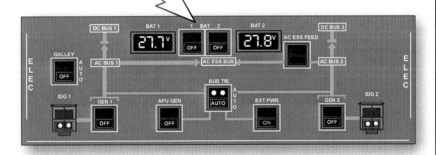

4. After 10 seconds, the battery charging current
MUST BE BELOW 60 AMPS and DECREASING.
If not, contact maintenance

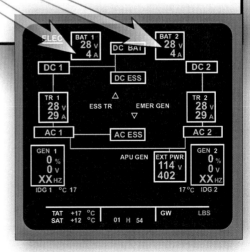

19 **FUEL PUMP SWITCHES** .... **ON**

There are 6 pump switches to turn on.

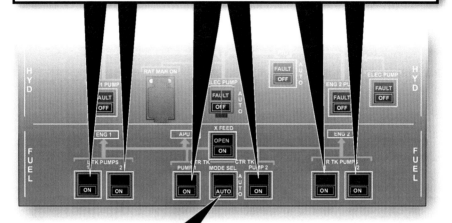

20 **FUEL MODE SELECTOR** .... **AUTO**

This will **ARM** the center tank pumps for automatic operation in the following conditions.

NOTE 1: If there is fuel in the CENTER TANK, the center tank pumps will run EXCEPT when the SLATS are extended.
NOTE 2: The pumps turn OFF 5 minutes after center tank low level is reached.
NOTE 3: Even with the slats extended, the pumps will run for 2 minutes after EACH engine reaches idle.

WHAT PILOTS CAN SCREW UP

They could leave this switch in **MANUAL**.
Manual mode will allow manual control of the **CENTER TANK PUMPS** using the **CTR TK PUMP** switches; but more importantly, it will deselect the **AUTO** mode..

> If this switch is inadvertently left in **MANUAL**, none of the automatic features will operate.
> *This is NOT a good thing.*

published by UNIVERSITY of TEMECULA PRESS, Inc.

21 **ENGINE 1 and ENGINE 2**
FIRE TEST SWITCHES .... PUSH

OBSERVE:

- Associated Engine **FIRE** switch illuminates
- **SQUIB** light illuminates
- **DISCH** light illuminates
- **MASTER WARN** lights FLASH
- **CRC** (continuous repetitive chime) sounds
- **ECAM ENG FIRE** warning activates
- Engine **FIRE** light illuminates on the control pedestal

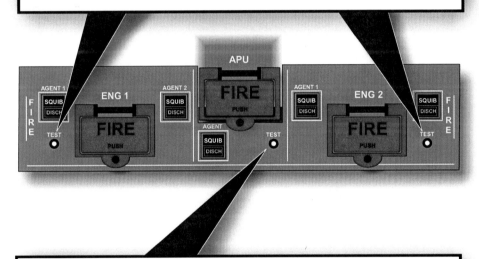

22 **APU FIRE TEST SWITCH .... PUSH**

OBSERVE:

- **APU FIRE** switch illuminates
- **SQUIB** light illuminates
- **DISCH** light illuminates
- **MASTER WARN** lights FLASH
- **CRC** (Continuous Repetitive Chime) sounds
- **ECAM APU FIRE** warning activates

24 OVERHEAD MAINTENANCE PANEL .... CHECK

All you are to do is check and see if there are any lights visible. If there are any lights on, contact maintenance.

NOTE: This panel is for Maintenance use ONLY!

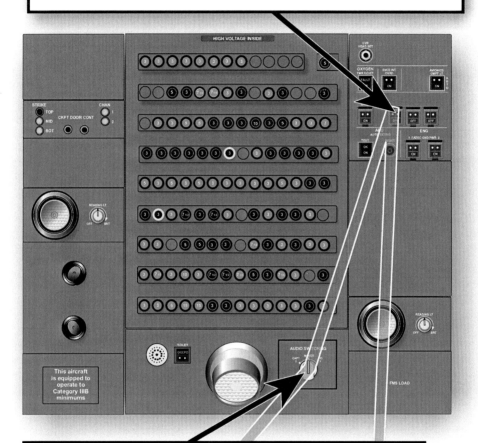

23 AUDIO SWITCHING SELECTOR .... NORMAL

published by UNIVERSITY of TEMECULA PRESS, Inc.

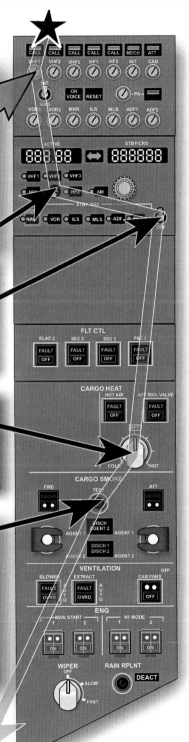

 25 **OBSERVERS AUDIO CONTROL panel .... SET**

1. Ensure the **VHF 1** reception knob is released **OUT**.

2. **VOLUME** is set to **MID-LEVEL**.

3. **ALL** other reception knobs are **OFF**.

26 **OBSERVERS RMP .... SET**

Ensure that the **RMP** is **ON** and The **SEL** light is **NOT** illuminated.

27 **AFT CARGO HEAT .... MID RANGE**

This switch on the **A320** *ONLY*.

28 **CARGO SMOKE test button ....**

PUSH and HOLD 3 seconds

OBSERVE:
-*SMOKE* lights illuminate *TWICE* with associated *ECAM* message.
-*DISCH* lights illuminate

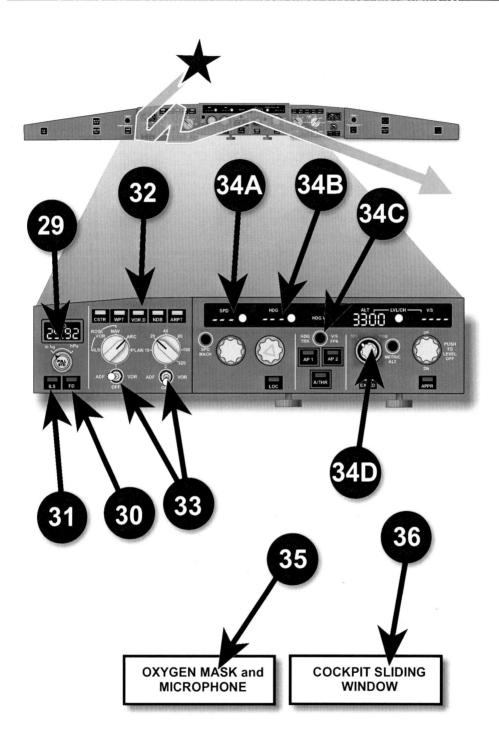

OXYGEN MASK and MICROPHONE

COCKPIT SLIDING WINDOW

29 · BAROMETRIC REFERENCE .... SET

Obtain the current field barometric setting (**QNH**)

*1. This will require the use of a **RADIO**, or the **DCDU** (**Datalink Control and DisplayUnit**)/**ACARS**/Printer to obtain the **ATIS**. or*
*2. Call **ATC** for the current field barometric altimeter setting.*

When the barometric setting is dialed into the unit, it is only displayed once on lower right corner of the PFD. The Indicated Altitude is also displayed on the PFD.

30 · FLIGHT DIRECTOR BUTTON .... ON

MUST BE ARMED in order to engage certain important AUTO-PILOT modes! This ARMS the climb and nav modes.

31 · ILS/LS BUTTON .... AS REQUIRED

This is not normally required nor desired to be displayed on the PFD or the ND during departure.
If, however, the ILS localizer or the ILS DME is required to comply with departure procedures, then this switch must be selected in order to be displayed.

32 · EFIS CONTROL PANEL .... SET as required

Personal preference is allowed, of course; BUT here are some recommendations:
- ARC for straight out departures
- ROSE NAV if turns back over the field are anticipated
- I personally prefer 40 nm range, but 10 or 20 is OK.

33 · VOR/ADF SELECTORS .... AS REQUIRED

The VOR and/or ADF is not normally required nor desired to be displayed on the PFD or the ND during departure.
If, however, the VOR and/or the ADF is required to comply with departure procedures, then this switch must be selected in order to be displayed.

STOP!!

We cannot continue without having the **MCDC/FMGC** initialization complete.

The **FMGC** cannot be operated until the **ADIRS** (Inertial reference system) has been initialized; and that takes about 10 minutes from the time it was turned to "**NAV**."
We can tell the unit is ready for use when the **PFD** and **ND** displays are operating.

WE CANNOT CONTINUE UNTIL
FMGC IS INITIALIZED

This is a good time to get out your charts, pencil, flashlight, earpiece, and all that other pilot stuff you are gonna need.

34   FCU (Flight Control Unit) .... CHECK

34A The **SPEED/MACH** indicator may be indicating some speed such as "100". **PUSH** the selector and Verify that the window is displaying "**DASHES**."

34B Verify that the **HEADING/TRACK** window is displaying "**DASHES**."

34C **HDG-V/S / TRK-FPA** selector button: Select **HDG-V/S**

34D Set **INITIAL ALTITUDE** or Expected **ALTITUDE**. Pushing or pulling the selector has no effect.

published by UNIVERSITY of TEMECULA PRESS, Inc.

35 OXYGEN MASK and MICROPHONE .... TEST

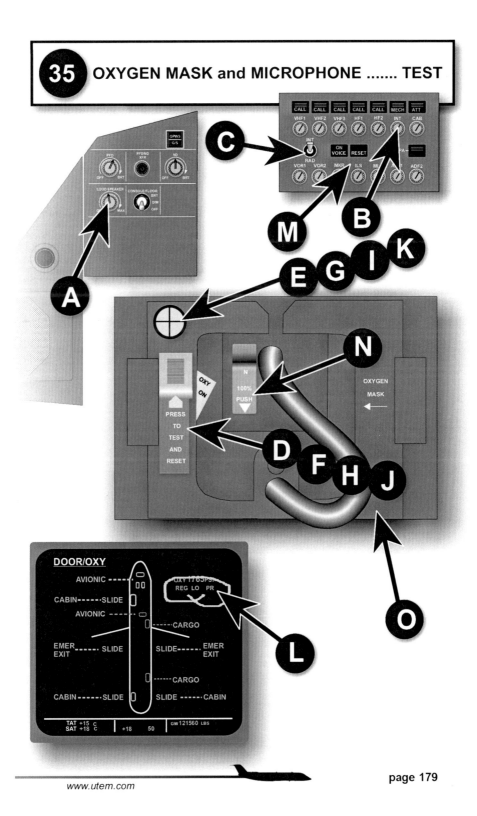

OXYGEN MASK and MICROPHONE .... TEST

This is an "every flight" item; however, this test is NOT required on subsequent flights IF the pilot stays on the same jet.

WARNING

*The test is performed **WITHOUT** removing the mask from the enclosure. If you insist on removing the mask, get ready for a protracted effort similar to that of attempting to stuff a 100 pound anaconda into a Cracker Jack box.*

BEWARE:

Before you begin the test,
MAKE SURE the other guys INT reception knob is *OFF!*
... or run the risk of blowing his brains out.

DO THESE STEPS:

A   LOUDSPEAKER .... ON

B   INT reception knob ...... ON

C   INT/RAD switch selected to ..... INT

D   Press-to-test and reset
SLIDE LEVER .... PUSH and *HOLD*

Accomplish the following three items while holding the **SLIDE LEVER.**

E   "BLINKER" FLOWMETER .... OBSERVE

It should turn **YELLOW** momentarily, and then turns **BLACK**. This indicates the regulator is leak tight.

F   REGULATOR EMERGENCY/
Press-to-test .... PRESS and RELEASE

G   LOOK and LISTEN

Verify the sound of oxygen flow across the mask microphone and **FLOW INDICATOR** turns **YELLOW**.

H   Press-to-test and reset
SLIDE LEVER .... RELEASE

I   Verify the **BLINKER FLOWMETER** is **BLACK** and all oxygen flow ceases.

published by UNIVERSITY of TEMECULA PRESS, Inc.

J

REGULATOR EMERGENCY/
Press-to-test .... PRESS and RELEASE

K

VERIFY ...the FLOW indicator stays BLACK,
indicating NO OXYGEN flow,

L

upper ECAM DOOR page .... CHECK

Verify the REGUL LO PR message is NOT displayed. This check
should be made AFTER all masks have been checked to ensure the
LOW PRESSURE valve is OPEN.

NOTE:
*Residual pressure in the line between the low pressure valve and the masks may be
sufficient to accomplish a mask test with the valve closed.*

M

AUDIO CONTROL PANEL .... RESET

The idea is to restore the audio panel to its original set-up.

RETURN INT/RAD switch to NEUTRAL, and
RETURN other pilot's INT RECEPTION knob to its original position.

OXYGEN MASK .... SET

N

N/100% LEVER .... VERIFY 100%

O

ENCLOSURE DOORS ..... VERIFY CLOSED

36

SLIDING WINDOW .... CLOSE and LOCK

Check that the RED UNLOCKING button is fully
popped out and the window does not open.

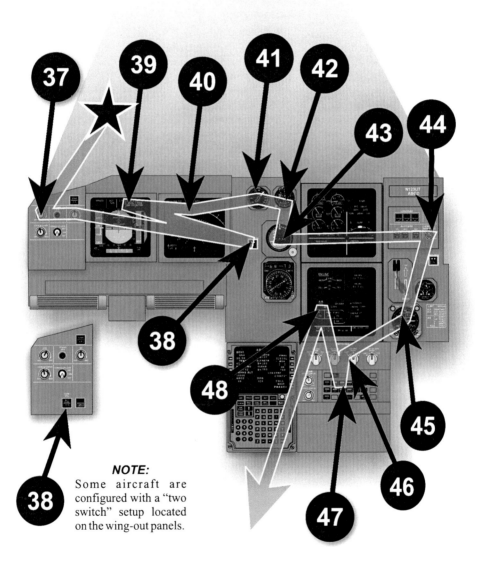

NOTE:
Some aircraft are configured with a "two switch" setup located on the wing-out panels.

published by UNIVERSITY of TEMECULA PRESS, Inc.

37 PFD and ND brightness .... As required
Ensure EGPWS and RADAR DISPLAYS visible

The two brightness control knobs manually control the respective illumination level.

If a **PFD FAILS** or is shut **OFF,** then the **PFD** display will shift automatically to the respective **ND**. When this happens, you can display the **PFD** or the **ND** on the "other" **LCD** screen using the **PFD/ND XFR** switch.

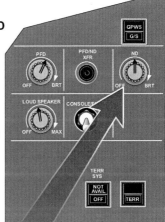

NOTE: *Once the **PFD/ND XFR** switch is depressed, the brightness controls shift. That is, the **PFD** controls the **ND**, and the **ND** controls the **PFD** display brightness.*

The **ND** selector has an **OUTER SELECTOR** that controls the brightness of the weather **RADAR** and the **EGPWS** image only.

NOTE: *The outer selector of the **ND** brightness selector **MUST BE ON** and **BRIGHT** to ensure the **EGPWS** pop-up feature is visible in the event of a windshear.*

---

38 EGPWS TERRAIN SYSTEM SWITCH (TERR or TERR ON ND)
(if installed) .... verify ON

BIG AREA OF CONFUSION!

There are at least two DIFFERENT locations for the **EGPWS TERR ON SWITCH** and the switch functions slightly differently for each configuration. Also, the switch has at least two different names.

UA configuration

NOTE: *In the **UA configuration**, turning on the Radar automatically deselects the terrain display. The switch must then be **MANUALLY** reselected to display terrain.*
*In the **Airbus configuration**, **EGPWS** must be MANUALLY deselected in order to display the **RADAR**.*

AIRBUS type A

PILOT SCREW UP: *If the radar won't display on the **ND**, assume that it is inoperative. Simply deselect the **TERR** or **TERR ON ND** switch with the radar set turned on ... and VOILA!*

AIRBUS type B

39 # PFD .... CHECK

1. Verify **PFD** displayed on the appropriate Display Screen.
2. No flags displayed
3. Verify **IAS** correct
4. Verify **FMA** correct
5. Verify **INITIAL TARGET ALTITUDE**
6. Verify **VSI** correct
7. Verify Altimeter setting (**QNH**) correct
8. Verify Attitude is correct
9. Verify **HEADING** agrees with **ND, DDRMI,** and **STBY COMPASS**.

NOTE:
The altimeters should read
ELEVATION PLUS 10 FEET AGL.
This is difficult, because we seldom know the exact elevation of the airplanes
position **UNLESS** at the runway end where it is noted on the approach plate
runway diagram.
If the altimeters do not read with
WITHIN +/- 25 FEET OF ELEVATION
and agree with each other
WITHIN 20 FEET
then maintenance action is ***REQUIRED*!**

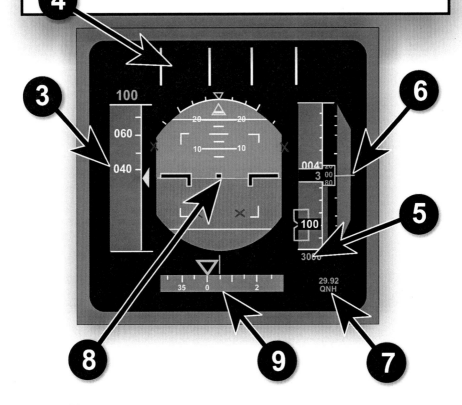

published by UNIVERSITY of TEMECULA PRESS, Inc.

40 **ND** .... **CHECK**

1. Verify **PFD** displayed on the appropriate **DISPLAY SCREEN**.
2. No flags displayed

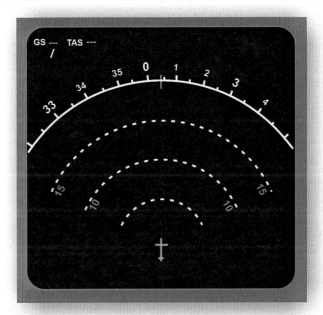

41 **STBY AIRSPEED INDICATOR** .... **CHECK**

If the indication is not less than 60 knots; notify maintenance.

4 plastic carets (bugs) should remain grouped together at the top of the instrument.

**IF ANY BUGS ARE MISSING
A DEFERRAL IS REQUIRED.**

STANDBY ALTIMETER .... CHECK

42

> The STANDBY ALTIMETER should read
> *WITHIN +/- 300 FEET of*
> *ACTUAL ELEVATION.*
> If the unit is outside of the tolerance,
> **CONTACT MAINTENANCE.**

DISCUSSION:

This has always been an area of ambiguity, since the only place where the pilot can be absolutely certain of the altitude is taxiing over the take-off threshold. That altitude is printed on the approach plate. Other references to the airport altitude are specifically located at airport geographical center, tower, etc. Some airports, however, actually paint the altitude in the ramp area. A call to the Tower can usually get the ramp altitude.

4 plastic carets (bugs) should remain grouped together at the top of the instrument.

NOTE

**IF ANY BUGS ARE MISSING
A DEFERRAL IS REQUIRED.**

HAPPY NOTE:
The **ALTIMETER VIBRATOR** *is inoperative on the ground*

---

43 ## STBY ATTITUDE INDICATOR .... CHECK

The **INDICATION** should be
- **ERECT** (indicating level flight)
- **NO FLAG**

If the standby attitude indication is cocked or not level,
PULL THE CAGING KNOB OUT
until the indicator becomes level. It is not unusual to see this "spun down" condition on airplanes that have been sitting without power for awhile.

If, after "caging" the unit, the instrument will not maintain a "level indication," suspect that the dedicated instrument rechargeable battery is faulty or depleted.
CALL MAINTENANCE.

published by UNIVERSITY of TEMECULA PRESS, Inc.

44 ANTISKID and NOSE WHEEL STEERING switch .... ON

Antiskid is automatically de-selected when the airplane speed is below 20 kts, even with the switch **ON**.

The **NOSEWHEEL STEERING** is **ELECTRICALLY** controlled and **HYDRAULICALLY** operated. There is **NO** hydraulic pressure to the nosewheel steering until:
- *NOSE GEAR DOORS are CLOSED*
- *A/SKID & N/W STRG switch ON*
- *TOWING CONTROL LEVER NORMAL*
- *At least ONE ENGINE RUNNING*
- *MAIN LANDING GEAR compressed.*

45 CLOCK .... CHECK/SET

NOTE: *There are two types of clocks: a GOOD one and a BAD one. The good one is digital and requires no attention. The bad one (displayed here) is difficult for a pilot to understand.* Verify that the time and date agrees with **UTC** time and date. One available source we have for the **UTC** time is the **HF** radio. *WHOOOPS!*

> ## WARNING:
> ## DO NOT OPERATE THE HF RADIOS
> ### during fueling operations.

A little personal warning here ... this sucker is **DIFFICULT** to understand ...and I absolutely GUARANTEE that if you start fiddling with the switches you are going to get it all screwed up and waste a lot of valuable time trying to get the thing to run properly.

The crux of the problem is the UTC selector. To help you out, here are the definitions for the dual function switch settings:

HSD = Hours/days
MSM = Minutes/Months
HLDY = Hold/Year
RUN = Begins normal operation

The DATE button selects between the available dual function settings. Selecting the switch will cause the clock to advance one unit per second.
Go ahead, I dare you to try and set it.

46 SWITCHING PANEL selectors .... NORMAL

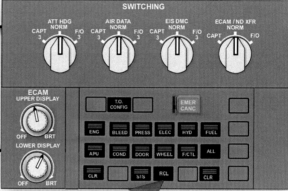

47 ECAM
Warning/Caution messages ..... RECALL

PUSH THE RCL (recall) KEY FOR ABOUT 5 SECONDS. This
will cause messages that have been cleared by the **CLR** key or cancelled
by the **EMER CANC** key to reappear.
If no messages, **NORMAL** appears on the *UPPER ECAM* memo.

48 ECAM STS (STATUS) PAGE ....CHECK

PUSH THE STS KEY. If there are **NO** status messages,
NORMAL is displayed for 5 seconds on the **UPPER ECAM** memo.

AFTER IRSs ARE ALIGNED

If there are status messages:
- Determine if they affect dispatch
- Determine if they require maintenance action
- Verify if **FAULT** or **MAINT** messages are **OK** with **MRD**.
- Verify if any **FAULT** or **MAINT** messages that
  MUST be cleared or deferred.

NOTE:
MAINT (CLASS II) MESSAGES ARE NOT FLIGHT CRITICAL;
HOWEVER, THEY MUST BE CLEARED OR
DEFERRED PRIOR TO DISPATCH.

FYI (For Your Information): *The display of MAINT*
messages is inhibited after engine start.

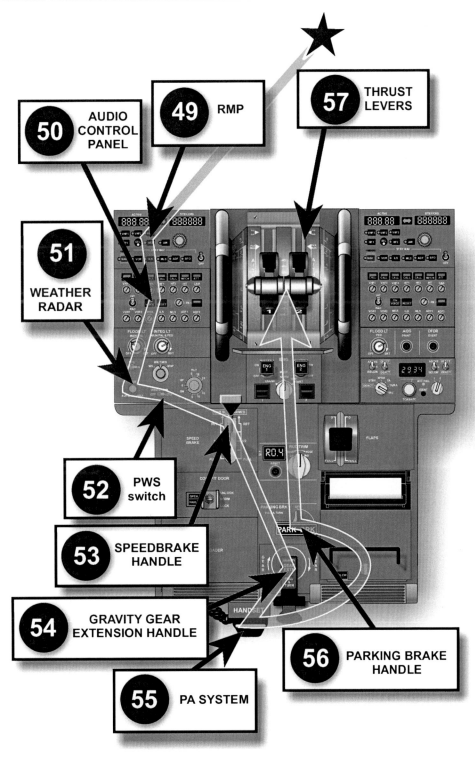

★

57 THRUST LEVERS

49 RMP

50 AUDIO CONTROL PANEL

51 WEATHER RADAR

52 PWS switch

53 SPEEDBRAKE HANDLE

54 GRAVITY GEAR EXTENSION HANDLE

55 PA SYSTEM

56 PARKING BRAKE HANDLE

49

RMP (Radio Management Panel) .... SET

1. Verify **RMP** selector switch is **ON**.
2. **GREEN NAV** light should be **OFF**.

In general, VHF 1 is used for ATC. VHF 2 is used for Company, ATIS, and other communications such as CPDLC (Controller Pilot Datalink). VHF 3 is reserved for ACARS/ATSU.

WARNING
DO NOT OPERATE
HF RADIOS
during fueling
operations.

FURTHER WARNING:
Ensure that personnel stay a minimum of 6 feet away from the vertical stabilizer antenna while the HF system is being tested.

50

ACP (Audio Control Panel) ....As Required

There are a couple of items to be aware of.
To **AVOID HOT MIKE** on frequency .... deselect the VHF 1 whenever you are not monitoring it or have left your seat.

Another point, if you are not going to have your headset on, it might be useful to monitor the Flight Attendant switch (ATT button).

published by UNIVERSITY of TEMECULA PRESS, Inc.

51

WEATHER RADAR .... OFF

Verify that the **POWER SWITCH** is in the **OFF** position.

Verify that the
GAIN selector is in
the **AUTO** position.

Just a note in
passing. There are
TWO different
cockpit layouts I
know of that have
different techniques
for viewing the **WX RADAR/EGPWS** on the **ND**:

The Airbus configuration requires that you "deselect" the **EGPWS** to view
the radar return. You do this by depressing the **TERR** or **TERR ON ND**
switch located on the forward instrument panel. There is a separate selector
for each pilot.

The "**OTHER**" configuration is a "two switch" set-up (Installed on UA
airplanes) that automatically deselects the **EGPWS** display when you select
the radar **ON**. There is also a separate selector for each pilot.

On both systems, even with the radar or **EGPWS** displays deselected, if you
should encounter an **EGPWS** warning, the **EGPWS** display will
automatically display on the **ND**.

*Now, here is a problem ... you MUST HAVE the intensity of the display set
high enough for it to be viewed ... and the EPGWS intensity selector is on
the "wing-out" panel on the outer ring of the ND brightness selector.*

52

PWS (Predictive Wind Shear) .... OFF

WARNING
**The WEATHER RADAR and
the PWS (predictive Wind Shear)
MUST BE OFF !!!**
*There exists a radiation hazard to
ground personnel and First Officers
doing their walk-around.*

WEATHER RADAR ops

This *WILL NOT* be a definitive guide to operating the **WEATHER   RADAR**. Learning to operate the **WX RADAR** is a continually developing art form, and learned best by actually operating the set over a long period of time. What we will present here are just some of the pilot information necessary to "get you started."

RULE NUMBER ONE:
AVOID SEVERE WEATHER.

The weather radar is designed as one of your tools to _keep you out of_ severe weather situations and not intended to be used as a penetration tool.

WARNING:
DO NOT OPERATE THE RADAR when:
- Personnel within 15 feet of the radar antenna.
- while fueling or defueling.
- Facing walls or metal buildings where "bounce back" can burn out the set.

HOW CAN A PILOT SCREW UP?

If you can't get the darned thing to work, consider these two things *BEFORE* you get the maintenance guy to come out and embarrass you.

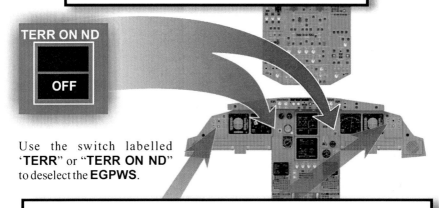

1. In the Airbus configuration, the **EGPWS** must be manually deselected in order to display the **WX RADAR** return on the **ND**.

TERR ON ND

OFF

Use the switch labelled '**TERR**" or "**TERR ON ND**" to deselect the **EGPWS**.

2. Sometimes, if the brightness is not balanced properly, you cannot see the return on the **ND**. While your first impulse might be to think the radar is not working, adjust the **ND BRIGHTNESS CONTROL KNOB** on the forward panels. These are turned all the way down when the airplane is secured.

53 SPEEDBRAKE LEVER ...RETRACT, DISARM

Verify that the **SPEEDBRAKE** lever is full forward in the **RET** position
AND
the lever is down in the stowed detent.

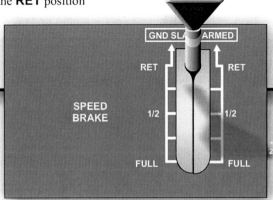

54 GRAVITY GEAR EXTENSION HANDLE .... STOWED

Sometimes in the sim, you will follow a crew whose arduous encounter may have included a manual gear extension. Make certain that the handle is stowed ...and that the systems actuated have been reset.

When the crank is turned, the hydraulic pressure is shut off, Main gear is "locked" down, (and most importantly)

NOSE WHEEL STEERING IS DEACTIVATED.

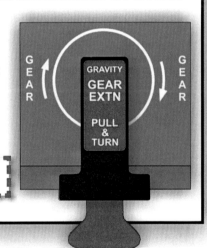

55 PASSENGER ADDRESS SYSTEM ..... CHECK

Pick up the handset and make a PA announcement to check the clarity, volume, and overall operation of the unit.

56 **PARKING BRAKE HANDLE .... SET**

THIS IS A **BIG DEAL!**

Even IF PARKING BRAKE HANDLE IS ON
Then we still have to **_CONFIRM_** that the parking brake is SET.

The PARKING BRAKE switch is actually ONLY an electric switch

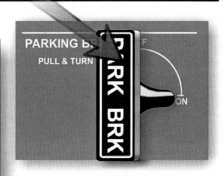

NOTE:
The parking brake should be set IF:
- **RAMP IS ICY**
- **WIND SPEED or GUSTS OF 40 KTS or greater.**

CAUTION:
The _ONLY_ confirmation that the parking brakes are SET is an indication of **PARKING BRAKE PRESSURE** on the **PARKING BRAKES AND ACCU PRESS** indicators.

If the pressure indicators are "**OUT OF THE GREEN BAND**" and indicating yellow system pressure ... then, and only then, can we assume the parking brakes are **SET**.

IF PARKING BRAKE HANDLE IS OFF
consider the cause. It could have been left OFF to allow for brake cooling.

ADDITIONAL NOTE:
If the brakes are OFF (released) then the BRAKE WEAR indicators will not be accurate when observed during the exterior inspection.

YOU MUST REMEMBER
to confirm that the parking brake is **SET** prior to accomplishing the **BEFORE START CHECKLIST.**

published by UNIVERSITY of TEMECULA PRESS, Inc.

57 THRUST LEVERS .... IDLE

The Thrust Levers
should be "standing up"
in the **IDLE** position.

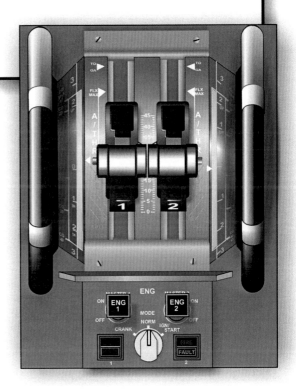

There are 5 positions defined
- **TOGA (TAKE-OFF GO AROUND)**
- **FLEX (FLEXIBLE TEMPERATURE)**
- **MCT (MAXIMUM CONTINUOUS)**
- **CL (CLIMB)**
- **FORWARD IDLE**

END of the flow:
COCKPIT PREPARATION - CAPTAIN

WHEEEEW!

EXTERIOR INSPECTION

ALSO CALLED A
PILOT WALK-AROUND

THE DIVERSION EXCLUSION:
"If a flight is diverted to another station, it may be difficult to accomplish a pilot walk-around due to station overload, a lack of stairs or loading bridge, foreign/station restrictions, etc. In this rare instance, the Captain may use discretion to depart the station without accomplishing a pilot walk-around. If the Captain deems a walk-around necessary, it will be done using any means available, including having a qualified line mechanic substitute for the pilot, or waiting for the station to provide stairs or a loading bridge."

While it is known to pilots as a walk-around ... on balmy days it could actually be a "stroll around" or in bad weather, a "run around". It is **ALWAYS ACCOMPLISHED** (exception noted above) before the initial flight of the day and between every subsequent flight segment. The inspection can be accomplished by either the Captain or a designated crew member ... normally by the First Officer (Duh!).
This book will not describe the routine exterior inspection as that is illustrated in other venues and is not typically a part of the simulator ride. However,
ALL CREW MEMBERS (INCLUDING CAPTAIN) WILL BE RESPONSIBLE FOR DEMONSTRATING KNOWLEDGE OF ITEMS ON THE EXTERIOR INSPECTION.

Before starting the exterior inspection
FIRST STEP 1: Wing Light Switch ...... ON

After exterior inspection complete
LAST STEP 2: Wing Light Switch ...... OFF

After completing the "walk-around" ... the First Officer rushes to the cockpit, stows their raincoat, gets out their flight kit and "flying stuff," adjusts their seat, and makes a "nest" and then does the ...
FIRST OFFICER'S COCKPIT SET-UP

FIRST OFFICER'S COCKPIT SETUP

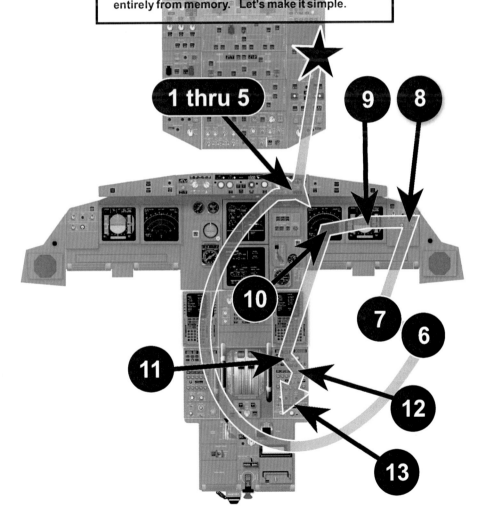

Even though there are only 13 steps to the First Officer's Cockpit setup, they also have to be done entirely from memory. Let's make it simple.

1 thru 5

9

8

10

7

6

11

12

13

5 EASY PIECES

Start your set-up with the **EFIS CONTROL PANEL**.
There are 5 things to set.

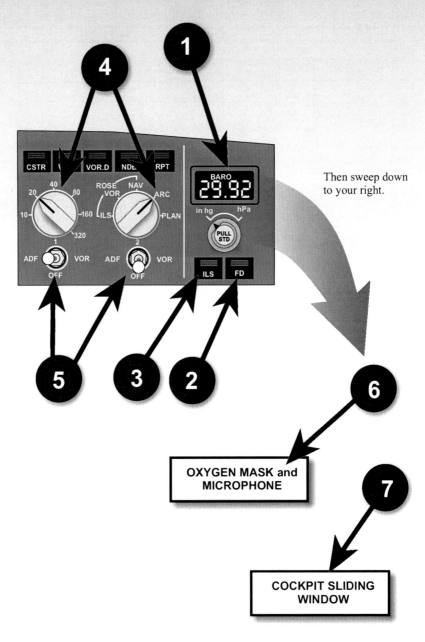

Then sweep down
to your right.

OXYGEN MASK and MICROPHONE

COCKPIT SLIDING WINDOW

published by UNIVERSITY of TEMECULA PRESS, Inc.

1 **BAROMETRIC REFERENCE** .... **SET**

Obtain the current barometric altimeter setting.

***1. This will require the use of a RADIO,
or the DCDU (DataLink Control and Display
Unit)/ACARS/Printer to obtain the ATIS. or***

2. Call ATC for the current field barometric altimeter setting.

When the barometric altimeter setting is dialed into the unit, it is
displayed on lower right corner of the **PFD**.

2 **FLIGHT DIRECTOR BUTTON** .... **ON**

MUST BE ARMED in order to engage certain important
AUTOPILOT modes! This **ARMS** the climb and nav modes.

3 **ILS/LS BUTTON** .... **AS REQUIRED**

This is not normally required nor desired to be displayed on
the **PFD** or the **ND** during departure.
*If, however, the **ILS** localizer or the **ILS DME** is required to
comply with departure procedures, then this switch must be selected
in order to be displayed.*

4 **EFIS CONTROL PANEL** .... **SET**

Personal preference is allowed, of course; BUT here are some
recommendations:
- **ARC** for straight out departures
- **ROSE NAV** if turns back over the field are anticipated
- A good start is 40 nm range, but 10 or 20 is OK.

5 **VOR/ADF SELECTORS** .... **AS REQUIRED**

The **VOR** and/or **ADF** is not normally required nor desired
to be displayed on the **PFD** or the **ND** during departure.
*If, however, the **VOR** and/or the **ADF** is required to comply
with departure procedures, then this switch must be selected
in order to be displayed.*

6 OXYGEN MASK and MICROPHONE .... TEST

This is an "every flight" item; however, this test is **NOT**
required on subsequent flights IF the pilot stays on the same jet.

WARNING

The test is performed **WITHOUT** *removing the mask from the enclosure. If*
you insist on removing the mask, get ready for a protracted effort similar to
that of attempting to stuff a 120 pound boa constrictor into a tobacco can.

BEWARE:

Before you begin the test,
MAKE SURE the other guys INT reception knob is *OFF!*
... or run the risk of blowing his brains out.

DO THESE STEPS:

A LOUDSPEAKER .... ON

B INT reception knob .... ON

C INT/RAD switch selected to .... INT

D Press-to-test and reset
SLIDE LEVER .... PUSH and *HOLD*
Hold down the **SLIDE LEVER** *while you do the next three steps.*

E BLINKER FLOWMETER .... OBSERVE

It should turn **YELLOW** momentarily, and then turns
BLACK. This indicates the regulator is leak tight.

F REGULATOR EMERGENCY/
Press-to-test .... PRESS and RELEASE

G LOOK and LISTEN .... VERIFY
Verify the sound of oxygen flow across the mask microphone
and **FLOW INDICATOR** turns **YELLOW**.

H Press-to-test and reset
SLIDE LEVER .... RELEASE

I BLINKER FLOWMETER .... OBSERVE
Verify the **BLINKER FLOWMETER** is **BLACK** and
all oxygen flow ceases.

published by UNIVERSITY of TEMECULA PRESS, Inc.

J **REGULATOR EMERGENCY/**
Press-to-test .... PRESS and RELEASE

K **BLINKER FLOWMETER ....VERIFY**
The **BLINKER FLOWMETER** indicator stays **BLACK**,
indicating **NO OXYGEN** flow,

L **LOWER ECAM DOOR page .... CHECK**
Verify the **REGUL LO PR** message is **NOT** displayed. This
check should be made **AFTER** all masks have been checked to
ensure the **LOW PRESSURE** valve is **OPEN**.
NOTE:
Residual pressure in the line between the low pressure valve and the
masks may be sufficient to accomplish a mask test with the valve closed.

M **AUDIO CONTROL PANEL .... RESET**
The idea is to restore the audio panel to its original setup.

RETURN INT/RAD switch to **NEUTRAL**, and
RETURN other pilot's **INT RECEPTION** knob to its original position.

OXYGEN MASK

N **N/100% LEVER .... VERIFY 100%**

O **ENCLOSURE DOORS .... VERIFY CLOSED**

SLIDING WINDOW

7 **SLIDING WINDOW ...... CLOSE and LOCK**
Check that the **RED UNLOCKING** button is fully
popped out and the window does not open.

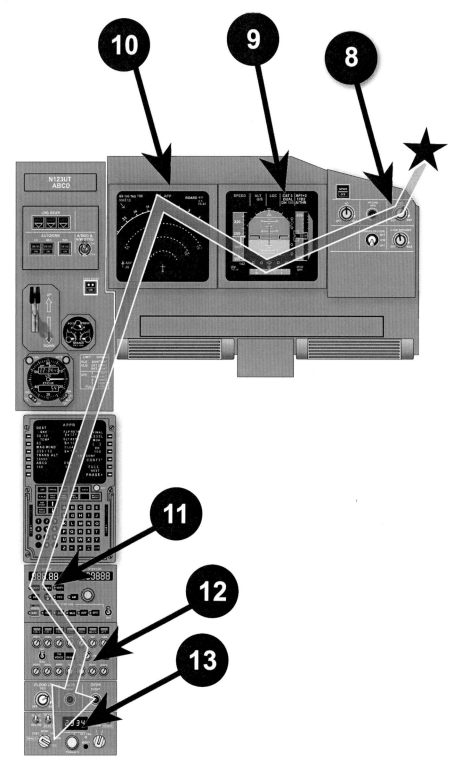

page 202

⑧ PFD and ND brightness .... As required
Ensure EGPWS and RADAR DISPLAYS visible

The two brightness control knobs manually control the respective illumination level.

IF a **PFD FAILS** or is shut **OFF**, then the **PFD** display will shift automatically to the respective **ND**. When this happens, you can display the **PFD** or the **ND** on the "other" **LCD** screen using the **PFD/ND XFR** switch.

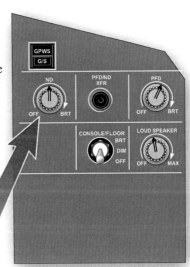

NOTE: *Once the* **PFD/ND XFR** *switch is depressed, the brightness controls shift. That is, the* **PFD** *controls the* **ND***, and the* **ND** *controls the* **PFD** *display brightness.*

The **ND** selector has an **OUTER SELECTOR** that controls the brightness of the **WEATHER RADAR** and the **EGPWS** image only.

NOTE: *The outer selector of the* **ND** *brightness selector* **MUST BE ON** *and* **BRIGHT** *to ensure the* **EGPWS** *pop-up feature is visible in the event of a windshear.*

NOTE:
Some aircraft (UA type) are configured with a "two switch" setup located on the wing-out panels.

---

9 **PFD** .... **CHECK**

A. Verify **PFD** displayed on the appropriate **DISPLAY.**
B. No flags displayed.
C. Verify **IAS** correct.
D. Verify **FMA** correct.
E. Verify **INITIAL TARGET ALTITUDE.**
F. Verify **VSI** correct (indicator horizontal).
G. Verify **ALTIMETER SETTING (QNH)**:Info from **ATIS**).
H. Verify Attitude is correct (No roll or pitch indicated).
I. Verify **HEADING** agrees with **ND, DDRMI,** and **STBY COMPASS**.

NOTE:

The altimeters should read
ELEVATION PLUS 10 FEET AGL.
This is difficult, because we seldom know the exact elevation of the airplane's
position **UNLESS** at the runway end where it is noted on the approach plate
runway diagram.
If the altimeters do not read with
WITHIN +/- 25 FEET OF ELEVATION
and agree with each other
WITHIN 20 FEET
then maintenance action ***REQUIRED!***

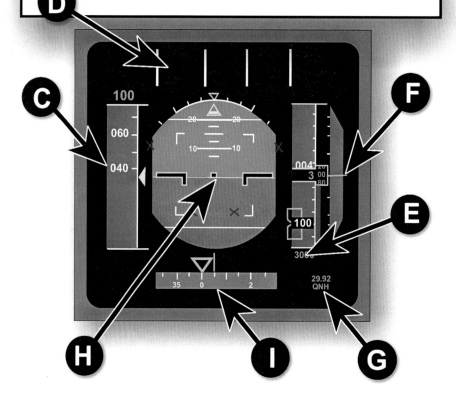

published by UNIVERSITY of TEMECULA PRESS, Inc.

10 **ND** .... **CHECK**
1. Verify **PFD** displayed on the appropriate **DISPLAY**.
2. No flags displayed

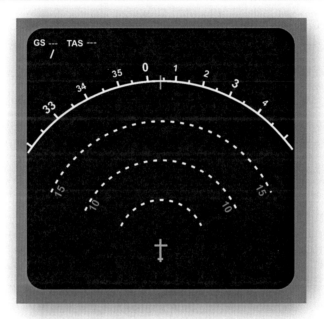

Shown here is the **ARC MODE** Of course, the **ND** will be
indicating an image depicting whatever is set up on the **EFIS
CONTROL PANEL (ECP)**.

RMP (Radio Management Panel) .... SET

1. Verify **RMP** selector switch is **ON**.
2. **GREEN NAV** light should be **OFF**.

In general, VHF 1 or CPDLC (Controller Pilot Datalink) is used for ATC, VHF 2 is used for Company, ATIS, and other communications. VHF 3 is reserved for ACARS/ATSU.

WARNING
DO NOT OPERATE HF RADIOS during fueling operations.

FURTHER WARNING:
Ensure that personnel stay a minimum of 6 feet away from the vertical stabilizer antenna while the HF system is being tested.

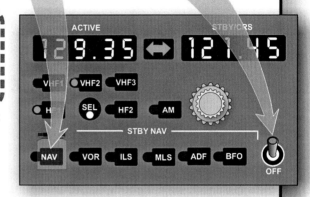

ACP (Audio Control Panel) ....As Required

There are a couple of items to be aware of.
To **AVOID HOT MIKE** on frequency .... deselect the **VHF 1** whenever you are not monitoring it or have left your seat.

Another point, if you are not going to have your headset on, it might be useful to monitor the Flight Attendant switch (ATT button).

published by UNIVERSITY of TEMECULA PRESS, Inc.

13 **TRANSPONDER MODE .... STANDBY**

We want to ensure that the transponder does **_NOT_** clutter the **ATC** system with unexpected returns on their radar equipment. Particularly such codes as 7700.

When Transponder selector is placed in **STBY,** the message **TCAS STBY** displays in green on the upper **ECAM EWD**.

UPPER ECAM EWD
(Engine/Warning Display)

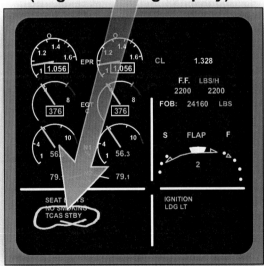

END OF COCKPIT PREPARATION
- FIRST OFFICER

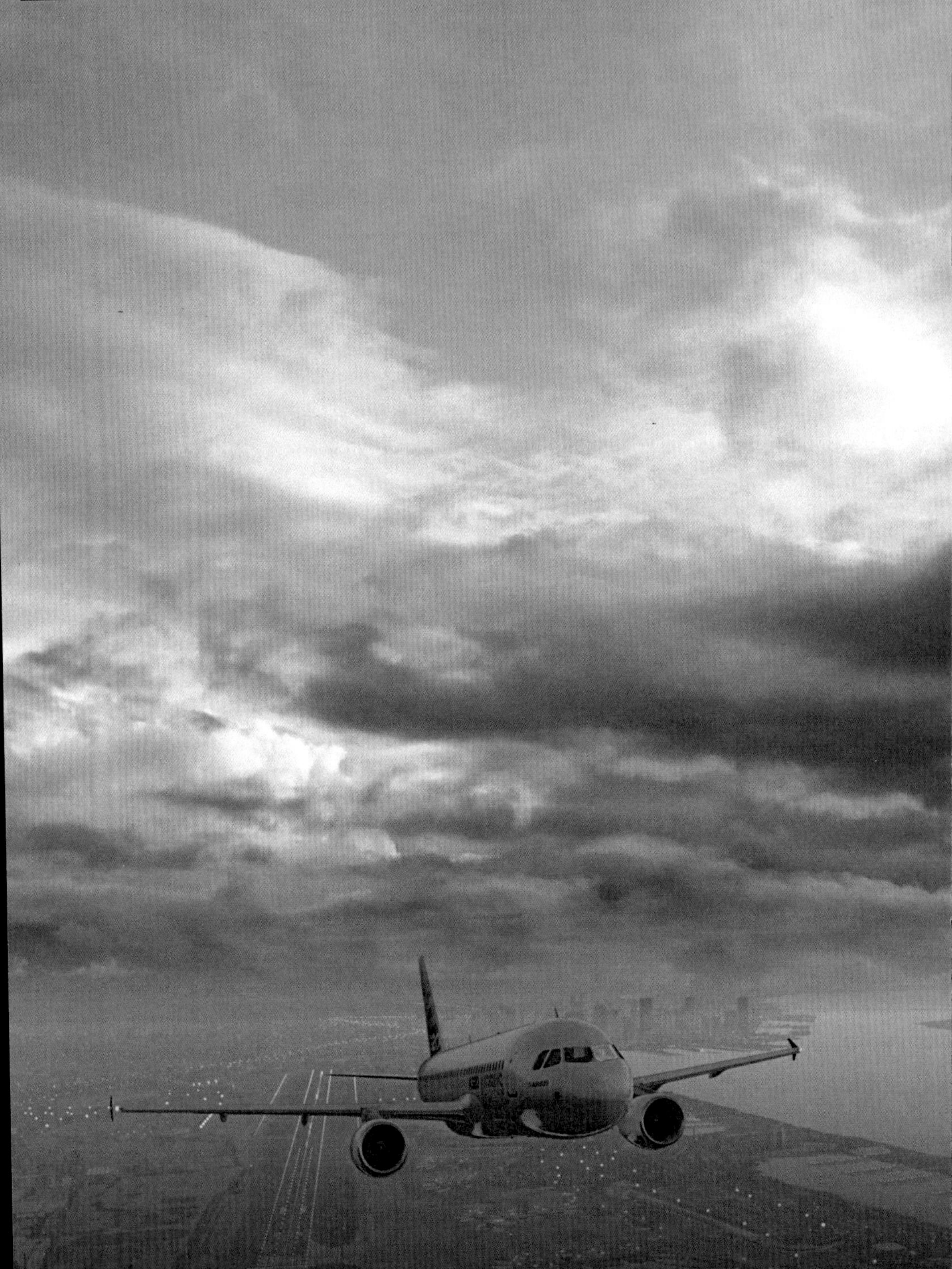

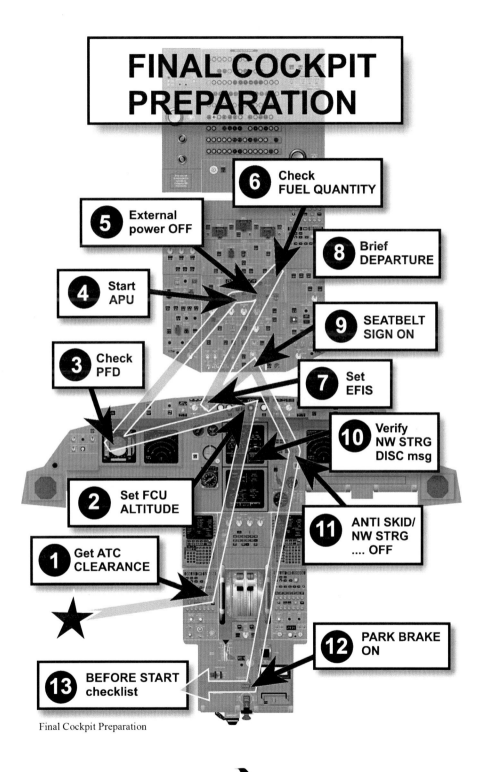

FINAL COCKPIT PREPARATION

5 External power OFF

6 Check FUEL QUANTITY

4 Start APU

8 Brief DEPARTURE

3 Check PFD

9 SEATBELT SIGN ON

7 Set EFIS

2 Set FCU ALTITUDE

10 Verify NW STRG DISC msg

1 Get ATC CLEARANCE

11 ANTI SKID/ NW STRG .... OFF

12 PARK BRAKE ON

13 BEFORE START checklist

Final Cockpit Preparation

About 20 minutes prior to pushback ...
or as indicated on the airport information sheet ...

1. GET ATC CLEARANCE

There are basically two ordinary ways to get the clearance.

Using the VHF radio, and
Using the center CDU and PDC

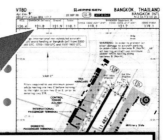

1: DETERMINE desired frequency (In this case we will use the 10-9 page to obtain CLEARANCE DELIVERY frequency)

4. DEPRESS the FREQUENCY TRANSFER SWITCH to make the selected frequency active.
NOTE:
The frequency that was the "old" active frequency, now becomes the standby.

2. SELECT RADIO SWITCH for the radio to be tuned.

3. DIAL IN FREQUENCY using the STANDBY FREQUENCY SELECTOR KNOB.

5. PUSH appropriate button to select the appropriate transmitter.
NOTE: Only one switch can be selected at a time.

6. ADJUST associated receiver volume control knob.

7. *HAVE OTHER PILOT MONITOR* the clearance.

8. Make transmission and request clearance.
Use either:
SIDESTICK switch,
REMOTE pendant, or
DEPRESS INT/RAD switch .

9. *WRITE IT DOWN*. Be prepared for a rapid transmission from the controller. Sometimes the "Aviation English" will be difficult to interpret. Make certain that you understand and obtain a complete clearance.

published by UNIVERSITY of TEMECULA PRESS, Inc.

GETTING THE CLEARANCE using PDC technique

Another (**BETTER**) way to get the clearance is using the **ACARS CDU**. Those airports where this service is available will be indicated on the 10-9 or 11-1 airport pages by the notation **PDC** or **CPDLC** in the legend of the airport diagram page. The initial call-up frequency at a station where a **PDC** or **CPDLC** has been received will be on **ATIS**, **AIRPORT PAGE REMARKS** or **NOTAM**.

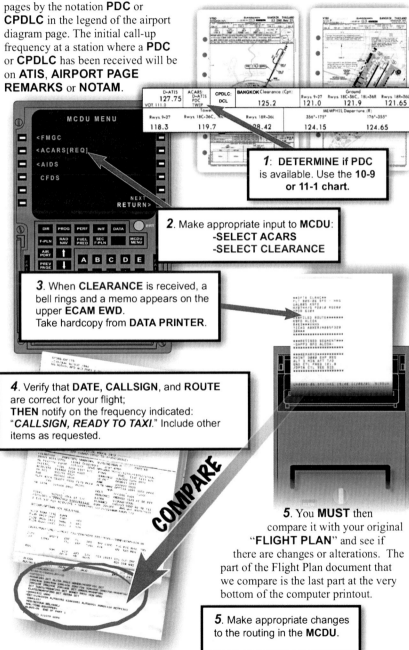

1: DETERMINE if PDC is available. Use the **10-9** or **11-1 chart.**

2. Make appropriate input to **MCDU**:
-SELECT ACARS
-SELECT CLEARANCE

3. When **CLEARANCE** is received, a bell rings and a memo appears on the upper **ECAM EWD**.
Take hardcopy from **DATA PRINTER**.

4. Verify that **DATE, CALLSIGN**, and **ROUTE** are correct for your flight;
THEN notify on the frequency indicated:
"*CALLSIGN, READY TO TAXI.*" Include other items as requested.

5. You **MUST** then compare it with your original "**FLIGHT PLAN**" and see if there are changes or alterations. The part of the Flight Plan document that we compare is the last part at the very bottom of the computer printout.

5. Make appropriate changes to the routing in the **MCDU**.

2. FCU Altitude

Set the first altitude restriction on your clearance or the lowest restriction depicted on the departure SID. Ensure that you have been assigned an altitude.
You will *NEVER* be cleared without a target altitude.

GOOD TECHNIQUE: Check that the FCU altitude selected is annunciated on the PFD.

IMPORTANT STEP

3. PFD

Both pilots verify that:
1. **V2**,
2. **V1**,
3. **CLB MODE** is **ARMED**,
4. **NAV MODE** is **ARMED**
5. **FCU ALTITUDE** displayed.

4. APU .... START (if not already running)

Since we have previously discussed starting the APU, I will let you refer to that page for information about this topic. Once the **APU AVAIL** light is illuminated you may switch to APU power... *BUT* (read next step).

5. EXTERNAL POWER switch .... OFF

Once the APU is started, it WILL NOT take the BUS automatically. The EXTERNAL POWER must be disconnected manually.

WARNING:

Select the external power OFF using the switch BEFORE notifying the ground person "cleared to disconnect." If the EXTERNAL power source is still powering the airplane, there will be a BIG ZAAAAPPPOOOO when the plug is pulled ...and the potential exists for injury to the ground personnel.

6 FUEL quantity .... CHECK

Since the person who actually performs the fueling will come to the cockpit, you cannot control the timing for this check. I recommend strongly, that when the fueller comes to the cockpit ... **STOP** what you are doing and take the time to ensure your fuel load. Once you have the final fueling information, you can perform the necessary calculations as outlined in company procedures.

7 EFIS control panel .... SET

Depending on the departure requirements, each situation may involve a different set of parameters. Generally, use a setting with

- **ARC** as display mode and
- **20 or 40 nm.**

8 DEPARTURE briefing ....

Depending on the departure requirements, each situation may involve a different set of parameters. Take a moment and list some of the items you might include in **YOUR** brief.

9 SEATBELT SIGN.. ON

Some Captains will take a moment and make an announcement drawing the passenger's attention to the illumination of the sign.
If you do: **KEEP IT BRIEF** as this is a critical phase of the loading of the cabin and you don't want to detract from that activity.

10 NW STRG DISC message .... VERIFY
(IF NOSE LANDING GEAR BYPASS PIN is installed)

When the Ground maintenance personnel hook up the tow bar for pushback, they will insert the Nose Wheel steering bypass pin and disconnect the nosewheel steering. It is that indication that we are looking for that will confirm the airplane is configured for push.

WARNING: Before pushback, the **ECAM** message NW STRG DISC **MUST BE DISPLAYED.**

11 A/SKID & N/W STRG switch .... OFF

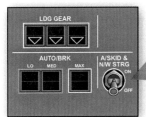

Once we are sure that the nosewheel bypass pin is inserted and the Nosewheel steering has been disconnected, then we can turn **OFF** the hydraulic pressure to the nosewheel steering so that the pushback can be accomplished.

Once you do that, the **ECAM** shows the message **BRAKES ANTI SKID/NWS ... OFF.**
We then have to clear that message and check that the **ECAM** screens are showing **NORMAL** indications in preparation for engine start.

published by UNIVERSITY of TEMECULA PRESS, Inc.

12   PARKING BRAKE HANDLE .... ON

EVEN IF THE PARKING BRAKE HANDLE IS ON:
We still have to **_CONFIRM_** that the parking brake is set.

The PARKING BRAKE selector handle is actually ONLY an electric switch.

CAUTION:

The **ONLY** confirmation that the parking brakes are set is an indication of **PARKING BRAKE PRESSURE** on the **PARKING BRAKES AND ACCU PRESS** indicators.

---

13   BEFORE START CHECKLIST ..... COMPLETE

Departure brief	Complete
MCDU/FMGC and Radios ...	Programmed, set, verified
ADIRS	Nav, aligned
Fuel panel	___ Pumps on, crossfeed closed
Fuel quantity	___ #, cleared with ___ #
Cabin signs	On
Oxygen check	Complete
Engine master switches	Off
Parking Brake	Set, pressure normal
Altimeters	_____ in/hPa, set
Airspeed	G.W.___, FLAPS___, V1, VR, V2, set

PREPARATION FOR PUSHBACK

There are three scenarios that will play at this point:

1. Start engines at Gate before pushback,
2. Start engines during pushback,
3. Start engines after pushback.

We are sitting there ready to go fly. We have already completed the "**BEFORE START CHECKLIST**" and perhaps have even started the engines, and are waiting for the signal to leave the gate.

Just prior to PUSHBACK
(or when prompted by the pushback crew)

Do these FOUR STEPS:

STEP 1: (**C**) **DOORS and SLIDES** ....Verify **CLOSED** and **ARMED**.
This will require co-ordination with the Flight Attendants or Purser. They will initiate the call-up using the interphone.
Check the **DOORS** page of the **ECAM** to confirm doors closed.

STEP 2: **CABIN PREPARATION** .... Verify **COMPLETE**.
This will usually be accomplished by conversation with the Flight Attendants or Purser. They will also provide additional information at this point; such as final passenger count, specials, and could get a coffee request from you.

STEP 3: (**F/O**) **Cockpit door** .... verify **CLOSED and LOCKED**.
Check Flight Operations Manual for details.

STEP 4: (**C,F/O**) **BEFORE PUSHBACK CHECKLIST** .... complete

BEFORE PUSHBACK CHECKLIST

CHALLENGE [F]	RESPONSE
Sliding windows	Closed, locked [C, F/O]
Doors, slides	Closed, armed [C]
Cabin preparation	Complete [C]

CHECKLIST COMPLETE

published by UNIVERSITY of TEMECULA PRESS, Inc.

The signal to begin the pus-back is initiated by the Ground Person. Generally, they will establish communication with a cheery "Hello" or some such, but here is the bare-bones dialog that you can expect.

GROUND	CAPTAIN
"Ground to Cockpit, predeparture check complete"	"Stand-by (if not ready)" or "Before Pushback Checklist complete" or"Brakes released, Hold the Push"
"Roger, cleared to push, Ramp is clear."	"Nose wheel steering disconnect message is displayed. Brakes released. Cleared to push"
"Cleared to start engine(s)." This command will be given at the sole discretion of the ground crew."	"Roger, Cleared to start engine(s)."
"Set brakes".	"Brakes set, Pressure normal."
"Tow bar disconnected" "Disconnecting Headset, Watch for Salute." (If a delay is required such as to load late bags, the ground will advise crew: "Standby.")	"Disconnect Headset" (at Captain's discretion) If you detect a problem or potential problem, keep the ground person on the line until you resolve the situation.
Ground person will walk away from the airplane, then at a safe distance turn and: Stand at attention and Salute. Release from guidance signal: Both arms extended in direction of taxi.	Acknowledge Salute by turning the NOSE light switch to TAXI, then OFF.

When **PUSHBACK CLEARANCE** *received*
from the Ground Pushback Personnel:

Then do these FIVE STEPS:

STEP 1: (F/O) PUSHBACK CLEARANCE .... OBTAIN.
Use the appropriate frequency from the Flight Operations Manual
or the Airport pages.

F/O NOTE:
Be aware that the Captain **WILL** **NOT** be monitoring the pushback frequency.

STEP 2: (F/O) BEACON SWITCH .... ON
The beacon should be **ON** any time:
- *the airplane is moving or*
- *the engines are running.*

STEP 3: (F/O) TRANSPONDER MODE SELECTOR........................ XPDR.
Placing the transponder to the **XPDR** position on the ground allows the
transponder to respond to selective interrogation modes of mode S; at some
airports with ground control radar transponder capability.
In flight, with **XPDR** selected, the transponder will switch to **ON** automatically.
This also places the **TCAS** to Standby.

STEP 4: (C) PARKING BRAKES .... RELEASE.
Just a reminder for those coming over from "other" airplanes. Releasing the
brakes involves **ONLY** turning the brakes selector to **OFF** ... and checking the
BRAKE PRESS gauges go to the "green band" indication.

DO NOT RELEASE BRAKES UNTIL CLEARANCE RECEIVED FROM:
- THE GOUND PUSHBACK CREW, ... OR IN SOME CASES
- TOWER, GROUND CONTROL, OR RAMP CONTROLLING AGENCY.

STEP 5: (C) NOTIFY GROUND PERSONNEL:
"CLEARED TO PUSH, BRAKES RELEASED."

published by UNIVERSITY of TEMECULA PRESS, Inc.

ENGINE START

There is not one single way to start the engines on the **Airbus A320**. There are several different techniques and here are some:
- **GROUND PNEUMATIC start**
- **CROSSBLEED START**
- **MANUAL ENGINE START**
- **STORED AIR GROUND START**
- **START VALVE MANUAL OPERATION**
- **INFLIGHT ENGINE START**

and all of these may be encountered on a checkride. Since reference to the appropriate **ADDITIONAL** and **IRREGULAR** procedure by using the **FLIGHT MANUAL** as a reference is not only suggested but required, I have elected to exclude these from our discussion at this point and will concentrate solely on the

- **NORMAL ENGINE START using AUTOSTART.**

WHAT IS AUTOSTART?

This is pure engineering magic and is referred to as **AUTOSTART**. Some hidden and mysterious doo-dad called the **FADEC** (*Full Authority Digital Engine control*) does everything. It controls the **START VALVE, BOTH IGNITERS**, and h**IGH PRESSURE VALVE**. It also monitors **N1, N2, EGT**, and further has the ability to detect **HUNG STARTS, STALLS**, and **NO STARTS**. *Amazing!* **AS LONG AS N2 IS BELOW 50%,** the **FADEC** will automatically **ABORT THE START** if it sees anything improper and then, amazingly, automatically **CONTINUES TO CRANK THE ENGINE** if it is needed to cool it and eliminate residual fuel vapors. If, however, **N2** is above 50%, the **FADEC** will no longer do all that monitoring and will not abort the start.

Another feature is that during an automatic start, if the residual **EGT is above 250°C**, the amazing **FADEC** will crank the engine until the EGT decreases below $250°C$ before initiating the start sequence. Unfortunately, there is **NO ECAM MESSAGE** to indicate this.

> *IF AN ABORTED START OCCURS*, a manual start may be attempted. However it will be necessary to;
> - Report the failed automatic start attempt (use the radio or ACARS),
> - Make a LOGBOOK entry,
> - Obtain clearance to continue the flight from Company Maintenance
> - get "NEW" MRD (Maintenance Release Document).
> BEFORE you can continue with the flight.
>
> **DO NOT TAKE OFF WITH A DIRTY LOGBOOK.**

Some
LIMITATIONS
associated with starting

STARTER DUTY CYCLE	ON	OFF
CONSECUTIVE STARTING ATTEMPTS *Measure timing from start valve opening until closing.*	2 minutes	15 seconds
	2 minutes	15 seconds
	1 minute	30 minutes
CONTINUOUS CRANKING	4 minutes	30 minutes

*IF start valve open for more than 2 minutes, then the **ENG MASTER** switch **MUST BE SELECTED OFF** for **30 minutes**.*

Maximum Starter re-engagement **RPM**	10% N2

MINIMUM PNEUMATIC AIR PRESSURE FOR STARTER

Minimum **DUCT PRESSURE** while starter rotating (PSI)	GREEN

ENGINE and THRUST MAXIMUM	TIME LIMIT	INSTR MARKING	EGT (°C)
START	*See limits above*	RED	**635**
TAKE-OFF / GO-AROUND	**5** minutes	RED	**635**
MAXIMUM CONTINUOUS	UNLIMITED	AMBER	**610**

NOTE: *Time limit is maximum operating time at thrust setting.*

RPM - MAXIMUM

N1 and N2 rotors	100 %

CAUTION:
If N2 vibration exceeds "5"
(indicated with an accompanying pulsating GREEN indicator)
and does NOT decrease after engine start ...
SHUT DOWN THE ENGINE and contact maintenance.

published by UNIVERSITY of TEMECULA PRESS, Inc.

OIL LIMITATIONS

Minimum **OIL PRESSURE**	**60 PSI**
Minimum **OIL QUANTITY** before START	**17 Quarts**
Minimum **OIL QUANTITY** at IDLE RPM	**12 Quarts**
Maximum **OIL TEMP** (continuous operation)	**155°C**
Maximum **OIL TEMP** (up to 15 minutes)	**165°C**
Minimum **OIL TEMP** (prior to start)	**-40°C**
Minimum **OIL TEMP** (prior to exceeding idle RPM)	**-10°C**
Minimum **OIL TEMP** (prior to takeoff)	**+50°C**

The FADEC is NOT available to SHUT DOWN an engine after 50% N2 has been reached.

If an **ENG 1(2) FAIL** message appears after 50% N2 , but prior to reaching idle speed, then a manual start may be required. *This requires a maintenance logbook entry and a new maintenance release to continue.*

If a cargo door is opened after the first engine has been started (common occurrence to accommodate late passenger bag loading)
WAIT 1 MINUTE
after the door is closed before starting the second engine.

COLD WEATHER START COMMENT:

During cold weather (and after anti-icing) start engines using the normal procedures. However, be alert that starting problems are more frequent during cold weather. Oil pressure may rise slowly and then go to higher than normal readings until it warms up. Remember, Oil pressure MUST BE within normal range for take-off:
60 PSI minimum

CAUTION:

If there is no oil pressure indicated by the time the engine reaches stabilized idle, follow the **ECAM** procedures.

The ENGINE START FLOW

Let's take a moment and review some of the information that is part of the engine start. The Check Captain may give you a hypothetical situation or thought problem to resolve. Here are a couple of common examples.

For example, the Check Pilot might provide you with updated wind information that indicates a strong "**TAILWIND**". If you receive that information during the pushback, communicate with the ground personnel that you would prefer a "tail downwind" for the start.
If the Check-guy prompts you with a simulated question from the ground guy, "Captain, which direction do you want the jet to face."
Take that as a clue that the wind might be a factor that could caused a potential compressor stall.
"Put the tail downwind."

Another example might be: A high temperature or high altitude situation may not provide enough pneumatic duct pressure for the start. It may be necessary to unload the pneumatic air requirements on the airplane: turn off the packs, maybe make an announcement to the passengers. Be creative in your response. Show

Expect a start problem

Review the list of start and engine limitations on the next page.

Since we will be using **SPECIFIC** engine and **SPECIFIC** engine starting techniques used at a **SPECIFIC** airline for this demonstration, you may find that the procedures at your airline differ somewhat from those specified here. Don't get your underwear in a bunch, keep in mind that the learning curve can be enhanced by taking the material here and (with a ball point pen) making whatever changes you deem worthy right in the margins of the text.

The A320 has two **IAE V2527-A5** high bypass turbofan engines. Each engine can produce 26,500 pounds of thrust.
We will also reference the **A319** and it has two **IAE V2522-A5** engines, rated at 22,000 pounds of thrust.
Each engine is equipped with a "**FULL AUTHORITY DIGITAL ENGINE CONTROL**" (**FADEC**) for engine management.

Put your aircraft type and engine configuration in this box for reference.

published by UNIVERSITY of TEMECULA PRESS, Inc.

HOW TO START THE ENGINES

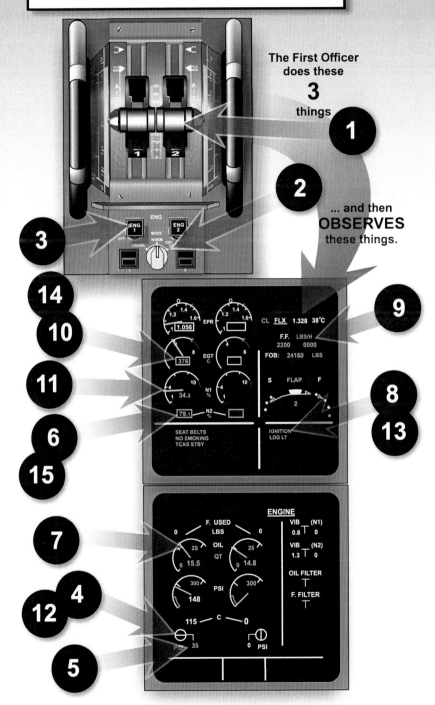

The First Officer does these

3

things

... and then

OBSERVES these things.

FIRST OFFICER does these three things:

1 (F/O) THRUST LEVERS
Verfiy at **IDLE**

2 (F/O) ENGINE MODE SELECTOR Select **IGNITION/START**:
This will:
- Display **ENG** page on lower **ECAM**
- Power up the **FADEC**
- **AMBER XXXX**s disappear from indicators (except N1 and N2)
- **ENG MASTER** switch is armed.
- The **PACK** valves close.
*If the **ENG MASTER** switch is not selected within 30 seconds, the pack valves reopen. They reclose when switch selected on.*

3 (F/O) ENGINE MASTER SWITCH............................ ON

FIRST OFFICER OBSERVES

4 START VALVE .... OPEN
*The start valve indicator will display a **HORIZONTAL LINE** when the start valve **OPENS**. A **VERTICAL LINE** indicates the valve is **CLOSED**.*

5 ENGINE DUCT BLEED PRESSURE .... GREEN
*This displays the **PNUEMATIC AIR DUCT BLEED PRESSURE** upstream from the **PRE-COOLER**. When **N2 EXCEEDS 10%** with the **ENGINE START VALVE NOT CLOSED** and the **PRESSURE IS BELOW 21 PSI**; then the value becomes **AMBER**. Also becomes **AMBER** when **BLEED OVER-PRESSURE IS DETECTED**.*

6 N2 ....INCREASES
*During engine start brightness intensifies and a gray box surrounds the figure. If it **exceeds 100%**, the value turns **RED** and a **RED CROSS APPEARS**. This indication remains during the whole flight segment.*

7 OIL PRESSURE .... INCREASES
*Either pointer or value will indicate the increase. If **above 390 PSI**, the value will "**PULSE.**" **BELOW 80 PSI** becomes **AMBER**, and **RED BELOW 60 PSI**.*

published by UNIVERSITY of TEMECULA PRESS, Inc.

30 Seconds after ENG MASTER switch ON:

8 IGNITION .... ON
*The **ECAM** message will read "**IGNITION**". The **FADEC** will introduce ignition approximately 30 seconds after the **ENG MASTER** is selected **ON**. The start valve will close and the ignition will cut off when **N2 reaches 43%**.*

9 ENGINE FUEL FLOW .... VERIFY
*The indicators will display the **FUEL FLOW (LBS/HR)** for each engine.*

10 EGT ....INCREASES
WITHIN 20 SECONDS AFTER FUEL FLOW INDICATION.
*Normally displays in **GREEN**. If **EGT** exceeds **610°C**. display turns **AMBER**. If **635°C** is exceeded, display turns **RED**.*

11 N1 starts increasing .... **BEFORE** 34% N2
*Normally displays in **GREEN**. When **N1** exceeds rating limit, it pulses in **AMBER**. It pulses in **RED** when **N1 EXCEEDS 100%**.*

AT 43% N2

12 START VALVE .... CLOSE

13 IGNITION .... OFF

14 EGT .... DECREASES

WHEN N2 STABILIZED AT GROUND IDLE ...

15 GRAY BOX AROUND N2 ....DISAPPEARS
This is the end of the start.

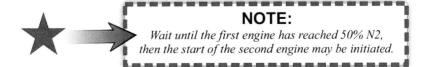

NOTE:
Wait until the first engine has reached 50% N2, then the start of the second engine may be initiated.

QRC*
* QUICK REFERENCE CHECKLIST

TAILPIPE TORCHING
DURING START / SHUTDOWN

There is no bell, siren, caution light or flashing warning ... there is no cockpit indication that relates to this "*EMERGENCY*." Your indication will come from the ground personnel who will be observing the start. It is even possible that a passenger or Flight Attendant may give you a call telling you what they are observing.
The Captain will have to make a judgement about the severity of the situation. At risk is NOT taking the situation seriously, but the alternative is overreacting to a non-event.
The first step is to "*IDENTIFY IF THERE IS A PROBLEM*."

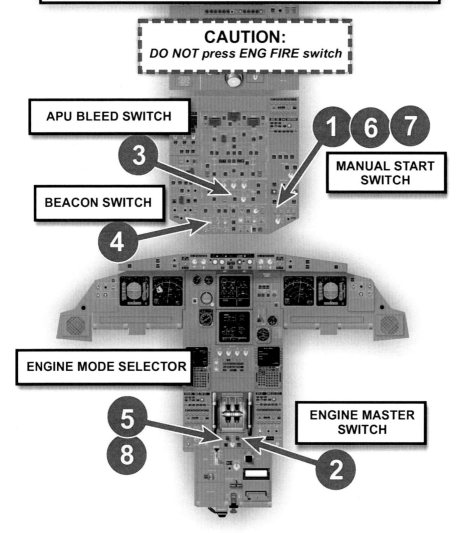

CAUTION:
DO NOT press ENG FIRE switch

APU BLEED SWITCH

3

1 **6** **7**

MANUAL START SWITCH

BEACON SWITCH

4

ENGINE MODE SELECTOR

5
8

ENGINE MASTER SWITCH

2

published by UNIVERSITY of TEMECULA PRESS, Inc.

STEP 1: MANUAL START SWITCH ..... OFF

Unless you are doing a manual start,
these switches should be **OFF** already.
These switches will *OPEN the START VALVE* if:
- **ENG MODE** selector is in
  either **CRANK** or **IGN/START,** and
- **N2** less than **15%**.

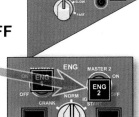

STEP 2: ENG MASTER SWITCH ..... OFF

This will:
- **CLOSE HP** and **LP** fuel valves,
- **TURN OFF** ignition
- Reset **FADEC**

This step will STOP any flow of fuel into the engine.

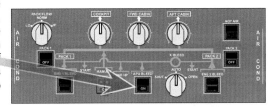

STEP 3: BLEED AIR PRESSURE .... ESTABLISH

During a start there should be
bleed air available; however,
during shutdown, it is possible
that the last engine shut down
would be left without bleed air of
some sort. Unless ground air is
available, then the only way to
get bleed air, is to start the **APU**.

STEP 4: BEACON SWITCH .... ON

The beacon should be "**ON**" for ALL operations already.

STEP 5: ENG MODE .... CRANK

The start valve will **OPEN** if:
- **ENG MAN START** switch is on, and
- **N2** is less than **10%**.

NOTE: *Ignition is NOT supplied*

STEP 6: MANUAL START ..... ON

The start valve will **OPEN** if:
- **ENG MODE** selector is **CRANK** or **IGN/START**, and
- **N2** is less than **15%**.

NOTE: Blue **ON** light indicates **START VALVE** open.

Start the chronometer, since there is a 4 minute time restriction for **NORMAL**
starter cranking operations. If required, of course, crank all you need. Crank the
engine and "blow" the fire and residual fuel out of the tailpipe.

WHEN FIRE IS OUT

STEP 7: MANUAL START SWITCH .... OFF

STEP 8: ENGINE MODE SELECTOR .... NORMAL

▬▬▬▬ *END OF QRC CHECKLIST* **▬▬▬▬**

AFTER START CLEANUP
FIRST OFFICER does these SEVEN things:

1 **(F/O) ENG MODE selector** .... **NORMAL**
When the Mode selector is placed to **NORMAL**, the **LOWER ECAM** replaces the **ENG** page with the **WHEEL** page. This is a check for the crew, that if the **IGN/START** switch is selected, the **ENG** page will be displayed. *Whoooops!*

2 **(F/O) GROUND SPOILERS:** .... **ARM**

If Ground Spoilers are **ARMED**, then they will extend automatically during a rejected take-off **WHEN**:
- **Wheel speed greater than 72 knots,**
- **BOTH thrust levers are in FORWARD IDLE**

The indication that the Ground Spoilers are **ARMED** is a **GREEN MEMO** in the upper **ECAM: SPLRS ARM**

3 **(F/O) RUDDER TRIM** .... **ZERO**
If there is a leftover trim setting from the previous leg, consider only rolling out about half of that amount.

4 **(F/O) PITCH TRIM** .... **SET**
Use the **TRIM WHEEL** on the **THRUST CONTROL PANEL** to manually set the value.
CAUTION NOTE: *When you set the trim using the "trim wheel" it is advisable to use an* **OPEN HAND** *so that the trim wheel won't pinch or* **"BITE"** *your fingers.*
The figure is in percent **MAC** and is provided in the "Final Weights." Note that the information may be available from dispatch via **RADIO/ACARS** after taxi-out updated "final" **MAC** data is sent.

5 **(F/O) APU BLEED switch** .... **AS REQUIRED**
The **APU** bleed switch is located on the overhead panel on the **AIR** control panel. If planning an engine shutdown due to lengthy taxi delays, it might be useful to remain on **APU** air.

6 **(F/O) APU MASTER switch** .... **AS REQUIRED**
APU may be left running if extended ground delays requiring engine shutdown are expected.

published by UNIVERSITY of TEMECULA PRESS, Inc.

(F/O) ENGINE ANTI-ICE .... AS REQUIRED
Be aware that with **ENGINE ANTI-ICE** selected:
- **MAXIMUM N1** is limited
- **CONTINUOUS IGNITION** is provided
- **MINIMUM** idle **RPM** is increased.

There is always the question as to whether or not **ANTI-ICE** is required. Here are the specific guidelines:

"**Engine anti-ice MUST be on during ALL GROUND and FLIGHT operations when icing conditions exist or are anticipated, except during climb and cruise when the temperature is below -40° C SAT.**"

"**Engine anti-ice MUST be on PRIOR TO AND DURING descent in icing conditions, including temperatures BELOW -40° C SAT.**"

What is the definition of **ICING CONDITIONS**?

"**Icing conditions exist during GROUND OPERATIONS, for TAKE-OFF, and INFLIGHT**"

when
-**TEMPERATURE is 10° C or below, and**
-**VISIBLE MOISTURE is** present in any form including *clouds, fog or mist with visibility of 1 mile or less, rain, snow, sleet, or ice crystals.*
-**SURFACE CLUTTER** while operating on ramps, taxiways, or runways *where surface snow, standing water, or slush may be ingested by the engines or freeze on the engines, nacelles, or engine sensor probes.*

What pilots screw up:
They think that icing conditions exist at 32°F.

10°C = 50°F

Icing conditions exist at 50°F.

COLD WEATHER NOTES

ENGINE START

Start engines normally, there is no specific procedure for starting an engine in cold weather; however, staring problems are encountered more often during cold weather. A big problem is **COLD OIL**:

- Oil pressure may rise more slowly than normal,
- Oil pressure may reach higher than normal pressure until it warms,
- Oil pressure must be in normal range for take-off.
- Oil Temperature **MUST BE above 50°C**
  to provide enough heat to de-ice the fuel during take-off.

> ### CAUTION
> *If there is **NO OIL PRESSURE**
> indication by the time the engine
> reaches stabilized idle,
> follow the **ECAM** procedures.*

GROUND DE-ICING/ANTI-ICING

The Captain is responsible for ensuring that the airplane is not dispatched with adhering precipitation on **CRITICAL SURFACES**. In order to meet that requirement, the Captain has several tools at his disposal, such as:

- Avoid operating in conditions deemed unacceptable,
- Ground de-icing to remove the adhering precipitation,
- Anti-icing to inhibit accumulation,
- a visual wing inspection.

GROUND DE-ICING comments

It is beyond the scope of this book to outline the steps necessary for evaluating essential ground deicing limitations and the subsequent interpretation of **HOLDOVER TABLE** data.

> ### CAUTION
> *Single Engine taxi NOT authorized in icing conditions.*

In icing conditions,
TAXI WITH THE FLAPS RETRACTED, and
AVOID OTHER AIRPLANE BLOWBACK.
until approaching the runway.
This is to avoid losing the layer of deicing material lying on the wings,

- Taxi with flaps retracted,
- Maintain greater than normal separation from preceding airplanes and
- Taxi at slower speeds. Avoid holding too closely to another airplane in

the takeoff queue; because there is the potential for blowback causing the deicing

published by UNIVERSITY of TEMECULA PRESS, Inc.

ANTI-ICE PENALTIES

There is **NO GROSS WEIGHT** penalty
when using **ENGINE ANTI-ICE** for **TAKE-OFF**.

NOTE:

When using anti-ice with a reduced thrust takeoff,
SUBTRACT 5° C from the flex temperature BEFORE entering it into
the **MCDU (PERF page)**. This is to ensure that the **FADEC** calculates
the correct reduced **EPR**.

VISUAL WING INSPECTION

Even if the airplane was de-iced in preparation for take-off and if the holding
time HAS NOT expired, and there is any question as to the need for additional
de-icing, then:

It is the Captain's responsibility to make a visual inspection of the wing
surfaces. The Captain may designate another member of the cockpit crew.
(Observer Member of the Crew (OMC) are also considered appropriate)

Here are the inspection criteria:

- Flaps set for take-off.
- Within 5 minutes of the take-off time.
- The inspection takes place from inside the cabin
  from the most advantageous windows
  (normally marked with black triangles):

        A320: Second window forward of the overwing emergency exits,
        A319: Sixth window aft of the overwing emergency exits.

ENGINE ICE discussion

Ice may build up on parts of the engine while the rest of the airplane shows no visible
accumulation. Here's how that happens: during ground operations in idle, as the air
enters the engine inlet, it accelerates and the pressure drops causing the temperature to
drop resulting in ice potentially forming on the interior parts of the engine.

50% N1

Periodic engine run-ups should be based on the
existing weather conditions rather than on visible
airframe ice. Periodic engine run-ups are required
even though the engine anti-ice is on.

*When in weather requiring engine anti-ice,
you should run-up to a minimum of 50% N1. The purpose is to SHED ICE.
Shedding ice is dependent on the rotational speed of the N1 rotor. There is
no requirement to sustain the high RPM, just to achieve 50%, even
momentarily. The amount of ice shed is not proportional to the amount of
N1 rotor speed. Thrust settings below 50% are not effective in shedding
ice.*

ENGINE RUN-UP comments

As soon as you can after leaving the gate area but not more than 10 minutes after
engine start ... the first run-up should be accomplished. The interval between run-
ups should not exceed 10 minutes. To avoid lateral slipping problems, it is
suggested that both engines be run up simultaneously.

If the airplane slides, move to another location where there is drier pavement.

ENGINE RUN-UP

During **ICING CONDITIONS**, it is considered Standard Operating Procedure (SOP) to perform an engine run-up just prior to take-off. When in position on the runway just before you begin the take-off roll:

- Set Parking Brake,
- Run both engines up to 50%,
- Check all primary engine instruments for normal operation,
- Release Brakes,
- Initiate the take-off.

If engine indications are NOT normal:
- Reduce thrust to idle, then
- Perform a second run-up.

If OK, GO ... if not taxi clear of the runway and contact maintenance.

CAUTION
DO NOT RELY ON HOLDING
THE BRAKE PEDALS DURING RUN-UPS.
Airplane movement occurring while you are preoccupied with monitoring the engine instruments is a real possibility. On really icy surfaces, brakes may not be able to restrict the movement of the airplane at run-up power settings ... be prepared to limit thrust.

PITCH UP PROBLEM

I'm just going to mention this as an awareness item. The potential is for a tail strike ... or if there is an asymmetrical lift vector, it could induce a roll and the potential for a pod strike.

During ICING conditions, a combination of
- Contaminated leading edge, and
- Faster than normal rate of rotation
  ($3°$ per second is considered normal).
can possibly result in a "spontaneous" pitch up.

WING ANTI-ICE

Since the wing anti-ice can be used effectively as a de-icer,
conditions permitting, plan to turn it on **WING ANT-ICE AFTER** first power reduction.

If the take-off is to be made with **ENGINE BLEEDS OFF**, do not turn on wing anti-ice until **AFTER** the engine bleeds have been turned **ON**.

WARNING
Prolonged operation in icing conditions greater than light would be appropriate
ONLY IN AN EMERGENCY !

published by UNIVERSITY of TEMECULA PRESS, Inc.

DANGER !

PREMATURE TAXI. Right here is one of the most dangerous places in the flight evolution. It is a place where the pilot must NOT get pushed or do things in a rush. The ground crew, the jet, and the pilot's career are in great jeopardy

... *DO NOT SCREW THIS UP!*

Every year there are literally hundreds of crews around the world that start their taxi **BEFORE** they are ready. The flight crews get preoccupied with getting their jet "out on time" or are desperately trying to get in the line-up for takeoff before Brand X, or ....
THIS IS A MOMENT OF CRITICAL PRESSURE.

There are **2 PROBLEMS**

 Premature **TAXI** with push-back crew still "hooked up."

 Start **TAXI** with the **NW STRG DISC** message displayed on the ECAM.

WARNING

The Captain *MUST NOT* request a taxi clearance *UNTIL*:

- **NW STRG DISC** message no longer on **ECAM**, and

- Guide man gives BOTH
  SALUTE SIGNAL, and
  RELEASE FROM GUIDANCE SIGNAL.

If the Captain **CANNOT PHYSICALLY** see the guideperson ... it is permissible for the First Officer, with the concurrence of the Captain, to view the salute and advise the Captain.
HOWEVER ... **ONLY** the Captain can acknowledge the salute by
FLASHING THE NOSEWHEEL TAXI LIGHT ON AND OFF
to signal "*Ready for release from the guideperson to taxi*".

published by UNIVERSITY of TEMECULA PRESS, Inc.

One major airline is so concerned, they have developed a seven step procedure that *MUST BE COMPLETED BEFORE* the Captain is to release the parking brake.

Here is one solution proposed by a major airline:
THE 7 STEP GATE DEPARTURE PROCEDURE

STEP 1: [C] *"I have a salute..."* The Captain verifies, announces, and **PHYSICALLY** returns the guideman salute. This indicates that all personnel are clear of the aircraft.

STEP 2: [C] *" And a release from guidance"* ... The Captain verifies and announces he has the signal to taxi. This signal means that in the guideman's opinion, the airplane may commence taxi without further guidance from him. *IT DOES NOT MEAN* that the airplane is cleared to taxi. The Captain responds to the ground personnel by "flashing" the **TAXI LIGHT**.

STEP 3: [C] ANTISKID and NOSEWHEEL Steering switch .... ON
If you try to taxi with this switch OFF, you will have
NO NOSEWHEEL STEERING and NO ALTERNATE BRAKES.

NOTE:
YOU MUST "RELEASE" ALL STEERING AND BRAKE PEDAL INPUTS BEFORE TURNING ON THIS SWITCH.

STEP 4: [C,F/O] Audio Control Panels .... Each pilot sets their own panel.

STOP ...WARNING!
DO NOT *set up the Audio Control Panels until the Captain announces the she/he has a"Salute and a release from guidance." This has proven to be a place where* **PILOTS SCREW UP**.

STEP 5: [C] *Politely request "Taxi Clearance, Please."*
(I put that "polite" thing in there myself.)

STEP 6: [F/O] Obtain the taxi clearance.
The First Officer **WILL NOT** call for the taxi clearance until **BOTH** pilots are ready to copy and confirm the information. **DO NOT** request taxi clearance in anticipation of taxi **PRIOR TO** the request from the Captain. Experience has shown that this is one of the places where confusion results in a potential unsafe operation.

STEP 7: [C] Captain may now release the parking brake.
Turn the handle off and observe the brake pressure gauges move to "**ZERO**".

TAXI STUFF

THE CAPTAIN *ALWAYS* STEERS THE AIRPLANE.

However, the First Officer may steer the airplane if a **SAFETY** consideration arises; **BUT**

- **ONLY** using rudder pedals, and
- **ONLY** on a straight segment of the taxiway.

If, however, there is an **EMERGENCY**, of course, the First Officer has the capability to steer the airplane from her/his side of the cockpit ... and in that case may use the tiller bar.

What is the problem here and why do these restrictions exist? Here is

NOSEWHEEL STEERING TILLER
technical information.

These are some of the boring technical details. The **NOSEWHEEL STEERING TILLER** is **ELECTRICALLY** controlled by a computer (**BSCU**) and **HYDRAULICALLY** operated by the **GREEN** hydraulic system. When we are ready to taxi, and only when all the criteria for operation are satisfied, then the nosewheel steering is operable.

You can steer the airplane using either:
- **STEERING TILLERS**
- **RUDDER PEDALS** ...and, of course,
- **AUTOPILOT** (effective only on Autoland rollout).

THE BIG STEERING PROBLEM

The big problem is that the pilot input (rudders or tiller bars) from both sides is "**ALGEBRAICALLY SUMMED**." This means that if "both" pilots are trying to steer with either the rudders or the tiller bars at the same time ... the resulting effect is a virtually **UNCONTROLLABLE** situation ... and the resulting oversteer can result in a runway excursion.

The steering sensitivity changes with the speed of the airplane, that is,

THE FASTER THE JET GOES,
THE LESS SENSITIVE IS THE STEERING.

The **TILLER** steering is +/- 75° up to 20 kts and decreases to 0° at 70 kts.
The **RUDDER** steering is +/- 6° up to 40 kts and decreases to 0° at 130 kts.

The **NOSE WHEEL STEERING SYSTEM**: Pilots call it ...

The "TILLER".

There are two "**TILLER CONTROL WHEELS or BARS**" in the cockpit, on each outboard side. This does **NOT** mean that the Frst Officer is expected to steer the airplane. So here is the *FIRST RULE OF AIRBUS STEERING*:

> **ALWAYS, ONLY** the **CAPTAIN is**
> expected use the **TILLER!!!**

There is **NO ROUTINE SOP** where the First Officer is required to use the tiller bar. However (and this is a corollary to the first rule) In an **EMERGENCY** or if the Captain becomes incapacitated or unable to steer the airplane, then the First Officer is expected to exercise judgement before taking over the tiller. *DUH!*

Here is a HUGE PILOT SCREW UP!

Likewise, The First Officer (co-pilot) should NOT be using the rudders to control the airplane trajectory before the Captain announces that the First Officer has control during the initial take-off.

The reason: If **BOTH PILOTS** attempt to control the airplane heading at the same time, the input will be **ALGEBRAICALLY ADDED** and that can result in an uncontrollable situation quickly developing.

The **SECOND RULE** of **AIRBUS** steering is like the first rule.

> **ONLY ONE PILOT** is allowed on the
> steering tiller or rudders at any time.

Clearly, during routine operations it is important that the crew to ensure that they **KNOW** who is controlling the airplane before they attempt to steer the airplane.

PEDAL DISCONNECT

> In the center of the "**TILLER WHEEL**" is a "**PEDAL DISC**" button. If that button is held in the depressed position, the **RUDDER PEDALS** are disconnected from the **NOSEWHEEL STEERING**. The Captain can still steer the airplane using the wheel.

The only time that this feature is used is during the **PRE-FLIGHT FLIGHT CONTROL** check. The way it is designed to operate is that the First Officer announces that he is about to conduct the flight control check and the Captain responds and depresses and hold down the **PEDAL DISC** button. That is the way it works in Fantasyland.

If the flight control check is initiated during taxi **WITHOUT PEDAL DISC** depressed ... there is the possibility that there will result a potential loss of control of the airplane. I'm just saying ....

MAXIMUM TAXI THRUST

Maximum *recommended* breakaway thrust is:

40% N1
Do NOT exceed 40% N1 within congested areas unless cleared by appropriate personnel.

Airplane response to engine thrust may be slow, particularly with a heavy airplane. So the technique is to add the thrust and wait for it to take effect before adding additional thrust.

NOTE: The ability of the airplane to start moving may be impeded by having the tiller cranked hard over so that the nose-gear acts like a brake.

DO NOT ride the brakes to control taxi speed. The technique is to reduce excess speed with a steady application of brake and then release brake.
Repeat as necessary.

BLIND SPOTS

Like any airplane, there are areas where the pilots cannot see. Since **the Captain does the taxiing**, he has to look across cockpit, particularly when making right turns ... this is a **SIGNIFICANT** problem and virtually **REQUIRES** that the First Officer be involved in "clearing" the area. If obstacle clearance is in doubt in the **RAMP AREA, wing walkers are advised**.

ENGINE POD CLEARANCE

The airplane Engine pod is only 21 inches above the surface and is 20 feet from the centerline. **BE EXTREMELY CAREFUL** if there are obstructions, such as snow piles from the snowplows, along the edge of the taxiway.

AIRCRAFT CLEARANCE IN TURN

The **ARC of the TAIL** is several feet greater than the arc of the airplane **NOSE**.
The **ARC of the OUTSIDE WINGTIP** is greater than that of the **TAIL**.

PROHIBITED FROM MAKING 180° TURN ON STANDARD 75 FOOT TAXIWAY.

The geometry of the airplane dictates that the nose wheel should be outside of the centerline when making a turn to keep the main gear centered. Add that the pilots sit about 10 feet in front of the nosewheels. The minimum pavement required to make a 180° turn is 80 feet, so the airplane is PROHIBITED from making a 180° turn on a standard 75-foot taxiway

GROUNDSPEED IN TURNS

Use the **GROUNDSPEED** readout on the **ND** (Navigation Display) to monitor taxi speed. Here are the **MAXIMUM** recommended speeds:

```
- STRAIGHT AHEAD .................. 25 Kts
- TURNS up to 45° ...................... 25 Kts
- TURNS greater than 45° .......... 10 Kts
```

published by UNIVERSITY of TEMECULA PRESS, Inc.

WARNING !!!

DO NOT move the flaps or flight controls until airplane is **MOVING** under its own power and is **CLEAR** of ground personnel and equipment.

OVERSTEER TENDENCY

The nosewheel steering system is electrically controlled and incorporates a non-linear relationship between tiller bar deflection and nose wheel deflection. What is meant by this is that the tiller becomes increasingly sensitive when exceeding $60°$ of deflection. This can contribute to a tendency to overcontrol the turn.

HOW PILOTS CAN SCREW THIS UP!

DURING TAXI IN ICING.

The result of this oversteer tendency can be disastrous on an icy taxiway. If the nose gear starts to slip and the Captain responds by increasing the steering input in order to try and regain control. NOT GOOD! BAD IDEA!

DIFFERENTIAL BRAKING MAY BE MORE EFFECTIVE THAN NOSE WHEEL STEERING ON VERY SLIPPERY SURFACES.

NOSEWHEEL SLIPPAGE DURING TURNS

Since the nose gear strut is angled forward, as you turn the Nosewheel Steering tiller and the angle of deflection increases, the outside tire is lifted off the ground, resulting in only one tire being more in contact with the pavement than the other. This reduces the amount of tire footprint and contributes to nosewheel slippage.

Now there is an understatement. Particularly in icing or slippery taxiway conditions, you will need all the "rubber on the road" that you can get. Cranking the Nosewheel Steering Tiller around reduces the rubber footprint by an amount proportional to the angle of the Nosewheel Steering Tiller. The tighter the turn, the less rubber on the asphalt.

Differential thrust can assist in maintaining airplane momentum through a turn.

TAXI OUT
FLOW

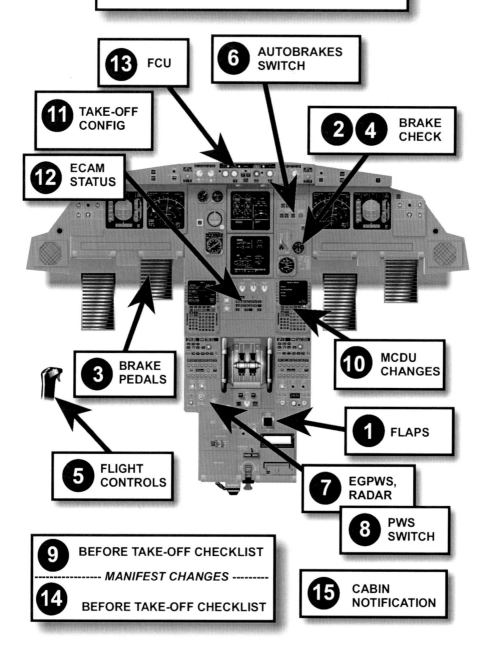

13 FCU

6 AUTOBRAKES SWITCH

11 TAKE-OFF CONFIG

2 **4** BRAKE CHECK

12 ECAM STATUS

3 BRAKE PEDALS

10 MCDU CHANGES

1 FLAPS

5 FLIGHT CONTROLS

7 EGPWS, RADAR

8 PWS SWITCH

9 BEFORE TAKE-OFF CHECKLIST

----------------- *MANIFEST CHANGES* ---------

14 BEFORE TAKE-OFF CHECKLIST

15 CABIN NOTIFICATION

published by UNIVERSITY of TEMECULA PRESS, Inc.

(F/O) FLAPS .... SET
Move **FLAP** selector to the **TAKE-OFF** setting;
VERIFY Flap handle position is the same as the **FLAP INDICATOR**
on the upper **ECAM**.

NOTE:

*The following discussion is intended as an example **ONLY** for one specific airline's approach. I do not know exactly how **EVERY** other airline selects the take-off runways; but since Airbus has actually certificated the airplane to operate using "**Optimized V-Speeds**" I can only guess that other operators use similar techniques to comply with their airplane certification.*

FLAP SELECTION DISCUSSION:

Airbus certified their airplanes using something called **OPTIMIZED V-SPEEDS**. This is different from old-school techniques such as "balanced field" that have been used for years by other airplane companies. It greatly simplifies flap selection and works sorta like this. The Airline engineering staff (SFOEG for the UAL guys) takes each runway and makes a database that preselects the appropriate take-off flap settings predicated on weight and "optimum V1" so as to take advantage of the full runway length. As a general statement, here are the broad guidelines used for applying flap choices (doesn't necessarily cover all situations):

FLAPS 1 - Use for long runways where **BRAKE ENERGY** could be a factor. For example a **HIGH ALTITUDE** airport like Denver, Colorado. Flap 1 V1 speeds are lower than Flap 2 V1 speeds for a given weight. The upside is that these lower V1speeds provide a better brake energy limit; the downside is that the lower V2 results in a reduced performance limit weight because of the reduced climb gradient.

FLAPS 2 - Where long runway is available and **BRAKE ENERGY** and stopping the airplane on the runway is **NOT** the major concern. Flaps 2 "generally" provides the **BEST PERFORMANCE LIMIT WEIGHT** due to the increased climb gradient.

FLAPS 3 - A Short runway where you might want the least take-off roll. Flaps 3 provides the best runway limit weight for shorter runways.

IMPROVED FLAPS V-SPEEDS - (Generally speaking) Provides the greatest take-off weight capability. However, these procedures are designed to be used **ONLY** if the actual take-off weight is greater than the maximum allowable gross weight for the runway in question using normal flaps and V-speeds. Typically used on
       - Short runways where runway limit weight needs to be maximized,
or
       - Long runways at high altitude runways
         where performance limit needs to be maximized.

So ... all that is interesting, but WHERE do I get a take-off flap setting?

Since the flap settings are already derived and the **FMGC** has all the necessary information resident in its database to accomplish a calculation, the information can be derived by using the **MCDU** to yield the solution.

TECHNIQUE 1: Use the **ACARS** function. This is the easiest way.

STEP 1. Pull up the **RWY DATA** page.
STEP 2: The **ONLY** required entry is the runway. Enter the runway number.
> *This is a little tricky and here is the protocol for that*:
> Enter the runway number. For example; 33
> or for single digit runways only enter the single digit,
> such as 9. *Do NOT enter the zero in front of the 9*.
> If there is a following modifier, enter it; such as 35L.
> You can enter two digit if appropriate; such as 16L.

STEP 3: Since you have only entered the runway and nothing else,
the **FMGC** will use this logic to determine appropriate Flap configuration.
- If reduced thrust **NOT** available,
   it will select the lowest flap setting possible.
- If reduced thrust IS available,
   it will select the flap setting with the highest assumed temperature.
- If assumed temperatures are the same.
   it will select for the lowest flap setting.

TECHNIQUE 2: Use the **EPR/ATOG** message

STEP 1. Compare the "**ASSUMED TEMPERATURES**" with the choices for available flap settings. If the assumed temperatures are different, select for the flap setting that has the **HIGHEST** assumed temperature.

WHY THIS WORKS:
The **ASSUMED TEMPERATURE** represents the measure of the take-off "pad" or "buffer" available. So, the higher the assumed temperature, the greater that "safety margin."

---

published by UNIVERSITY of TEMECULA PRESS, Inc.

THIS IS A BIG, BIG DEAL!!!
UNDERSTAND THIS !

THE BRAKE CHECK
(or more appropriately, the BSCU check)

DISCUSSION:

The **BIG** problem with this system is not some hydraulic line blowing up or leaking or coming undone ... but rather the dreaded failure of the **BSCU (BRAKE and STEERING CONTROL UNIT)** computer.

---

2 (C) BRAKES .... CHECK
The **BRAKE CHECK** must be performed after the airplane is moving.

HOW TO DO THE BRAKE CHECK:

3 STEP 1: [C] Press the **BRAKE PEDALS**
(top of the rudder pedals) smoothly.

4 STEP 2: [C] YELLOW system parking
brake pressure .... Verify "**ZERO**"

DISCUSSION:

This system is very difficult for a mere human pilot to understand. Let's talk about the situation.

The way the hydraulics are plumbed on the Airbus;
- The **GREEN** system powers the "**NORMAL BRAKES**", and
- The **YELLOW** system supplies pressure to the **PARKING BRAKE** and the **ALT BRAKES**.

Here is where the pilots get confused. That little gauge on the instrument panel is for the "**PARKING BRAKE**" and represents the **YELLOW** system pressure being supplied to the **PARKING** and **ALT** brake system **ONLY**.
If we depress the "**TOE**" brakes on the rudder pedals, **GREEN** system pressure is supplied to the brakes. Since there is no gauge on the instrument panel to monitor that pressure, the brake pressure gauge should indicate "**ZERO**" pressure to the parking/alt brakes from the **YELLOW** system. In a kinda negative proof way, it indicates a "normal" brake situation.

BOTTOM LINE:
If you depress the "toe" brakes and the airplane stops, the system is operating normally **ONLY IF** there is "**ZERO**" pressure indication on the (parking) **BRAKE PRESS** gauge."

DISCUSSION:

As soon as we can after getting the salute and release from guidance, we want to determine if the **BSCU** *is working properly.* **DO NOT** *get jammin' down the taxiway and then do the* **BRAKE/STEERING CHECK**. *Do it while you are still creeping along at some snail pace.*

BIG PROBLEM!!!

IF EITHER OR BOTH
THE BRAKE and/or NOSEWHEEL STEERING FAIL

DO NOT TURN THE
A/SKID & N/W STRG switch OFF
until
RELEASING TOE BRAKE PRESSURE

DISCUSSION:
If you were to turn off the A/SKID & N/W STRG switch OFF with the TOE brakes even a teensy-tiny bit depressed.
WHAM!!!

The brakes apply **MAX** *braking immediately and the airplane feels like it has hit a brick wall. Even at very small forward speeds the effect is truly memorable. The flight attendants particularly will forever reserve a place for you in their memories.*

(C) BRAKES .... immediately RELEASE
Remove **ALL** (Did I say **ALL**!!!) pressure from the toe brakes.

(F/O) A/SKID & N/W STRG switch ....OFF
Right here is where the problem can occur. The First Officer **MUST** coordinate with the Captain to ensure **ALL** pressure is removed from the **TOE** brakes. The problem is that the Captain is trying to regain braking by pushing harder on the toe brakes ... it is counterintuitive for him to release the pressure momentarily so the "switch" can be turned **OFF**. Then..

(C) USE TOE BRAKES TO ACTIVATE ALTERNATE BRAKING and STEERING.
Do not continue taxiing. Use differential braking pressure to steer the airplane and bring the airplane to a stop. *DO NOT EXCEED 1000 PSI on the BRAKES and ACCU PRESS gauge.*
If for some reason, the alternate system doesn't activate and the toe brakes still don't work, you can use successive short parking brake applications to slow and stop the airplane. Once you are stopped ...

(C) SET PARKING BRAKE.
Get outside assistance via radio to either repair (reset **BSCU**) or tow to maintenance area.

---

published by UNIVERSITY of TEMECULA PRESS, Inc.

When there is an appropriate lull in the activities, the Captain will call for ...

⑤ THE FLIGHT CONTROL CHECK [CAPT,F/O]

The **ECAM F/CTL** page will be automatically displayed whenever flight control inputs are detected. It will remain displayed for 20 seconds after the last input.
NOTE: The control check MUST be performed in the required order.
Both pilots will be involved in the check, with the First Officer "**HEAD DOWN**." The Captain **MUST** maintain situational awareness during the check and not run into anything.

HOW TO DO THE FLIGHT CONTROL CHECK:

STEP 1: Captain announces and moves sidestick "**UP (BACK) and DOWN (FORWARD) and NEUTRAL**".
First Officer verifies full and proper movement of control surfaces on the **ECAM F/CTL** page, and responds "**CHECK**."

STEP 2: Captain announces and moves sidestick "**LEFT and RIGHT and NEUTRAL**".
First Officer verifies full and proper movement of control surfaces on the **ECAM F/CTL** page, and responds "**CHECK**". All the spoiler panels should be retracted.

NOTE: Ailerons will "**DROOP**" if the flaps are extended.

STEP 3: Captain will press the **PEDALS DISC** center selector switch on the Steering Tiller; and apply **FULL LEFT** and **FULL RIGHT** and **NEUTRAL** rudder while maintaining forward direction with the Steering Tiller.
The First Officer will follow through on the rudder pedals and verify full and proper movement of the control surface on the **ECAM F/CTL** page, and responds "**CHECK**."

STEP 4: First Officer then verifies "**LEFT, RIGHT, NEUTRAL**" using the right side sidestick.

WARNING:
YOU MUST ensure that the GROUND SPOILERS are RETRACTED before ARMING THE AUTOBRAKES.

⑥ [F/O] AUTOBRAKES SWITCH .... MAXIMUM
The only time we select **MAX** is for take-off. It is used for take-off **ONLY**!

WHAT PILOTS SCREW UP!

If the ground spoilers are extended even a teensy bit; when you arm the auto-brakes ...
THE AUTOBRAKES WILL ACTIVATE IMMEDIATELY TO MAX!
WHOOOOPS !!!! ...another chance to "HIT A BRICK WALL!"

---

7 [F/O] EGPWS and RADAR displays ..... SELECT (as required)

    If the use of the weather radar is required; then either or both pilots may select the **TERR** or **TERR ON ND** switch **OFF**. If weather radar is not to be used; then both pilots should select **TERR** or **TERR ON ND**.

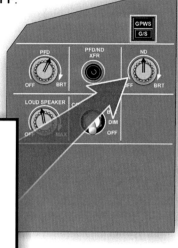

NOTE:
Even if both pilots are in the weather radar display mode, the terrain display pop-up feature is still available.

The **ND** selector has an **OUTER SELECTOR** that controls the brightness of the weather **RADAR** and the **EGPWS** image only.

NOTE:
The outer selector of the ND brightness selector MUST BE ON and BRIGHT to ensure the EGPWS pop-up feature is visible in the event of a windshear.

---

8 [F/O] PWS SWITCH .... AUTO

9 [C,F/O] BEFORE TAKE-OFF CHECKLIST ....COMPLETE
(Down to manifest changes)

BEFORE TAKE-OFF CHECKLIST

CHALLENGE [F/O]	RESPONSE
Control check	Complete [C,F/O]
Engine anti-ice	On/off [C]
Autobrakes	Max [C]
Flaps	___Planned____indicated, detent [C]
Engine Mode Selector	Normal/ignition start [C]

----------------- *MANIFEST CHANGES* -----------------

published by UNIVERSITY of TEMECULA PRESS, Inc.

DANGER ZONE

Right here is where the flight crew gets really over powered with the crush of "getting it all done". Particularly during a short taxi, the First Officer can easily get into task saturation. Each separate item **MUST** be completed properly before proceeding to the next ... **HOWEVER**, that seems impossible since the crew does **NOT** set the pacing of the task stream. **ATC** is giving information that demands attention, the Load Planner is passing streams of data that must be checked and entered appropriately, the Flight Attendant is needing your attention and has important information, an **ECAM** warning appears, and on and on.

This is
FIRST OFFICER
BUSY TIME !

The Captain is the moderator and controlling agent. The First Officer will be **"HEAD DOWN"** and up to their elbows in alligators. *The Captain MUST maintain*

SITUATIONAL AWARENESS

If necessary, coordinate with **ATC** (Ground Control), taxi clear of the taxiway, set the parking brake and resolve any issues.

Here is the **OFFICIAL** model for
WORKLOAD MANAGEMENT:

- PLAN
- PRIORITIZE
- SEQUENCE
- ASSIGN

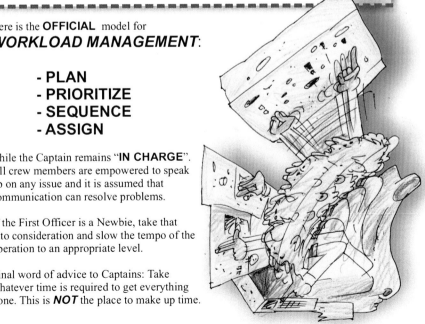

while the Captain remains **"IN CHARGE"**. All crew members are empowered to speak up on any issue and it is assumed that communication can resolve problems.

If the First Officer is a Newbie, take that into consideration and slow the tempo of the operation to an appropriate level.

Final word of advice to Captains: Take whatever time is required to get everything done. This is **NOT** the place to make up time.

10 [F/O] RUNWAY and/or ROUTE CHANGES
(if appropriate) ....ENTER

Runway and or route changes are made on the **MCDU F-PLAN page**. It can be kinda tricky.

Go to the F-PLAN page and re-enter the departure runway using a **LATERAL REVISION** off the first fix. In our case: **LFPG27L**.

Route changes can be entered directly on the **F-PLAN** page, use the **CLR** feature to delete "old" routing. This is fairly intuitive and doesn't need much explanation. If you screw things up, you can always use the **SEC F-PLAN** that we had copied just for this situation.

WHAT PILOTS SCREW UP:
They try to change runways on the **PERF** page. While this seems like a simple solution, it will **NOT** work. You have to make the runway/route changes on the **F-PLAN** page.
DO NOT MAKE RUNWAY CHANGE ON PERF PAGE.

LISTEN UP: another *POTENTIAL SCREW UP*
There is a very special feature of the Airbus MCDU that operates on the **F-PLAN** page. It is called **AUTO STRINGING**. This is intended as a speed tool, but until you understand it, you will be baffled when you first see it work.

Hey, Where'd all my fixes go?
Here is a description of this feature.
When a waypoint is inserted into a flight plan, such as during a lateral revision, and the same waypoint occurs in a SID, STAR, or transition routing ... the FMGC automatically removes the intervening waypoints and connects the two common waypoints.

If a waypoint on the selected STAR is an IAF for the selected approach, the FMGC will autostring the two together, thereby deleting the STAR waypoints that are beyond the IAF (Initial Approach Fix).

AUTOSTRINGING MAY NOT REFLECT YOUR ACTUAL ATC CLEARANCE, YOU MUST VERIFY ROUTING AFTER A CHANGE.

published by UNIVERSITY of TEMECULA PRESS, Inc.

DO NOT TAKE OFF WITHOUT THE FINAL WEIGHTS.

The final weight manifest **_MUST BE_** received and the changes made (if appropriate) prior to crossing the runway threshold. Generally, these changes are received while the airplane is taxiing to the runway. The information can be passed to the airplane using either voice radio or cockpit printer.

CONFIRM THAT THE CHANGES YOU HAVE ARE THE CORRECT CHANGES FOR YOUR FLIGHT !

[F/O] FINAL WEIGHTS .... ENTER

> **NOTE:** *Once the second engine is already started, it will not be possible to access the* **INIT B** *page, Use the* **FUEL PRED** *page for weight changes.*

1. If the final weights were not entered prior to engine start,
   enter the airplane's actual gross weight on the FUEL PRED page
   by adding the final ZFW to the actual fuel on board.

2. **_ALWAYS_** enter the final CG.

3. If the CG is forward of 25%,
   use the forward CG flowcharts in the Take-off Performance chapter.

4. Verbally advise the Captain of any weight changes and
   if there are any V-speed changes and final CG.

5. Reset the stabilizer trim, if necessary, and confirm rudder trim is zero.

[F/O] TAKEOFF PERFORMANCE .... CONFIRM

After you get the final weights;
- **VERIFY** that the takeoff performance is acceptable, and
- **MODIFY** V-speeds for the actual gross weight, if required.

IMPORTANT NOTE:

If the actual weight of the airplane is too heavy for the current **FLEX** **TEMPERATURE**, *use the* **ACARS** *to obtain "new" flex thrust takeoff data.*

[C,F/O] FLIGHT PLAN PAGE on MCDU .... SELECT

While there is no "hard and fast" rule about this, it is recommended that both pilots select the F-PLAN page for take-off.

11 [F/O] TAKE-OFF CONFIGURATION PAGE .... SELECT (on ECAM)

Verify at least two entries:
- **NORMAL** is displayed.
- **FLAP SETTING** is correct.

12 [F/O] ECAM STATUS .... CHECK

If **STS** (Status Page on ECAM) is NOT DISPLAYED .... disregard this step.

13 **[F/O] FCU** .... **CHECK**
Ensure that the **FCU** is setup as follows:

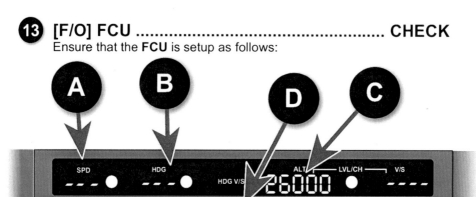

A. SPEED WINDOW .... DISPLAY "WHITE DOT" and dashes
With the "dashes and dot" displayed, the "hidden" value selected will be the speed displayed on the **PERF/CLIMB** page in the **MCDU**. If an undesired airspeed is displayed, "**PUSH**" the selector knob to display the "dashes and dot"..

B. HEADING/NAV .... Verify
OPTION 1: If you are going to use **NAV** for your departure heading, then all you have to do is leave the "white dot and dashes" in the window.
At 30 feet, the **NAV** will engage and the airplane will start an aggressive turn towards the next waypoint.

OPTION 2: Pull the **HDG SEL** knob in order to fly runway heading. Ensure that the airplane's heading indicator is on the runway heading, then, at **30 feet RWY TRK** will engage.

OPTION 3: You may preset a desired after take-off heading.

TECHNIQUE
Setting runway heading in the display is desirable for a couple of reasons.
1. In the event of an engine failure, we would want runway heading since that will represent protected (clear of obstacles) airspace up to 1,500 feet.
2. Turns at extremely low altitudes are undesirable.

C. ALTITUDE .... Verify
Set in the NEXT cleared altitude.

D. HEADING-VS/TRK-FPA .... Verify
Select HDG TRK or V/S FPA

published by UNIVERSITY of TEMECULA PRESS, Inc.

(14) [C,F/O]
BEFORE TAKE-OFF CHECKLIST........
COMPLETE DOWN TO FINAL ITEMS.

----------------- *MANIFEST CHANGES* -----------------

Trim	____%, Zero, set [F]
Weight, speeds	Checked [F], set [C,F]
FMGCs, Radios	Programmed, set for departure [C,F]
EGPWS, Radar displays	Terrain/weather [C,F]
PWS	Auto [F]
Thrust	____Flex/TOGA EPR, set [C]
FCU ... Managed heading, heading ___/nav, altitude____, set [C]	
Takeoff configuration	Normal [F]
ECAM status check	Complete [F]

----------------- *FINAL ITEMS* -----------------

ABOUT 2 MINUTES BEFORE DEPARTURE

(15) [F/O] CABIN NOTIFICATION .... ACCOMPLISH

The announcement should be a "stand alone" message. By that I mean, the only thing you want to say in this message is:
"FLIGHT ATTENDANTS PREPARE FOR TAKEOFF"
or some such statement.
Do not include other material in this announcement.

When APPROACHING TAKE-OFF RUNWAY or "Cleared to HOLD SHORT"

[F/O] TRANSPONDER .... TRAFFIC

[F/O] TAKE-OFF MEMO.. CHECK

Verify all the lines in the TAKE-OFF memo are GREEN

[C,F/O] BEFORE TAKE-OFF CHECKLIST.............................. COMPLETE

----------------- *FINAL ITEMS* -----------------

Cabin notification	Complete [F]
Transponder	Traffic [F]
Takeoff memo	Green [F]

This is the moment of truth:

At this point in the flight evolution, we have to ask ourselves this question:

> ## IS THERE ANY REASON
> ## WHY I SHOULD NOT TAKE OFF?

If there is **ANY** ambiguity that might affect the successful resolution of the take-off or the flight, we **MUST** confess, get a clearance to taxi clear, park the airplane, and resolve that ambiguity. *This is what the Check Pilot is going to want to see. She/he will want to see you evaluate the situation and resolve the potential problem.*

DISCUSSION:

This is a sad but true fact, there are so many restrictions to flight in commercial aviation that are hidden in a huge pile of manuals and handbooks, that it is virtually impossible for a mere human pilot to have every one of the impediments committed to memory and available for instantaneous recall ... much less even know where to look. Plus they are constantly being changed and altered into a continuously evolving mountain of obscure and eclectic knowledge. Don't expect the ultimate solution here, but let's list just a few of the items that you will be responsible for.

NOTE: *If your airline has different ones, cross these out, write your restriction in the box, continually add to your own personal list. Make it a hobby.*

◼ WIND

Takeoff/landing CROSSWIND guidelines

"REPORTED" Braking action	TAKEOFF	LANDING
GOOD	*See CROSSWIND LIMITS in next table*	
FAIR/MEDIUM	**25**	**25**
POOR	**15**	**15**
NIL/UNRELIABLE	OPERATIONS *NOT RECOMMENDED*	

NOTE: *The ICAO term for FAIR is MEDIUM, NIL is UNRELIABLE*

MAXIMUM "demonstrated" CROSSWINDS
... with FLIGHT CONTROLS in NORMAL or DIRECT LAW (with or without yaw damper).

	A320		A319	
WIND DIRECTION	TAKEOFF	LANDING	TAKEOFF	LANDING
CROSSWIND	**29 Knots**	**33 Knots**	**29 Knots**	**33 Knots**
CROSSWIND with GUSTS	**38 Knots**			
TAILWIND	**15 Knots**	**10 Knots**	**10 Knots**	

published by UNIVERSITY of TEMECULA PRESS, Inc.

Just when you thought you were all ready to take-off ...

> *"... if the weather conditions at the airport of take-off are below the landing minima in the certificate holder' operations specifications for that airport (to include increased landing minima in the case of newly qualified Captains with high minimums), no person may dispatch or release an airplane from that airport unless the dispatch or flight release specifies an alternate airport located within the following distances from the airport of take-off..."*
> **CFR part 121.617**

Here is what that said.

*IF you cannot return and land at the same airport
because the weather is below landing minimums
then you must designate a TAKE-OFF ALTERNATE.*

TAKE-OFF ALTERNATE REQUIRED
When:

WEATHER AT
DEPARTURE AIRPORT is
BELOW LANDING MINIMUMS

for
A319 / A320
TAKE-OFF ALTERNATE must be within

370 NM

*1 HR NORMAL CRUISE
with
1 ENG INOP*

 NEW or HIGH MINIMUM CAPTAINS must use their minimums in this determination.

 If you decide to designate a **TAKE-OFF** alternate **AFTER** filing your release;
- *you MUST have the concurrence of the DISPATCHER and*
- *WRITE THAT ALTERNATE ON YOUR ORIGINAL COPY OF THE FLIGHT RELEASE DOCUMENT.*

 If after dispatch, an **ALTERNATE** or a different or additional alternate is added to the flight release, that alternate *MUST BE WRITTEN ON YOUR ORIGINAL FLIGHT RELEASE DOCUMENT*.

■ *MICROBURST:*
The #1 reason NOT TO T/O is a MICROBURST ALERT from ATC.

■

DO NOT TAKE-OFF if:
STANDING WATER ... over 1/2 inch
SLUSH .... over 1/2 inch
WET SNOW .... over 1 inch
DRY SNOW .... over 4 inches

■
Here is the **OFFICIAL** definition of *CLUTTER* (a form of runway contamination):

STANDING WATER of 1/8 inch
SLUSH of 1/8 inch or greater
WET SNOW of 1/4 inch or greater
DRY SNOW of 1 inch or greater

Further, less than the amounts listed in the definition above are not considered clutter and no weight or V speed restrictions are required.

NOTE: *If "clutter" exists, it may require adjustment to the V speeds. Check your Flight Operations Manual for guidelines.*

■ ICING and FREEZING PRECIPITATION:

	LIGHT	MODERATE	HEAVY
FREEZING RAIN	OK	NO-OP	NO-OP
FREEZING DRIZZLE	OK	OK	NO-OP
SNOW	OK	OK	OK

NOTE: *I have heard that "ICE PELLETS" have been added to this list (... but I can't confirm that).*

■ *IF BRAKING ACTION NIL:*
Take off NOT RECOMMENDED.

■ *AIRCRAFT SYSTEMS NOT READY:*
Either checklist NOT completed, or
Warning light or horn,
Flight Attendants NOT ready,
Ambiguity in clearance or routing,
Other NO BRAINERS!

■ *WEIGHT of AIRPLANE TOO GREAT*
for the existing runway conditions.

published by UNIVERSITY of TEMECULA PRESS, Inc.

■ CHARTS, NOTAMS, PIREPS, and so forth.

There is information on the charts for almost every contingency. Engine failure after take-off, the climb corridor, noise abatement, and so forth. **BRIEF EVERY APPLICABLE PART**. The Check Captain will be looking for that.

Also, be aware that there are **TAKE-OFF MINIMUMS**. In general, and this is just a statement from me, you will have to look at the individual chart ... Take-off minimums look something like this: 600-600-600; Where they are describing the three parts of the takeoff runway using "landing" nomenclature. By that I mean **TDZ** (touchdown zone), **MID** (midfield), **ROLLOUT** (far end). For example; if there is a fog bank blowing onto the runway, and the rollout end becomes less than 600 RVR; it would be controlling and you could not take-off.

Be Alert.

■ ETC., ETC., ETC.

I can't think of every imaginable thing that we would have to consider before taking off ... and each airline and airplane model has their own set of rules; besides they are constantly changing. So, I am leaving part of this page blank for you to write some of the restrictions to take-off that you can come up with.

Here are two suggested briefing guides that are used at a major aircarrier for their pilots to use during the check-ride. It leads you to believe that these are the only items essential to pass the checkride. I personally used these only as a prompting mechanism as there are missing items as well as superfluous items on the list.

BUT

that being said, it is a good place to start, and I suggest you make up a similar list to jog your memory.

TAKE-OFF DATA BRIEFING

☐ NOSE NUMBER matches LOGBOOK and MAINTENANCE RELEASE.

☐ RELEASE NUMBER is correct for paperwork.

☐ ZFW/TOGW matches MCDU

☐ TRIM SETTING.

☐ BLEED CONFIGURATION.

☐ FLAP SETTING.

☐ EPR/N1.

☐ RUNWAY LIMIT/PERFORMANCE LIMIT.

☐ WIND CORRECTION.

☐ T or EOSID PROCEDURES.

PRE-DEPARTURE BRIEFING

☐ CREW DUTIES.

☐ FLIGHT PLAN CHANGES.

☐ NOTAMS/BULLETINS.

☐ WINDSHEAR.

☐ RUNWAY CONDITIONS.

☐ REJECTED TAKE-OFF PLAN.

☐ ENGINE FAILURE PROFILE.

☐ CLEARANCE.

☐ SID.

☐ EOSID or T-PROCEDURE.

☐ TAKEOFF PROFILE.

☐ TERRAIN / OBSTACLES.

☐ TRANSITION ALTITUDE.

☐ TRAFFIC WATCH.

☐ OBSERVER BRIEF.

published by UNIVERSITY of TEMECULA PRESS, Inc.

EOSID, "T" procedure, E-route,
and other Single Engine Escape Techniques

Unless otherwise noted, every runway that you will fly out of will have the following criteria:

> *"Terrain clearance will be ensured if you fly the extended runway centerline up to 1,500 feet AFE."*

Some airlines and airports have made provision for special routing after take-off in the event of an engine failure. They are concerned that airplane performance may be seriously jeopardized by loss of an engine to the point where the "normal" departure becomes questionable where terrain and obstacle clearance is concerned ... so in accordance with directives from the controlling agencies (FAA, EASA, or ...) they sent their engineering personnel to every airport where they thought there might be a problem and devised an alternate escape procedure, contingency plan, special departure procedure, "T" procedure, etc. for every airport/runway they expected to use. The officially used title for these procedures is ...

EOSID
Engine Out Standard Instrument Departure

There are basically two types of EOSID (Engine Out Standard Instrument Departure) procedures:
- **EOSID**; which will reposition you for an immediate return to land.
- **Special EOSID** (EMERGENCY TURN) which presumes avoidance of obstacles due to lack of performance.

Definition of EOSID: *"An EOSID is a departure procedure diverging from SID published by the local authorities, to be flown in case of engine failure. The EOSID is produced by the operator ...". "Local authorities [may] propose themselves the EOSID for their particular airport (e.g.: Innsbruck)."*

"T" page, "E-route", and
other Company Developed Procedures

Some airlines felt that these were not enough and so they added some of their own procedures where the EOSID were considered inadequate. These "special" procedures are not necessarily recognized by the various control agencies (Towers, Departure Controls) where the airline operates. As a result, if you are attempting to fly some "T" or EOSID procedure ... you will be required to either obtain a clearance ... or declare an emergency and state your intentions.

For example: *"ABC Tower, this is XYZ123, we have experienced an engine failure/fire and I am declaring an emergency. I am turning to a heading of 123 degrees, etc."*

BIG CONFUSING AREA
If there is both a contingency procedure such as a "T" page and a conflicting EOSID ... which one should the pilot fly?

You need to sort this out NOW, before you are up to you eye-lashes in a pool of alligators. Here are some thoughts.

HOW DOES *EOSID* WORK?

To determine if you have an EOSID
routing in the database:
FIRST, select the departure runway,
THEN scroll to the bottom of the list
of available **SIDs**.
IF the last entry is **EOSID**, then you
have an assigned Engine-Out routing
available in the database.

To preview the **EOSID** routing,
- select it on the **SID** page, or
another way to do it is to simply
- Select **PLAN** on the **EFIS**
CONTROL selector panel

The **EOSID** routing will be displayed in
YELLOW (temporary)and will not change
to **GREEN** (active) until:
- Engine failure detected, and
- **INSERT*** (**LSK 6R**) is
selected.

The **DIVERSION WAYPOINT** is the last waypoint common to
both the **SID** and the **EOSID**, and is the point where the **EOSID**
diverges from the **SID**. In our example, that point is "**PLANT**".

CASE 1

If engine fails prior to the DIVERSION WAYPOINT:
The **EOSID** will **AUTOMATICALLY** display on the **ND** in **YELLOW**
(Temporary) and may be either **INSERTED** or **ERASED**.
If inserted:
The **EOSID** becomes the **ACTIVE FLIGHT PLAN (NAV or HDG ok)**.

CASE 2

If engine fails AFTER the DIVERSION WAYPOINT or if there is
NO DIVERSION POINT:
(such as might occur during the ENGINE FIRE scenario.)
The **EOSID** routing will **AUTOMATICALLY** display on the **ND** in
YELLOW, BUT it *CANNOT* be inserted. It can be used, however, as
pilot information, and the pilot may:
- continue to fly the original **SID** (using **HDG or NAV**),
- Return to and fly the **EOSID** routing using the **HDG** select,
- Fly another escape routing and determine terrain clearance.
(such as in VMC conditions).

published by UNIVERSITY of TEMECULA PRESS, Inc.

> "**NO EOSID**" displayed on the **SID** queue of the runway page means there is no "**ENGINE OUT SID**" available in the **MCDU/FMGC** database. That does **NOT**, however, relieve you of the responsibility of briefing (and subsequently flying) an engine out routing. Also, if there is a "**T**" page or other escape procedure listed in your company materials, then you must use that routing. Either way, you should be aware of and brief the routing you will utilize should there be an engine failure on/after take-off.

Since the **EOSID**s are developed (in most cases) by the airline operator, the routing will most likely be the same as any other published "escape" procedure (such as "**T**" procedure). Therefore, we will refer to these Single Engine escape procedures as **EOSID**.

Thoughts about *EOSID.*

1. An **EOSID** needs to be considered for **EVERY TAKEOFF, NORMAL APPROACH**, and specifically for **ENGINE-OUT** approaches. The idea here is to treat potential engine failure for both landing as well as take-off.

2. Some Captains say that they "expect" an engine failure on **EVERY** take-off and missed approach and brief accordingly. I think that is prudent and I would **EXPECT** that on a checkride every Captain candidate would include a discussion about what he intends to do in the case of an engine failure/fire.

3. If executing an **MCDU/FMGC** database described **EOSID**, be aware of the steps necessary to recall and be able to expeditiously insert that **EOSID** routing as the **MCDU F-PLAN** page.

4. If confronted with both a "**T**" (company contingency plan) or **EOSID**, decide **BEFORE** attempting the takeoff or approach and brief accordingly. Note that some **EOSID**s are not in the **MCDU/FMGC** database but are described on the airport approach plates.

5. Consider that a "**SPECIAL EOSID**" is published so as to preclude contact with an obstacle (referred to as crashing) such as some earthbound structure or landmark and does **NOT** imply that there is a single engine situation.

6. Consider that the **EOSID** is designed to safely return you to the airport for landing.

ENTERING THE CONFINES OF THE RUNWAY

When we finally receive the clearance from the tower to enter the confines of the runway, **CONTROL TOWER** will issue a clearance like:

CALLSIGN, RUNWAY, "LINE UP AND WAIT".

Anytime the airplane has entered ANY runway environment; it is some company's policy to "**TURN ON THE LIGHTS**".

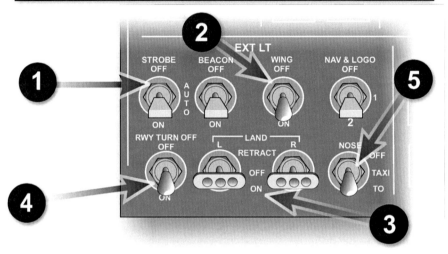

1. [C] STROBE LIGHT SWITCH .... ON
2. [C] WING LIGHT SWITCH .... ON
3. [C] LANDING LIGHT SWITCHES .... ON
4. [C] RUNWAY TURNOFF LIGHT SWITCH .... ON
5. [C] NOSE LIGHT SWITCH .... ON

Unless cleared for a "**ROLLING TAKE-OFF**", come to a **FULL STOP** ... The Captain will steer into position and align the airplane on the runway centerline.

DO NOT RELY ON "HOLDING" THE BRAKES
SET THE PARKING BRAKE

[C] PARKING BRAKE .... SET, CHECK PRESSURE.

published by UNIVERSITY of TEMECULA PRESS, Inc.

GENERAL COMMENTS
regarding the TAKE-OFF

It is Company SOP that **BOTH** flight directors be on for **ALL** takeoffs, if available. At least one flight director MUST BE ON for the SRS to operate.

> ### WARNING:
> ### DO NOT USE THE STEERING TILLER
> ### DURING TAKE-OFF ROLL !

Maintain directional control using the rudder. Remember that the rudder pedal controls nosewheel steering and that it does so in a continuously diminishing way. That is: steering authority starts to decrease above 40 kts and is **completely removed by 130 kts.**

Rolling Takeoffs are OK. While they don't increase the takeoff capability, they do expedite takeoff, make for a smoother transition, and reduce (somewhat) the potential for **FOD** (Foreign Object Damage).

TAIL STRIKE

Outside of running off the runway by using the **STEERING TILLER** during the take-off roll, the **MOST FEARED** event is the dreaded **TAILSTRIKE**. Oh sure, there are a lot of reasons this could occur:
Early rotation, Erroneously **LOW Vr**, Flaps set improperly, Trying to get off to avoid birds or obstacles, Directional Control problems due to gusty winds, etc.

BUT the *NUMBER ONE REASON* a tailstrike could occur is:

 ### BOTH PILOTS MAKING
SIMULTANEOUS STICK INPUTS !!!

Pilots aren't stupid (usually) so how could this occur? The **NUMBER ONE REASON** is that both pilots think that they are supposed to be doing the take-off.
THIS IS A BIG DEAL!!!

> ### IMPORTANT:
> Captain makes a statement confirming who is going to make the takeoff and the status of the brakes:
> ### "I (You) have control of the airplane,
> ### and the parking brakes are (are not) set".
> The First Officer acknowledges a transfer of control.

STOP!

LET'S TAKE A BREAK
FOR A TIMELY DISCUSSION

GROUND SKOOL

At this point in our conversation, we need to talk a little about philosophy, Airbus philosophy 101 to be exact. To develop a fundamental understanding of the Airbus flight paradigm we need to go back to ground school.

What I am going to try and do here is to describe what those fabulous engineers over at Airbus did to create what may be the most modern and cutting edge jet in the world. Their boss gave them a "clean sheet of paper" and the mandate to be as creative as they wanted. What they came up with is nothing short of genius.

Here is what I think their thought process was (in an abbreviated version). They figured that since the airplane is going to be an airliner and the primary mission is to fly from one known airport to another known airport, they decided to define a "typical" flight profile. They then divided that perfect profile into individual "phases." Since each part or phase has individual requirements, a definitive starting point and a conclusion, they built these into the computerized heart of the airplane (FMGC) the necessary parameters for each individual segment of what is a continuous chain of phases.

> THE SECRET OF THE AIRBUS IS PHASES!

This concept is a lot like DOMINOES ... one falls into the next, and once it has fallen, going back is difficult.

PHASES

UP↑

DOWN ↓

Once we get a handle on that and understand how the modeling for their airborne computer driven airplane is constructed, filling in the details becomes a piece of cake.

While the Airbus jet is certainly designed to operate in what has become the ubiquitous "old fashioned" VOR-AIRWAYS network; they made it entirely compatible with the old school while at the same time giving it the flexibility and adaptability to be entirely at home with the latest emerging technologies and airborne guidance technologies. The airplane is easy to hand-fly, and it also has been given a computerized fly-by-wire capability that makes what was formerly either extremely difficult or impossible ... well, almost easy.

published by **UNIVERSITY of TEMECULA PRESS, Inc.**

INTRODUCING
The concept of  **PHASES**

In order to create their unique and exquisite solution to the flight paradigm, the Airbus Engineering team divided a typical, perfect flight evolution into parts that they called "**PHASES.**" There are at least eight major phases and the ones we will consider in our discussion are:

- PREFLIGHT (TAXI)
- TAKE-OFF
- CLIMB (CLB)
- CRUISE (CRZ)
- DESCENT (DES)
- APPROACH (APPR)
- LANDING
- GO-AROUND

Each phase is separate from the one before and the one after. Each has a unique set of operating parameters and considerations. Each phase is separated from the next one by a unique "**PHASE TRIGGER.**"

IMPORTANT NOTE:
Each of these separate and distinct phase kernels has a specific beginning and ending. The **MCDU/FMGC** *requires* each phase to be completed before it will go to the next phase of the flight operation sequence.

*For an example of failing to "trigger" the next phase; let's say that you had initially programmed a cruise altitude of FL 330 on the **INIT A** page of the **MCDU/FMGC**, but decided during the climb phase that you would instead make your final cruise altitude FL 310. The **MCDU/FMGC** would not actuate the phase trigger (reaching cruise altitude) nor transition to the **CRZ** phase and therefore none of the subsequent automatic features would operate ... such as **DES** (descent) phase indicators and profiles.*

Therefore, we have to be aware of these things called the **PHASE TRIGGERS**. These are the events that tell the computer to switch to the next "phase" of operation. If the airplane does NOT execute these trigger events, it **WILL NOT** progress to the next phase. On the next page, I have made a list of the phase triggers I have identified.

So, to simplify, let me restate the situation:
1. A flight is divided into **PHASES**.
2. Each phase has a "**PHASE TRIGGER**" that initiates that phase.
3. You must complete one phase to go to the next.
4. An incomplete chain of phases does *NOT* allow complete use of the automated features.

That is the approach we will take in our tutorial. We will construct a flight plan that is a "typical" routing and describe how it could be flown "perfectly." The goal is to make each flight just like the preceding one... similar and perfect.

Understanding and implementing the idea of phases is crucial to understanding how to fly an Airbus. If you can "get" this, you can become an Airbus Ace.

PHASE TRANSITION

a simplified list of PHASE TRIGGERS

PHASE TRANSITION	PHASE TRIGGERS
PREFLIGHT to TAKE-OFF	*Thrust levers to either the FLX or TOGA detent.*
TAKE-OFF to CLIMB	*Reaching the ACCEL level entered on the PERF page.*
CLIMB to CRUISE	*At programmed cruise altitude entered on the PERF page.*
CRUISE to DESCENT	*Manual activation of descent. Leaving cruise altitude.*
DESCENT to APPROACH	*Manually "ACTIVATE and CONFIRM APPR" on PERF page.*
APPROACH to LANDING	*Disconnect Auto-pilot, or Aircraft touchdown*
APPROACH to GO-AROUND	*TOGA detent on the thrust levers during the approach phase.*
LANDING to COMPLETION OF FLIGHT	*30 seconds after landing; and goes Back to PREFLIGHT when INIT or PERF key is pressed*

*These "triggers" I have listed here are not a complete list ...**BUT** they are the ones that pilots "normally" use to operate the jet. Be aware that some limitations and necessary flight control selections are not referenced here.*

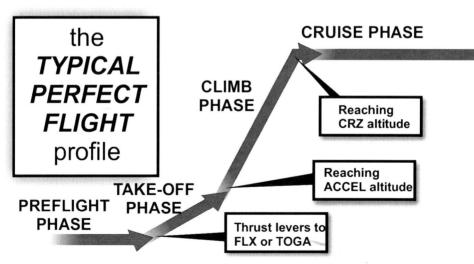

the
TYPICAL PERFECT FLIGHT
profile

CRUISE PHASE

CLIMB PHASE

Reaching CRZ altitude

Reaching ACCEL altitude

TAKE-OFF PHASE

PREFLIGHT PHASE

Thrust levers to FLX or TOGA

published by UNIVERSITY of TEMECULA PRESS, Inc.

A quick overview of the
PHASE *OPERATING CRITERIA*

Let's take a quick and dirty look at each phase in isolation and try and identify some of the unique requirements and operating criteria that exist. This is just to give us a feel for a more detailed look to follow.

PREFLIGHT PHASE: During the preflight (taxi) phase, the thrust levers act just like any other airplane. The pilot has **FULL MANUAL** control and can move them and expect the engines to respond in kind.

During taxi, the **PFD** will display the "**IRON CROSS**" and it will move in response to the stick. Note that there is NO flight director in the taxi phase.

TAKE-OFF PHASE: Once the thrust levers are moved manually into either the **FLX** or **TOGA** detent, the **FADEC** takes control of the thrust and the pilot no longer controls the thrust of the airplane directly.
NOTE: *The pilot can physically retard the thrust levers, taking the **FADEC** out of the **FLX/TOGA** mode while still on the ground and return to taxi phase operations. This is for aborted take-offs.*

The **PFD** "**IRON CROSS**" will disappear and there will be no Flight Director; however, a single green "runway heading"lineup indicator line will become visible on the **PFD**. Depending on how the airplane is configured, either when the airplane is airborne and the landing gear oleos extend, or when **SRS** (throttles to **FLX or TOGA** detent) selected, then the Flight Directors will be displayed on the PFDs.

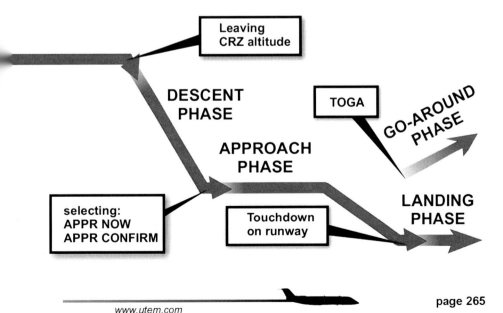

CLIMB PHASE: During the climb phase, the airspeed target on the speed tape will automatically reflect the value selected on the PERF/CLB page of the MCDU or a managed airspeed of 250 kts below 10,000 feet. At 10,000 feet, the managed airspeed will slew towards ECON (unless another value had been selected on the CLB page). The FCU will display a "selected" airspeed if one has been selected, or it will display white dot and dashes if it is allowed to be managed.
To revert to managed airspeed from the indicated selected airspeed, the pilot has to "PUSH" the airspeed selector on the FCU.

The airplane will turn towards the next waypoint on the F-PLAN page *IMMEDIATELY* when the autopilot is selected unless the FCU has a selected heading displayed.

CRUISE PHASE: During the cruise phase, the airplane will remain at the managed altitude until the pilot *PHYSICALLY* initiates a descent. Even though a lower altitude may be set into the FCU prior to the descent point (Hockey stick), the airplane will not leave the cruise altitude at the descent point or after without input from the pilot.

This requires a little finesse, and I will suggest that you start your descent (PUSH the ALT knob) about 5 miles prior to the descent point using the managed autoflight technique. This will cause the FMGC to establish a 1,000 fpm descent rate until it intercepts the calculated descent profile as indicated on the PFD altitude tape by the "VNAV descent profile indicator" donut.
If you should elect to manually control the descent (PULL the ALT knob), be aware that all the automated descent indications and crossing altitude/airspeed controls are eliminated.

APPROACH PHASE: During the approach phase, we will use the automation to fly the airplane to a landing. The steps to do this are simple to remember:
    - Select ILS. When the desired ILS identifier appears on the PFD, this will cause the "descent profile indicator" to be removed and the glideslope and localizer indices to be displayed.
    - Select LOC.
    - Within about about 10 miles from the airport, select "APPR PHASE" and then select "CONFIRM APPR". This will cause the airspeed target symbol on the PFD to slew to GREEN DOT ("0" flap or clean maneuvering) airspeed and the airplane will slow to that speed.
Selection of flaps will cause the airspeed bug to slew and the airspeed to constantly decrease to maintain green dot airspeed.
    - When the localizer starts to move, select APPR on the FCU.
    - If below 8,000 feet, select the second autopilot.
      This will arm the autoland mode.
    - When the glideslope is one dot from the horizon,
      select gear and landing flap.
    - At 400 feet the autoland will engage.
    - At "RETARD" ...pilot must MANUALLY select
      the thrust levers to the reverse gate, and
    - on touchdown, MANUALLY select REVERSE.
    - Airplane "should" track centerline.
      Once slowed and ready to exit the runway,
      deselect the autopilot and that will trigger the taxi phase.

published by UNIVERSITY of TEMECULA PRESS, Inc.

GO-AROUND PHASE: If, during the **APPROACH** phase, the thrust levers are manually placed into the **TO/GA** detent, the airplane enters the **GO-AROUND** phase.

If **BOTH** autopilots are engaged (such as during an autoland or **CAT III** approach) they will remain engaged until:
Either another **LATERAL or VERTICAL** mode is annunciated. **THEN**
the #2 Autopilot will disengage.

If the airplane should touch down during the go-around evolution, it will continue the go-around.

INTRODUCING *the CONCEPT OF*

MINIMUM GROUND SPEED
... or as the pilots call it:

GS MINI

The Airbus engineers looked at the way that other aircraft manufacturers had handled the unique situation surrounding windshear during the approach and decided that they had a better idea. What they came up with is simple and exquisite: Minimum Ground Speed.

PILOT ACTION REQUIRED:
1: Place **LATEST** winds in the **PERF/APPR** page
2: Allow the airplane to fly the approach using **MANAGED** airspeed, and the **MCDU/FMGC** will do all the rest. It is a no-brainer.

What that does for us: Flying from a headwind condition into a microburst that then results in a tailwind condition, the airplane will maintain a constant final operating airspeed with enhanced stall margin. We ensure we are taking advantage of this feature by flying the **MANAGED APPROACH SPEED**. It will calculate the **GS MINI** automatically.

HOW TO SHUT OFF THE GS MINI
If we **PULL** the **AIRSPEED** knob and fly "**SELECTED**" airspeed, then the **GS MINI** feature is deselected.

SAMPLE CALCULATION:

LATEST WIND = 270/15
RUNWAY 27
Vref = 148 KTS

V_{REF} = V_{LS} = **148 KTS** (*obtained from MCDU*)
NOTE: *HW addition is NEVER less than 5*
V_{APP} = V_{LS} + 1/3 LATEST HW = _____ KTS.
GS MINI = V_{APP} - HW = _____ KTS.
V_{TGT} = GS MINI + IRS WIND = _____ KTS.

$V_{TGT}*$
MANAGED DYNAMIC TARGET SPEED
Point A = _____ Kts
Point B = _____ Kts
Point C = _____ Kts

A
+30 kts

B
0 kts

C
-30 kts

Actual (IRS) Headwind component

V_{TGT} (TARGET) BUG SPEED CAN NEVER BE LESS THAN V_{APP}.

---

published by UNIVERSITY of TEMECULA PRESS, Inc.

GS MINI *continued*

There are some problems using the **GS MINI**:

1. Managed speed fluxuates when flying the approach.

2. Speeds selected by the **GS MINI** may be slower than desired by the pilot.

3. Speeds flown may be significantly slower than the flow of traffic and as a result prompts calls from **ATC** for speed increases.

As a result, many pilots revert to manual control of the airspeed during the approach phase..

Vapp (Approach speed) = **VLS + 5 and/or* 1/3 HW** on **LATEST** winds (placed in **MCDU** by pilot).
* "or" = Newer A320s,
*"and" = Older A320s.

You can find the relevant airspeeds listed on the **MCDU**. Simply select the **PERF** page and using the **<PHASE** selector scroll to the **APPR** page. Once you are on that page, you can enter the **ATIS or LATEST TOWER** winds, and the **MCDU/FMGC** will calculate the **MANAGED AIRSPEED TARGET** (V$_{TGT}$) using the **GROUNDSPEED MINIMUM** technique ... and do it

```
              A P P R
  Q N H       FLP RETR        FINAL
 [    ]       F = 1 5 6        2 7 L
  T E M P     SLT RETR         M D A
 [    ]       S = 1 8 6       [    ]
  MAG WIND    CLEAN            D H
 2 7 0 °/ 1 0   O = 2 2 0     [    ]
  T R A N S A L T             LDG CONF
 6 0 0 0                      CONFIG 3°
  V A P P        V L S
 1 5 6          1 4 8          F U L L
  P R E V                      N E X T
 < P H A S E                  P H A S E >
```

VLS is **Minimum Selectable Speed.**
While you can actually select a lower airspeed, it is the lowest speed the auto-flight will fly, and is the lowest speed you can fly with a "safe" margin above stall.

Vref = **VLS** for the flaps at "**FULL CONFIGURATION**".
*All irregular procedures base adjustments using **VLS** for **CONFIG FULL**.*

SIDEBAR FYI NOTE:
There are two selectable V$_{LS}$ speeds. You can make your selection using the **LSK 4R** or **LSK 5R**, it will toggle between Landing Configuration **3°** and **FULL**.

PILOT ACTION:
All the pilot has to do is "manually" enter the **LATEST** winds.

V$_{APP}$ WILL *NOT* EXCEED V$_{LS}$ BY MORE THAN 20 KTS.

GS MINI (**Minimized Ground speed**) = **Vapp - Headwind in MCDU.**
(**LATEST** winds placed there by the pilot).
There is no place to monitor Mini GS.

ACTUAL HEADWIND is derived by the **FMGC** from "real time " observation using onboard sensors (IRS).

V$_{APP}$ minus Mini-GS plus IRS WIND =
The MANAGED TARGET AIRSPEED (V$_{TGT}$)

GS MINI the **ACTUAL HEADWIND COMPONENT**
(derived from the IRS) becomes the dynamic, constantly changing, managed **V$_{TGT}$** (**TARGET**) **BUG SPEED.**

V$_{TGT}$ (TARGET) BUG SPEED CAN *NEVER* BE LESS THAN V$_{APP}$.

SRS
SPEED REFERENCE SYSTEM

The Speed Reference System is a fundamental mode of the **MCDU/FMGC** and one which we as pilots need to understand. We will be using the SRS for every flight. It is strictly a pitch mode and controls the airplane's airspeed during high thrust settings by using pitch commands.

At least ONE autopilot or flight director MUST be on.

> **CHECK-GUY QUESTION:** HOW DO WE ARM THE SRS?

The **SRS** operates in two venues:
- **TAKE-OFF,** and
- **GO-AROUND.**

For **TAKE-OFF**, the **SRS** system is ***ARMED*** when
- **V2** is entered in the **MCDU (PERF page)**, and
- **FLAPS NOT at "0"** or to put it another way; there **MUST** be some flaps selected.

The **SRS** system is then ***SELECTED*** when:
- **THRUST LEVER** is moved to the **FLX/MCT** position, (with **FLEX** temperature set in **MCDU/FMGC**), or
- **THRUST LEVER** is moved to **TOGA** position.

During the Go-Around, manually moving the thrust levers to the **TOGA** position when the flap lever is **NOT in "0"** position, will select the **SRS** mode.

When selected, it will provide pitch information for one of four basic airspeeds:
- **Take-off with 2 engines** .... **V2 + 10 KTS.**
- **Take-off with ENG failure after V1** .... Speed at time of failure, but not less than **V2**.
- **Go-Around phase** .... speed existing at the time of the Go-Around but not less than **Vapp** (Approach Speed).

To recap: These are the four target airspeeds:

4
- **V2 + 10**
- **V2** (in event of an engine failure)
- **Vapp** (approach speed)
- **Speed at time of selection**

NOTE:
*The **SRS** will allow the speed to decrease below these figures in an attempt to maintain a* **minimum climb rate of 120 fpm.**

published by UNIVERSITY of TEMECULA PRESS, Inc.

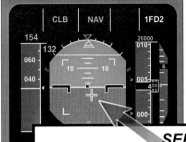

When you initially take the runway, you will notice that the airplane will not be displaying the Flight Director ... in fact, a lot of information will not be displayed. Here is what you can expect to see before the thrust levers are pushed to the takeoff power position and the **SRS** system is engaged.

SERIOUS NOTE:

One particular **IMPORTANT** item on the **PFD** to be aware of is the so-called "**IRON CROSS**". It is the joystick/flight control position indicator. We should be aware of the location of that indicator **BEFORE** we push up the thrust levers and select the **SRS**, since it directly affects the control of the direction in which the airplane will accelerate. We want that Iron Cross centered horizontally on the **PFD** initially and not cocked off to the side.

SPEED REFERENCE SYSTEM (SRS).

Selecting the **SRS** is accomplished by pushing the thrust levers to the takeoff position and is the **PHASE TRIGGER** for going from the **TAXI** to the **TAKEOFF PHASE**.

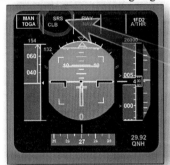

Pushing the thrust levers to the **TOGA/FLX** position will cause the **SRS** to become engaged and annunciated on the **PFD**. The Check Pilot will expect you to be aware of that engagement indication on the **FMA** (Flight Mode Annunciator) panel.

SRS (Speed Reference System) is a **BIG DEAL** on the Airbus. The Checkperson wants you to know about it. Here are few facts to make you look like you know what you are talking about.

(1) At least **ONE FLIGHT DIRECTOR or AUTOPILOT** must be **ON** for **SRS** to operate.

(2) It is **ARMED** when you program **V2** on the **MCDU/FGMC** and
- the **FLAPS** are **NOT at "0"** position.

(3) It is **ENGAGED** when
- the thrust levers are placed in **TOGA** or
- **FLX/MCT** with a flex temp set.

> **7** THINGS TO KNOW ABOUT THE SRS.

(4) The pitch bar initially indicates **10 degrees** until the aircraft becomes airborne, then: the **SRS** system commands the pitch to maintain airspeed during two venues;

TAKE-OFF AND GO-AROUND:

(5) - Normal 2 engine take-off ... **V2 + 10 KTS.**

(6) - Single engine take-off ... Speed existing at time of the engine failure **BUT not less than V2 KTS**.

(7) - Go-around ...Speed existing at the time of the Go-around **BUT not less than Vapp**.

NOTE: *the SRS will allow the speed to decrease to maintain a minimum of* **120 FPM climb***. It will always struggle to maintain a positive rate of climb.*

AUTOTHRUST STUFF

There are only 5 Thrust Lever positions defined by stops or detents:

5

MAX REVERSE
FORWARD IDLE
CLIMB (CL)
FLEX/MAX CONTINUOUS THRUST (FLX/MCT)
TAKE-OFF/GO-AROUND (TOGA)

The **AUTOTHRUST** system is **ARMED** on the ground by:

setting the thrust lever to **TO/GA** if at least one flight director is on.

setting the thrust lever to **FLX** if at least one flight director is on and a **FLEX** temperature has been entered in the **MCDU/FMGC**.

Moving the Thrust Levers forward to the **TOGA/FLEX** position will "**SELECT**" the **AUTOTHRUST (A/THR) ON**.

NOTE:
The autothrust system **WILL NOT ARM** when the thrust levers are advanced for takeoff
IF
BOTH FLIGHT DIRECTORS ARE OFF

The **AUTOTHRUST** system is **ARMED IN FLIGHT** by:
Pushing the A/THR button when the thrust levers are not in the engagement range.

The **AUTOTHRUST** system is **ENGAGED IN FLIGHT** by:

Setting thrust levers in the engagement range with the auto-thrust armed.

Pushing the A/THR button when the thrust levers are in the engagement range.

Activating ALPHA FLOOR, regardless of position or arming status.

published by UNIVERSITY of TEMECULA PRESS, Inc.

There are actually two distinct parts to the Take-off:

SPOOL-UP and ROTATION phase

Spooling up the engines is pretake-off phase, however, once the engines have
- **TOGA/FLX** selected, and
- **SRS** is annunciated,
the jet enters the **TAKE-OFF** phase..

DISCUSSION ABOUT THE KOZ
(*KEEP OUT ZONE*)

On "some" Airbus engines there is an idiosyncracy that occurs on the **_GROUND ONLY_**. During operations in this specific **RPM** range, the lip of the cowl interferes with the flow of air and the engine spool-up can be interrupted. Not a problem in the air. The **FADEC** has a built-in feature which does not allow the engine to stabilize in this range;

HOWEVER, if you elect to "manually" spool-up the engines, be aware that you "**COULD**" get an asymmetric thrust application if your thrust application is done **TOO SLOWLY**!!.

YIPE!!

The solution is to let the automation spool up the engines.

KEEP OUT ZONE (KOZ)
61% to 74% N1
*The **FADEC** wil not allow engine to stabilize in this range because it produces stress on the fan blades.*

Moving the Thrust Levers forward to the **TOGA/FLEX** position will "**SELECT**" the **AUTOTHRUST (A/THR) ON**.

THE LAWS

Airbus has designated the term "**LAWS**" to indicate levels of automated flight envelope protection available with degraded flight control capability.

There are 5 levels or LAWS;
- *NORMAL LAW*
- *ALTERNATE LAW*
- *ALTERNATE LAW (without speed stability)*
- *DIRECT LAW*
- *MECHANICAL BACK-UP*.

These LAWS operate in two modes:
- *GROUND MODE and*
- *FLIGHT MODE*.

My personal view is that "memorizing" the parameters of protection for each of the laws, let alone trying to determine which LAW you are actually operating under when there is an emergency failure involving airplane control, is asking too much of a mere mortal airline pilot.

THE ONLY IMPORTANT PRIORITY CONCERN OF THE PILOT IS TO
FLY THE AIRPLANE.

NORMAL LAW

If everything is operating **NORMALLY** and everything is fine, then the airplane is said to be operating in "**NORMAL LAW**". This is the highest level of automated protection available and provides three axes protection envelopes for:
- *LOAD FACTOR LIMITATION*
- *PITCH ATTITUDE PROTECTION*
- *HIGH ANGLE OF ATTACK PROTECTION*
- *HIGH SPEED PROTECTION*
- *BANK ANGLE PROTECTION*.

When operating in "**NORMAL LAW**", regardless of the pilot's input, the computers prevent excessive maneuvers and maintain the airplane within the limits of a "safe" envelope in pitch and roll.

HOWEVER:
THE RUDDER HAS NO PROTECTION IN ANY LAW.

published by UNIVERSITY of TEMECULA PRESS, Inc.

THE *NORMAL LAW* PROTECTION LIST

In **NORMAL LAW**, when everything is going right and all the flight control computers are up and running, here is what the airplane sees as **LIMITATIONS** that require it to do something. There is a **GROUND** mode and a **FLIGHT** mode ... but who really is concerned about the **GROUND** mode ... so we will concentrate on the **FLIGHT** mode.

FLIGHT MODE NORMAL LAW

The **FLIGHT MODE** is active from **LIFTOFF** until
FLARE MODE engages during landing at **50 FEET RA**.

PITCH

The pitch mode constantly trims the **ELEVATOR** and **STABILIZER** to maintain 1 G load on the side stick at neutral and with wings level. If the pilot moves the sidestick, the pitch mode trims the pitch to maintain a load factor proportional to the sidestick deflection *regardless of airspeed*. The pitch trim is automatic with or without the autopilot engaged.

LOAD FACTOR LIMITS:

The pitch trim tries to keep the airplane within these limits:
> **+2.5g to -1.0g (Trailing edge flaps retracted)**
> **+2.0g to 0.0g (Trailing edge flaps extended).**

PITCH ATTITUDE LIMITS:

The pitch is maintained to these limits:
> **30° NOSE-UP reducing to 25° at low speed (with flaps 0 to 3)**
> **25° NOSE-UP reducing to 20° at low speed (with flaps FULL)**
> **15° NOSE DOWN**

The **FLIGHT DIRECTOR BARS** are removed from view when
the pitch exceeds **25° UP** or **13° DOWN**.

∝ PROT (ALPHA PROT or A.PROTECTION)

HIGH ANGLE OF ATTACK PROTECTION

This is called the ∝ (alpha) protection mode and includes three angle of attack functions:
> - Alpha Protection (∝ Prot)
> - Alpha Floor (∝ Floor)
> - Alpha Maximum (∝ Max)

> ### *When Angle of Attack gets to be greater than " ∝ Prot":*
> **STUFF HAPPENS**!!! This event is usually a surprise to the pilot.

> - AUTOPILOT .... **DISCONNECTS**
> - SPEED BRAKES .... **RETRACT**
> - NOSE-UP PITCH TRIM .... **INHIBITED**
> - BANK ANGLE LIMIT .... **reduced from 67° to 45°**
> - ANGLE of ATTACK .... **is set by sidestick deflection:**

IMPORTANT NOTES

1. ∝ **MAX CANNOT** be exceeded
even if the stick is held full back against the stop.
2. If **ANGLE OF ATTACK PROTECTION** is active,
the sidestick must be pushed forward to return to normal mode.

THE *DEGRADED LAWS* PROTECTION LIST

Anything not In **NORMAL LAW** is operating in some *DEGRADED LAW mode*. Now, I don't know about you, but there are times when I am aviating and things are not going well that I don't want to have to revert to some memory item that doesn't make any difference anyway. That is pretty much the way I think about identifying which "**LAW**" the airplane is operating in. I think it is adequate to know if you are in **NORMAL LAW** or simply in any of the other **DEGRADED LAWS**.

So, I am not going to spend much time on trying to sort out the various laws. Things are either **NORMAL** or they are **NOT**.

Here are some generalizations regarding **DEGRADED LAWS**:

    - *THE AIRPLANE CAN BE STALLED !*
    - There are radically **REDUCED** protections.
    - **Vmo** is reduced to 320 KIAS
    - Expect **no YAW DAMPING**.
    - The **SPEED TAPE** on the **PFD** may be modified with the addition of
      a black and red barber pole indicating stall warning speed.

... and some other stuff that will be totally confusing since the information load is different depending on the nature and extent of the failures.

Bottom line assessment ... if the airplane gets so screwed up in attitude, airspeed, control failure, or other unknown triggers that it winds up in some **ABNORMAL** or **ALTERNATE LAW** ... it probably cannot return to **NORMAL LAW** *even if the situation is corrected*.

> *EXPECT the remainder of the flight*
> *to be flown in some degraded mode*
> *such as ALTERNATE MODE.*

THE ABSOLUTE WORSE CASE LAW
MECHANICAL BACKUP

Even if you should experience a
"COMPLETE LOSS OF ELECTRONIC FLIGHT CONTROL SIGNALS" ...
THE AIRPLANE IS STILL CERTIFIED FOR FLIGHT.
You can EXPECT this situation only to be demonstrated during training;
but if you should have the Check-Pilot from Hell, here are the flight tools available.

    - **PITCH** is controlled using the **MANUAL TRIM WHEEL**
    ☀ *(Available ONLY if hydraulic power is available)*,
    - **LATERAL** control using the **RUDDER PEDALS**
    The rudder pedals command rudder surface movement via cables.
    ☀ *("Available ONLY if hydraulic power is available.")*

> **THE COCKPIT INDICATION OF THIS SITUATION IS:**
> - a red **MAN PITCH TRIM ONLY** warning on the **PFD**.

published by UNIVERSITY of TEMECULA PRESS, Inc.

DANGER ZONE

FLASHING
TOGA LK
WARNING

If Airspeed slows to the top of the "**BRICKS**" at the bottom of the airspeed tape, then:

- "**A-FLOOR**" (boxed green) momentarily flashes on the **PFD**, but is almost immediately replaced with a flashing **TOGA LK** (green) annunciation.

- **THRUST** goes to **TOGA** regardless of other factors, even if you are hand flying and not using the thrust management system in any kind of automatic mode, and stays frozen there until ...

ACTION BY THE PILOT CHANGES IT.

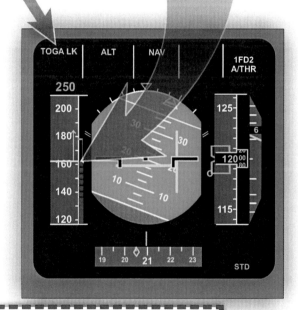

I'M SCREAMING AT YOU:
*Even though the **A/THR** button is illuminated, the thrust is frozen in **TOGA**.*

As a result, even after you regain control of the airplane, the airspeed will continue to increase until the airplane overspeeds and the jet is in jeopardy of being destroyed.

... unless you regain control of the thrust and turn off the TOGA LOCK.

HOW TO TURN OFF
"TOGA LOCK"

SIMPLE ANSWER:
TURN OFF THE AUTOTHRUST SYSTEM.

The **AUTOTHRUST** system. It can be **DISENGAGED IN FLIGHT** by:

1. Pushing the **A/THR** button on the **FCU** panel,

OR

2. Pushing **EITHER** disconnect button on the sides of the **THRUST LEVERS.** These are referred to as the **INSTINCTIVE SWITCHES**.

PANIC ANSWER

STEP 1: *FLY THE AIRPLANE !!!*
Once you have sorta recovered and the airspeed is increasing, *THEN* you need to think about getting the thrust back to a normal situation.

TOGA **STEP 2**: "**MATCH THE DONUTS**" ... by that I mean physically push the thrust lever to the full forward position so that the little white circles at the top of the thrust indicators "**MATCH**" the thrust indicator settings shown on the **UPPER ECAM**. This is done by pushing the thrust levers to the full stop forward.

CLICK **STEP 3**: "**DISCONNECT THE A/THR**" ... You can click the "**INSTICTIVE SWITCH**" ... **BUT** here is *PILOT SCREW-UP* warning. *DO NOT HOLD THE SWITCH IN* ... if held more than 15 seconds the **A/THR** will be rendered inoperative for the rest of the flight segment. *TECHNIQUE COMMENT*: Use the **FCU** switch. It is simpler just to push it once (**OFF**) and a second time (**ON**) ... **CLICK-CLICK**.

CLICK **STEP 4**: "**RE-ENGAGE THE A/THR**" ... Once you have the thrust lever full forward, push the A/THR switch on the FCU and observe:

- **A/THR** in WHITE on the PFD FMA, *AND*
- **A/THR** button on the FCU illuminated.

CL **STEP 5**: "**RESET THE A/THR**" ... Pull the thrust levers "**G-E-N-T-L-Y**" back to the **CL** detent.
NOTE: In the air, there are **NO KOZ** ("Keep Out Zone") considerations.

published by UNIVERSITY of TEMECULA PRESS, Inc.

HOW PILOTS CAN SCREW UP
and get into TOGA-LK

DISCUSSION:

There are a couple of places where 'Bus pilots can get into **A-FLOOR** situations and get the **TOGA LK** annunciated. Here are a couple of screw-ups for you to think about:

AFTER TAKE-OFF: A level off right after take-off and before the "**LVR CLB**" reduction, with the thrust levers still at take-off setting (**TOGA** or **FLX**), will result in airspeed building rapidly towards overspeed. If the pilot chooses to control the excess thrust by **MANUALLY** retarding the thrust levers to IDLE ... this will **DESELECT** the Autothrust mode (**A/THR** switches off automatically).

Here is where pilots screw up; as the airspeeds slows, they will place the thrust levers towards the **CL** detent, thinking that the thrust is now in **AUTOTHRUST** mode. *IT IS NOT!* Since the A/THR mode is "**STILL**" deselected. As a result the airspeed may decay slowly, perhaps unnoticed, until "**A.FLOOR**" is annunciated.

OMIGOSH!!!!!

LOW ALTITUDE, LOW AIRSPEED, LOW ENERGY ... not a happy place.

AT ALTITUDE: There are two high altitude
situations that are built into this airplane that can bite your butt:

SITUATION 1: If the airplane is at 31,000 feet or higher and the airspeed is less than .75 Mach; If the spoilers are deployed more than ½, you can get **A.FLOOR** protection. You may say, *"Yeah, but, if the autopilot is on, the spoilers are automatically limited to ½ extension."*

However, if the pilot pulls the speedbrake lever to "**FULL**" and then for some reason turns **OFF** the autopilot, the protection is removed and the speedbrakes immediately extend to full and the **A .FLOOR** could be annunciated along with all that other exciting stuff.

WOW!!! BIG SURPRISE!

SITUATION 2: You are cruising along above **FL 250 at ECON MACH** and you get an **RA**. A voice starts yelling at you,"**TRAFFIC, TRAFFIC**" followed by "**INCREASE CLIMB, INCREASE CLIMB**". *OMIGOSH* ... there he is on the **ND** ... and closing. You swiftly reach up to the **FCU**, set in a higher altitude and depress the **EXPED** switch.

WHOOPS!!!

Here is the problem. In **EXPED** mode, the airspeed will target "**GREEN DOT**" in a climb. The **MACH** number for a "green dot" airspeed is below minimum stall speed above **FL 250** ... so, guess what ... The pilot could be looking at Alpha protection, **A FLOOR, TOGA LOCK**. I can't even imagine what a surprise this would be.

Have a nice day.

CHECK PILOTS LOVE this stuff.

What would happen if the airplane got really slow and the pilots didn't notice it? Normally, the airplane would stall and probably crash ... but those wily engineers at Airbus, never trusting pilots to be constantly paying close attention, built a "**FAIL SAFE**" feature into their airplane. They called it "∝" (Greek letter for **ALPHA) FLOOR**." Generally, pilots don't write Greek, so it is referred to as "**A.FLOOR**" on the **FMA** (**PFD**) and the **UPPER ECAM E/WD**. It is called **ALPHA FLOOR** when being referred to in writing.

∝ *(ALPHA) FLOOR*
DEMONSTRATION:

Airline pilots are required to demonstrate an **A.FLOOR** initiation and recovery procedure during their checkride. It is an interesting and useful exercise since it demonstrates both the limitations and the utility of this Airbus feature.

A.FLOOR DEMONSTRATION setup

To set up the airplane for this demonstration, here is a recommended procedure ... of course, this is just a simple sample of one of the many ways a pilot can screw up and get in this position. Here are the steps:

STEP 2- Retard thrust.

STEP 1- Disengage **AUTO-PILOT** and **A/THR**.

STEP 3- Let airspeed decay to "green dot".

STEP 4- Simulate "pop-up" traffic and make an aggressive avoidance maneuver UP and LEFT.

STEP 5- As the airspeed decays towards the "red bricks", **A.FLOOR** will annunciate momentarily on **PFD/FMA** (flashing) and **ECAM/E/WD**; then be replaced with a flashing **TOGA LK**. Note that even though the Thrust will immediately increase to **TOGA**, the Selected thrust lever position setting will remain. There is *NO AUTOMATIC THRUST LEVER MOVEMENT.*

HERE IS THE BOTTOM LINE

What happens at "TOGA LK" is:
  1. The thrust goes to TOGA and without regard for other factors and
  2. Stays frozen there until action by the pilot changes it.

published by UNIVERSITY of TEMECULA PRESS, Inc.

a suggested

A.FLOOR RECOVERY *technique*

When **A.FLOOR** is activated, the airplane will be in a position of extremis and requires **EXTREMELY** sensitive control inputs to avoid **UPSET** and **STALL** related problems. Let me put it this way: "*YOU ARE ABOUT TO DIE.*" At this point, the pilot **MUST** concentrate on recovery ONLY!!!. These events occur so rapidly, that your recovery must be swiftly and accurately completed.

STEP 1- Reduce angle of attack by pushing the stick gently forward. *(In a real life situation, this will disconnect the autopilot and you will be treated to the warning horn)*. A green flashing **TOGA LK** should immediately annunciate on the **PFD** and the THRUST will go to **TOGA** regardless of any other factors.

STEP 2- *FLY THE AIRPLANE* so that the airspeed begins to increase towards the "green dot." This is the most difficult part. I *STRONGLY* suggest that you remove any rolling tendencies or aileron/spoiler input, and level the wings. G-E-N-T-L-Y lower the nose and allow the airplane to fly out of the **A.FLOOR** situation.

CAUTION:
Once you have recovered, the airplane will continue to accelerate **VERY** rapidly, and you are now faced with a potential **OVERSPEED** situation.

WHEN AIRPLANE IS UNDER CONTROL

STEP 3- **PUSH** throttles to the forward stop (**TOGA**).
We do this to match the **THRUST LEVER** setting to the **ACTUAL** thrust setting.
REMINDER: The thrust is **ALREADY** at **TOGA**.

Shut OFF the TOGA-LK

STEP 4- Disengage **A/THR** (use the **FCU** button).
This will turn off the **TOGA LK**
...and after a very short delay

STEP 5- Re-select the **A/THR** (use the **FCU** button).

A simple way to think about this step is to push the **A/THR** button twice. (Shut it off, and then back on).

STEP 6- Ensure the thrust levers are placed in **CL** detent once again. Physically move the thrust levers to the **CL** detent and observe **CL** indicated on the **ECAM**.

STEP 7: Stabilize flight, get auto-pilot re-engaged (if necessary) and re-establish normal flight inbound to the next fix.

PART TWO

All that stuff that went before was just preparation for the 'ride.

THE
SIM RIDE

or

PSYCHOMOTOR SKILLS

demonstration

LET'S DO IT!

IT'S A PIECE OF CAKE!

IT'S TIME TO SHOW 'EM WHAT YOU GOT!

HOW TO **TAKE OFF**
When take-off clearance is received:

1   PARKING BRAKE handle .... OFF

Turn handle on the lower console to **OFF** and check that the gauge under the gear handle goes to "**ZERO**".

BIG PROBLEM:

NOTE: *If the pressure does not go to zero, consider a potential* **BDDV** *(Brake Dual Distribution Valve) failure. Do not* **TAKEOFF** *or try and taxi, reset the brake and get assistance in clearing the runway. Your flight is over until the* **BDDV** *is changed.*

DO NOT TAKE OFF !!!

2   THRUST LEVERS .... FLEX or TOGA

Once more, Let's go over that.
Technique for advancing the thrust levers:

- Advance levers to about **1.05 EPR** and
- allow engines to stabilize at about **50% N1**.
- Then "rapidly" move the thrust lever through the **KOZ** (Keep Out Zone) and smoothly to the **FLEX or TOGA** notch.

BIG PROBLEM: IF YOU MOVE THE THRUST LEVERS TOO SLOWLY THROUGH THE KOZ, THERE IS THE POTENTIAL FOR A MISMATCHED OR ASYMMETRICAL THRUST.

YIPE!! *That event could cause the airplane to exit the runway and ruin your whole day. It is essential that you monitor the thrust throughout the spoolup venue and make corrections as necessary.*

DISCUSSION:

The **THRUST LEVERS** are being operated manually at this point and will remain so until the **CL** detent is selected after take-off. Even though **TOGA or FLX** is annunciated, the pilot has full control of the thrust levers and can abort a take-off or pull the thrust levers to idle at **ANY TIME!**

Target: Have THRUST LEVERS set by 40 KNOTS

Planning to have the Thrust set by 40 knots is a good target, and covers the worst case scenario where you have a crosswind greater than 20 knots or a tailwind.

TIP!

Here is a recommendation: If you have elected to use the **FLX** setting for take-off, and get an **ECAM** warning, select **TOGA**. The reasons for the warning might be flex temperature not entered in **MCDU** or the **FLEX** annunciation on the **UPPER ECAM** changes to **TOGA**. Whatever the cause, if you select **TOGA**, the warning will more than likely be cancelled.

TIMEOUT

Let's take a moment and talk about the pitch bar on the Flight Director. Initially, it appears to be pitching up and then down and back up again ... what's with that?

In simple terms, the Flight Director pitch bar is trying to cause the nose of the airplane to move up or down. This is usually to comply with an airspeed command initiated from either the **MCDU/FMGC** or the pilot.

Here's the **BASIC** Flight Director paradigm:
If the requested airspeed is **GREATER** than the indicated airspeed, the nose should be pitched over to gain airspeed.
If the requested airspeed is **LESS THAN** the indicated airspeed, the nose is pitched up to lose airspeed.

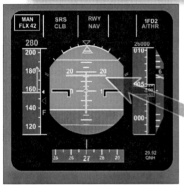

The actual Flight Director pitch bar will be fixed at 10 degrees initially and does not actually become operable until the airplane has become airborne; you will already be in your rotation when the bar starts to move, and here is the first $OM_IGO{}^SH$ moment. The Flight Director pitch bar will initially respond to the speed tape requested airspeed (**SRS** on the magenta triangle) with a **RADICAL PITCH UP** command. **IGNORE** the pitch bar command...
***PITCH TOWARDS 12.5 (single engine)
to 15 DEGREES!
DO NOT INITIALLY FOLLOW
THE FLIGHT DIRECTOR PITCH BAR.***

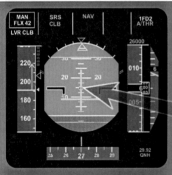

Once the airplane has climbed out of the **ACCEL** altitude that is set on the **PERF/CLB** page, the target airspeed will slew to either: **250 kts** or (if requested) "**0**" flap speed. We had selected "0" clean maneuvering (**GREEN DOT**) airspeed because it complied with the speed restriction imposed by the "**Class B**" airspace. However, don't follow that pitch bar! **REMAIN FOCUSED AT 12.5 to 15 DEGREES** pitch until the pitch bar comes down almost to the airplane symbol ...then: You may engage the autopilot if airplane **above 100 feet with SRS annunciated.**

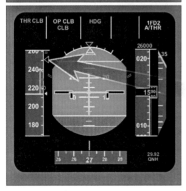

Passing about 3,000 ft **AFE**, if you are cleared to resume normal airspeed, select **250 KTS** below 10,000 feet for the climb-out. You do that by **PUSHING** the **SPD** knob on the **FCU**. It should indicate "**WHITE DOT**" and the target indicator will slew to **250 kts**.
If we have the autopilot engaged, the pitch indicator should remain centered as the airplane automatically adjusts attitude to maintain the target airspeed (pitches down to increase airspeed). If manually flying the jet, **FOLLOW THE PITCH BAR.**

published by UNIVERSITY of TEMECULA PRESS, Inc.

ITS TIME TO ...

SPOOL 'EM UP

SET TAKE-OFF THRUST

Move the **THRUST** levers to the **FLX** or **TOGA** detent. Check the upper right corner of the **ECAM** for the appropriate **THRUST SETTING** annunciation.

TECHNIQUE:

Manually ease the throttles to about **1.05 EPR**, and allow engines to stabilize at the 12 o'clock position, then more aggressively push the thrust levers to the **TOGA or FLX** detent. The idea is to let the **FADEC** (engine controlling computer) complete the spool up of the engines through the **KOZ**. then **RELEASE** the **BRAKES**.

NOTE:

Slowly pushing up the thrust levers manually through the **KOZ** (Keep Out Zone) may result in asymmetric power application.

Here is a recommended crosswind technique:

IF CROSSWIND AT OR BELOW 20 KTS with NO TAILWIND

Use ½ forward stick deflection until about 80 knots, then slowly release back pressure on the side stick so that the iron cross reaches a neutral position at about 100 knots.

IF CROSSWIND GREATER THAN 20 KNOTS OR THERE IS A TAILWIND.

Maintain FULL FORWARD stick deflection until 80 knots, then slowly ease side stick pressure so as to be at neutral by 100 knots.

When the Thrust levers are in the appropriate **TAKE-OFF** detent, the **PFD/FMA** will indicate that the **SRS** (Speed Reference System) is now selected.

Target is to have take-off thrust set by 40 knots

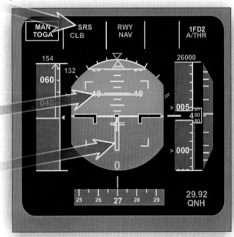

Notice that only the Flight Director pitch bar will be displayed. It is not controlled by the Flight Director at this point but only indicates a fixed 10 degree pitch.

The single green "runway heading" indicator should be displayed.

AFTER
TAKE-OFF THRUST
HAS BEEN SET

CHECK
4 THINGS

1. FLIGHT MODE ANNUNCIATORS .... both pilots confirm proper indications.

- White boxed **THRUST** setting (**MAN** over **TOGA** or **FLX/TEMP**). If you have selected **FLX**, but the **FLEX TEMP** has not been entered in the **MCDU/FMGC**, an **ECAM** warning will occur. A quick solution is to select **TOGA** rather than try to insert a flex temp.

- **SRS _MUST_** be annunciated for the system to be armed.

- **LNAV** selections. If Heading indicator has been pulled, then **HDG** or **RWY** (runway heading) will be the operating heading indication (**GREEN**). otherwise **NAV** will be armed (**BLUE**)

- **BLANK**

- "**1FD2**" indicating flight directors armed. At least one flight director must be armed for the **SRS** to operate. **A/THR** (**BLUE**) indicating the autothrust is armed.

2. EPR SETTINGS .... When the thrust levers are moved to the take-off setting (**FLX** or **TOGA**), that setting is indicated on the upper right of the upper **ECAM**, and the "**WHITE DONUTS**" will move to the desired thrust settings on the engine indicators. As the engines spool up, the thrust indicators should move to match the donuts.

NOTE: *Be aware of the proper target "donut" settings before making the thrust selection.*

3. CALL OUT ABNORMAL SITUATIONS .... The **MEMO** pad on the **UPPER ECAM** will be your target instrument. It will annunciate any abnormal or emergency situation in its computerized brain. However, if you see a situation or indication that you think should be addressed, whether annunciated or not, "**CALL IT OUT**!" This is **THE** place to correct any item that you feel affects the outcome of the take-off.

4. ENG page should automatically replace the **WHEEL p**age on the lower **ECAM.** If it does not, then manually select the **ENG** page using the **ECAM** selector panel.

Note about **T.O. INHIBIT** (**MAGENTA**) indication. This feature is active from the application of take-off power to 1,500 feet or for 2 minutes. It stops some aural warnings, cabin interphone (including emergency calls) and most **ECAM** indications. At 80 knots even more **ECAM messages are inhibited** leaving only a few **VERY CRITICAL** items uninhibited.

published by UNIVERSITY of TEMECULA PRESS, Inc.

THE ROTATION PART OF THE TAKE-OFF
TAKING-OFF to INITIAL CLIMB

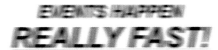

REALLY FAST!

Once the jet starts to move, it will be in a continually accelerating mode and the flow of events will become an overpowering wave unless we "pre-think" and make a plan. Let's discuss what will happen and see if we can come up with a method to deal with the situation.

TRACK CENTERLINE: The airplane may or may not track exactly down the runway. So the first order of business is to make corrections to the airplane's take-off vector that coincide with the confines of the runway.

LOOK "DOWN THE RUNWAY" towards the horizon and make your corrections based on that sight picture.

Push forward on the stick very *gently* and move the pitch indicator (Flight Director **MAY NOT** be displayed yet) to a point just below the horizon indicator on the **PFD**. This will help prevent an undesired early rotation and possible "**TAIL STRIKE**".

   at 80 KTS: Relax any forward pressure so as to be at **NEUTRAL BY 100 KTS.**

at V1: On the **PFD** speed scale, the little "**1**" is our "**GO/NO GO**" speed. It is important in the real world that we are aware of what is happening during the speed buildup to **V1**. Are there warning lights, or fire indications, or engines failing, or ???

> **at VR**: Start an extremely gentle rotation towards our initial pitch attitude of **12.5 to 15 degrees**. Pitch towards **V2+10 kts airspeed**. The rate of rotation should be about 2 to 3 degrees per second. The potential for **TAIL STRIKE** is highest right here.

Initially, **YOU MAY NOT HAVE A FLIGHT DIRECTOR,** but as the airplane rotates and the gear oleo extends, the Flight Director bars will be displayed.

at **12.5 to 15 degrees pitch on the PFD** ... **HOLD THAT SIGHT PICTURE.**
Use every bit of your excess brain power to keep from chasing the Flight Director pitch bar. Stay at 12.5 to 15 degree, wings level.
DO NOT FOLLOW THE F/D PITCH BAR initially!

> Initially, when the thrust levers are placed in the take-off (**SRS**) detent, the pitch bar goes to **10 degrees pitch up**.
> ### *- THE FLIGHT DIRECTOR BARS*
> ### *WILL NOT BE DISPLAYED INITIALLY*.

NOTE:
Leaving **ACCEL** altitude, the pitch bar will move to display either:
- The speed we have preset on the **MCDU PERF/CLIMB** page
  ("green dot"/ 0 flap maneuvering) or
- **250 KTS BELOW 10,000 FEET**.

some TAKEOFF check-ride protocols

> **CAPTAIN'S HAND MUST BE ON THE THRUST LEVERS UNTIL V1 IS ANNOUNCED BY PM (Pilot Monitoring).**
>
> The Captain should be "SPRING-LOADED" to the abort position.

at 80 KNOTS

The **PM** (Pilot Monitoring) calls out **"80 KNOTS, THRUST SET**."
This callout verifies:

- **THRUST is actually set at TOGA/FLX.**

PM *checks the* **UPPER ECAM** *for indications.*

- **AIRSPEED indications have been cross-checked.**

PM *glances at 3 locations to check the* **AIRSPEED**.
Speed tape on both pilots PFD and Standby Airspeed indicator.

- **NO ECAM MEMO or other abnormal indications** ... IF SO "**CALL THEM OUT**".

If there are abnormals ... abandon the take-off, stop the airplane, exit the runway, evaluate the situation. Normally reverse thrust and high speed abort techniques are usually NOT desired nor required.
A "**HOT BRAKES**" situation is normally not experienced in aborts **below 80 knots**.

at V1

The **PM** (Pilot Monitoring) calls out **"V1"** <u>**5 KNOTS BEFORE**</u> reaching the V1 speed.
EXPLANATION: *The ability to stop on the runway is predicated on initiating the abort* **AT or BEFORE** *V1. Aborts after V1 should be avoided. By the time the PM makes the call and the Captain moves his hand ... takes about 5 knots.*

<u>**The Captain's hand should be removed from the thrust levers AT V1**</u>.
The reasons are:

- Reinforces the "**GO**" decision,
- Prevent an instinctive abort above V1.
- Normally, **NEITHER** pilot's hand should be on the thrust levers between **V1** and the **GEAR-UP** call.

Brief discussion: *I think we are all aware of the crew that managed to save an airplane with a last minute abort* **AFTER V1** *when another airplane pulled on the runway in front of them in a foggy situation. Enough said about that, use your head!*

at VR and V2

The **PM** calls out **"VR"** and **"V2"** as those speeds are reached.

LET THE FUN BEGIN!

published by UNIVERSITY of TEMECULA PRESS, Inc.

One of 5

things is about to happen to you !

Let's examine in some detail how the different **TAKE-OFF** scenarios will unfold ... and what we should do in each case.

- **LOW SPEED ABORT**

- **HIGH SPEED ABORT**

- **V1 CUT (Engine fail on runway).**

- **V2 CUT (Engine failure after take-off)**

- **NORMAL TAKE-OFF**

Every flight, every checkride, every take-off, every day the pilot is faced with the same terrifying reality ... things may not go as planned. And you can bet that the Check Captain will be just waiting to make something miserable happen to you. So you simply **MUST BE PREPARED** and have your mind focused, ready to react.

We pilots are like a highly trained athlete ready to spring, prepared for the unexpected, and ready to handle any situation ... aren't we?

YO MAMA!

Let's look at a few of the potential situations, and before we get caught up in trying to invent the wheel while we have our panties in a bunch ... let's make a plan for each situation and be ready to respond crisply and succinctly enough to convince the Check Person that we know what we are doing. It is always embarrassing to thrash around, screaming and shouting and in general looking like you don't know what is going on.

"LOW SPEED ABORT"
Rejecting take-off below 80 knots

Aborting a take-off before reaching 80 Kts is generally considered no big deal. In fact, I can almost guarantee that the Check Captain is going to give you a potential reject situation to see how you respond. I would make the assessment that almost anything could trigger a low speed abort.
*In this speed range, if you are uncertain whether to stop or not ...**STOP!***

THE CAPTAIN IS EXPECTED TO MAKE ALL ABORTS !

 If Captain decides to abort ... She/He should announce **LOUDLY**:
"***I HAVE THE AIRPLANE ... ABORTING!***"
The First Officer (if making the take-off) should respond, and
remove ***ANY CONTROL INPUTS!!!.***

AUTOBRAKE will normally NOT deploy since it only activates above 72 Knots. Use "normal" toe brakes to slow the airplane and exit the runway.

[F/O] Notify **TOWER** or Controlling Agency!
1. Expeditiously state your intention to **ABORT**.
2. State **RUNWAY** and position.
2. Be prepared to request assistance, such as **Fire Department.**

[C,F/O] Treat situation as a landing roll and accomplish routine post landing procedures since the situation is not an emergency nor does it require any irregular handling.

IMPORTANT NOTE:
If the slow speed abort procedures are completed
and a subsequent take-off is planned:
RESET BOTH FLIGHT DIRECTORS.

Generally speaking, a low speed abort will not require abnormal braking ... therefore, it is unlikely that there will be a residual tire temperature problem. Delaying subsequent departure for tire and brake cooling is *probably* not required. *For the record, I would*
monitor the ***ECAM WHEEL*** page and
check the ***REJECTED TAKE-OFF*** cooling chart
*... this tells the check person that you are aware of a potential **HOT BRAKE** problem.*
NOTE: ECAM temperature indications may be slow to respond.

HOWEVER ...
There was some reason that you aborted the take-off. ***DO NOT*** forget to resolve that ambiguity before you start preparations for another take-off.

COMMON PILOT SCREW-UP:

During the checkride, the crew is so relieved and satisfied when they complete a successful abort, that they completely overlook the need to resolve the reason for the abort in the first place. There is a lot going on.

---

published by UNIVERSITY of TEMECULA PRESS, Inc.

"HIGH SPEED ABORT"
Rejecting take-off between 80 knots and V1

The **HIGH SPEED ABORT** is arguably the **MOST DANGEROUS** event in commercial aviation.
The current airline thinking is: "*If it will fly ... continue the take-off.*"
There are exceptions such as FIRE/ENGINE FAILURE before V1.

THE CAPTAIN IS EXPECTED TO MAKE ALL ABORTS !

If Captain decides to abort ... She/He should announce **LOUDLY**:
"*I HAVE THE AIRPLANE ... ABORTING!*"
The First Officer (if making the take-off) should respond, and remove **ANY CONTROL INPUTS!!!**.

Generally speaking, the decision to abort in this speed regime should be made only if the failure involved would impair the ability of the airplane to fly.

CAPTAIN DOES THIS:

[C] Aggressively move thrust levers to FULL REVERSE.
The use of less than maximum reverse is OK.

MONITOR AUTOBRAKE.
The **AUTOBRAKE** will come on at **MAX** (if selected) when:
1. Groundspeed greater than 72 knots, and
2. Thrust Levers command ground spoilers to activate by being pulled to idle.
If autobrake **FAILS** to actuate, apply maximum "toe" braking.

FIRST OFFICER DOES THIS:

[F/O] Notify TOWER
1. Expeditiously state your intention to ABORT.
2. State **RUNWAY** and position.
2. Be prepared to request assistance, such as Fire Department.
Make **PA** to **Flight Attendants/PAX "REMAIN SEATED"**. If the cockpit fails to provide direction and there is no **PA** announcement made, you can expect the **F/A** to initiate an evacuation on their own initiative..

Maintenance action required when:
1. **AUTOBRAKES or MAXIMUM MANUAL** braking used.
2. **TEMP** between **TWO BRAKES ON SAME GEAR** is greater that **150°C**.
3. **TEMPERATURE** of one of those two brakes is **>or= 600°C or <= 60°C**.
4. **ANY BRAKE** temperature exceeds **900°C (A319, A320); 800°C (A321)**.

If **BRAKES HOT** ECAM message remains after parking ... request that **ALL** gear be chocked so that brakes can be released. The Check Captain will expect you to
CONSULT THE BRAKE COOLING TIME TABLES.

Here is "my" V1 cut profile. It is not put forth as an official or SOP concept. It is just my idea and might work for you.

"V1 CUT"
Engine Failure after V1
Airplane on the ground

Once you have passed V1 airspeed, the Captain's hand should been removed from the thrust levers. When indication of an "**ENGINE FAILURE**" is observed, the pilot noting the failure says; "**ENGINE FAILURE**."

At time of engine failure, between **V1** and **V2**; here are the **PFD** indications.

BETA TARGET:
Sideslip index changes to "**BLUE**" when:
- **CONF 1,2, or 3** selected, *AND*
- **ANY** engine EPR exceeds **1.25**, *AND*
- Difference of **EPRs > .25**

GROUND ROLL COMMAND BAR:
Flight Director may not be visible, but the ground roll command bar will provide lateral guidance based on"**RUNWAY TRACK**" memorized by **FMGS** before engine failure. Continue to maintain visual tracking (look at far end of the runway) as long as possible.

TOGA = If taking off in **FLEX**, consider pushing thrust levers to **TOGA**.
(*TOGA not required as a/c is certificated SE FLEX*).
TALK = **PM** to **TOWER**: "**ENGINE FAILURE**"
TURN if required by **EOSID** procedure or "**T**" procedure turn, tell **TOWER**.
TRIM = Rudder takes about 20 seconds (A320), 30 seconds (A319).

4-Ts
TOGA
TALK
TURN
TRIM

@ positive climb

PITCH 12.5 degrees
GEAR UP
CENTER BETA target

Autopilot OK:
Above 100 feet;
IF
- In **TRIM**, and
- **SRS** on FMA

Speed **V2 or greater**

There is no requirement to rotate "exactly" at **VR**.
TIP! Keep nose wheel grounded for a few knots beyond **VR** if you need it.

KEEP NOSEWHEEL GROUNDED until at least **VR**.

NOTE: *MAX TIRE SPEED* 195 Kts.

PFD indications:
MAN
FLX 42
SRS CLB | RWY
1FD2
A/THR
180 | 153
160
140
120
100
10 — 10
29.92 QNH
25 26 27 28 29

published by UNIVERSITY of TEMECULA PRESS, Inc.

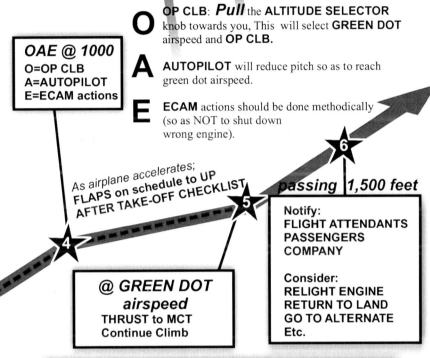

O **OP CLB**: *Pull* the **ALTITUDE SELECTOR** knob towards you, This will select **GREEN DOT** airspeed and **OP CLB**.

A **AUTOPILOT** will reduce pitch so as to reach green dot airspeed.

E **ECAM** actions should be done methodically (so as NOT to shut down wrong engine).

OAE @ 1000
O=OP CLB
A=AUTOPILOT
E=ECAM actions

As airplane accelerates;
FLAPS on schedule to UP
AFTER TAKE-OFF CHECKLIST,

passing 1,500 feet

Notify:
FLIGHT ATTENDANTS
PASSENGERS
COMPANY

Consider:
RELIGHT ENGINE
RETURN TO LAND
GO TO ALTERNATE
Etc.

@ GREEN DOT
airspeed
THRUST to MCT
Continue Climb

READ THIS:
Select **MCT** (Max Continuous Thrust) on "good" engine:
NOTE: If **FLEX** was used for take-off, to select **MCT** you **MUST**:
    1. Move thrust lever from **FLX** to **TOGA**, and then
    2. Move thrust lever back to **MCT**.
If you **DO NOT** go to **TOGA** first, you will remain in **FLX**.

At airspeeds less than **GREEN DOT,** bank angles are limited to 15°. I have indicated that with a dashed line.
- - - - - - - - - - - - -
After 500 feet, when the Flight Director or autopilot is on, bank angle limited to "commanded" bank angle.

Terrain clearance is **ONLY** ensured by climbing to 1,500 AFE while tracking the extended **RUNWAY CENTERLINE**.

"V1 CUT" bad techniques and stupid screw-ups.

Arguably, the most busted event on the checkride is the **V1-CUT**! It is indeed a challenging and confusing event and demands that the pilot use his pilot bag of skills to the fullest. It involves thinking and understanding as well as the ability to actually fly the airplane using your hands ... it is a dreaded and feared event. But let me guide you through the process and see if we can conquer the beast. Here is my list of ...

THE BIG *5* V1-CUT SCREW-UPS

Although by no means all the ways a clever and determined pilot can screw up.

Presented in the order of their appearance ... drum roll please.

SCREW-UP # 1 ... ABORTS AFTER V1.

As the airplane goes hurtling down the simulator runway, once you have taken your hands off the thrust levers 5 seconds before V1 ... **DO NOT REACH UP AND PULL THE THRUST LEVERS BACK**. Do not attempt to abort the take-off at or after **V1** ... at this point (**V1**) you should visualize yourself as "committed to fly."

DISCUSSION: *Attempts to abort after V1 are always an improper response in the sim. I realize, however, that in the real world there have been "airplane saves" by alert crews who have aborted after V1 to avoid disastrous situations. However, an abort after V1 is not something you want to be talking about in the debrief after a simulator session.*

SCREW-UP # 2 ... PUSHES WRONG RUDDER.

Even though the nosewheel of the airplane is on the ground, the most important control input is from the **RUDDERS**. The rudder is very effective on this airplane and it really isn't necessary to know which engine has failed. All you have to do is keep the nose of the airplane headed down the runway. You don't want to get "walking" the rudders and the airplane wallowing from one side to the other as you try to figure out which rudder to push. It should be intuitive. **DO NOT THINK ABOUT WHICH LEG TO PUSH** ... just ease in the rudder that makes the nose go where you want.
In a catastrophic engine failure, there is no question about which rudder to push, and it will take almost full extension to control the heading. Push the rudder so that the nose of the jet goes in the direction you want. Use enough input to make the correction you want, then "lock" your leg to everything but teensy-tiny corrections.

TIP! *Right rudder makes the nose go right, and left rudder makes the nose go left.*

OBSERVATION: For some reason, pilots have gouges such as "working foot - working engine", or they try to figure out by looking at the engine gauges which rudder to push. I have actually observed some guys during the sim-ride using the 50-50 technique (they push one rudder knowing they have a 50% chance of being wrong). Pretty ugly ... and 50% of the time the airplane (Simulator) exits the runway.

published by UNIVERSITY of TEMECULA PRESS, Inc.

SCREW-UP # 3 ... ROTATES BEFORE VR.

I can almost guarantee that the first time the other pilot screams "ENGINE FAILURE" your first instinct will be to ease back on the stick. If you do that and the nosewheel loses its grip, the jet will head off the runway and across the airport grass like a scared rabbit.

DO NOT ROTATE WHEN THE OTHER PILOT YELLS ENGINE FAILURE.

It is my opinion that there should actually be a slight downward pressure on the nosewheel to aid in controlling the tendency of the airplane to swerve off the runway. I also advocate keeping the nosewheel on the runway for a few seconds after **VR**. There is no requirement to initiate rotation right at **VR**, and a few seconds beyond that actually helps in the evolution.

DISCUSSION: Maximum tire speed is 195 Knots. You can stay in contact with the runway until reaching that limit. The only requirement is that you get airborne before the end of the runway passes under the nose.

SCREW-UP # 4 ... POOR ROTATION TECHNIQUE.

When you initiate the rotation, the airplane will hesitate slightly at about 8 to 10 degrees. It does this because the airflow to the elevators is disturbed by the wings. Some awareness on your part is required to "pull" the nose through the burble and then return immediately to normal rotation pressures.
You are aiming for about 2 to 3 degrees per second.

1. If you rotate too aggressively, the tail will drag the runway. The tail can strike the runway even though the main landing gear are actually in the air.
A TAIL STRIKE IS NOT GOOD!
2. If you fail to complete the rotation to 12.5 degrees, the airplane will fly "more or less" level at 8 to 10 degrees. This can result in contact with Mother Earth off the end of the runway. This is called Controlled Flight Into Terrain and
CFIT IS NOT GOOD!
3. Keeping the back pressure in for too long, and exceeding 12.5 degrees will result in a loss of airspeed, the rudder losing effectiveness, the nose of the airplane slewing uncontrollably into the "bad" engine, you will stall and crash.
A STALL AND CRASH IS NOT GOOD!

SCREW-UP # 5 ... NO PREPARED PROCEDURE.

Probably the most pitiful thing to observe is some pilot trying to invent the wheel as the airplane is charging down the runway with one engine spooling down. Without a plan, without a set of ideas already set in his mind, the hapless airplane driver is along for the ride. Trying to accomplish this procedure without a methodically thought out plan and a series of specific milestones is simply checkride suicide.

MAKE A PLAN BEFORE YOU FLY!

I have presented my ideas about what a plan "could" look like, but it is up to you to sit down and go through the steps to create a plan that works for you. Once you have that plan, you will have to go over it again and again to firmly set the details in your memory. ...and then go over it some more until you are ready to puke. I GUARANTEE that your brain will turn to putty the first time you are confronted with this situation and you will have little or no brainpower left over to improvise.

"V2 CUT"
Engine Failure after Airplane Off Ground,
Single Engine approach, or Engine Fails during go-around.

RULE NUMBER 1 is *FLY THE AIRPLANE* !

While this situation is generally depicted as happening right after take-off, it also could occur on a **MISSED APPROACH**. It could be the result of the Check Captain screwing up (selecting the engine failure too late). All this doesn't matter. You will be expected to fly the airplane and avoid contact with the earth.

LOWER NOSE: Make your initial target pitch 12.5 degrees. **DO NOT** follow the **PITCH BAR** on the **FLIGHT DIRECTOR** initially. If **SRS** is **NOT** displayed, maintain speed **NO LOWER** than **V2**.

LEVEL WINGS: Use the Flight Director **ROLL** indicator for guidance.

CENTER BETA TARGET: Use the **RUDDER** to center the **BLUE** "beta target" index on the bottom of the yaw indicator (Sailboat).

TRIM: The **RUDDER** to maintain the "beta target" index centered.

4-Ts
TOGA
TALK
TURN
TRIM

TOGA = If taking off in **FLEX**, consider **TOGA**.
(TOGA not required as a/c is certificated SE FLEX).
TALK = PM to **TOWER**: "*ENGINE FAILURE*"
TURN if required by **EOSID** or "T" procedure turn, tell **TOWER**.
TRIM = RUDDER takes about
20 seconds (A320), 30 seconds (A319).

If GO-AROUND ... TOGA

PITCH 12.5 degrees
@ POSITIVE CLIMB
GEAR UP
CENTER BETA target

Auto-pilot OK:
Above 100 feet;
IF
- In **TRIM**, and
- **SRS** on **FMA**

Speed **V2** or greater

Auto-pilot OK:
Above 100 feet; IF
- In **TRIM**, and
- **SRS** on FMA

published by UNIVERSITY of TEMECULA PRESS, Inc.

OP CLB: *Pull* the **ALTITUDE SELECTOR** knob towards you, This will select **GREEN DOT** airspeed and **OP CLB**.

O

OAE @ 1000
O=OP CLB
A=AUTOPILOT
E=ECAM actions

A **AUTOPILOT** will reduce pitch so as to reach green dot airspeed.

E **ECAM** actions should be done methodically (so as NOT to shut down wrong engine).

As airplane accelerates;
FLAPS on schedule to UP
AFTER TAKE-OFF CHECKLIST

passing 1,500 feet

Notify:
FLIGHT ATTENDANTS
PASSENGERS
COMPANY

Consider:
RELIGHT ENGINE
RETURN TO LAND
GO TO ALTERNATE
Etc.

@ GREEN DOT
airspeed
THRUST to MCT
Continue Climb

READ THIS:

Select **MCT** (Max Continuous Thrust) on "good" engine:
NOTE: If **FLEX** was used for take-off, to select **MCT** you **MUST**:
  1. Move thrust lever from **FLX** to **TOGA**, and then
  2. Move thrust lever back to **MCT**.
If you **DO NOT** go to **TOGA** first, you will remain in **FLX**.

At airspeeds less than **GREEN DOT**, bank angles are limited to 15°. I have indicated that with a dashed line.

- - - - - - - - - - - -

After 500 feet, when the Flight Director or autopilot is on, bank angle limited to "commanded" bank angle.

Terrain clearance is **ONLY** ensured by climbing to 1,500 AFE while tracking the extended **RUNWAY CENTERLINE**.

SPECIAL CASE:
ENGINE FIRE ON TAKE-OFF

A potential "Checkride from HELL" event. If you get an engine fire warning after V1, the Check Pilot will be looking for you to continue the initial part of the take-off profile **WITHOUT SHUTTING DOWN THE ENGINE**. It is too easy to get involved with shutting off the engine at a low altitude ... and while becoming preoccupied with the shutdown and get slow, or worse yet - **FLY INTO THE GROUND**.

In this situation, you may have a fire warning, BUT you are not single engine yet ... and you can pick your spot. It is a judgement call on your part and I am not trying to set SOP, but normally, waiting until out of about 500 feet before shutting down the engine and fighting the fire is desirable.

REMINDER:

You can do a perfect engine shutdown procedure, but if you **CFIT** (Controlled Flight Into Terrain) you will be trying to explain the event in the debrief while scheduling your recheck.

Once you shut 'er down, you can revert to **EOSID** routing and Single Engine procedures and checklists.

This is a Captain to Captain discussion about aborting after V1. I think we have all heard about the courageous crew that aborted after V1 to avoid contact with another airplane that had taxied onto the runway in the fog ... and they got stopped and saved the day. Heroes no doubt.

And there is not a pilot among us that wouldn't try to do the same thing in that situation ... but late aborts are probably the **MOST DANGEROUS EVENT IN AVIATION**. You probably do not want to be trying to explain your late abort decision to the Check Airman in the debrief. Here is the official position of one major air carrier:

WARNING:
"In the HIGH SPEED REGIME, especially at speeds near V1, a decision to reject should NOT be based on the perceived ability that the airplane can be stopped. The decision to reject should be made ONLY if the failure involved would impair the ability of the airplane to be safely flown."

published by UNIVERSITY of TEMECULA PRESS, Inc.

"NORMAL TAKE-OFF"

One thing you can expect on your checkride is a "normal take-off". Unfortunately, the check guy isn't going to tell you which of the many flight profiles you are going to fly is the "normal" one. Here is a simple profile that represents a

STANDARD NOISE ABATEMENT TAKE-OFF.

Cruise Altitude

PUSH SPD selector on FCU.

3,000 Feet AFE

250 Knots to 10,000 Feet
ECON above 10,000 Feet

Green Dot airspeed

800 Feet AFE

Thrust Levers to "CL" detent.
Retract flaps on schedule.
'After Take-off Checklist"

Set THR RED/ACC altitude
800/800 AFE on PERF page.

HDG or NAV

V2 + 10 Knots

Manually advance thrust
levers to 1.05 EPR

Advance thrust levers to
TOGA/FLX detent.

Autopilot "ON".
@ 100 feet if SRS annunciated,
@ 500 feet, if no SRS.

Call out FMAs (TOGA or
FLX/TEMP)

Target pitch ... 15 degrees.
@ "positive climb" ... "GEAR UP".

"80 Knots, Thrust set"
"V1, VR, V2"

ROTATION technique

The Pilot Flying will rotate the airplane smoothly and gently. The movements are barely perceptible and should produce about $2°$ to $3°$ per second of nose vertical pitch change. You want to target $12.5°$ (single engine) to about $15°$ up. You want to slowly arrive at the SRS pitch command on the PFD.

TAIL-STRIKE

11.5° *PITCH* JET HITS EARTH
(13.5 degrees for the A319)

WINGTIP or ENGINE POD SCRAPE

Particularly in a gusty crosswind, there may be a tendency to over-control the ailerons as the airplane comes un-stuck and begins flying. It is possible to "Hit or drag a pod or a wingtip" since the engine is a mere 21 inches above the runway surface.

at 16° ROLL JET HITS EARTH

CROSSWIND

TAKE-OFF LIMITS

Demonstrated maximum with flight controls in either normal or direct law with or without yaw damper.

BRAKING ACTION: GOOD	A320/A319
CROSSWIND	29 KNOTS
CROSSWIND with GUSTS	38 KNOTS
TAILWIND	15 / 10 KNOTS

REPORTED BRAKING ACTION	ALL MODELS
FAIR/MEDIUM	25 KNOTS
POOR	15 KNOTS
NIL/UNRELIABLE	OPERATIONS NOT RECOMMENDED

As the airplane is accelerating, the situation is very fluid and several factors are changing. For one:

- **RUDDER** actuated **NOSEWHEEL** steering has more effect at lower airspeed. Using the rudder pedals, at 40 knots the input is +/- $6°$ and gradually diminishes until at 130 knots there is $0°$ input to the nosewheel steering from the rudders.

"POSITIVE CLIMB"

Either the Pilot Monitoring (**PM**) or the Pilot Flying (**PF**) will call out; "**POSITIVE CLIMB**," when the airplane indicates that it has physically left the earth. That requires a check of **BOTH** the **IVSI** on the right side of the **PFD** instrument, **AND** a check of the barometric (Standby) **ALTIMETER**.

"GEAR UP"

The Pilot Flying (**PF**) will call out; "**GEAR UP**," and the Pilot Monitoring (**PM**) will respond "**GEAR UP**" and then place the gear handle to the **UP** position.

NOTE: Selecting the **LANDING GEAR** handle **UP** only actuates an electrical switch and it **is NOT** directly tied to any cable or mechanical device. There are two **LGCIU** (Landing Gear Control and Interface Units) that monitor proximity sensors and that provides information for the **ECAM** and other gear indicators.

at 260 KNOTS

When airspeed below 260 Knots, selecting the gear **UP** or **DOWN** will perform all the normal functions of the gear and gear doors.
When airspeed greater than 260 Knots, a **HYDRAULIC SAFETY VALVE** cuts off any fluid to the gear actuation mechanism.

NORMAL RETRACTION

GEAR INDICATIONS:
- Automatic braking is applied to main gear.
- Landing gear locked in Wheel Wells **MECHANICALLY**.

The gear are "**DOWN AND LOCKED**"

The gear are "**UNLOCKED**" or "**IN TRANSIT**"

No indication if the gear are "**LOCKED UP**"

The "**WHEEL SYNOPTIC - LOWER ECAM**" showing the gear door positions as locked. The lack of a "wheel" depiction indicates that the **GEAR** is **LOCKED UP**.

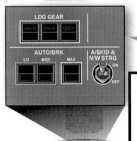

YEAH, BUT ARE THE GEAR UP?
If there is **NO GEAR INDICATION** on either the **LANDING GEAR PANEL** or the **ECAM WHEEL** synoptic page indications, then we are to assume that the **GEAR** are **UP** and **LOCKED**.

After raising the **GEAR HANDLE**
DISARM the GROUND SPOILERS.

Discussion about engaging **THE AUTOPILOT**.

If **SRS** is annunciated, the autopilot may be engaged when above **100 Feet.**
If **SRS NOT** annunciated,
The autopilot may not be engaged until passing **500 Feet.**

Either pilot may engage the auto-pilot. I personally think it is better to have **BOTH** pilots involved, but during periods of high task loading, it sometimes make sense for the **PF** to engage the autopilot.

It is **SOP** for the **PF** (Pilot Flying) to verify engagement by observing the **FMA** annunciation on the **PFD**. Just because the little light goes on in the FCU switch does not mean that the auto-pilot is engaged.

NOTE: *On your checkride, the Check Captain may ask you if your autopilot is engaged, and she is expecting you to reference the **PFD FMA**, not the **FCU**.*

How to turn on **THE AUTOPILOT**.

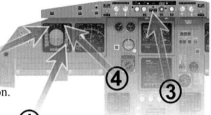

1.Check altitude
2. If above 100 feet but below 500 feet,
  check the **PFD FMA** for **SRS** annunciation.
3. Depress the **AP 1** button on the **FCU**.
4. Verify autopilot engaged on the **PFD FMA**.

There are basically TWO ways to control the heading of the jet:
  1. **PULL** the **HDG/TRK** selector button on the **FCU** and
    Manually select a heading (such as Runway heading), or
  2. **PUSH** the **HDG/TRK** selector on the **FCU** to select
    NAV mode and fly the **MCDU/FMGC** defined pathway.

It is my opinion that on a checkride, **ALWAYS** consider selecting the **RWY** or **HDG** and attempt to track outbound on the extended centerline since we are always expecting an engine failure. This will give us obstacle clearance up to 1,500 feet.

BIG PROBLEM.

If the first waypoint or fix is to the side of the extended runway centerline, and you have elected to fly a "**NAV**" mode for the **LNAV** or Lateral Navigation, then when you select the autopilot **ON**, *the airplane will turn immediately towards that initial fix*. If there are obstacles such as the tower in your projected departure path, then there is a possibility that the airplane my pass over, in the near vicinity of, or through the tower. Not a good thing. It is, therefore, generally considered "**GOOD CAPTAIN PRACTICE**" to limit all significant turns to **400 feet AGL and above,** particularly in restricted visibility situations.

SITUATIONAL AWARENESS

at 30 FEET

Once airborne, the selected heading mode will engage at 30 feet **AGL**.
If we hadn't set anything in the **FCU**, it will default to **NAV**.
If we had selected a heading, then that would be visible on the **FCU**.
If we had "pulled" the selector, then **RWY TRK** would be the operative heading.

at ACCEL or ALT*

SRS is (normally) the operating pitch mode up to the acceleration altitude that is set in the **PERF** page. At this point, the **FMGC** transitions to the **CLIMB PHASE** and the pitch mode target speed shifts to

- Climb speed programmed by the pilot in the **CLB PERF** page
  (usually **GREEN DOT** speed), or
- 250 Knots below 10,000 Feet **AGL**.

at "flashing" LVR CLB on the FMA

1. Look at speed trend arrow on the **PFD** and it should be indicating an acceleration. Reduce the pitch slightly if necessary.

2. Monitor the **UPPER ECAM** for the **THRUST** indication.
   It should be **TOGA** or **FLX**.

3. Pull the **THRUST LEVERS** back until **CL** is the indicated operating mode. The thrust levers should be **in the CL detent** on the thrust lever quadrant. Once in this detent, the application of thrust is automatically controlled. The thrust levers no longer physically move, but the thrust will be constantly changing to accommodate the requirements of automated flight and to maintain the airspeed and pitch commands from the **MCDU/FMGC** (computer).
It is pure magic.

> *The thrust levers will remain in the **CL** detent for the remainder of the flight until they are retarded for landing.*

COMMENT:

This is a truly unique capability ... and fantastic. The pilots are not required to adjust the thrust levers manually but may make speed and pitch commands using only the **FCU** and **MCDU/FMGC** which will result in the thrust responding automatically. Once you see this system in action, you will find it becomes second nature to depend on it and you quickly become used to it. It is virtually foolproof.

BUT ... how can a pilot screw it up?

wOW!

ONE OF THE "*BIG TEN*" PILOT SCREW-UPs

BIG MONSTER PROBLEM.

GOOF UP PART # 1.

When responding to the flashing "**LVR CLB**" on the **PFD**, if the thrust levers are inadvertently retarded back *beyond* the CL detent, the engines will spool down accordingly ... and if pulled into the IDLE range, they will spool down all the way to idle. ***The A/THR will disconnect***.

GOOF UP PART # 2.

If you push the thrust levers back towards the **CL** detent, even though **CL** may be the annunciated thrust lever setting, the thrust will remain in manual control because the **A/THR** is deselected..
This is ***NOT A GOOD THING***.
To "reengage" the automated "**CL**" mode, you must rearm the **A/THR** mode. Either push the thrust levers forward beyond the **CL** detent into the engagement zone, and then retard back to the **CL** detent.
Or reselect **A/THR** on the **FCU** with the thrust levers in the **CL** position.

GOOF UP PART # 3.

If you do not do this, and do not recognize that the thrust is in manual ... even with **CL** annunciated ... the airspeed will possibly decay into the "**RED BRICKS**" and you will get an **A.FLOOR** annunciation and the thrust will go to **TOGA LOCK**.
Or ... it could generate an overspeed situation and the airplane's integrity could be compromised. Either way, that will pretty much be the end of your checkride.

Here is the way the simulator problem can develop:

1. After take-off, you accept a low altitude level off.
2. With the thrust levers set at **TOGA/FLX**, the airspeed increases **VERY** rapidly.
3. Airspeed approaches **Vmax**, and
4. Pilot manually retards the thrust levers to **IDLE**.
    Whoops! BIG MISTAKE!!!
5. Airspeed diminishes to **Vmin** (the Red Bricks) and **A.FLOOR** is annunciated.
6. Thrust goes to **TOGA LK** with thrust levers physically in idle position.
7. Airspeed increases to **Vmax**.
8. Pilot becomes confused and doesn't know what to do.
9. Airspeed overspeeds.
10. Airplane comes apart, pilot busts checkride.

SITUATIONAL AWARENESS

published by UNIVERSITY of TEMECULA PRESS, Inc.

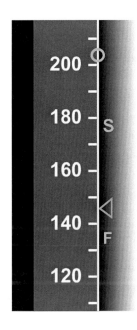

RAISING THE FLAPS

The Pilot Flying (**PF**) calls for the flaps using the airspeed cues on the **PFD**. Once the airspeed is greater than:
- "**F**" speed, the **PF** may call for "**FLAPS 1**,"
- "**S**" speed, the **PF** may call for "**FLAPS UP**."

NOTE:

"**F**" speed is displayed only if the take-off is made with the flaps in **configuration 2 or 3**.

Once the flaps have fully retracted, the **ECAM ENG** page is automatically replaced with the **ECAM CRUISE** page.

AFTER TAKE-OFF CHECKLIST

Pilot Monitoring (**PM**) will complete the After Take-off Checklist without response.

AFTER TAKE-OFF CHECKLIST ..... COMPLETE

(To be checked ALOUD by the Pilot Monitoring)

Landing Gear.. UP
Flaps .... UP
ECAM memo .... Checked

at 3,000 Feet AFE (*Above Field Elevation*)
SELECT MANAGED SPEED

Depending on whether you are restricted to a specific airspeed or not (possibly in Class "B" airspace) it is generally accepted that you may accelerate to 250 Knots below 10,000 feet. 10,000 feet and above you will (probably) be cleared to accelerate to your desired climb airspeed (normally **ECON**).

The **MCDU/FMGC** has already been programmed for all this, so all you have to do is select "**MANAGED**" airspeed by **PUSHING the SPD knob on the FCU**.

The target airspeed pointer will turn to **MAGENTA** and slew to the appropriate setting.

LOUSY WEATHER OPS during
CLIMB PHASE

If no icing forecast is but encountered during the flight, notify the **ATC** controller, of course, and don't forget to send an **ACARS** message to the Dispatcher

USE OF ENGINE ANTI-ICE in CLIMB and CRUISE

Engine anti-ice **MUST** be used during **CLIMB and CRUISE** in icing conditions *EXCEPT* when the temperatures are below -40°C SAT.

I would mention this now for future reference that in the descent, when in icing conditions, the engine anti-ice *MUST BE ON* prior to and during long descents *EVEN IF* the temperature is below **-40° C/F SAT** (Static Air Temperature).

CAUTION

DO NOT DELAY the use of engine anti-ice until ice buildup is visible from the cockpit. *SEVERE* engine damage or flame-out can result.

ENGINE VIBRATION concerns

If an increase in vibration occurs due to icing, here is what should happen. The engine fan section should automatically shed the ice and the vibration should decrease. Normally, **OK** to continue.
BUT
if the vibration does **NOT** decrease,
go to the flight manual for guidance and procedures.

WING ANTI-ICE guidelines

Ice accumulation on the visual ice indicator, cockpit window frame, windshield center post, or on the wiper arm indicates structural icing and the need for wing anti-ice.

There are two ways to use the wing anti-ice system:
- as a de-icing system. This provides
    the cleanest airfoil, least run-back, and least thrust and fuel penalty.
- as an anti-icing. Use this method
    when in extended operations in icing conditions such as holding.

WARNING

The Deicing and Anti-icing equipment **IS NOT** intended to permit extended operations in other than **LIGHT ICING**. If icing conditions of greater than **LIGHT** are encountered or expected to develop ...

EXIT THE AREA IMMEDIATELY!

Prolonged operations in **ICING CONDITIONS GREAT THAN LIGHT** are appropriate *ONLY IN AN EMERGENCY SITUATION*.

---

published by UNIVERSITY of TEMECULA PRESS, Inc.

CLIMB PHASE

MEMORY REFRESHER:

The **CLIMB PHASE** begins when the airplane climbs through the **ACCEL ALT** that we had selected on the **MCDU/FMGC**. The **CLIMB PHASE** terminates **ONLY** when the airplane *REACHES* the **CRUISE ALT** we had selected on the **MCDU/FMGC**. Intermediate "**CLEARED TO**" altitudes that we select on the **FCU DO NOT** satisfy the **FMGC** (computer brains) that we have reached **CRUISE PHASE** unless that altitude coincides with the cruise altitude selected in the **MCDU**.

BIG PROBLEM!
BUSTING YOUR ALTITUDE

During the entire time that you will be airborne, you will constantly be receiving altitude changes. Either they come from **ATC** or are printed on the **SID/STAR** and approach charts. There are actually **TWO** problems in this situation.

1 - Setting the correct altitude, and
2 - Ensuring the altitude remains correctly set during the selection of the vertical mode.

This is strictly technique and not necessarily SOP, but try this. When an altitude change is received,

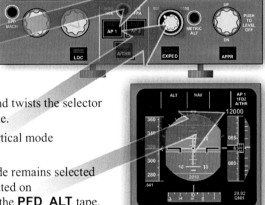

1. The **PF** points at the **FCU** altitude window and reads back the **CLEARED TO** altitude.

2. The **PM** repeats the altitude and twists the selector to set that **CLEARED TO** altitude.

3. The **PF** selects the desired vertical mode (push or pull the knob) and,

4. Confirms that the target altitude remains selected by reference to the altitude indicated on the top (or bottom if descent) of the **PFD ALT** tape.

Discussion: Since they started employing the automated systems, altitude excursions have greatly diminished ... *BUT*, the problem still persists. The solution seems to be in getting **BOTH** pilots involved in the setting the new cleared to altitude. It may seem redundant and unimportant, but I suggest that you make "**SOME**" routine a habit pattern. Especially during high task loading situations, specifically the approach part of the flight.

SITUATIONAL AWARENESS

LIGHTS (before 250 Kts)

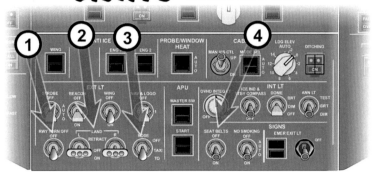

1. LANDING LIGHT SWITCHES .... **RETRACT** before **250 kts** (suggested).
When to turn out the lights is largely a matter of pilot preference and conditions. However, the **LANDING LIGHT SWITCHES** should be retracted **BEFORE** reaching **250 kts**. The maximum retraction/extension speed limit of the landing lights is Vmo, 350 kts, but they create some noticeable vibration effects above 250 kts ... and that "suggests" a speed restriction be observed for passenger comfort.

2. RUNWAY TURNOFF LIGHT SWITCH .... **OFF.**

3. NOSE LIGHT SWITCH .... **OFF.**
This switch controls both the taxi and take-off light. When the nose gear is retracted, both lights automatically shut off.

4. SEAT BELT SIGNS .... **OFF (at Captain's discretion).**
Normally this is shut down as soon as flight conditions permit. This will allow the Flight Attendants to conduct their in-flight duties.

PASSING TRANSITION ALTITUDE
(In the US, this is always 18,000 Feet)

1. Both pilots set altimeters to **STD** (Pull the **EFIS** control panel **BARO** switch).

2. Captain sets the **STANDBY ALTIMETER to 29.92 in Hg/1013 hPa**. You do that using the knob on the instrument and observing the window in the display.

HOW CAN A PILOT SCREW THIS UP???
Sometimes, if a **DESTINATION** altimeter setting is known, it can be preselected on the instrument so that it can be easily retrieved during the approach phase. **BIG PROBLEM** if you forget to select **STD**.
You will BUST YOUR ALTITUDE!!! Really ugly.
This occurs with alarming frequency, so:
"Pilots are not allowed to preset the destination altimeter setting *UNDER* the airplane is in **ALT CRZ** or at selected cruise altitude."

---

published by UNIVERSITY of TEMECULA PRESS, Inc.

PASSING **18,000 Feet**

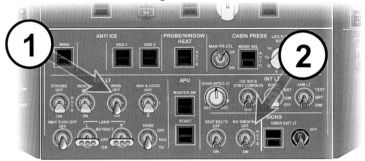

1. [Captain] Turn the
WING LIGHTS switch ..... **OFF**

2. [PM] **NO SMOKING** SIGN
..... cycle **AUTO** then back to **ON**.
If the flight is going to cruise
below 18,000 Feet, then cycle it when
you are level at the cruise altitude. The
idea is to activate the "chime" to signal
the Flight Attendants that the
"**STERILE COCKPIT**" is no longer in
effect. It has nothing to do with smoking.

3. [Captain] "Verify" **APU** .... **OFF**

The official technique for "verifying" that the
APU is **OFF**: select the **ECAM APU** page.
Look at the "**N**" to see if it is "turning", and
look at the "**EGT**" to see if it is "burning".
The **BLEED AIR** switch is programmed to
close when the **APU** shuts down without
action from the pilot.
If you see the bleed air switch indication
"**OPEN**" with the **APU** not running, then
further investigation is in order.

> *You do NOT want to be airborne*
> *with the APU off and the*
> *APU BLEED AIR switch OPEN*
> *simultaneously.*

---

4. [PM] **MANUALLY TUNED** navaids.
Go to the **RADIO NAV** page of the **MCDU**
and clear any manually tuned navaids;
unless, of course, they are being used ....
DUH!
To clear them, use the **CLR** key.

If the radio frequency has been
"**MANUALLY**" tuned, **LS** (line select) **CLR**
to the frequency line will return to the
AUTO-TUNE navaid from the database.

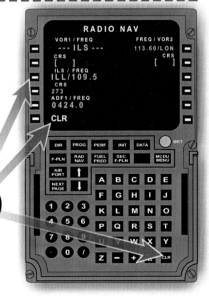

DOING THE CLIMB

The autoflight will initially climb at 250 Knots airspeed unless MCDU/FMGC was set up with another airspeed such as GREEN DOT airspeed) until reaching 10,000 feet MSL, where the nose will pitch over and the airplane will accelerate to ECON climb airspeed (Somewhere around 280 - 300 Knots).

INTERMEDIATE LEVEL OFF (ALT)
versus
CRUISE ALTITUDE (ALT CRZ)

Once the airplane reaches a target altitude we have set on the **FCU**; look at the **PFD** (Primary Flight Display) . Across the top is the **FMA**, and the second annunciation from the left should read "**ALT.**" Once **ALT** (or **ALT CRZ**) is annunciated, we are **OK** to preset another **FCU** target altitude in preparation for an anticipated descent or climb, and the airplane will remain at that altitude.

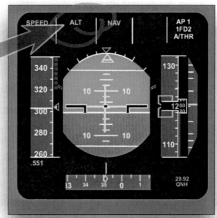

Look at the **ND** (Navigation Display) . The projected point on the green route line depicted by a bent **ARROW** (referred to as a "Hockey Stick) is the point where the airplane will reach the cruise altitude that has been preselected on the **PROG** page (FL260 in our example). Once the jet reaches this point in the route, it should be at the point where it will capture the ALTITUDE, annunciating **ALT CRZ** on the **PFD**, and enter the cruise phase.

Once **ALT** or **ALT CRZ** is annunciated, even with a different target altitude set in the **FCU** display, the airplane will remain at altitude, waiting for the signal to descend. You may preselect higher or lower altitudes when the **PFD FMA** is indicating **ALT***, **ALT**, or **ALT CRZ** and the airplane will remain at altitude, waiting patiently for your command.

DO NOT PUSH OR PULL THE ALTITUDE SELECTOR UNTIL READY TO CHANGE ALTITUDE.

published by UNIVERSITY of TEMECULA PRESS, Inc.

ONE OF THE *"BIG 10"* PILOT SCREW-UPs

Climb phase is initiated when the airplane climbs through the **ACCEL** altitude and continues until the airplane "captures" the **CRUISE** altitude that was displayed on the **PROG** page during the **MCDU** preflight setup. If the airplane is allowed to climb all the way to the planned cruise altitude, the **MCDU PROG** page will automatically shift to **ECON CRZ** page and the jet will then be in the **CRUISE** phase.

HOWEVER ...

What if the airplane does not reach the planned cruise altitude set in the **MCDU**? If the jet reaches an **FCU** selected target altitude that is **BELOW** the planned **MCDU PROG** page altitude, then even though **ALT** will be annunciated in the **PFD**, the flight algorithm will still remain in **CLIMB** phase. You will still be operating in **CLIMB PHASE**. This is *NOT GOOD*!

There is a simple way to resolve the situation, it is called re-cruising. Here is what you do:

HOW TO RE-CRUISE IN CLIMB:

A simple solution to this problem is to reset the airplane's actual altitude on the **MCDU PROG page** to create a "new" cruise altitude. You access the proper page by selecting the **PROG PAGE** key on the **MCDU** and the **XXX CRZ** page will be displayed. Type the new cuise altitude to the scratchpad and line select it to **LSK 1L**.

Once the new altitude is substituted for the "old" one, the airplane will then re-transition to a new **CRUISE PHASE**. This is called "**RE-CRUISING**".

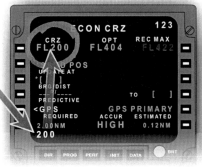

EXAMPLE: *Say you have initially set FL260 (26,000 feet) in the **MCDU** as your planned cruise altitude, but during the climb, you decide for some reason (let's say that there is turbulence reported at that altitude) to opt to cruise at a lower altitude (Let's say FL200). You set the lower altitude in the **FCU** and the jet levels off at that altitude.*

WHOOPS! *In order to complete the Airbus phase algorithm, you must tell the **FMGC** about your new cruise altitude. It is easy, just go to the **PROG** page and, simply change the cruise altitude to reflect your new cruise altitude (in our example FL200).*

*The **PROG** page will reflect the appropriate cruise phase page, such as **ECON CRZ**.*

SITUATION 1:

Once the airplane is established in cruise at the planned altitude; then when and if you decide to continue your climb to another higher altitude.

> **1** - Set your new **HIGHER** altitude in the **FCU** altitude window.
> **2** - **PUSH** the **ALT** selector button (selecting managed mode).
> **3** - The "new" selected cruise altitude will
>   **AUTOMATICALLY** be inserted in the **PROG** page.
> **4** - The **PROG** page will shift to **CLB**.
> **5** - A message across the bottom of the **MCDU** will say:
>   "**NEW CRZ ALT ENTERED.**"
> **6** - The airplane will start a climb to the new higher cruise altitude.

SITUATION 2:

With the airplane is established in cruise at the planned altitude; then if you decide to descend to a lower altitude and the airplane is more than 200 NM from the destination:

> **1** - Set your new **LOWER** altitude in the **FCU** altitude window.
> **2** - PUSH the **ALT** selector button (selecting managed mode).
> **3** - The "new" selected cruise altitude will
>   **AUTOMATICALLY** be inserted in the **PROG** and **INIT** page.
> **4** - The **PROG** page will shift to **DES**.
> **5** - A message across the bottom of the **MCDU** will say:
>   "**NEW CRZ ALT ENTERED.**"
> **6**-The airplane will start a descent to the new lower cruise altitude.

WHEN A PILOT
SCREWS UP!

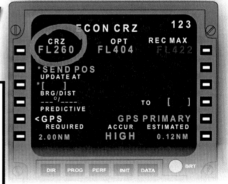

If you "**ACCIDENTALLY**" start the descent or push the "**APPCH NOW**" key, and change your mind ...

SITUATION 3:

If the **DESCENT** or **APPROACH** **PHASE** is inadvertently activated, the **CRUISE PHASE** can be recovered by reentering your previous cruise flight level on the **PROG** or **INIT** page.

SITUATION 4:

If **ENGINE FAILURE** occurs, **PROG** page automatically displays the recommended **EO** (Engine Out) altitude. That would be the single engine altitude computed for **LONG RANGE CRUISE** (LRC) speed at **MAX CONTINUOUS THRUST** and **ANTI-ICING OFF**. Useful information when performing a **DRIFTDOWN**.

VNAV stuff

HOCKEY STICKS
TOP OF CLIMB (T/C) and TOP OF DESCENT (T/D)

As we continue our flight profile, we can see two little "bent arrows" on the green route line on the **ND**. These are the "**TOP OF CLIMB**" and "**TOP OF DESCENT**" indicators. They are placed there by the **FMGC** in response to the flight parameters that we have entered (or allowed to be defaulted) when we loaded the **MCDU**.

Referred to as "hockey sticks, they are **ONLY** indicators and are used for planning purposes.

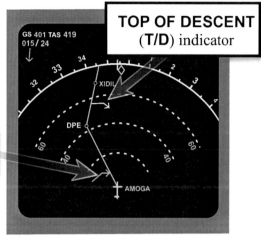

TOP OF DESCENT (T/D) indicator

TOP OF CLIMB (T/C) indicator

THE "TOP OF CLIMB" INDICATOR

"Top-of-climb" indicates where the airplane will reach the "**PLANNED**" cruise altitude that was set in the **INIT A** page and we can now view in the **PROG** page. Note that the airplane will automatically level off **ONLY** at the **FCU** displayed altitude, not necessarily the "hockey stick" point. The **PFD/FMA** will annunciate "**ALT**" **ONLY** when the auto-pilot captures the **FCU** selected altitude.

If, and this is the case most of the time, the Planned Altitude on the **INIT A** or **PROG** page and the **FCU** selected altitude are the same, then the airplane will level off, capture and annunciate **ALT CRZ**, and the jet will transition to the CRUISE PHASE.

THE "TOP OF DESCENT" INDICATOR

"Top-of-descent" indicator **ONLY** displays the point where a managed descent profile, if started at this point, will meet the constraints that are displayed on the **F-PLAN** page. The actual initiation of the descent **REQUIRES** manual input from the pilot. It is a two step process:

1- SET LOWER ALTITUDE IN THE FCU
2- PUSH THE ALT SELECTOR BUTTON

A managed descent is desirable in this airplane since in that mode it gives an indication of the relationship of the airplane to the "planned" flight path. There is a **V/DEV (MAGENTA DONUT)** that appears on the Altitude Tape of the **PFD**, and you can monitor the vertical progress on the **PROG** page during the descent.

It is generally considered good practice to start the descent using the managed technique described above about 5 miles prior to the T-D point.

The airplane will assume a fixed descent rate (about 1,000 fpm) until is flies into the descent profile and from that point on, it will capture and fly that profile.

If you get a late start and overfly the **T/D** point, use the OP DES technique. Pull the selector and the airplane will descend at idle thrust (**THR IDLE** on **FMA**).

CRUISE PHASE
(After level off)

> **MEMORY REFRESHER**:
> The **CRUISE PHASE** begins when the airplane level offs at the **CRUISE ALTITUDE** that is indicated on the **PROG** page. This is indicated by the **PFD/FMA** annunciator indicating **ALT CRZ**.

In **RVSM**, it is recommended that the **AUTOPILOT** be used to make the actual cruise altitude capture and continue to be engaged during cruise. Except where disengagement is required such as during **TURBULENCE** or **TRIMMING**. It is absolutely essential that the airplane capture and remain as close to the cleared cruise altitude / flight level as possible.

After level off complete, it is considered **SOP** (Standard Operating Procedure) to perform an altimeter check. Altimeters *MUST BE* within 200 feet of each other.

DISCUSSION ABOUT RVSM
(Reduced Vertical Separation Minimum)

RVSM extends the altitude where **1,000 foot** vertical separation between airplanes exists from **FL 290 to FL 410** inclusive. This is predicated on the increased accuracy of the pressure sensitive altimeter. There are two potential problems.

DANGER 1: Above transition altitude, if the altimeters are **NOT** set to **STD** or **29.92 in Hg** or **1013 hPa**, then the airplane will **NOT** actually be cruising at the appropriate altitude.

DANGER 2: The altimeters **MUST BE WITHIN 200 FEET** of each other or the airplane is not in compliance with the **FAA** operational requirements.

DO THESE
7
THINGS
AFTER LEVEL-OFF

1. LEVEL OFF .... Verify
2. ALTIMETERS ....Check
3. CRUISE WINDS .... Enter
4. ECAM MEMO .... Review
5. ECAM SYSTEM PAGES .... Review
6. FLIGHT PROGRESS .... Monitor
7. FUEL .... Monitor.

published by UNIVERSITY of TEMECULA PRESS, Inc.

LNAV stuff:
HEADING SELECT:

For this discussion, we are only considering autopilot controlled flight. This is not a hand flown, autopilot off discussion. At almost any point in a flight (and that includes holding) you can revert to manually selected heading control and steer the airplane in any direction. This can occur during climb, cruise, descent and most of the approach phases of flight.

Here's how you do that:
STEP 1 -Turn the heading selector knob to the desired heading.
STEP 2 - **PULL** the heading selector knob.
STEP 3 - Airplane will turn immediately to that heading.

There can be some complexity to this. Let me clear the air a little. Once you **PULL** the heading selector button, here are the three rules:

> **RULE 1** - If the selected heading is different from that
> of the airplane track **PRIOR TO PULLING** the knob,
> the airplane will turn in the shortest direction towards the selected heading.

> **RULE 2** - If the knob is pulled **DURING** a turn
> (heading may not be visible), then the airplane will
> roll out on the existing heading.

> **RULE 3** - If the heading is selected **AFTER** the knob is pulled,
> then the airplane will turn to the selected heading in the direction
> that the selector was turned.

LIMITATIONS TO RULE 3:

*If you **PUSH** the **HEADING SELECTOR** knob, and the airplane is within capture criteria, it will turn, intercept, and fly the blue course line. The **PFD** annunciation will be **NAV**.*

*If you **PUSH** the **HEADING SELECTOR** knob, and the selected airplane heading/position is outside the capture criteria, the airplane will remain in open mode, and the **PFD** will annunciate **HDG**.*

BIG MEMORY ITEM !

PUSH towards airplane ... to select **AUTOPILOT** (*MANAGED*)control.

PULL towards pilot .... to select **PILOT** (*SELECTED*) control.

LNAV stuff:

GOING DIRECT:

Programming the airplane to go directly to a fix is pretty straight forward.

SITUATION ONE: If the fix is already on your flight plan (**F-PLAN** page), then it is a simple two step process:

STEP 1 - Select the **DIR** key.
This will place a *[   ] bracket in the top of the queue.

STEP 2 - LSK the desired **FIX**.
The airplane will **IMMEDIATELY** place that fix at the top of the **F-PLAN** queue, and the airplane will go directly towards the new fix.

SITUATION TWO: If the desired fix is NOT already in your flight plan queue, and we want to make it the **NEXT** or **GO TO** waypoint, then we would

STEP 1 - Type the desired fix in the scratchpad.

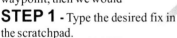

FROM		123
	UTC	SPD / ALT
*[ ]		
	TRK123 1NM	
AMOGA	0009	298/ FL258
	44	
(T/D)	0015	.42/
		2
DPE	0015	.63/ FL253
---F-PLN DISCONTINUITY---		
DEST	TIME DIST	EFOB
EGLL	____ 201	--.-
ABC		↑

DIR PROG PERF INIT DATA   BRT

F-PLN RAD NAV FUEL PRED SEC F-PLN MCDU MENU

AIR PORT ↑

NOTE: *There are a few different ways to write the new fix:*
LAT/LONG,
P/B/D (place/bearing/distance),
P-B/P-B (place-bearing/place-bearing),
PD (Place-distance along the track waypoint; for example BIG/-10 is a waypoint ten miles before BIG along our track).

STEP 2 - Select the **DIR** key. This will open the *[   ] at **LSK 1L**.

STEP 3 - **LSK 1L** to place the new fix at the top of the queue in the brackets.

STEP 4 - Resolve "**DUPLICATE NAMES**" conflict if it exists.

STEP 5 - Review "**YELLOW TMPY**" screen, and if correct.

STEP 6 - Select **INSERT***.

STEP 7 - Remove **F-PLAN DISCONTINUITY**.

WHAT CAN A PILOT SCREW UP?

Taking **ENROUTE REDIRECT ROUTINGS**, even from **ATC**, **MUST ALWAYS** involve a calculation regarding the ability of the airplane to fly above the terrain on a Single Engine. Even though this information may be covered in the **METHOD 1 and 2** calculations included on your flight plan, those are specifically for the "planned routing". **BE AWARE**: This is a favorite Check Pilot ploy to evaluate your awareness. A simple "Cleared direct to ---" and when you hear that, get out your chart and look for **MOCA** (Minimum Obstacle Clearance Altitude), **MEA** (Minimum enroute altitude) or other terrain indications between you and the new waypoint that are above your single engine altitude, even if you are operating on both engines.

IF ...THEN: I can tell you, **IF** you do not check for terrain clearance; **THEN** the Check guy will fail an engine and ... whoooops! Things get ugly.

---

published by UNIVERSITY of TEMECULA PRESS, Inc.

LNAV stuff: # LATERAL REVISION:

If you line select a fix that is in the Flight Plan queue (**MCDU F-PLN** page), you will get the **LAT REV** page. This is the key that unlocks many mysterious secrets of the Airbus **MCDU/FMGC**. Here are just some of the things you can do from the **LATERAL REVISION** (**LAT REV**) page.

> -**NEXT WPT** (Next Waypoint)
> -**HOLD** (Holding)
> -**VIA/GO TO** (used for placing Airways/Endpoint)
> -**NEW DEST** (New Destination ... divert or alternate)
> -**ENABLE ALTN** (make selected alternate the destination)

We have already used the **LATERAL REVISION** technique in our preflight planning, and now we can see where it is also a powerful inflight management tool. I would draw your attention to the usefulness of this **LATERAL REVISION** tool in diversion scenarios where we need to reselect an alternate or diversion airport or re-file the flight path routing, particularly during weather diversion or **EMERGENCY** situations.

NEXT WAYPOINT:

If we want to insert a new fix/waypoint into the queue after another waypoint, then we could use the **LATERAL REVISION** method.

STEP 1 - Line Select the fix that we want to insert the new fix **AFTER**. In our example: **DPE**. Then observe that the **LAT REV** page is displayed.

STEP 2 - Type the desired fix in the scratchpad. For example: **ABC**.

*IMPORTANT: Do Step 1 **BEFORE** Step 2. That is; select the **FIX** for lateral reversion **BEFORE** typing the new fix into the scratch pad.*

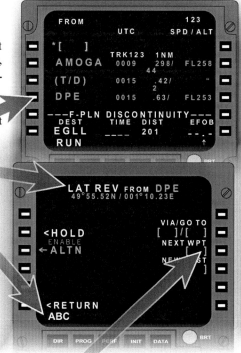

STEP 3 - LSK3R "NEXT WPT".

STEP 4 - Resolve "**DUPLICATE NAMES**" conflict if it exists.

STEP 5 - Review "**YELLOW TMPY**" screen, and if correct.

STEP 6 - Select **INSERT***.

STEP 7 - Remove **F-PLAN DISCONTINUITY**.

LNAV stuff:

REVIEW: Select **F-PLN** page on the **MCDU** and line select a fix using the keys on the left side of the **MCDU**. This is called a **LATERAL REVISION**.

VIA/GO TO:

This is a technique by which a pilot can enter an airway/waypoint endpoint from the lateral revision point. Here is an example to illustrate this feature. Say you have been cleared from **DPE** via **UM605** to **SFD**.

Perform a lateral revision from **DPE** and use the **VIA/GO TO** entry. Place the entry like this: **UM605/SFD** in the [   ]/[   ] brackets.

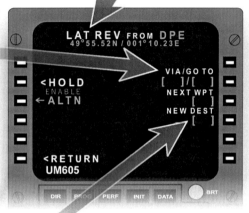

We can use this technique during pre-flight planning and setup as well as during flight enroute changes, such as diversions and reroutes.

NOTE: You **CANNOT** perform airway to airway reroutes by entering notation like this: **J45/J133**.

NEW DEST:

The "New Destination" feature allows the pilot to quickly change the direction of the flight. Doing so automatically creates a temporary flight path. This feature is available **ONLY** when you use waypoints in the active flight plan.

What that means is that you will have a routing to the new destination directly from one of the waypoints that exist in the flight plan.

Destination identifiers are four digit **ICAO** letters; for example **EGCC**.

DISCUSSION:

Using the "New Destination" feature inflight for ordinary operations such as arrival destination not available, fuel considerations, passenger medical emergency, reroute from **ATC**, and so forth is all pretty routine, but for the checkride we must be prepared for the **EMERGENCY** that demands an immediate landing. If in **ETOPS** or **METHOD 1 or 2** restricted, the decision of which runway or airport to select will be a critical part of the decision paradigm.

If IMMEDIATE landing is required (e.g: Both engines fail), then:

- **ATC** may be your best resource.
- **DO NOT** overlook the dispatcher as an aid for making your selection.
- The **AIRPORT SELECTOR** on the **ND**. It will display airports that are long enough for you to land (usually 6,000 feet plus).

published by UNIVERSITY of TEMECULA PRESS, Inc.

IF YOU GOTTA LAND ASAP ...

If you have set in a lower altitude in the **FCU** for a descent, and you are frantically trying to start the descent using the managed (**PUSHING** the alt selector knob) and it simply won't select... chances are you never got to cruise altitude (check **PROG** page), but are actually trying to start your descent while the airplane is still in the **CLIMB** phase instead of the **CRUISE** phase, you may want to perform a "**RE-CRUISE**". Or you could simply **PULL** the **ALT** selector button and start an **OP DES** descent.

RE-CRUISING IN DESCENT:

If the airplane is allowed to remain in **CLIMB** phase by leveling off before reaching the planned cruise altitude that is entered on the **PROG** page, or the climb is interrupted before it is complete; then a "managed" descent can not be initiated. The managed descent milestones and profile limits will not be available to either the displays or the **FMGC** during the descent. This is **NOT GOOD**!
What does it mean? It means that if you descend using the autopilot in **OPEN (OP DES)** mode, the descent will not be controlled to respond to any of the managed control points for the descent. The airplane will simply assume a descent path predicated on a fixed descent rate. I offer the argument that while **OP DES** is a perfectly good descent technique, it might be helpful to restore the managed mode for the descent.

A simple solution to this problem is to reset the cruise altitude on the **PROG** page to a "new" cruise altitude that is lower than the current actual altitude of the airplane, even if already started in the descent using **OP DES**. As the airplane passes through the "new" cruise altitude, the airplane's computer will detect that it has left the cruise altitude and transition to **DESCENT** mode. This will allow the managed descent mode to be activated restoring the managed mode parameters. You must then reselect the managed mode (**PUSH** the **ALT** selector).
Wheeeew! Saved again! This is also referred to as "**RE-CRUISING**".

> **EXAMPLE**: Say you are in the climb, but you level off prior to reaching your cruise altitude. This might happen, for example, if you were to encounter a situation (emergency or major system failure) requiring immediate descent for landing. The problem occurs more commonly, however, when a pilot simply "forgets" to re-cruise after changing his planned cruise altitude. I would point out that there is no prohibition against making the descent using **OPEN DESCENT** mode. However, descents from higher altitude that are "on course" would benefit from a re-cruise.
> In my opinion, it is desirable to re-cruise for no other reason than regain the **VDEV** descent profile indicator (magenta donut).

REMINDER:
If you **RE-CRUISE** in **OP DES** descent, even though the "managed" descent capability is restored when you pass through the "new cruise altitude" it does **NOT** automatically become the selected mode of operation. You will have to reselect the managed mode (once it becomes available) by pushing the **ALT** selector button.

LNAV stuff:

HOLDING

HOW TO GET INTO HOLDING:

Any discussion regarding **HOLDING** must include a link to the **LATERAL REVISION** page. The first few times you try to find the **HOLD PAGE,** you notice that there is no hold key on the Airbus. Those wily engineers decided to cleverly hide the "**HOLD**" command on the **LAT REV** page. Once you get used to it, you will see that there is a logic behind this.

SITUATION 1: HOLD AT YOUR PRESENT POSITION.

STEP 1: Open the **F-PLAN** page.
STEP 2: LSK 1L; that is Line Select the top waypoint in the queue.
This will open the **LAT REV** page.
STEP 3: LSK 3L <HOLD.
STEP 4: This will reveal the **COMPUTED HOLD at PPOS** page.
Look at the parameters and change them if desired.
STEP 5: LSK 6R INSERT*.
STEP 6: The Holding pattern will be displayed on the **ND** in **GREEN,** and the airplane will immediately start a turn so as to fly that pattern.

SITUATION 2: HOLD AT A WAYPOINT IN YOUR ROUTE.

STEP 1: Open the **F-PLAN** page.
STEP 2: LSK the desired waypoint in the queue.
This will open the **LAT REV** page.
STEP 3: LSK 3L <HOLD.
STEP 4: This will reveal the **COMPUTED HOLD at ---** page.
Look at the parameters and change them if desired.
STEP 5: LSK 6R INSERT*.
STEP 6: The Holding pattern will be displayed on the **ND** in **GREEN** at the selected waypoint. When the airplane arrives at that waypoint it will enter the holding pattern.

SITUATION 3 HOLD AT OFF ROUTE WAY-POINT.

STEP 1: Open the **F-PLAN** page.
STEP 2: Select the **DIR** key.
This will place ***[   ]** at the top of the queue.
STEP 3: Place waypoint/fix name in scratchpad.
STEP 4: LSK 1L. This will place the new waypoint/fix at **LSK 2L** position (second in the queue).
STEP 5: LSK 2L. This will display the **LAT REV** page
STEP 6: LSK 3L <HOLD.
STEP 7: This will reveal the **COMPUTED HOLD at ---** page.
Look at the parameters and change them if desired.
STEP 8: LSK 6R INSERT*.
STEP 9: The Holding pattern will be displayed on the **ND** in **GREEN** at the new selected waypoint.

published by UNIVERSITY of TEMECULA PRESS, Inc.

HOW TO GET OUT OF HOLDING:

There are a few ways to depart the holding pattern. We will discuss only five of them.

TWO 2 "LEAST DESIRABLE" TECHNIQUES:

1 - Shut off the auto-pilot and **HAND FLY.** While always an option, it is a brute force solution and leaves us with the problem of how to return to our "route".

2 - **HEADING** select, and using the **OPEN** mode, steer out of the holding pattern. We have to re-shuffle the queue on the **F-PLAN** page to return to our original flight planned route. Not particularly pretty.

"OK" TECHNIQUE

An "acceptable" technique is to use the **CLR** key to delete the holding fix. This is risky because **unless you have a clearance from present position to the next way-point,** when you delete the holding fix, the airplane will proceed from the position it was when the fix was deleted directly to the next fix ... and may, during that evolution, leave the confines of the established holding area.

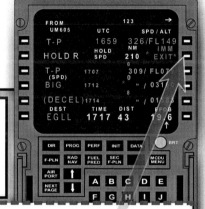

"GOOD" TECHNIQUE:

This is perhaps the most logical to use. Use the '**DIR**" key and select the holding fix. Some care must be taken so that the airplane doesn't make a turn that leaves the confines of the holding pattern.

THE MOST ELEGANT TECHNIQUE:

This is the technique the Check Pilot will be looking for.

Once you enter the holding pattern, the **F-PLAN** page will display an entry "**IMM EXIT***" at **LSK 2R**. If you select that entry (**LSK 2R**) it will toggle to "**RESUME HOLD***" and the jet will start a turn so as to make the most expeditious return to the holding fix and continue on the original routing. Really cool .... and the technique that is the most desirable.

REQUIRED "HOLDING" REPORTS:

ENTERING HOLD:
1. **FIX**
2. **TIME**
3. **ALTITUDE**
LEAVING HOLD:
1. **TIME**
2. **ALTITUDE** ; **Resume normal operating speed.**

What pilots generally screw up! They fail to report:
- **ALTITUDE ENTERING HOLDING,**
- **LEAVING ALTITUDE WHILE IN HOLDING,**
- **ARRIVING AT ALTITUDE IN HOLDING.**

Occasionally the airplane is unable to enter the holding pattern **AT** the assigned altitude. These are **IMPORTANT** since the controller **CANNOT** discriminate between airplanes that are in holding because of the transponder clutter. She/He relies solely on your radio reports.

GETTING READY FOR THE ...
APPROACH DESCENT

GETTING HIGH !!!! YIPE!!!

If you are higher than 10,000 feet above the field altitude, inside of 30 miles from the landing runway, and going faster than 250 kts ...
YOU ARE ALREADY SCREWED!!!

At this point in our flight, we should be thinking about and getting ready to descend and land. To somehow simplify and make certain we don't forget anything, we need a simple way to gather our thoughts and get everything ready to make the approach and land. In the world of airline flying, pilots have developed "gouges" (pronounced **GOW-JEZ**) to help them remember how to complete some of the more complex tasks. These crutches are usually acronym driven. By that I mean they are a sequence of letters, each one representing a more complex task.

I am suggesting that you should develop a memory device to use. here is one that some pilots use: "**A-I-R-B-A-G**".

It is simple and will help focus your thoughts. It works really well in emergencies as well as ordinary garden variety flight profiles.

A-I-R-B-A-G

A- **ATIS**
I - **I**nstall the approach
R- **R**adios setup
B- **B**rief the approach
A- **A**pproach Descent checklist
G- **G**o **A**round and **A**lternate

Here is what the concept is, and it applies to both a routine flight as well as an emergency/irregularity situation where you brain turns to useless putty. Having something to fall back on to ensure that you have done invaluable.
So, here are the details.

OMIGOSH !!!
I NEED AN
AIRBAG !

So, when your brain turns to putty and you can't think of what to do next ...
A-I-R-B-A-G.

A stands for **ATIS.** Every airport (almost) has a radio frequency that continuously broadcasts an Automatic Terminal Information Service, or **ATIS**. It contains important stuff we would need to know to plan our landing. The frequency for the **ATIS** is, of course, right on the **APPROACH PLATE** for the airport.

Use the number 2 radio so as not to interfere with **ATC** communications.

STEP 1: Use the knob to set the requested frequency in the **STBY/CRS** window.

STEP 2: Select the frequency to the ACTIVE window by depressing the double headed arrow "transfer key".

STEP 3: Ensure **VHF 1** button is selected and has a green activate light illuminated.

STEP 4: Select the **VHF 1 "CALL"** button and ensure that the volume knob is turned up.

When within radio range (about 195 NM or line of sight), the **ATIS** should become audible. Copy the **ATIS**.

Place a copy of it in a place where both pilots can refer to it during the approach.

Some comments about the ATIS:

Generally speaking, the **ATIS** transmitter is located at the airfield. This qualifies it as a "**LOCAL FACILITY**". The **ATIS** broadcast uses a **VHF** transmitter, which means that it is line of sight and as such usually can't be received outside of about **200 NM** from the airport, depending on your altitude. Expect at that range for the transmission to sometimes be scratchy and broken, particularly if a human person is reading the weather and is difficult to understand.

Other sources for the weather such as **ACARS** for the weather, and a **METAR**, may be copied using the **HF** (High Frequency) radio. While these can be monitored at virtually any distance from the airport, they are not suitable for use if flying the **APPROACH NAV APPROACH** procedure because of the requirement that:

> "The *ALTIMETER SETTING MUST BE FROM A LOCAL FACILITY*.

Of course, the current Control Tower for the airport of intended landing issues the weather information that is the **MOST AUTHORITATIVE** and supercedes the others during the execution of the approach.

I - R

stands for **INSTALL THE APPROACH and RADIOS.** Once we have the **ATIS** information, we have enough data to install the approach. Once these details are added to the **FMGC**, it will allow the computer to make more accurate **ETA/EFOB** calculations.

To facilitate the process and make life easier, let's use the "**REVERSE Z**" to help cover all pages in a coherent order: **F-PLAN ... NAV RAD ... PROG ... PERF.**

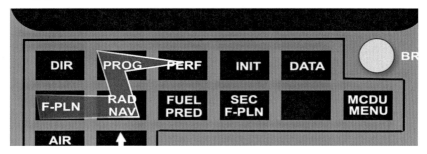

First ...

Select the **F-PLAN PAGE.**

To install the runway, we will do a lateral revision of the destination airport.
Here's how we do that:

Select **EITHER** the **GREEN EGLL** (In our example diagram, just under the "**F-PLN DISCONTINUITY**" line) ... or the **WHITE EGLL** that is on the bottom line of the **MCDU** display.

For this exercise, we will line select the **WHITE EGLL** (**LSK 6L**).

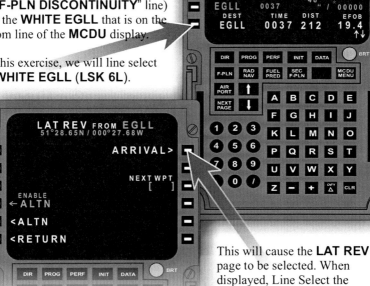

This will cause the **LAT REV** page to be selected. When displayed, Line Select the **ARRIVAL** prompt (**LSK 1R**).

This page will reveal the available approaches; Line Select the desired approach/runway. We can get that from the **ATIS** or Tower. For our example **ILS27L** is indicated.

★ *For the non-ILS APPROACH-NAV approach we would have to see a "line selectable" entry for that specific approach: such as VOR27L.*

NOTE: we may have to use the **SLEW KEYS** to scroll the selections until the desired runway (in our case ILS27L) is revealed.

Once selected, this will reveal the next page which includes a list of the available **STAR**s (**S**tandard **T**erminal **A**rrival **A**rrival) procedures.

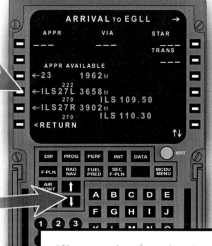

If known, select the assigned **STAR** and other transition information including "**VIA**s". **NOTE**: *If a waypoint on the selected STAR is an IAF for the approach selected, the FMGC will auto-string them, and in the process DELETE the STAR waypoints that are beyond the IAF. If this is a problem, select NO VIA.*

Select the **INSERT*** key.

Remove any **F-PLAN DISCONTINUITY** lines that may have been inserted.

Remember how to do that: *Select CLR to the scratchpad, then Line Select the F-PLN DISCONTINUITY.*

IMPORTANT
Check the F-PLAN pages for speeds and altitude constraints and see that they agree with the approach chart restrictions. Add other constraints and restrictions if required using the **VERTICAL REVISION** technique (Line Select right column of fix information line on the **MCDU** display).

INSTALLING AN ALTERNATE

For this example, we will assume that you **HAVE NOT** already programmed an alternate in the **INIT A** page at the beginning of this flight. My comment about this would be that it is probably a good idea to **ALWAYS** designate your alternate during the initial **MCDU** set-up.

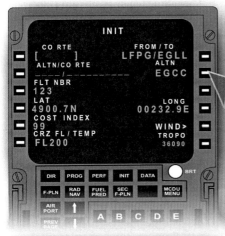

Go to the **INIT** page. The **INIT A** page has a place to insert the selected **ALTN** (Alternate) destination. Placing the four digit **ICAO** identifier in that position (**LSK 2R**) automatically adds that airport to the end of the queue on the **F-PLN** page.

For our example trip, I have arbitrarily designated Manchester (**EGCC**) as our Alternate for London's Heathrow (**EGLL**).

HOWEVER, IF YOU DIDN'T DO THAT ...

If you didn't do that at the beginning of the flight, you will find that the **INIT PAGE** is "locked out" and you can no longer access that page for input,

So ... here is one alternative for inputting the alternate. Take the routing from your destination (**EGLL**) to your alternate (**EGCC**).

EGLL.HON.LOVEL.EGCC

Enter the fixes into the **MCDU** below the **END OF F-PLAN**

DISCONTINUITY line and before the **EGCC**. I prefer having at least one fix for the **MCDU/FMGC** to use. This, at least, gives me somewhere to point the airplane after the missed approach.

published by UNIVERSITY of TEMECULA PRESS, Inc.

Ret up the **RADIOS**. This activity takes place primarily on the **RAD NAV** page of the **MCDU**.

An idiosyncrasy of the Airbus system is that the radio set already knows what the frequencies are for the approach selected on the **F-PLAN** page; therefore, if you have selected either an **ILS**, a **VOR** or an **NDB** (selected as **ADF** on the **EFIS** Control Panel and **MCDU**) from the queue, then it will know which radios to tune and what the frequencies are. Here are some limitations and restrictions:

NDB (referred to as **ADF** on the **MCDU**)

These approaches are displayed on the **ND** and the **DDRMI**. They are auto-tuned **_ONLY_** when an **NDB (ADF)** approach is selected from the database during the lateral revision of the destination on the **F-PLAN** page, **AND** the first fix of the selected approach is the "**TO**" waypoint. Generally they are slow to tune and so we will usually **MANUALLY TUNE** the **NDB**s.

VOR DME

Can be displayed on the **ND**s and the **DDRMI**.

ILS DME

Can be displayed on the **ND**s and the **DDRMI**.

VOR

VOR 1 and **2** bearing information can be displayed on both the **ND**s and the **DDRMI CDI** (Course Deviation Indicator).

Other available approaches will be listed in the queue in the **MCDU**.

The **ILS CAT III B** is *THE* approach that this airplane was designed to fly. It is the only approach that can be flown to a landing using the autoland system in weather down to 300 RVR and be landed without obtaining visual contact with the runway or runway environment. It is the approach of choice for Airbus crews.

NOTE: Flying an **AUTOLAND** approach **REQUIRES** two autopilots. Single autopilot **ILS** approaches require the autopilot be shut off at minimums and the landing hand flown.

The **ILS/FREQ** line will display the **ID/FREQ/HEADING** when the runway information received is suitable for navigation. That will also be repeated on the **PFD** lower left corner in the radio cluster display. Once that appears, you may engage the **APPR** mode on the **FCU**. However, until that information is displayed, the **APPR** mode will be locked out. It has been my experience that the radio cluster does not tune until within about 10 or 20 miles of the airport ... also; the radio cluster will not display the information until the **EFIS** Control Panel has the **ILS** button selected.

CONFIRMING ILS RADIO TUNED
to the proper frequency.

The **RAD NAV** key selects the **RADIO NAV** page and indicates which radios have been tuned ... and since the Airbus incorporates an "**AUTOTUNE**" system, we have to look at this page to see which radios are tuned to what frequencies.

Since we are **MOST** interested that the computer will be tuned to the **ILS** for the **RUNWAY** we have indicated we are going to land on, we look at the **LSK 3L**. When it has a four digit (sometimes three or even two digits depending on the radio facility) identifier (such as **IDPP**) and that coincides with our expected runway **ID**, then we can assume that it is tuned to the appropriate **ILS** frequency.

This will match the information displayed on the **PFD** lower left corner. This is called the **RADIO CLUSTER**, and will display the tuned **ILS** when it is identified and ready for use.

DISCUSSION: This will all happen within about **20 NM** of the landing airport, so you have to be alert. We have the option of manually tuning the radios. To do this, it requires a **RUNWAY IDENTIFIER** that will positively identify that radio facility. With out the **ID**, course MUST BE manually entered.

HOW PILOTS CAN SCREW IT UP!

IF ANY RMP IS SELECTED TO NAV, the fields on the **RAD NAV** page will be **BLANK on both MCDUs !**

published by UNIVERSITY of TEMECULA PRESS, Inc.

Next ...

Select the **PROG PAGE**.

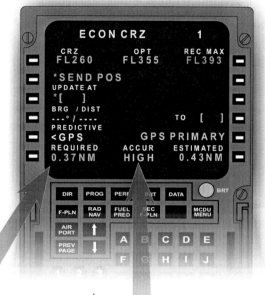

If flying a **LINE SELECTABLE** non-ILS approach, then use the **APPROACH-NAV-APPROACH** procedure. However, for ALL Non-ILS approaches, it will be necessary to check the following two required items to ensure that the airplane systems meet the minimum requirements for executing the approach.

ITEM 1: The **RNP**.

The **RNP** (Required Navigation Performance) is related to the preciseness of the ability of the airplane to accurately predict its position. Here are the actual requirements:

> *- Prior to initiating the FAS (Final Approach Segment) we check the RNP within 5 NM of the FAF. It should have a default value of 0.37 (unless a non-standard RNP is published and manually entered).*
> *- If the RNP is below 0.36, the ILS approach MUST BE auto-coupled.*

If **GPS** is required for the approach, there will be a notation right on the **APPROACH PLATE**. Then **GPS** must be installed and must be **PRIMARY** for navigation.

ITEM 2:
The **ACCURACY**.
The accuracy of the system MUST BE HIGH.
- Inside the FAF, if the **ANP** (Actual Navigation Performance) goes below the **RNP**, a **MISSED APPROACH** must be executed. This is indicated by a **LOW ACCURACY** message on the ND and the MCDU.

another boring **DISCUSSION:**

When **EPE** (Estimated Position Error) is greater than the **RNP**, then **NAV** accuracy is LOW and **NAV ACCUR DOWNGRADE** is annunciated on the **ND**.

Some approaches may specifiy a nonstandard RNP, which must be entered into **LINE 6L** on the **PROG PAGE** before the beginning of the FAS.

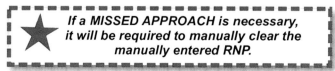

> *If a MISSED APPROACH is necessary, it will be required to manually clear the manually entered RNP.*

COMPLETE THE PERF / APPR PAGE

Select the **MCDU PERF** page, it should appear and be labeled **APPR**.

1: Enter the **ALTIMETER SETTING**.
Must be from a "LOCAL" at landing airport source.
QNH at dest is entered in either **in/Hg or hPa**.
Beyond 180 NM from the destination, green brackets will be displayed.
Within 180 NM, four amber boxes will appear.

2: Enter the **TEMPERATURE**.
Enter in **C°**. This information is
used to refine the descent profile.
*APPROACH-NAV approach
restriction > -15°C.*

3: Place the wind component
(don't include gusts) from the
ATIS in the appropriate entry
(**LSK 3L**). This is the only pilot
input required to arm the **GS
Mini** (Minimized ground speed)
feature of the Airbus computer.

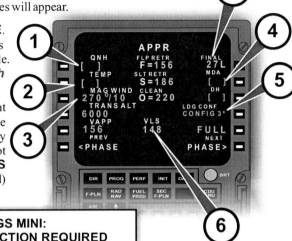

```
                    APPR
      QNH       FLP RETR        FINAL
    [    ]       F=156           27L
      TEMP      SLT RETR        MDA
    [    ]       S=186         [    ]
    MAG WIND    CLEAN           DH
   270°/10      O=220         [    ]
   TRANS ALT                  LDG CONF
   6000                       CONFIG 3*
   VAPP          VLS
   156           148           FULL
     PREV                        NEXT
   <PHASE                     PHASE>
```

```
+--------------------------------------+
|            To ARM GS MINI:           |
|   THE ONLY PILOT ACTION REQUIRED     |
|    "manually" enter the ATIS winds.  |
+--------------------------------------+
```

4: Enter the **MDA** or **DH**.

ILS	**CAT I:** barometric minimums in the **MDA** field.
	CAT II/III: Radio altimeter in the DH field.
APPCH-NAV	DH in the **MDA** field
CDAP or CDFA	**MDA PLUS 50 FEET** in the **MDA** field.

NOTE: *If a runway change is made, it will erase these entries for MDA and DH.*

5: Check **LANDING CONFIGURATION**:
If landing with **FLAPS 3, Select CONF 3** to obtain the correct approach speeds.
This is the flap setting at which the airplane will slow to managed approach speed.

```
+--------------------------------------------------------------+
|  6: IMPORTANT AIRSPEED NOTE:                                  |
|  If an IRREGULAR or EMERGENCY procedure requires an approach  |
|  speed modification, the additional speed increment must be   |
|  added to the VLS for CONF FULL, even if the landing is to be |
|  accomplished using another flap setting. VLS is computed by  |
|  the FMGC for LANDING 3 or FULL. It cannot be modified by     |
|  the pilots. VREF equals VLS for LANDING CONFIG FULL.         |
+--------------------------------------------------------------+
```

7: Confirm **RUNWAY** assignment. However, changes to the runway **CANNOT** be made on this page. Use the **F-PLAN** page lateral revision to destination to change runway.

AIRBAG continued

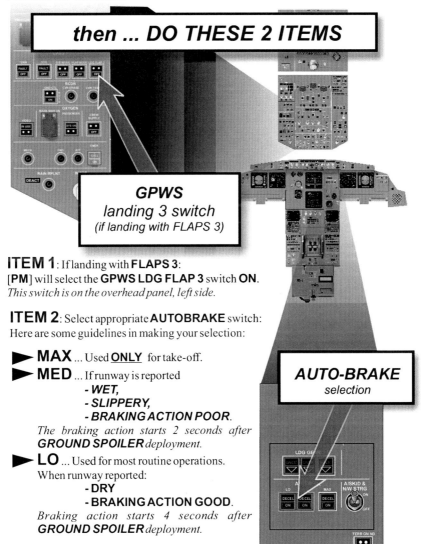

then ... DO THESE 2 ITEMS

GPWS
landing 3 switch
(if landing with FLAPS 3)

ITEM 1: If landing with **FLAPS 3**:
[**PM**] will select the **GPWS LDG FLAP 3** switch **ON**.
This switch is on the overhead panel, left side.

ITEM 2: Select appropriate **AUTOBRAKE** switch:
Here are some guidelines in making your selection:

▶ **MAX** ... Used **ONLY** for take-off.

▶ **MED** ... If runway is reported
　　　　- WET,
　　　　- SLIPPERY,
　　　　- BRAKING ACTION POOR.
The braking action starts 2 seconds after
GROUND SPOILER *deployment.*

▶ **LO** ... Used for most routine operations.
When runway reported:
　　　　- DRY
　　　　- BRAKING ACTION GOOD.
Braking action starts 4 seconds after
GROUND SPOILER *deployment.*

AUTO-BRAKE
selection

NOTE: **GROUND SPOILER** extension occurs
automatically when **BOTH GEAR** have touched down, and
　　　　- **BOTH THRUST LEVERS** in forward idle
　　　　　when system is **ARMED**, or
　　　　- **REVERSE THRUST SELECTED ON ONE ENG** with
　　　　　OTHER THRUST LEVER at idle
　　　　　if ground spoilers **NOT ARMED**.
During **AUTOLAND**, ground spoilers extend at half speed,
1 second after **BOTH** main landing gear touch down.

AIRBAG *continued*

B stands for **BRIEF THE APPROACH.** I don't want to bore you with redundant information; however, let's just identify a few of the items that we might want to review before starting the approach and include in a shared **PILOT BRIEF**.

Airport elevation = 83 feet
ATIS frequency = 128.075
Tower frequency = 118.5
ILS ID = I-LL
ILS freq = 109.5
ILS heading = 273
GSIA (Glide Slope Intercept Altitude)= 2,500 feet
A/S restriction = 210 Kts

Be especially alert to the notes that are scattered all over the chart, such as:
The **MSA** (Minimum Sector Altitude) **25 NM** circle will show highest obstacle in that sector.

The "brief" should include a clear description of what you intend to do in a normal take-off situation ... and a description of what your plans are if you lose an engine or have to return to the field..
Something like this: *"I'm going to fly a CAT III B approach to runway 27L at Heathrow airport in London. The ILS frequency is ... and so forth and on and on ... blah, blah, blah."*

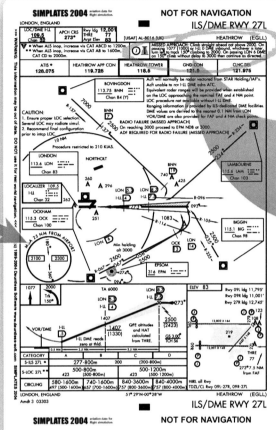

Call for the APPROACH DESCENT checklist: Here is the place where we want to complete all the Before Landing items that we can.

APPROACH DESCENT CHECKLIST

APPROACH BRIEFING .... Complete
MCDU/FMGCs, radios .... Programmed, set for approach
EGPWS, radar displays........................... Terrain/weather
Auto brakes ....Lo/med/off

.... TRANSITION LEVEL ....

Altimeters .... _____ in Hg/hPa, set

published by UNIVERSITY of TEMECULA PRESS, Inc.

AIRBAG continued

G **GO-AROUND and GET OFF**: Brief what you intend to do if the landing doesn't work out and you have to execute the **GO-AROUND** or **MISSED APPROACH** procedure. Also brief what you intend to do if the approach works out **OK**.

DO NOT FLY THIS PROCEDURE

without coordination with **ATC**. This would be the expected procedure during a **LOST COMM** situation, but remember that if you are at a busy airport (ie, **KORD**) that there are multiple runways in use and you need to be alert to the needs of the controlling agency (**APPROACH or the TOWER**).

Take a moment and go over what you would do if you were to execute a missed approach (also called a go-around or overshoot). You can create your own procedure, or ... Here are some of the Overshoot steps that I have identified:

GO-AROUND *REVIEW*

STEP 1: "**GO-AROUND THRUST**" - Select **TOGA** thrust.

STEP 2: **PITCH 15° up**. If auto-pilot ON, monitor pitch.

STEP 3: "**FLAPS**" - Raise flaps one notch .

STEP 4: "**GEAR UP**" - when Positive climb established.
After raising the gear:

STEP 5: "**SET MISSED APPROACH ALTITUDE**" if not already done.

When **ALT*** or **OP CLB** annunciated or
Flashing **LVR CLB** alerts pilot, change thrust to the CL detent.

STEP 6: **THRUST to "CL"** .

Then go to the **FCU** and **EFIS Control Panel** and do 4 things:

STEP 7: **FLIGHT DIRECTOR** verify ON

STEP 8: **HDG - V/S** mode - verify ON

STEP 9: **AUTOTHRUST** - verify ON

STEP 10: **AUTOPILOT** verify ON

NOTE: Terrain and Obstacle clearance is assured up to 1,500 feet AGL, *IF* we track the runway centerline. **TOGA** will select and fly the airplane track at the time of selection; this is approximately runway heading.

AIRBAG continued

Review and brief these procedures ...

When to set THE MISSED APPROACH ALTITUDE

ILS	After **GLIDE SLOPE** capture.
APPCH-NAV	When **FINAL APP** is engaged.
CDAP or CDFA	After jet **BEGINS FINAL DESCENT** (and is below Missed Approach Altitude).

Since we are considering what to do in case we have to "Go-around" it would be useful to have someplace for the airplane to go-around to. There are basically three options:

- an alternate.
- accept vectors and reenter the destination airport traffic pattern and be directed by ATC to another landing approach.
- go into holding "somewhere" and decide what you are going to do when there.

2 NON-STANDARD ACTIONS
that must be completed during the go-around:

1 **RESELECT HDG-V/S mode,**
if the approach was flown using the **TRK-FPA** mode (The **BIRD**).

2 **CLEAR ANY MANUALLY ENTERED RNP.**
If an **RNP** was manually entered during the approach, either because a nonstandard **RNP** was specified on the approach plate or the **RNP** value was improper (less than 0.37).

HOW TO TURN OFF "GO-AROUND PHASE"
and return to a NORMAL CLIMB PHASE

Once we have accomplished the missed approach and are climbing through about 1,500 feet **AGL**, we need to get control of the airplane so that we can continue a normal climb using a normal climb phase technique. Here is how to get the airplane back into the **CLIMB PHASE**.

When we have an active **GO-AROUND PHASE**, we can reactivate the **CLIMB PHASE** by:
- Selecting a **NEW DESTINATION FIX**, and
- Entering a **NEW CRZ FL** on the **PROG** page.

End of A-I-R-B-A-G briefing

published by UNIVERSITY of TEMECULA PRESS, Inc.

approaching the *TOP OF DESCENT (T/D)*

There are seven things we will be discussing that should be accomplished prior to the top of the descent. These things are in addition to the **A-I-R-B-A-G** items that we have discussed:

1. **EGPWS** and **RADAR** displays .... Setup.
2. **NORMAL** or **BELOW** on the **TCAS** .... Select.
3. **LANDING ELEVATION** .... Verify.
4. **NAVIGATION ACCURACY** .... Check.
5. **SEAT BELT SIGN** switch .... ON.
6. **ECAM STATUS** .... check.
7. **APPROACH DESCENT CHECKLIST** .... complete to transition level line.

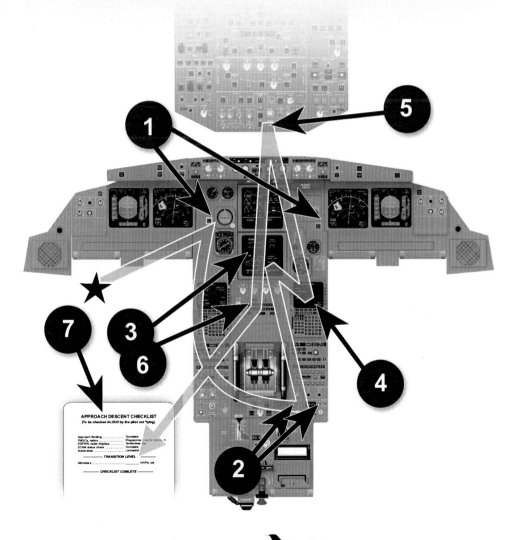

1. EGPWS and RADAR displays

EGPWS (Enhanced Ground Proximity Warning System) and the **WEATHER RADAR (WX RADAR)**.

We will consider both these systems, as operating one affects the operation of the other. Here's the secret reason why.

Turn OFF the EGPWS display, to turn ON the radar display.

In the Airbus configuration, the **EGPWS** must be manually deselected in order to display the **WX RADAR** return on the **ND**.

Use the switch labelled '**TERR**" or "**TERR ON ND**" to de-select the **EGPWS** and therefore allow the **RADAR** return to be displayed on the **ND**. That's how you get the radar to display.

If **WX RADAR** not required; both pilots should select
TERR or **TERR ON ND** .... **ON.**

If **WX RADAR** is required; either/or both may select
TERR or **TERR ON ND** switch .... **OFF.**

Even if BOTH pilots are using the **WX RADAR**, the **EGPWS** "pop-up" feature is still available.

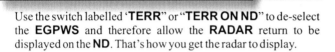

If weather is a "potential factor" during the descent, and it is my experience that it *ALWAYS* is a possibility, turn on the **WEATHER RADAR**. While operation is fairly intuitive, it is actually a complex art-form and requires many hours of operation to master the subtleties of this device.

  RADAR RULE NUMBER ONE:
AVOID SEVERE WEATHER.

WHAT CAN A PILOT SCREW UP?

Sometimes, if the brightness is not balanced properly, you cannot see the return on the **ND**. While your first impulse might be to think the radar is not working, adjust the **ND BRIGHTNESS CONTROL KNOB** on the forward panels.

Discussion about
CFIT, EGPWS, GPWS , and POP-UP

During your training and check experience, your instructor or check person will **DEFINITELY** be required to include a **CFIT** (Controlled Flight Into Terrain) event.

Terrain warning is an area of confusion for the new Airbus pilot. Let's try to get a grip on this system because we definitely are going to encounter a terrain warning during the descent as a part of the training. Here is some information.

> There are two separate systems that operate independently:
> - **GPWS**, and
> - **EGPWS**.

GPWS SYSTEM

The **GPWS** is a **G**round **P**roximity **W**arning **S**ystem that has **NO DATABASE**, but relies on sensors located on the airplane itself. It monitors certain parameters and when it senses that the airplane is going to exceed these limits, issues a warning.
The GPWS is considered reliable and REQUIRES a response from the pilot.

EGPWS SYSTEM

The **EGPWS** is an **E**nhanced **G**round **P**roximity **W**arning **S**ystem and uses an onboard worldwide terrain **DATABASE**, **FMGC** position, and airplane flight path and altitude. The database contains all the runways in the world that are 3,500 feet or longer for which terrain issues exist. It is **INDEPENDENT** of the **GPWS** system. If the **EGPWS** fails to operate properly, it **DOES NOT** affect the **GPWS** systems operation. While primarily an **ND** display function, it also issues aural Caution and Warning alerts. Note that the **EGPWS** system does not account for man-made obstacles.

There is a "*POP-UP*" feature

Since the **EGPWS** must be deselected (depress **TERR** or **TERR ON ND** switch) in order to see the radar display, how would we be protected by the **EGPWS** if both pilots were monitoring the radar and we encountered a terrain conflict?
The answer is an automatic "pop-up" display feature. If an alert occurs, the **ND** display automatically changes to the **EGPWS** display, and the **EGPWS** then remains in view until either the threat no longer exists or the **TERR/TERR ON ND** switch is manually deselected.

a word about ...
TERRAIN DISPLAY and
SPURIOUS EGPWS WARNINGS

The background terrain display associated with the onboard database will sometimes provide spurious indications and nuisance alerts. The reasons for error are usually associated with position misalignment issues, such as map shift.

2. TRAFFIC DISPLAY SWITCH

Select **NORMAL (N)** or **BELOW** on the **TCAS.**

It is suggested that during descents that we orient the **TCAS** antenna **DOWN** in order to better assess traffic that may be in our path. Similarly, when in a climbing attitude, it is suggested that we tilt the antenna **UP (ABOVE)**.

There is one way we could screw up ... we could flip "**THE OTHER GUYS SWITCH!**" Whoops, Cockpit etiquette dictates that unless directed or specifically required, one pilot should not necessarily move the other pilot's controls.

3. LANDING ELEVATION .... Verify

Verify that the **LANDING ALTITUDE** shown on the **LOWER ECAM** cruise page is the same as that of the airport of intended landing. Normally, this would be the destination ... but in the case of a diversion, it would be some other place.

Entering the diversion airport in the **MCDU** will cause the **FMGC** to calculate a "new" altitude. We should check to see that the information is appropriate for the landing airport.

NOTE:

This same information is available on the **ECAM PRESS** page.

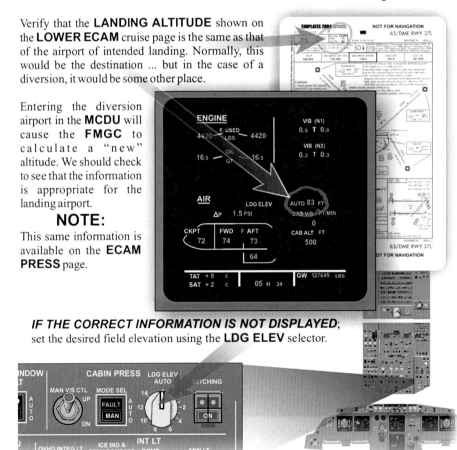

IF THE CORRECT INFORMATION IS NOT DISPLAYED; set the desired field elevation using the **LDG ELEV** selector.

published by UNIVERSITY of TEMECULA PRESS, Inc.

4. NAVIGATION ACCURACY check

There are several ways to do a **NAV GROSS ERROR** check. Here is a simple and quick method.

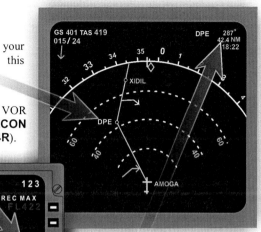

STEP 1: Select a **VOR** from your **ND** displayed flight plan. In this example, we'll use **DPE**.

STEP 2: Place your selected VOR (**DPE**) into the **PROG page / ECON CRZ** in the "**TO**" brackets (**LSK 4R**).

STEP 3: Compare the **FMGC** generated distance on the **PROG page** with the raw data distance displayed on the **ND**.

The **MAXIMUM** tolerance for a "**TERMINAL AREA**" accuracy check is **1 NM**.

LIMITATION:
In the **TERMINAL AREA** or **ON APPROACH**, **NAV** may be used only if

- the airplane is in **HIGH NAV ACCURACY** and

- the **NAV ACCURACY CHECK** was satisfactory.

5. *SEAT BELT SIGN switch*

The decision of when to place the **SEAT BELT sign ON** resides with the Captain; however, making the seat belt sign announcement and illumination prior to beginning the descent will help clear the aisles for the Flight Attendants, will free the cockpit crew, and will prepare for possible unexpected turbulence in the descent. All that being said, it is still up to the Captain as to the timing for the seat belt sign "ritual."

6. *ECAM STATUS page check*

The **ECAM STS** page will be displayed IF there is any anomaly that should require attention. If you select **STS** page, it should reflect the **NORMAL** status of the airplane's systems. An abnormal situation should cause the appropriate system page to be automatically displayed for your information and review.

Obviously, should an abnormal situation appear, you will be expected to make the appropriate response to the indication.

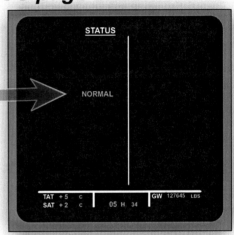

7. *APPROACH DESCENT checklist*

Complete the **APPROACH DESCENT** checklist to the **TRANSITION LEVEL** line.

APPROACH DESCENT CHECKLIST
(To be checked ALOUD by the Pilot Monitoring (PM))

Approach Briefing .... Complete
MCDU/FMGCs, radios .... Programmed, set for approach
EGPWS, Radar displays .... Terrain/weather
ECAM status check .... Complete
Autobrakes .... Lo/med/off

----------------- *TRANSITION LEVEL* -----------------

published by UNIVERSITY of TEMECULA PRESS, Inc.

STARTING THE DESCENT

DISCUSSION:

The Airbus **WILL NOT** initiate a descent on its own; it requires the pilot to **MANUALLY** tell it to start the descent, so there are two questions you ask yourself:
- When do we start the descent, and
- How do we start the descent.

WHEN ?

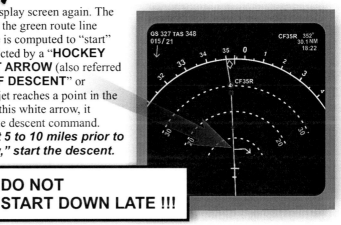

Look at the **ND** display screen again. The projected point on the green route line where the airplane is computed to "start" the descent is depicted by a "**HOCKEY STICK**" or **BENT ARROW** (also referred to as the "**TOP OF DESCENT**" or "**T/D**"). Once the jet reaches a point in the route just prior to this white arrow, it should be given the descent command. *I suggest about 5 to 10 miles prior to the "bent arrow," start the descent.*

DO NOT START DOWN LATE !!!

HOW ?
Once the descent clearance is received, and the target altitude is placed in the **FCU** and verified, there are two basic ways to descend. One is the "**MANAGED**" (**DES**) or automatic way. It is simple to initiate:

PUSH THE ALTITUDE SELECTOR KNOB.

One way you could screw up is to "**PULL**" the knob instead. That would initiate the second basic descent option, "**OP DES**" or Open Descent command. This method will require the pilot to control the descent instead of relying on the computer generated profile.

DISCUSSION:

If the **DES** mode is selected (**PUSH** the **FCU** altitude selector knob) prior to the hockey stick, the airplane will start to descend at about 1,000 **FPM**, gradually flying into the

projected ideal descent path and when able, it will intercept and descend on the computerized flight path indicated by the magenta "donut" (**V/DEV**) on the **PFD** Airspeed Tape. The jet will begin level off at **ALT*** so as to arrive on the altitude selected on the **FCU** altitude display (in our example 7,300 feet).

Normally, if everything went well, and we started down prior to the hockey stick or bent arrow, we would use DES (PUSH for managed descent) and life would be good.

BUT IF WE HAVE A PROBLEM AND NEED TO ...
GET DOWN RIGHT NOW!
OR if we just get a late start in the descent.

> *The most effective method of increasing the descent rate is to maintain a **HIGHER AIRSPEED** until **ALT*** and **THEN** decelerate rather than trying to slow up while in the descent.*

The two primary drag tools are:
- **SPEED BRAKE**, and
- **LANDING GEAR**

> **ABOVE 31,000** *feet, if airspeed less than than* **.75 MACH** *you* **MUST NOT** *use greater than* ½ **SPEEDBRAKE** *extension.*
> There is the possibility of activation of the high angle of attack or Alpha-Floor protection. **YIPE!**
> To preclude this possibility **the speedbrake deflection is limited to ONE HALF deflection with the autopilot engaged.**
>
> ### HOW A PILOT CAN SCREW THIS UP!
> If you shut off the autopilot, and pull the speedbrake to full deflection in this situation, you can get **ALPHA FLOOR** and the **THRUST LEVERS** may go to **TOGA LOCK.**

31,000 feet
DO NOT extend the gear above 250 Kts and 25,000 feet!
This is the maximum landing gear extend speed and altitude. If you attempt to **EXTEND** landing gear above **260 kts**, a **HYDRAULIC SAFETY VALVE** closes to prevent landing gear extension.

25,000 feet
DO NOT extend the FLAPS OR SLATS above 20,000 feet MSL!
This is the maximum **FLAP** extended altitude.

20,000 feet
ALT*

Retraction of the spoilers should begin about **ALT*** on the **PFD FMA**, and slowly continue until stowed.

There should be **NO SPOILERS DEPLOYED** as the thrust levers begin to increase the thrust.

1500 feet AGL

The **SPEED BRAKE/SPOILERS** have restrictions to use below 1,500 feet, and for the purposes of this discussion, we should consider this a target altitude for the retraction of the spoilers.

notes on using SPEEDBRAKE/FLAPS for drag.

☎ When extended, speed brakes increase the **VLS**.

☎ ***BIG PROBLEM!!!*** When the speed brakes are fully extended, the **VLS** may actually be higher than the **VFE** . What this means is that if you try to lower flaps with speedbrakes extended, you may overspeed the flaps.

> *You **ARE REQUIRED** to notify maintenance if VFE (Flap Extended Speed)is exceeded. Logbook entry REQUIRED after landing.*

It may be necessary, in this case, to retract the speedbrakes, decrease the rate of descent and allow the speed to decrease ***BEFORE*** selecting the flaps.

✎ ***FURTHER PROBLEM***: In-flight extension of the **SLATS** "increases" the engine idle speed and thrust with little noticeable increase in drag.

☎ Speedbrake rate of retraction is slower when going fast. May take as long as 25 seconds (50 seconds for A319) from full extension.t **ALT*** (just prior to reaching the level-off altitude) start gently and smoothly retracting the speed brake. AVOID aggressive speedbrake movement!

> Here are the ***SPEEDBRAKE LIMITATIONS***:
>
> **NO GREATER THAN ONE-HALF POSITION** when
> - *BELOW .75 MACH, and*
> - *ABOVE FL 310.*
> *POSSIBLE activation of* **NOT GOOD!**
> *the high angle of attack protection!*
>
> **INFLIGHT** with **SLATS RETRACTED**:
> - *DO NOT USE SPEEDBRAKE BELOW 200 KIAS!!!*

notes on using the GEAR for drag.

Extending the **LANDING GEAR** will provide a significant amount of drag and does **NOT** cause excessive noise or vibration in the cabin even at higher airspeeds. *"When airspeed is greater than 260 kts, a HYDRAULIC SAFETY VALVE cuts off the HYDRAULIC SUPPLY and LANDING GEAR CANNOT BE EXTENDED. HYD PRESS restored when airspeed below 260 KTS and landing Gear handle out of the UP position."*

> Here are the ***LANDING GEAR LIMITATIONS***:
>
> MAX SPEED to EXTEND THE GEAR (VLO)......................... 250 Knots
> MAX SPEED to RETRACT THE GEAR (VLO) .... 220 Knots
> MAX SPEED with the GEAR EXTENDED (VLE) ... 280 KIAS/ .67 MACH
>
> MAX EXTEND ALTITUDE ....25,000 feet MSL

Since we are on the subject of descents, I thought it would make sense to discuss the **EMERGENCY DESCENT** procedure at this point.

EMERGENCY DESCENT

This is an AUTOPILOT "ON" MANEUVER
IMMEDIATE ACTION ITEMS

1: O2 MASK and REGULATORS .... As required.

2: Crew communications .... Establish

3: FCU target altitude .... **SET either a safe altitude or 10,000 feet**.
The target descent altitude is to get the airplane down to 10,000 feet in order to meet the oxygen requirements for passenger survival. The biggest concern is **NOT** to hit any terrain, so we have to pick a heading that ensures terrain clearance. Reference to the navigation charts will indicate **MEA, MORA or MOCA** if descending on airways. In descents **OFF** airways to avoid traffic conflicts, use the **GRID MORA**. If under the control of **ATC**, request vectors "clear of terrain."

4: FCU EXPED switch .... **PUSH** and observe light illuminate.
It automatically engages managed speed.
The expedite function will generate commands to reach the altitude set in the **FCU** window with 'maximum vertical gradient". In descent, we can expect airspeed commands of **.80 M/ 340 KIAS**. To dis-engage EXPED, select a new vertical speed mode or selected speed.

5: HEADING .... **SET** as required.
Particularly when flying in **RVSM** (Reduced Vertical Separation Minima) it may be necessary to "get off the airways **ASAP**". So the initial descent heading will probably be 90 degrees to the current heading...then your main concerns will revert to terrain clearance.

FIRST ... CONCERN FOR TRAFFIC;
THEN CONCERN FOR TERRAIN.

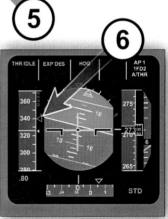

6:TARGET SPEED.... CONFIRM, .80M/340 kts
use the **PFD** indication.
Since we are using the **EXPED** switch, we can expect the speed triangle to be at **.80M/340 KIAS**.

7: THRUST .... **"CONFIRM"** in idle.

Potential problem. It is **VERY** desirable to continue to operate in **AUTOTHRUST** ... So **DO NOT** move the thrust levers manually to the idle detent. If you do move the thrust levers to the idle detent, the **A THR** will shut off and the potential for disaster becomes greatly increased. There is **NO REQUIREMENT** to touch the thrust levers during this evolution. We look at the **PFD / UPPER ECAM** to see what the thrust is.

NOTES:

The **FADEC** has three **IDLE** modes. When in **EXPED**, it uses the "**MODULATED**" mode which governs the thrust to maintain bleed system demands of the airplane. When in this idle mode, the word **IDLE** is displayed on the **UPPER ECAM**. (FYI: *The two other modes are* **APPROACH IDLE** *and* **REVERSE IDLE**).

> ## How can a pilot screw up?
> ## *PULLS THE THRUST LEVERS MANUALLY INTO THE IDLE DETENT !*

If the pilot looks at the **ECAM** and sees the display **CL** as well as **IDLE** and thinking that the thrust must be calling for something well above **IDLE** thrust .. **AND PULLS THE THRUST LEVERS TO THE IDLE DETENT!**. *OMIGOSH !* <u>Don't do that</u>*!* As long as **IDLE** is annunciated on the display between the instrument indicators and the thrust indicators reflect an idle indication, the engines

8: SPEEDBRAKES .... **EXTEND**

On autopilot, speedbrake extension is limited to ½ when altitude is above 31,000 feet.

> *The reason is that >F310 and <M.75 possibility of activation of the High Angle of Attack protection (ALPHA PROT) can occur if full extension is used on the speed brake. YIPE!!!.*

> ### This is an AUTOPILOT ON maneuver!
> ## *DO NOT TURN OFF AUTOPILOT*
> *... the speedbrake would go to full extension.*

9: TRANSPONDER 7700

10: ATC .... Advise

This is an obvious event if we are within radio range of the controlling agencies. If outside **VHF** communications range, such as **NATS** (North Atlantic Track System), use other airplanes to handle your communication as it may be a somewhat complex situation. Use whatever resource is available.

> Go to the **QRH** checklist to complete the **REFERENCE ITEMS**.

PASSING FL 180

WING LIGHTS switch .... ON

The idea of turning on the wing lights is to improve the ability of other airplanes to "**SEE YOU**." The **LANDING LIGHTS** have a suggested 250 kt limitation on extension.

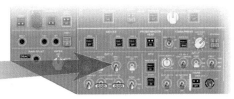

FYI: **FL180** is also the **TRANSITION LEVEL** for all of the US airspace as well as many other places in the world. Transition **ALTITUDE** can be much lower, such as **FL40 (4000 feet MSL)** in Paris, France; but I have never seen the transition level higher than **FL180**.

STERILE COCKPIT procedures begin.

DEFINITION OF STERILE COCKPIT:

NO flight crewmember may engage in **ANY** activity which distracts or interferes in any way with the proper conduct of duties. This would include:
- Radio calls for non-safety related purposes,
- Announcements to the passengers promoting company or points of interest,
- Paperwork unrelated to safe conduct of the flight,
- Eating meals or drinking beverages (**NO COFFEE OR COLA, etc**)
- Engaging in nonessential conversation,
- Reading materials not related directly with the proper conduct of the flight.

NO SMOKING switch ...... AUTO, then back to ON

Cycle the **NO SMOKING** sign when leaving **FL 180** or when leaving cruise altitude if it is lower than **FL 180**. Here is the reason: cycling the switch one time rings two chimes ... and this is the signal to the Cabin Attendants that this is the beginning of a **STERILE COCKPIT**.

Descending through
TRANSITION LEVEL

ALTIMETERS set and announce QNH (In/hPa)

There are three altimeters to set: Captains and First Officers on their respective **EFIS** control panels, and the Captain sets the **STANDBY ALTIMETER** Kollsman window.

APPROACH DESCENT checklist

Complete the APPROACH DESCENT checklist

```
----------------- TRANSITION LEVEL -----------------

   Altimeters ....................................... _____ in Hg/hPa, set

       -------------- CHECKLIST COMLETE --------------
```

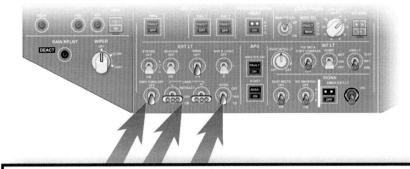

When slowed to 250 Kts
LANDING LIGHTS .... *ON*

During extension, the landing lights are pushed into the slipstream by little electric motors. Once extended, the speed restriction no longer applies.

RUNWAY TURNOFF LIGHTS .... *ON*
NOSE LIGHTS .... *ON*

CABIN NOTIFICATION

DO NOT FORGET THIS ANNOUNCEMENT! If you are flying with the cabin crew on subsequent legs and expect a cup of coffee, don't forget.. The Cabin Attendants will be waiting for this in order to get prepared for landing.

It is intended to be a "stand-alone" broadcast ... by this I mean, it is ONLY the following statement unaccompanied by any other comment:

> "*Flight Attendants prepare for landing.*"

Setting up the Captains comm panel can be time intrusive and complex, so I recommend that you use the handset located at the rear of the lower console.

WHAT CAN PILOTS SCREW UP!

In addition to forgetting the Cabin Attendants, there are two other possibilities here:

1. Broadcasting to the whole world your Cabin announcement. I am sure you have heard plenty of these broadcast on the **ATC** frequency. *DOH!* A good way to avoid this is to use the handset for cabin announcements.

2. The second screw up is to not get the handset properly reseated. This could keep the handset mic "**HOT**" and everything that is then said in the cockpit is broadcast to the cabin. This is ***NOT*** a good thing.

FLYING THE APPROACHES
AIRBUS STYLE

The Airbus A320 airliner in this discussion is certified to fly the following approaches to published minimums. They are in three broad procedure categories;

- **ILS** (precision approaches) which includes
CAT I, CAT II/III Autoland, ILS PRM (Precision Monitoring Approach).

- **APP NAV** approaches (managed) which includes
VOR, NDB, GPS, RNAV, RNP, and other emerging technologies as they are approved by controlling agencies. All must be line selectable.

- **CDA** approaches (selected) which includes **LOC** only, **SDF, LDA** without glideslope, **Back Course, ASRLOC**, and the **VOR** and **NDB if NOT** line selectable. **CDAP**s (Constant Descent Approach Profile) procedures that are known by several different acronyms.

One of the challenges is deciding which approach is to be flown using which technique. Here is an easy way.

ILS is to be flown like an ILS ... that one is easy.

If the approach is in the list on the F-PLAN page list of approaches when you do the LATERAL REVISION of the landing airport, then it is said to be "line-selectable." You use the managed or APP NAV approach technique.

All the rest of the non-precision approaches that use the CDA or CDAP techniques.

> WHAT'Z THE GEE-ESS-EYE-AY* FOR THIS APPROACH?

*GSIA is "GlideSlope Intercept Altitude"

INTRODUCTION

Probably the **MOST** challenging part of the flight evolution is that small segment between the Final Approach Fix (**FAF** or **GSIA**) and the Missed Approach Point (**MAP**) or Missed Approach Waypoint (**MAWP**). . Unfortunately, there exists a vast library of publications, manuals, periodicals, handouts, and other sources filled with a never-ending list of changing limitations and rules governing the operation of the approach segment. These are only clearly understood by one or two experts ... and they don't talk to pilots. So we are left with the daunting task of trying to sort out the situation for ourselves. In reality, all it is that pilots really want to do is **FLY SAFELY,** not bend the airplane, and stay out of the Chief Pilot's office. So, here is the **EXTREMELY** condensed version of **ONLY** what you absolutely need to know to slip by and pass your checkride.

Where this particular airplane model and type is concerned, there are only

THREE TYPES OF APPROACHES

(I'm **NOT** including **VISUAL APPROACHES** in this list)

There are the **ONLY** three general types of approaches we will discuss in this manual:

- **ILS** approaches,
- **APP NAV APPROACH**,
- **CDAP** or **CDFA** non-precision approaches.

ILS is the most common approach Airbus line pilots will fly. There are two basic levels of the ILS: **CAT I** and **CAT II/III**.

APPROACH NAV APPROACHES or MANAGED APPROACHES are basically **NON-ILS** (or non-precision) approaches that are "*LINE SELECTABLE*".
These include: **VOR, NDB, LOC BC** (back-course), **LOC, SDF, LDA** (without ground based glideslope), **RNAV**, and **GPS**.
In this approach, the **FMGC** will construct an onboard **FLIGHT PATH** that the airplane can fly without pilot input, just like a coupled **ILS**.

CDAP (Constant Descent Approach Procedure) or SELECTED MODE APPROACHES are basically "everything else".
Any Non-ILS approach that cannot be line selected must be categorized as a **CDAP** approach.
This **CDAP** technique requires the **PILOT** to control the vertical path to the runway using the **V/S-FPV** selector on the **FCU**. Using a reference to the **FPV** indicator (the "**BIRD**") or the Vertical Deviation Indicator (the "**DONUT**") to control the rate of descent.

INTRODUCING "APPCH PHASE".

REVIEW of APPCH PHASE:
Remember that selecting the **APPROACH PHASE** does **NOT** have anything to do with the selection of a specific approach or navaid tuning. All it does is manage the airspeed during flap extension by calculating and slowing to "**GREEN DOT**" airspeed.

This is possibly a new concept to some non-Airbus pilots; but is one of the features that 'Bus drivers appreciate about their jet. It is extremely labor saving and takes much of the work out of calculating the speeds during the very busy approach environment. Here is how to get it to work.

APPROACH PHASE
activated and confirmed

HOW TO SELECT the APPCH PHASE:

STEP 1: on the **MCDU**, Open the **PERF** page. It should have the title "**DES**" at the top. Line 6L (bottom line on the left hand side) should be "ACTIVATE **APPR PHASE**" in blue. If not displayed, select the "**NEXT PHASE**" entry at **LSK6R**.

STEP 2: Line select "ACTIVATE **APPR PHASE**".

STEP 3: The title should change to "CONFIRM **APPR PHASE**".

STEP 4: Select **LSK 6L** "CONFIRM **APPR PHASE**".

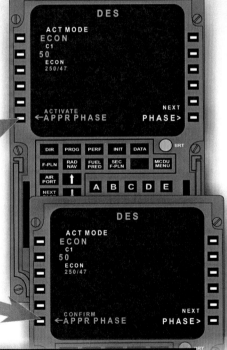

   ...OR if you forget all that ...

Alternately, the **APPCH PHASE** will **AUTOMATICALLY** activate when
- a managed **LATERAL MODE** is engaged, and
- the **DECEL** waypoint has been passed on the **ND**.

NOTE: *The DECEL waypoint will **NEVER** be above 7,200 feet AGL.*

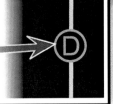

published by UNIVERSITY of TEMECULA PRESS, Inc.

"APPCH PHASE" *continued*

When the airspeed drops below **250 KTS** (which is the **MAXIMUM GEAR EXTEND** airspeed) you may lower the landing gear.

> **NOTE 1**: You are not allowed to extend the gear above **25,000** feet MSL.
> Generally, the landing gear is not extended until actually flying the ILS glideslope ... an exception is during descent using the gear as drag tool. A quick memory gouge is:
> **"OK TO EXTEND LANDING GEAR"**
> below **250 Kts** and **25,000 feet.**
>
> **NOTE 2**: Once the gear is **EXTENDED**, the airspeed limitation with the gear hanging out is: **280 Kts/.67 Mach.**
> **NOTE 3**: In order to **RETRACT** the landing gear the airspeed *MUST BE* below **220 Kts.**

DISCUSSION:

This is the part of the **PFD** that that tells you when it is OK to lower the flaps to the next setting ... and it is a teensy-tiny part of the instrument.

It is the **MAXIMUM FLAP SPEED** indicator and it looks like a small magenta "**EQUAL**" sign. You can barely see it ... it is insignificant visually, but **VERY IMPORTANT** to the operation of the airplane. **DO NOT** drop flaps to the "next" lowerflap setting until your airspeed is less that "▬▬".

HOW "APPCH PHASE" WORKS

As the airplane slows, and the airspeed drops below the "**MAXIMUM FLAP EXTEND**" airspeed indication for the next flap setting, if desired you are cleared to extend the flaps **ONE** notch.

When you extend the flaps, the green dot airspeed will slew to the next lower green dot airspeed, and the airplane will start to slow to that speed. As it does, the **MAXIMUM FLAP EXTEND** airspeed indicator slews also. When your airspeed drops below that indicated airspeed, select the next flap setting.

> ## NOTE:
>
> Some airline managements, in a panic that pilots will overspeed the flaps, have placed a restriction on lowering the flaps, here is a typical limit.
> *DO NOT LOWER FLAPS UNTIL AIRSPEED*
> *10 KNOTS BELOW THE MAGENTA EQUAL SIGN.*
>
> **GOOD TECHNIQUE** is to decelerate to near **GREEN DOT, S,** or **F** before selecting the flaps to minimize wear on the flaps/slats.

SIMILAR TERM CONFUSION

Let's clear out any confusion between "**ACTIVATING THE APPCH PHASE**" and "**ARMING THE APPCH**". Both are important and have major *SCREW-UP* possibilities.

ACTIVATING THE APPROACH PHASE

Activating and confirming the approach PHASE may be done on the **PERF APPR/DES** page of the **MCDU**. This will cause the **MANAGED AIRSPEED** to target the **GREEN DOT** with "**0**" **FLAP**. Further **APPROACH**. speed cues will be linked on the **PFD** Speed Tape according to the amount of **FLAP/SLAT** selected.

If, you screw up and accidentally select **APPCH** phase while in **CRZ** phase; the airplane will not enter the **DES** phase and will instead slow to managed speeds (in this case it will be "**GREEN DOT**").
You may accept that and use the **SPEED SELECT** to set the speed for the rest of the descent, bypassing the automated **SPEED** control features of the **MCDU/FMGC**, Or ... you can correct the situation and reenter the current cruise altitude on the **PROG PAGE** for the **CRZ** altitude. This will force the **MCDU/FMGC** back into the **CRUISE (CRZ) PHASE**. Alternatively, the airplane will automatically enter the **APPCH PHASE** during descent when it passes the (D).

Generally speaking, it is good Captain practice to **ACTIVATE** and **CONFIRM** the **APPR PHASE** below 10,000 Feet. The airplane is starting its slow-up anyway and that makes for a better fit into the ATC traffic flow. Just a suggestion.

> Here is the first point of confusion; Activating the **APP PHASE** can be done **AT ANY ALTITUDE**. However, **ARMING THE APPCH** must be accomplished *ONLY* **BELOW 8000 Feet AGL**.

ARMING THE APPCH

Arming the approach is accomplished by selecting **APPCH** on the **FCU** . These are the procedures to be aware of:

- On the **ILS**, do not arm the **ILS APPCH MODE** above **8,000** Feet.
  If you do, the autopilot and flight directors may disengage.
- On **APP NAV** approach, arm the **APPCH MODE** when at **FAF** altitude.
- On **CDAP** approaches, do not arm **APPCH MODE**,
  Pilot uses **FCU** to define glide path.

published by UNIVERSITY of TEMECULA PRESS, Inc.

DANGER

*KNOW what is the difference between a VNAV deviation indicator,
a V/DEV indicator and a Glide Slope deviation indicator?*

VERTICAL DEVIATION INDICATOR
and
VERTICAL NAVIGATION DEVIATION INDICATOR
versus
ILS GLIDESLOPE

Misunderstanding the difference could lead you to try and land below the surface
of the earth ...and this is NOT good. **YOU WILL DIE** ...and bust your checkride.

Here is the crux of the problem.

1. The ILS Glide Slope scale **CHANGES**, getting more sensitive the closer you get
to the ground.

2. The **VNAV** donut represents a computed vertical pathway predicated on
calculations from the FMGC. The range of the **VNAV** scale is **ALWAYS +/- 500
FEET**.

3. The **V/DEV** scale for the **Non-ILS Approach Nav** mode is predicated on a
"pseudo" glidepath constructed without reference to any fixed position on the earth.
The range of the **V/DEV** scale is **ALWAYS+/- 200 FEET**.

HERE IS THE PROBLEM. Since we fly about 90% of our approaches using the
ILS (or other **PRECISION APPROACH**), once we get into the **Non-PRECISION
APPROACH e**nvironment, it is very simple to get confused as to the relative
position of the airplane between the flight path and the ground.
Consider this situation:

Using either the **VNAV** or the **V/DEV** for a flight path; even if you
are at 240 feet on the **VNAV** (or 90 feet on the **V/DEV**) **AFE** point
in the published approach, but you are more than half scale below
the expected glide path ... **YOU ARE BELOW THE SURFACE
OF THE EARTH**! I mean you are dead. You have crashed.

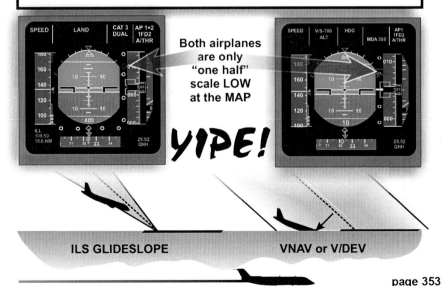

Both airplanes
are only
"one half"
scale LOW
at the MAP

YIPE!

ILS GLIDESLOPE   VNAV or V/DEV

Some notes regarding:

TRAILING EDGE FLAPS and LEADING EDGE SLATS

Four hydraulically operated **WING TIP BRAKES** are installed to **LOCK THE FLAPS AND/OR SLATS** in case of:
- *ASYMMETRY*
- *UNCOMMANDED OVERSPEED*
- *SYMMETRICAL RUNAWAY*
- *UN-COMMANDED MOVEMENT*

NOTE!

These **WING TIP BRAKES** <u>CANNOT</u> be reset in flight.

Similarly, a **FLAP DISCONNECT DETECTION SYSTEM** stops flap movement if excessive differential movement is detected between the inner and outer flaps on the same wing.

An **A-.LOCK** function **PREVENTS** initiation of **SLAT RETRACTION** from position 1 to 0 at a high angle of attack or low airspeed. *The inhibition is removed automatically when the angle of attack is reduced or airspeed increased*.

TAKE-OFF WITH FLAPS 1:

When **FLAPS 1** is selected for take-off **(1 + F)**, the trailing edge flaps **AUTOMATICALLY** retract to **0 at 210 Knots**.

TAKE-OFF OR GO-AROUND WITH FLAPS 2 OR 3:

1. When **FLAPS 1** is selected, the **1 + F** configuration is obtained if airspeed is **LESS THAN 210 Knots**.
2. The trailing edge flaps **AUTOMATICALLY** retract to configuration **0 at 210 Knots**.

FLAPS SELECTION IN FLIGHT:

1. When **FLAPS** lever is moved from 0 to 1 in flight, only the slats are extended.
2. After **FLAP** retraction, configuration **1 + F** is no longer available until the airspeed is **100 Knots or less**, **UNLESS FLAPS 2** or more has been previously selected.

POSITION	SLATS	FLAPS	MAX SPEED	USE FOR ...
1	18	0	230	INITIAL APPROACH
1(1+F)	18	10	215	TAKE-OFF
2	22	15	200	TAKE-OFF/APPROACH
3	22	20	185	TO/APPRCH/LAND
FULL	27	40	177	LANDING

published by UNIVERSITY of TEMECULA PRESS, Inc.

FINAL APPROACH steps

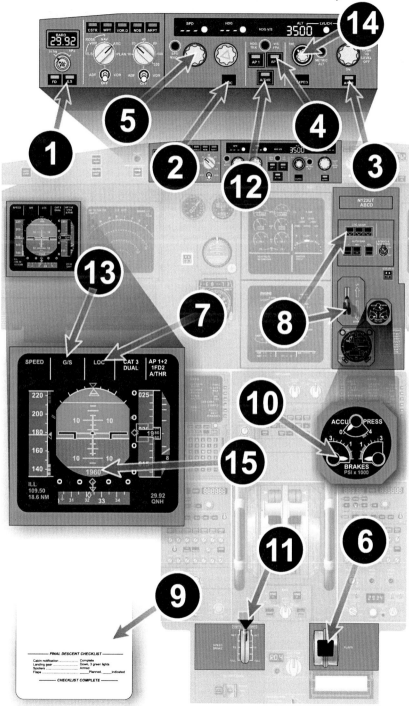

SETTING UP FOR THE TYPICAL

ILS
CAT III AUTOLAND

In order for the jet to automatically fly the glideslope and arrive at the runway ready to land, it has to be set up. Here are steps that make this rascal perform its magic.

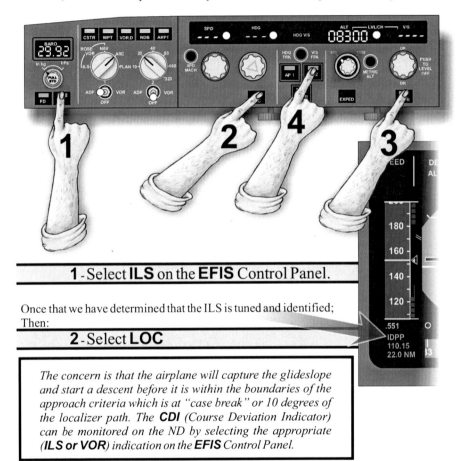

1 - Select **ILS** on the **EFIS** Control Panel.

Once that we have determined that the ILS is tuned and identified; Then:

2 - Select **LOC**

*The concern is that the airplane will capture the glideslope and start a descent before it is within the boundaries of the approach criteria which is at "case break" or 10 degrees of the localizer path. The **CDI** (Course Deviation Indicator) can be monitored on the ND by selecting the appropriate (**ILS or VOR**) indication on the **EFIS** Control Panel.*

(when within 10 degrees of capture), then....

3 - Select **APPR** on the **FCU,** and

4 - Select the second **AUTOPILOT(AP2)** on the **FCU.**

If everything works, the airplane will intercept the glideslope and the localizer and fly itself **AUTOMATICALLY** to the runway threshold. It is truly a sight to behold.

5. MANAGED speed .... SELECT

(on command from the PF).
If an airspeed is annunciated in the FCU, it will be necessary to PUSH the selector knob to transition to the managed mode. Managed speed is recommended unless **ATC** or other flight contingencies require a specific speed to be flown or set as a target. With **APPR PHASE** as the operative mode and managed airspeed, the airplane will slow to **GREEN DOT** airspeed.

6. FLAPS .....SELECT (on command).

Respect the limitation, 10 knots below the extend flap limit speed ("=" sign on the speed tape). Ideally, allowing the airspeed to decelerate to **GREEN DOT, S, or F** airspeed is desirable.
Once selected, the flap extension progress can be monitored on the **UPPER ECAM.**

7. [PF] "LOC" CAPTURE .... "ANNOUNCE".

[PF] **"LOC"** capture .... **"ANNOUNCE".**
When the localizer becomes the operative heading mode, the airplane is now considered to be within the confines of the approach.
The PF monitors the capture on the **FMA** on the **PFD** and states so.

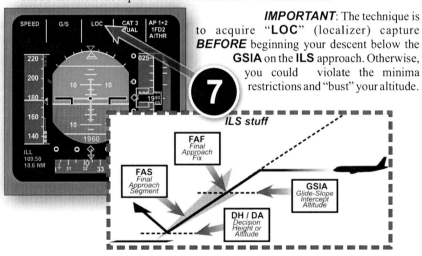

IMPORTANT: The technique is to acquire "**LOC**" (localizer) capture *BEFORE* beginning your descent below the **GSIA** on the **ILS** approach. Otherwise, you could violate the minima restrictions and "bust" your altitude.

ILS stuff

FAF
Final Approach Fix

FAS
Final Approach Segment

GSIA
Glide-Slope Intercept Altitude

DH / DA
Decision Height or Altitude

8. LANDING GEAR (on command from PF).............. DOWN

Exactly when to lower the landing gear is an artform. Only experience will give you the proper feel for when to actually "throw out the rollers". Some pilots use the technique of dropping the gear to coincide with the airplane's pushover as it intercepts the glideslope. They will put the handle down when the pitch indicator passes the lower dot on the PFD altitude tape..

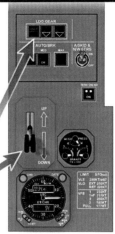

The **LDG GEAR** lights display proximity detector information received from **LGCIU 1**. They will be illuminated as long as **LGCIU 1** is electrically powered.

- The **RED UNLK** lights indicate that the gear IS NOT in the "selected" position.
- The **GREEN TRIANGLE** indicates the gear is down and locked.
- **DARK (BLANK)** indicator when **GEAR UP.**

The **RED DOWN ARROW** illuminates when the **LOWER ECAM L/G GEAR NOT DOWN** warning is activated.

This indicator comes on when *ANY GEAR IS NOT DOWN* and:

- *RAD ALT below 750 feet AGL with power back*
  regardless of flap position, or
- *RAD ALT below 750 feet AGL with*
  FLAPS 3 or FULL *selected, or*

9. FINAL DESCENT checklist .... COMPLETE.

------------ FINAL DESCENT CHECKLIST ------------

Cabin notification .... Complete
Landing gear .... Down, 3 green lights
Spoilers .... Armed
Flaps .... _____Planned, _____indicated

------------ CHECKLIST COMPLETE ------------

It is considered "**GOOD TECHNIQUE**" to include the words
**"GEAR DOWN,
FINAL DESCENT CHECKLIST"**
as a single phrase.

10. ALT and PARK BRAKE pressure .... ZERO.

NOTE: This gauge *ONLY* displays the yellow hydraulic system pressure that is supplied to parking and alternate brakes.

 With the landing gear down and the parking brake not set, the parking brake pressure gauge should indicate "**ZERO**".

published by UNIVERSITY of TEMECULA PRESS, Inc.

BRAKE and ACCUMULATOR check

One thing we will have to get used to as Airbus Pilots is this annoying 'Brake and Accumulator pressure indicator" check. It seems to be a constant concern that this system might have failed. ...and what would happen if it fails???

 The concern is that any pressure existing on the system gauge would indicate that the PARKING BRAKE may be set or partially engaged. We DO NOT want to have hydraulic pressure from the YELLOW system indicating on the BRAKE PRESSURE gauge.

AVOID ANY ACTION ON BRAKE PEDALS DURING FLIGHT

GOOD CAPTAIN TECHNIQUE

If we see that residual pressure has been accumulating or increasing on the BRAKE PRESSURE gauge, it might be a good idea to drop the gear a little early to allow time to try and fix the problem.

IF AFTER PLACING THE GEAR DOWN,

there is residual pressure indicating on the **BRAKES HYDRAULIC GAUGE**, *WE MAY HAVE A PROBLEM* !

Do this ONLY AFTER GEAR EXTENSION:

Depress the brake pedals several times. This may help decrease the pressure indication.

Leave the ANTISKID and NOSEWHEEL switch .... **ON.**

Then after landing:

IF PRESSURE REMAINS and AUTOBRAKES AVAILABLE:

Select **AUTOBRAKES** switch to **MED.**
This will cause the NORMAL brake system to take priority on landing and cancel the alternate pressure.

IF PRESSURE REMAINS and AUTOBRAKES ARE NOT AVAILABLE:

Apply **MANUAL BRAKING** just after touchdown.
What this does is cancel the alternative pressure by giving priority to the normal braking system source. Some asymmetry may occur, but it can be controlled by using differential braking.

11. GROUND SPOILERS .... ARM

Using the speedbrakes is allowed during the approach, even after
the completion of the Final Descent Checklist, BUT

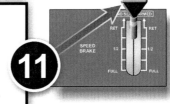

SPEEDBRAKES MUST BE
FULLY RETRACTED and
GROUND SPOILERS ARMED before:
- **FAF** (Final Approach Fix),
- **OM** (Outer Marker), or
- **1,000 Feet AGL** (on **VISUAL**).

12. AUTOTHRUST mode .... SPEED or OFF

NOTE: *OPEN DESCENT IS PROHIBITED* beyond the
- **FAF** or **FAP** on an instrument approach,
- **BELOW 1500 feet AGL** on a VISUAL APPROACH

Verify that either
- **SPEED** annunciated on the PFD, or
- **AUTOTHRUST** mode not selected.

Here's the details:
If operating in **OP DES** (OPEN DESCENT), the **A/THR** setting is **THR IDLE**.
If operating in **SPEED** mode, the **A/THR** mode system varies the thrust setting
to maintain speed (selected or managed).

So ... we want to either be in
SPEED mode or **A/THR ... OFF**.

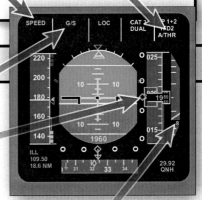

13. "GLIDESLOPE" capture
.... "ANNOUNCE".

Looking at the **PFD**, we want to observe
the glideslope indicator on the move
downwards towards the level pitch line, and
the **ANNUNCIATOR** change to **G/S** and
the aircraft pitch to maintain that indication.
*NOTE: capturing the glideslope does not
put the airplane into autoland mode. That
does not occur until descending below 400
feet AGL.*

The **PM** has the **SOP** assigned duty to "*monitor the sink/descent rate*".
Using the best **CRM** procedure and all communication skills at their command
(screaming is **OK** if required), inform the **PF** of any excessive rate or trend.

published by UNIVERSITY of TEMECULA PRESS, Inc.

14. MISSED APPROACH ALTITUDE .... SET on FCU.

IMPORTANT DISCUSSION:

Since the 3 different styles of approaches have been introduced, there may **_DEFINITELY_** be some confusion about when to set the missed approach altitude during the approach procedure.

Here are the protocols I am **_suggesting_**, These things change and maybe your airline has different criteria. Check these with your specific Company **OPSPECS** before you start using me for an excuse for your screwing up:

WHEN TO SET MISSED APPROACH ALTITUDE ON FCU	
- On **PRECISION (ILS)**:	**AT GLIDE SLOPE CAPTURE**.
- On **APPROACH NAV**:	When **FINAL APP** indicates **ENGAGED** on the **PFD FMA**.
- On **CDAP**:	After airplane begins **FINAL DESCENT**, and is **_BELOW_** the **MISSED APPROACH ALTITUDE**.

15. @ *1,000 feet AGL* *(RAD ALT on PFD)*.......... [PM] ANNOUNCE:

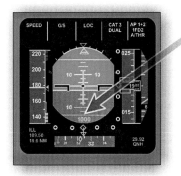

"1,000 FEET,
INSTRUMENTS CROSSCHECKED,
LANDING MEMO GREEN".

"Instruments crosschecked" means:
- **Radios,**
- **Autopilots,**
- **Flight Directors**

are correctly configured for the approach and have the appropriate indications.

If any **LANDING MEMO** item is not green,
- **CORRECT** the condition, or
- **PM** announce exception
(*"...landing memo green except for ___"*).

Some of those whacky

DEFINITIONS
used to define the APPROACH ELEMENTS.

FAF - Final Approach Fix.

In general, the Final Approach Fix for a non-ILS will be depicted on the approach plate by a "Maltese Cross" symbol. It is the point where the Final Approach Segment begins. *What pilots screw up:* They confuse the **FAF** with the **FPA** Intercept Point. Note that the descent does not actually begin until the airplane intercepts the Flight Path Angle for the approach.

FLY OFF SEGMENT.

In order to comply with constraints of the approach, it will be necessary to include a "Fly Off Segment" after the **FAF**. This will allow the airplane to intercept the computed **FPA**. We can tell if there is a significant "Fly Off Segment" by looking at the ND and observing a "**BLUE HOCKEY STICK**" after the **FAF**.

FPA - Flight Path Angle.

The Airbus **FMGC** has the remarkable capability to generate a "glideslope" from the database. It does this by taking a point 50 feet **TCH** (Threshold Crossing Point)) and extending it up to the **FAF** altitude. This is the basis for the Approach Nav approach to fly the vertical profile segment automatically.

In the **CDAP** approach, it is the **PILOT** who must define the **FPA** using either Rate of Descent or the **FPA** controls.

FAF Altitude - Final Approach Fix Altitude.

Since the Airbus FMGC only generates the flight path information from the FAF altitude to 50 feet .... the airplane ***MUST BE AT FAF ALTITUDE*** in order to use the Approach Nav Approach capability. This is the key to this approach.

FAS - Final Approach Segment

ILS FAS begins at a point where the **GSIA** and the **GLIDESLOPE** intersect and continues to the **MAP.**
Non-ILS FAS starts at the **FAF** and goes to the **MAP.**
NOTE: The Non-ILS descent from **FAF** altitude may not begin until intercepting the computed **FPA**.

MAP - Missed Approach Point

This is where the approach terminates ... you either **LAND** or you **GO-AROUND**. No other options. While several factors including Op Specs and company policy may dictate a higher altitude, the absolute minimum altitude that the airplane can descend to without landing is **50 Feet below MDA**. *PERIOD!!!!*

DA - Decision Altitude

In general, when flying the Non-ILS Approach, enter the **DA** in the **MDA** field of the **PERF APPR** page of the **MCDU**.
NOTE: For the **CDAP** approach, use the charted **DA + 50 feet**.

GSIA - Glide Slope Intercept Altitude

The **GSIA** is depicted on the Approach Plate.

published by UNIVERSITY of TEMECULA PRESS, Inc.

COMMON TERM USAGE:

Here are some of the elements of the approaches. I drew the diagrams to help us all get "on the same page" and talking about the same things. While I am trying to use commonly used terminology associated with this evolution, I realize that there is a wide variation in the labels that are placed on these items.

ILS

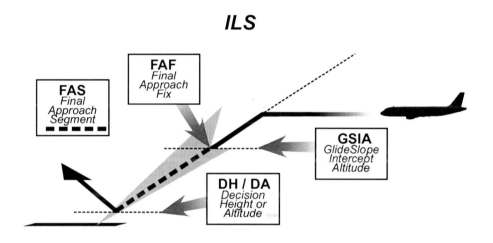

NON-ILS
Approach Nav and CDAP

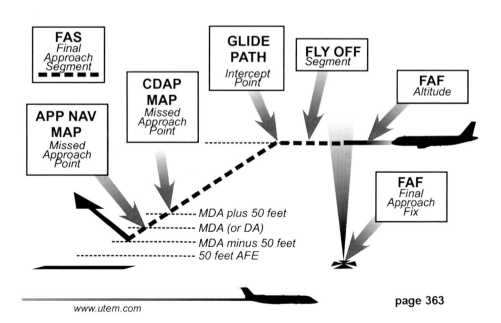

AIRBUS ILS
AUTOLAND

©MIKE RAY 2008

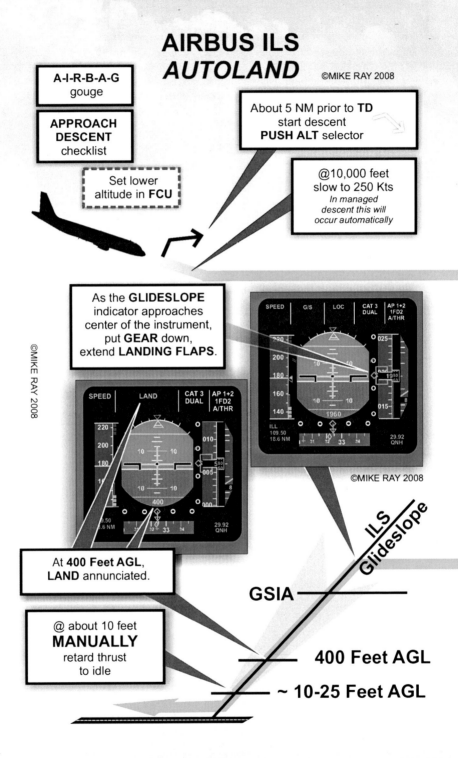

A-I-R-B-A-G
gouge

APPROACH DESCENT
checklist

Set lower altitude in **FCU**

About 5 NM prior to **TD**
start descent
PUSH ALT selector

@10,000 feet
slow to 250 Kts
In managed descent this will occur automatically

©MIKE RAY 2008

As the **GLIDESLOPE** indicator approaches center of the instrument, put **GEAR** down, extend **LANDING FLAPS**.

©MIKE RAY 2008

At **400 Feet AGL**, **LAND** annunciated.

@ about 10 feet
MANUALLY
retard thrust to idle

ILS Glideslope

GSIA

400 Feet AGL

~ 10-25 Feet AGL

published by UNIVERSITY of TEMECULA PRESS, Inc.

©MIKE RAY 2020

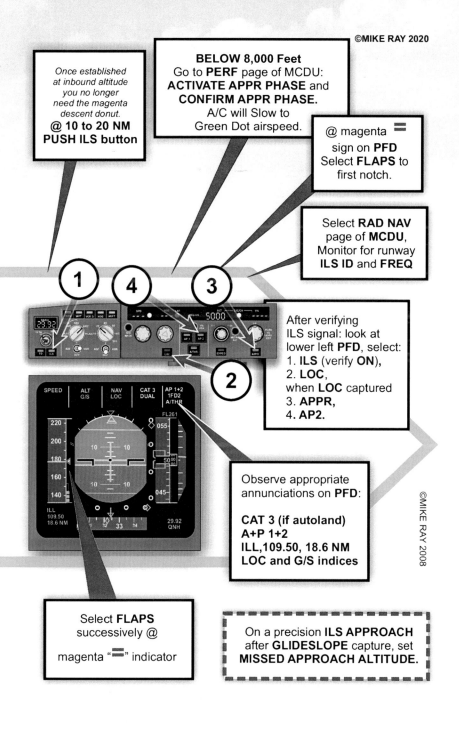

Once established at inbound altitude you no longer need the magenta descent donut.
@ 10 to 20 NM PUSH ILS button

BELOW 8,000 Feet
Go to **PERF** page of MCDU:
ACTIVATE APPR PHASE and
CONFIRM APPR PHASE.
A/C will Slow to
Green Dot airspeed.

@ magenta **=**
sign on **PFD**
Select **FLAPS** to
first notch.

Select **RAD NAV**
page of **MCDU**,
Monitor for runway
ILS ID and **FREQ**

After verifying
ILS signal: look at
lower left **PFD**, select:
1. **ILS** (verify **ON**),
2. **LOC,**
when **LOC** captured
3. **APPR,**
4. **AP2.**

SPEED | ALT G/S | NAV LOC | CAT 3 DUAL | AP 1+2 1FD2 A/THR

Observe appropriate
annunciations on **PFD**:

CAT 3 (if autoland)
A+P 1+2
ILL,109.50, 18.6 NM
LOC and G/S indices

©MIKE RAY 2008

Select **FLAPS**
successively @
magenta "**=**" indicator

On a precision **ILS APPROACH**
after **GLIDESLOPE** capture, set
MISSED APPROACH ALTITUDE.

FLYING THE
"APPROACH-NAV" APPROACH

REVIEW:

The Approach-Nav Approach is

> (1) **NON-ILS** (Non-precision) and
> (2) **LINE SELECTABLE**.

When you select the approach from the **F-PLAN** lateral revision of the **DEST** fix ... you *MUST* be able to "Line select" the approach with that name (for example **VOR14L**) from the list on that page ... it *MUST* be complete in the database. You *CANNOT* "build" the approach, add fixes, or manipulate the approach from the **FAF** (Final Approach Fix) inbound. The approaches in this category are:

> **VOR, NDB (ADF), GPS,** and **RNAV**.

Incredibly, the Airbus engineers were able to create a program that is able to construct a flight path that extends from a point 50 feet above the Threshold Crossing Height on the runway up a 3 degrees slope to a point that co-incides with the FAF altitude sometimes even higher).

What is even more amazing is that the airplane can actually hook-up and fly that pseudo-glideslope like an ILS and the PFD is equipped with the similar flight path indicators ... and even more astonishing is that the jet is certified by the FAA to do so down to 50 Feet AFE.

In order to accomplish this feat, there is a list of pre-approach criteria that must be met. Here is the list I have collected:

SYSTEM REQUIREMENTS:
If these requirements are not met
THE APPROACH IS NOT AUTHORIZED

AUTOPILOT MUST be USED IF: Ceiling and Visibility< 1000/3.
2 OPERATING FMGCs (*PFD FMA should show* **1FD2**)   **and**   **BOTH F/Ds MUST be ON.**
RAW DATA MUST BE MONITORED (*If available*)
APPROACH MUST BE DATABASE SELECTABLE
APPROACH CHART and CONSTRAINT ALTITUDES on F-PLAN PAGE MUST AGREE
RNP VALUES and ACCURACY BEFORE FAF; RNP=0.37, ACCURACY=HIGH.
TEMP MUST BE - 15°C or AS PUBLISHED.
ALTIMETER SETTING MUST BE FROM LOCAL SITE.
HDG-V/S MUST BE USED for the MISSED APPROACH
MUST CLEAR "PILOT INPUTTED RNP" ON CLIMBOUT IF MISSED APPROACH.

DO THE REVERSE "Z" ...

This seems like a daunting feat of memory on first glance ... but if you simply do the "**REVERSE Z**" in the "**A-I-R-B-U-S**" set-up, you will have accomplished the important parts of this task.

BIG SCREW-UP!

If you should be making the intercept using the speed selector; when you select the **NAV** mode, the speed will go to the one selected. If you don't check it, the chances are that the thrust will come on and the airplane will try to accelerate.

BRIEF THIS: DO NOT PUSH THE ILS/IL BUTTON!

If you push the **ILS/LS** button, the **RNAV** indications will be disabled and an amber **V/DEV** will start flashing on the **PFD**.

SET MINIMUMS	DH in the MDA field (PERF/APP page)
MANUALLY TUNE NAVAID	NDB (ADF) SPECIFICALLY
BEFORE ACTIVATING APPROACH	ENSURE SELECTED AIRSPEEDS ARE CONSISTENT
ARM NAV (LNAV)	WHEN "CLEARED FOR THE APPROACH"
MUST BE AT FAF ALTITUDE	BEFORE ARMING THE APPROACH
ARM APPCH (FCU)	WHEN AT FAF ALTITUDE
DESCEND TO FAF ALTITUDE	WHEN CLEARED and within 10° of FINAL COURSE or ON PUBLISHED FAS
CHECK RNP	Inside of 5 NM from FAF
BE FULLY CONFIGURED	NOT LESS THAN 2 NM from FAF
SET M/A ALTITUDE	When FINAL APP indicates ENGAGED on the PFD FMA.

The RNP Discussion:

There are 3 points to be made here.

POINT 1: Officially, 0.3 is required, but the Airbus computer will display **0.36** or **0.37**. Don't let this confuse you. If 0.37 is not displayed, manually enter 0.37 in **BOTH** **MCDU PROG** pages (**LSK 6L**). The **EPE** (Estimated Position Error) must be lower than the **RNP**. If it is, then the **PROG** page should display a required **ACCURACY** value of **HIGH**. If you don't have this situation, you will get a **NAV ACCURACY DOWNGRADE** message on the **MCDU**.

POINT 2: If this happens, you may select the autopilot for the other **FMGC** and see if that resolves the issue. That is to say, if **BOTH** FMGCs display an error message you will have to execute a **MISSED APPROACH**.

POINT 3: If a **MISSED APPROACH** becomes necessary for any reason ... guess what, the manually entered **RNP** must be cleared.

The FLY OFF segment discussion:

Since the computed vertical flight path "never" exactly coincides with the FAF ... there will "always" be a short horizontal segment where the jet flies past the **FAF** to intercept the vertical flight path. This is called the "**FLY OFF**". It will be identified by a "hockey stick" on the ND that goes from "white" to "blue" when **FINAL APP** is captured. Don't get all anxious when the jet doesn't start down right at the **FAF**.

BEFORE the FAF/FPA
The **FMA** indications on the **PFD** should be:
APP NAV (ARMED or ENGAGED) and
FINAL (ARMED).

Here is where the **V/DEV** indicator (called "**THE BRICK**") starts to become visible. It operates *ALMOST* like an **ILS** **GLIDE SLOPE** indicator.

PILOT GOUGE
"0.36 HIGH HOCKEY FINAL"

---

published by UNIVERSITY of TEMECULA PRESS, Inc.

"APPROACH-NAV" APPROACH
COMMENTS and SCREW-UPS!

MONITORING RAW DATA means:
- **DISPLAY the BEARING POINTERS**: On the **VOR, NDB (ADF)**
  use the switches on the **EFIS** control panel to select.
  ROSE mode **OK** for **VOR**.
- **CONFIRM TUNING** by observing identifiers on **PFD** and **ND**.
- **AURALLY CONFIRMED** by listening to the **IDENT** signal.
- **CONTINUOUSLY MONITOR THE AURAL SIGNAL**
  of the **NDB (ADF)** during the approach.

Normally fly the **APP-NAV** approach using
ONE AUTOPILOT AND BOTH FLIGHT DIRECTORS ON.
NOTE: The second autopilot will physically not engage. If both autopilots have failed, then a manual **F/D RNAV** is permitted.

THE APPROACH MUST BE LINE SELECTABLE. Only use the **EXACT** approach from the database ... ***DO NOT*** attempt to manually build, add, or delete waypoints inside the **FAF** to the runway.

Using **NAV** is **PROHIBITED for PROCEDURE TURN** course reversals. When the **F-PLAN** shows a **PROC T**, use the **HDG** or **TRK** mode to steer the procedure turn.

NAV mode may be engaged when on a heading that will intercept the final approach course to the **FAF/FAP**.

Only when ***"CLEARED FOR THE APPROACH"*** should you press the **APPR** button on the **FCU**.

Airplane must be **FULLY CONFIGURED**, the **FINAL DESCENT CHECKLIST** completed, and at **FINAL APPROACH SPEED** before **FAF/FAP**.

The **FMGC** computed **VERTICAL FLIGHT PATH** starts (or ends) at the published **FAF ALTITUDE**. The jet ***MUST BE AT*** *FAF ALTITUDE* to capture the flight path for the descent.

This is BIG !
*If you are flying an APPROACH NAV approach (a line selectable Non-ILS approach), you **MUST BE AT** the **FAF ALTITUDE** passing the FAF in order to intercept and acquire the glidepath.*

The **APP NAV APPROACH** procedure ***MUST BE USED*** for **VOR** and **NDB** approaches (if the requirements for an **APP NAV APPROACH** are met).

AIRBUS APP NAV Approach

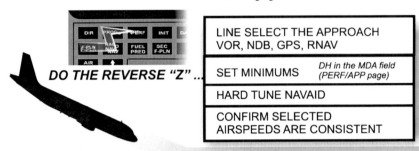

DO THE REVERSE "Z" ...

LINE SELECT THE APPROACH VOR, NDB, GPS, RNAV	
SET MINIMUMS	DH in the MDA field (PERF/APP page)
HARD TUNE NAVAID	
CONFIRM SELECTED AIRSPEEDS ARE CONSISTENT	

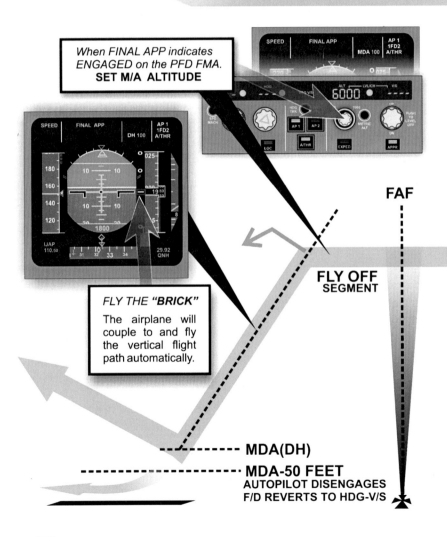

When FINAL APP indicates ENGAGED on the PFD FMA.
SET M/A ALTITUDE

FAF

FLY OFF
SEGMENT

FLY THE "BRICK"

The airplane will couple to and fly the vertical flight path automatically.

------- **MDA(DH)**

----------- **MDA-50 FEET**
AUTOPILOT DISENGAGES
F/D REVERTS TO HDG-V/S

BIG SCREW-UP!

FAILS TO ACTIVATE and CONFIRM!

If flying vectors to the intercept using manually set speeds, when selecting **NAV** mode, the speed goes to **250 Kts**.

WHEN "CLEARED FOR THE APPROACH" and ON INTERCEPT HEADING select NAV mode.

PUSH to **ARM LNAV**

NOT LESS THAN 2 NM from FAF

**BE FULLY CONFIGURED
GEAR DOWN
LANDING FLAPS
FINAL DESCENT CHECKLIST
APPROACH AIRSPEED**

WHEN CLEARED and Within 10° of FINAL COURSE or ON PUBLISHED FAS

**DESCEND TO
FAF ALTITUDE**

Inside of 5 NM from FAF

"0.36-HIGH-HOCKEY-FINAL"

WHEN AT FAF ALTITUDE
PUSH TO **ARM APPCH**

2 NM   5 NM

DO NOT PUSH THE ILS/IL BUTTON!

If you push the **ILS/LS** button, the **RNAV** indications will be disabled and an amber **V/DEV** will start flashing on the **PFD**.

FLYING THE CDAP APPROACH

TECHNICAL DETAILS

This approach may be selected whenever the **APP NAV** approach can't be flown.
Here are the reasons the **APP NAV** approach cannot be flown:

- The approach is based on a localizer, or
- The requirements for an **APP NAV** approach are not met.

Here are a list of approaches that may be flown using the **CDAP** procedure.

- **LOC** (**ILS** with glideslope out of service),
- **LDA** (without glideslope),
- **SDF**,
- **VOR**,
- **NDB** (**ADF**),
- **LOC BACK COURSE**,
- **ASR**, and other voice commanded approaches

DISCUSSION:

If the approach course is based on a
LOCALIZER FRONT COURSE,
then we use the **LATERAL (LNAV)** to track the **LOC** course.

If the approach course is **NOT** based on a
LOCALIZER FRONT COURSE,
then we would use **LNAV** in the **TRK** mode.

The **VNAV** (vertical path) in ALL CASES
is flown using the **FPA** to an adjusted **DA(CDAP DA)**.

---

what is the *ADJUSTED CDAP DA?*
ADD 50 feet to the **PUBLISHED MDA**.
Insert this **CDAP DA** on the **PERF APP PAGE** (**MDA** field).

PLAIN LANGUAGE TALK:

This approach is a lot like the **APP NAV** approach **BUT** the airplane does **NOT**
automatically follow a vertical segment after the **FAF**.

1. The pilot must decide **WHEN** to start down, and
2. **HOW FAST** to descend so as to remain on the "glide path".
3. The pilot controls the vertical descent segment
   using the **FPA-V/S** knob on the **FCU**.

There are two options for the descent control and indication, Either:

- **FPD** (Flight Path Director called "The Bird"), or
- Command Bars and Vertical Deviation Indicator (called the "Donut").

Unless you are **REALLY FAMILIAR** with flying that funny little
indicator some call the Bird (**FPD**), I would not attempt to try and learn
during the checkride. There is some complexity to understanding just
how it works. So when you start down on the 3 degree glideslope, look
for the vertical deviation indicator and "**FLY THE DONUT**".

---

published by UNIVERSITY of TEMECULA PRESS, Inc.

FLYING THE **CDAP** APPROACH

There are three questions that the pilot wants to know:
- How do I determine the FPA (Flight Path Angle?),
- When do I start down?,
- How do I "fly" the descent to MDA?

HOW TO DETERMINE THE FPA.

Here are FOUR methods:

METHOD 1: Look on the approach chart.

On "some" charts there will actually be a notation that states what the **FAS** (Final Approach Segment) flight path angle is. In our example, we can see that the **FPA** is 2.94°. We can also see that the FAS begins at the OUTER MARKER or 4 NM from touchdown point and 4.8 from the VORTAC (VOR). This tells us 2 ways to determine when to start down.

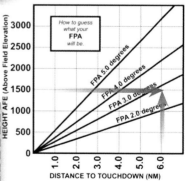

METHOD 2: Look at an ILS approach plate for the same runway. *If the FAF location and altitude is the same as the approach you are flying AND there are no step-down fixes;* then: Use the glide-slope angle published on the approach chart conversion table on the ILS approach plate.

In our example, departing the FAF at a 3 degrees FPA would get us to the runway threshold.

Gnd speed-Kts	70	90
GS	3.00° 377	485

MAP at D0.3 IFUI or
OWNER to MAP 4.6 3:

METHOD 3: Look in Flight Manual for appropriate graph or chart. Here is a "rough" chart I made for my use, yours may look a little different.

EXAMPLE: If the FAF is 6 NM from the runway and the FAF altitude is 1500 Feet AGL, then fly a FPA of 2.8°.

FLY OFF WARNING:
When using this technique, if glide-slope is excessively shallow (less than 2°) using the FAF as a starting point ... delay the descent to a point (FLY OFF) where a "normal" 3° descent can be made.

FLIGHT PATH ANGLE (FPA)

Chart: HEIGHT AFE (Above Field Elevation) vs. DISTANCE TO TOUCHDOWN (NM), showing FPA 5.0 degrees, FPA 4.0 degrees, FPA 3.0 degrees, FPA 2.0 degrees lines. Box: "How to guess what your FPA will be."

BEST
TECHNIQUE

METHOD 4 *(My personal favorite)*:
Still using our chart, Start with a 3 degrees glideslope. If, for example, the FAF altitude is 1500 Feet AGL, then you would have to start your descent (FAP) about 5.6 NM from the touchdown point.

FLYING THE **CDAP** APPROACH

WHEN TO START DOWN.

The Airbus has the remarkable capability to construct a "virtual" Flight Path Angle (**FPA**) that the pilot can select on the **FCU**. Once the distance is calculated for the departure from **FAF** altitude and this **FPA** (Flight Path Angle) is known, it is a simple extension of logic that if the airplane flies the **FPA** it should arrive close enough to the runway landing area to actually land the airplane.

Every approach **FAS** segments start after passing the **OUTER MARKER**. Most outer markers are identified by:

- **STATION PASSAGE,**
- **DME** from a **NAV RADIO,**
- **DISTANCE** on the **ND,**
- **AURAL SIGNAL** (Incessant beeping).

The distance **AFTER** the **FAF** for the descent point (**FAP**) is called the "**FLY OFF**. On some approaches, all you will have is the **CF** (Centerline Fix) on the **ND**. Some approaches use timed descent points and some use distance or radials from ground based navigation radios. Each **FAS** (Final Approach Segment) situation will be different. We have to determine **AND BRIEF** how we are going to determine our descent point (**FAP**).

It is recommended that IF a line selectable approach is available ...**USE IT!** It will have waypoints that can be used to measure your progress during the approach. If the approach is NOT line selectable, it may be good technique to insert waypoints into the **MCDU/FMGC** flight plan for progress milestones.

> Once you have decided how to identify the point
> where the descent **FPA** is to begin ... **BRIEF IT!**
> **PLAN TO START YOUR PUSHOVER ABOUT**
> **.3 NM BEFORE YOUR DESCENT POINT.**

THE FINAL APPROACH SEGMENT.

This final approach segment is (usually) flown using the autopilot and the **FCU**. Here is the 1-2-3.

STEP 1: Be **AT FAF ALTITUDE**, configured, on airspeed, Final Approach Checklist completed, and cleared for the approach.

STEP 2: Crossing the **FAF**: Contact Tower with report, start clock, etc.

STEP 3: Select the **FPA** button

STEP 4: Set in your **FPA** (Flight Path Angle).

CONFUSING NOTE: You then have 45 seconds to **PULL** the **V/S** knob towards you or the display reverts to dashes; BUT the value you set in is "**STILL ACTIVE**".

STEP 5: Approaching the descent point, which is about .3 miles before **FAP** (Final Approach Point),

> **PULL** the *Vertical Speed Selector knob*.

STEP 6: If you have set in some milestone waypoints,

> tweak the V/S knob if necessary to stay on the glideslope.

STEP 7: Once the airplane starts the descent and is actually below the missed approach altitude, *SET THE MISSED APPROACH ALTITUDE IN THE FCU*.

> Even if you have visual contact, continue to use the autopilot
> to control the airplane up to 50 feet below the published **MDA**.

FLYING THE **CDAP** APPROACH

CDAP OP SPECS and REVIEW ITEMS

The **VERTICAL PATHWAY** in all cases is flown using the **FPA** to an adjusted **DA**.

To determine the "adjusted" **CDAP DA** ... add 50 feet to the published MDA (Minimum Descent Altitude) and insert this adjusted **CDAP DA** on the **PERF/APPR** page in the MDA field.

On **FAS** (Final Approach Segment), **FPA** may be adjusted, *BUT NOT MORE THAN +/- 1 degree* from the predetermined angle. For example, you can adjust a 3 degree **FPA** from 2 to 4 degrees. If you require more than +/- 1 degree ... *GO AROUND* (DUH!!!).

Once established on final, a **MISSED APPROACH** is required if:
- Sustained raw data deviation exceeds 5 degrees,
- Loss of autopilot **IF REQUIRED** for the approach.

AUTOPILOT REQUIRED for the approach when:
- Ceiling reported less than 1,000 feet, or
- Visibility reported less than 3 miles, or
- Raw data not available.

Definition of "**RAW DATA**": Navigational information from ground-based Navaids.

Monitoring Raw Data: When raw data is displayed, pilots must confirm proper tuning by observing the decoded identifier on the **PFD** or **ND.** If the identifier **IS NOT** displayed, the pilot MUST use the **AURAL IDENTIFIER** ... and further, for the **NDB** (**ADF**), it *MUST BE CONTINUOUSLY MONITORED*!

- **LOC, LDA, SDF**: **ILS/IL** button must be selected
  to display localizer on the **PFD.**
- **LOC BACK COURSE**: **ROSE ILS** must be used to display
  the localizer on the ND. Because of *REVERSE SENSING*
  ... DO NOT SELECT ILS/LS button.
- **VOR and NDB**: Use the **VOR/ADF** switches on the **EFIS** control panel.
  ROSE VOR may be used if desired.

While the pilot determines and controls the vertical pathway to the runway, the **LATERAL PATH** is always flown using "raw data".

For a **CDAP**, the reported visibility must be above the published minimums to begin the **FAS**, with these exceptions:
- **NDB (ADF)** ... reported visibility *NOT LESS THAN 2 miles*.
- If weather less than **800/2** *MUST HAVE* an **EGPWS** operational.

ALL MISSED APPROACH/GO-AROUND As must be flown using the **HDG-V/S**. On some airplanes. advancing the thrust levers to **TOGA** will automatically change the **FD** mode to **HDG/V/S**. However, it is up to the pilot to monitor that situation.

FLYING THE **CDAP** APPROACH

KNOBS and BUTTONS review

ILS/IL switch SCREW-UP:

On the **APPROACH NAV** approach, we **NEVER** touch the **ILS/IL** selector!!! In fact, if a localizer is used for the approach ... we are forbidden from using the **APPROACH NAV** technique.

HOWEVER,

On the **CDAP**, if a localizer is to be used for navigation, we select the **ILS/IL** switch, BUT if we are flying a **LOC BACK COURSE** we **DO NOT** select the **ILS/IL** switch because of reverse sensing.

BUTTON A: There are two choices for vertical path mode ... you can set a Flight Path Angle (**FPA**) or a Vertical Speed (**V/S**). We make that selection by depressing the little black button in the middle of the unit.

KNOB B:

You can change the target altitude for the system using the **ALTITUDE SELECTOR** knob. It is a multifunction knob.

That is the easy part, here is where it gets complicated:

- **PUSH** will select **DES** mode allow the **FMGC** computer to climb or descend to the altitude selected on the **FCU** altitude window.
- **PULL** will select **OP DES** mode and allow the airplane to climb or descend in the most expeditious manner to the altitude in the **FCU**.
- **TURN** to select the target altitude.

KNOB C:

This is also a multifunction knob:
- **PUSH** the knob to **LEVEL OFF**.
- **PULL** the knob to **ACTIVATE** the selected vertical path mode.
- **TURN** the knob to change the value for the vertical path descent or climb (either **PFA** in degrees or **V/S** in feet per minute).

BIG SCREW UP!

When the **KNOB C (V/S knob)** is **PULLED**, the airplane will descend or climb at the **FPA** or **V/S** selected and try to go to the target altitude selected in the **FCU** altitude window and then level off.

If there is **NO INTERVENING SELECTED ALTITUDE** in the **FCU** altitude selector window, the airplane will continue to climb until it goes into **A.FLOOR/TOGA-LK** ... or if it is descending, it will

FLY RIGHT INTO THE EARTH !

The **CDAP** approach has the potential for this disaster. Since we will be descending at low altitude with the altitude set in the **FCU** window for the **MISSED APPROACH** altitude, we must

MAINTAIN SITUATIONAL AWARENESS!!!

---

published by UNIVERSITY of TEMECULA PRESS, Inc.

Personal observations and comments
SIMPLIFY - SIMPLIFY - SIMPLIFY

> Let me preface any personal comments with the caveat that the following comments are **NOT** to be interpreted as a suggestion that you deviate from any Standard Operating Procedures (**SOP**) or officially sanctioned information. This is just a "Captain-to Captain" conversation. *DO NOT* quote me on this but ...

SIMPLIFY THE PROCEDURES ... I feel that where it isn't necessary to complicate a subject ... that it shouldn't be done. Here is my first example:

When to set the Missed Approach altitude in the **FCU**. This debate has been raging for years and I have been watching it with amazement. Right at the point where the pilot is the most preoccupied, there is inserted in the procedure the requirement to set the missed approach altitude.
Look at the procedures presented in this book ...

WAY TOO COMPLICATED!

ILS	After **GLIDESLOPE** capture.
APPCH-NAV	When **FINAL APP** is engaged.
CDAP	After jet **BEGINS FINAL DESCENT** (and is below Missed Approach Altitude).

If I were King ...
Wouldn't it be much easier and certainly more simple if:

> *"When established at **FAF** altitude, **GSIA**, or intercept altitude inbound to the **FAF** (with **ALT** displayed on the **PFD FMA**) ... set the Missed Approach altitude."*

If you arrive at the **FAF** and the weather (or other considerations) make commencement of the approach undesireable, this would greatly simplify the problem of executing the Missed Approach at the **FAF**. Simply **PUSH** the Altitude Selector knob.

Another example would be the choice of **LANDING FLAP**. On this airplane and during a checkride ... why not simplify your life and select "**FULL**" flaps. This would avoid selecting that overhead switch (**GPWS LDG FLAP 3**), avoid changing the flap selection to **CONFIG 3** on the **PERF APPR** page, avoid the **VLS** speed change problem and all those other considerations associated with **FLAPS 3**.

Or how about during the sim-ride we dispense with that **FLEX** take-off. After you have demonstrated proficiency in calculating the flex temperature ... just use the **TOGA** position.

As so on ... as you become more familiar with the operation of the Airbus, you will see many places where you can simplify the operation. I have found that my brain freezes or turns to putty when I get past a certain amount of complications; particularly when I am new on a piece of equipment and particularly in a check-ride situation. But remember ...

ALWAYS BE SAFE.

AIRBUS CDAP Approach

DO THE REVERSE "Z" ...	VOR, NDB (ADF), LOC only, LDA, SDF, ASR IF flyingLOC back course, *GPWS G/S MODE - OFF*
	CDAP MINIMUMS published MDA plus 50 feet in MDA field (PERF/APP page)
	MANUALLY TUNE NAVAID
	PRE-COMPUTE FPA, or USE 3° and compute FAP (push-over)

DOING THE
PUSH-OVER

1: Be Configured, at FAF altitude, VAPP

2: BUTTON A select FPA,

3: ROTATE KNOB C-set FPA (3°).
If the knob is not pulled within 45 seconds, the window reverts to dashes BUT the value selected is still active..

4: Start clock, Report, etc.

5: PULL KNOB C at .3 NM before the FAP.

6: Tweak DESCENT rate using KNOB C.

7: Set KNOB B to MAA when below MAA. (Missed Approach Altitude).

FLY OFF SEGMENT

FAP *FAF*

⑤ ④ ③ ②

⑥

FAP minus.3NM

MAA - - - - - - - - - - - ⑦

CRITICAL POINT: At .3 NM before the **FAP** (Final Approach Point) ... *PULL* the **VERTICAL SPEED SELECTOR KNOB (KNOB C)**. Note that the **FAP** may be the **FAF** ... or to say that another way, If there is **NO FLYOFF**, then PULL the knob at .3 NM "before" the **FAF**.

published by UNIVERSITY of TEMECULA PRESS, Inc.

OK to use **NAV (PUSH KNOB)** up to the **FAF** if proper guidance available ... **BUT:**

DO NOT USE NAV between the **FAF and the RUNWAY!**

(pull knob - set headings)

SET FAF ALTITUDE in the FCU window and WHEN CLEARED ... **DESCEND TO FAF ALTITUDE (PULL KNOB)**

NOT LESS THAN 2 NM from FAF

BE FULLY CONFIGURED
GEAR DOWN
LANDING FLAPS
FINAL DESCENT CHECKLIST
APPROACH AIRSPEED

2 NM before FAF

(1)

CDAP approach
NOTES and SUGGESTIONS:

- If procedure turn is required, DO NOT USE **NAV** but rather steer around the turn using the **HDG SEL or TRK-FPA**.
- Select **TRK-FPA** before becoming established on the FINAL APPROACH COURSE.

- If approach based on a LOCALIZER FRONT COURSE **(LOC, LDA, or SDF)** then you can use the LOC mode for the lateral guidance.

- **DO NOT USE NAV** between FAF and the RUNWAY.
  OK to use "**LOC**" (see note above).

- Once established on the FAS, inside the FAF, *the lateral navigation **MUST BE** flown using "**RAW DATA**"*.

- If you are going to try and use **NAV** at any point in the approach
  ... ensure that the **F-PLAN** is properly sequenced.
  I recommend if there is any question that you select TRK-FPA early on and use TRK for the whole approach profile. Trying to use **NAV** in close on a **CDAP** is a recipe for disaster.

- **TRK** mode already has the wind correction.
  Just move the cursor to the direction you want to go.

LANDING the jet *(a quick overview)*

The **AUTOTHRUST** system should normally be used up to the point where "**RETARD**" (about 20 feet AFE) is called out by the automated voice. Then the thrust levers **MUST BE** manually pulled to the idle position.

However, and I am reluctant to even mention this, if thrust control is required, depress the instinctive disconnect button , and manually control the thrust. **DUH!!!**

8°	**DO NOT EXCEED 8° of PITCH** during the landing.

11.5°	**DO NOT** delay touchdown with a prolonged float to get a grease job: **TAIL STRIKES EARTH:** A320 @ 11.5° pitch; A319 @ 13.5°.

16°	**CROSSWIND LANDING: WING-TIP or ENGINE SCRAPE:** occurs at 16° of roll.

WARNING:
DO NOT ATTEMPT to GO-AROUND AFTER initiating REVERSE THRUST.

The landing sequence goes something like this:

@10 - 20 feet (AGL) *above ground level* — Select thrust levers to **IDLE** at the "**RETARD**" callout (20 feet AFE).

IF AUTOLAND ... Let airplane control the *ROTATION, TOUCHDOWN, AND ROLLOUT* to a complete stop

@ TOUCH DOWN — Select **REVERSERS**
AUTOBRAKING system will select **ON**
GROUNDSPOILERS will auto **EXTEND**.

@ 80 knots — Start coming out of reverse.

@ 60 knots — Be out of reverse

When SLOWED or STOPPED
THRUST LEVERS to idle
Raise **FLAPS** (Unless in icing)
Stow **GROUND SPOILERS**

TAXI SPEEDS
Use the **ND** groundspeed indicator.
Maximum recommended speeds:
- Straight Ahead ....25 Kts
- Turns less that 45° .... 25 Kts
- Turns greater that 45° .... 10 Kts

LANDING ROLLOUT

As airplane touches down and nosegear is gently grounded ...

1. VERIFY .... THRUST LEVERS to IDLE.

Use the **RUDDER** to maintain directional control and **AILERONS** to maintain wings level. These controls are effective down to about

60 KNOTS.
DO NOT USE NOSEWHEEL STEERING
above normal taxi speeds.

2. FULL REVERSE .... *after main gear touchdown.*

It is **OK** to reverse before nose gear touchdown,
but be aware that a slight pitchup may occur. Side-stick will easily control it.

3. GROUND SPOILERS................................. DEPLOYED

If they do not deploy, call out the abnormality and PF manually deploy spoilers if desired. Use of the spoilers is MOST EFFECTIVE at higher speeds. Note that it is NOT REQUIRED to meet calculated landing distances.

4. IDLE REVERSE........................ SELECT AT 80 KNOTS.

CAUTION:
Ensure forward idle reverse is achieved by
60 KNOTS.

Here is the problem: High thrust settings at low airspeeds have two results:
- Compressor stalls (Bang - bang - bang ... we have all heard that)
- **FOD** (Foreign Object Damage) .. and we have all seen it.

If desired, leave the reversers in "**IDLE REVERSE**" down to 25 knots.

5. ENGINE PARAMETERS .... MONITOR

The biggest concern is **ASYMMETRIC REVERSE THRUST** that would result in difficulty in steering. Other things to look for is excessive **EGT,** engine not in reverse.

6. AIRSPEED CALLOUTS ..... "60 KNOTS and 80 KNOTS"

7. THRUST LEVERS .... FORWARD IDLE

PROBLEM:
When deselecting reverse, the thrust levers have this resistance point that requires a little more pressure to overcome, and as a result, it is easy to inadvertently apply forward thrust by getting the thrust levers forward of the idle position.

8. BRAKES .... AS REQUIRED

Braking is normally recommended to be initially accomplished using the **AUTOBRAKE** system. Autobrakes use the **GREEN HYDRAULIC** system and initiation is activated by the extension of **GROUND SPOILERS**. Then, when the Pilot Flying depresses the top of the **RUDDER PEDALS**, the autobrakes will disconnect automatically and normal braking will occur.

WARNING:
Do **NOT** disengage the **AUTOBRAKES** using the **AUTOBRAKE** switch. Depressing the **RUDDER TOE BRAKE** will cause the **AUTOBRAKE** system to disconnect.

WARNING

If the **BRAKES** or **NOSEWHEEL STEERING** fails,

RELEASE THE BRAKE PEDALS
BEFORE
selecting the A/SKID and N/W STRG switch off

IF YOU DON'T, IT'S LIKE
HITTING A BRICK WALL!!

- BRAKE PEDALS .... IMMEDIATELY RELEASE
- A/SKID & N/W STRG switch .... OFF
- BRAKE PEDALS .... MODULATE

At this point, it is my opinion that the first thing to think about is:
- **STOPPING ON THE CONFINES OF THE RUNWAY.**

The secondary response is to
- **TAXI CLEAR OF THE RUNWAY.**

If there is any doubt, remain in position and
- ***NOTIFY THE TOWER OF YOUR ACTIONS!!!***

9. SET THE PARKING BRAKES.

We have continually encountered the **BSCU** failure problem during this manual flow discussion. It is a constant concern, and I would comment that I personally don't consider it a good Captain's decision to try and taxi or continue the trip with this issue.

Stop the airplane, set the parking brake, contact the appropriate **ATC** control agency. Once that is done, contact company maintenance and dispatch personnel and determine the contingency plan.

My personal view is that this **BSCU** problem, while it can achieve resolution with the flight crews, requires the coordination of appropriate personnel outside the cockpit.

TAXI-IN

> ### DO NOT EXCEED
> ## 40% N1
> #### when operating within congested areas

ENGINE COOL DOWN discussion:

The basic rule is:

3 MINUTES @ IDLE BEFORE SHUTDOWN

If you operate the engines above **IDLE**, then they should be motored for three minutes before shutdown. However, If the taxi time from landing to parking is less than three minutes, it is not necessary to motor the engines at the gate to achieve the three minutes.

WHEN CLEAR of the RUNWAY

The **NUMBER ONE** thing that the crew should be doing is listening to **ATC** (usually Tower or Ground Controller) for taxi instructions. While I don't say that you absolutely **CANNOT** be doing some of the runway exit flows, these are of secondary importance at this point.

The Captain has a fairly cursory list of items that involve shutting down the lights ... but the First Officer will be "head down" during part of this **FLOW.** The Captain **MUST** maintain situational awareness ... and if there is an ambiguity ... **STOP THE JET AND RESOLVE THE ISSUE.** This is very important where language differences between the crew and the controllers may make the situation questionable.

CAPTAIN ....TURNS OFF 5 LIGHT SWITCHES

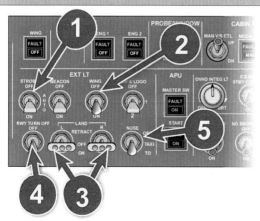

1. **STROBE LIGHTS**
2. **WING LIGHTS**

   The wing lights may

   be left on if desired.

3. **LANDING LIGHTS**
4. **RUNWAY TURNOFF LIGHTS**
5. **NOSE LIGHTS**

FIRST OFFICER FLOWS
When Clear of the Runway

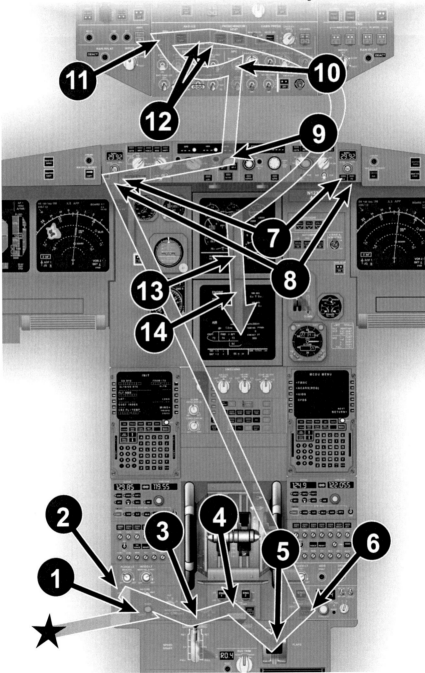

published by UNIVERSITY of TEMECULA PRESS, Inc.

FIRST OFFICER TAXI-IN FLOW

1. PWS (Predictive Wind Shear) **switch** .... **OFF**

2. WEATHER RADAR .... **OFF**

WARNING

The **WEATHER RADAR** and **PWS** must be
OFF
When operating in the ground environment around personnel.

3. GROUND SPOILERS .... **DISARM**
Verify the **SPEEDBRAKE** is in the **RET** position, and **DOWN**.

4. ENGINE MODE SELECTOR .... **NORMAL**

5. FLAPS .... **UP**

CAUTION

If there is the possibility of **ICE ACCUMULATION** on the **FLAPS**,
LEAVE THE FLAPS EXTENDED.
Notify the ramp that a flap inspection and potential de-icing may be necessary.

6. TRANSPONDER MODE SELECTOR .... **STBY**

7. ILS/LS BUTTONS .... **OFF**

8. FLIGHT DIRECTOR SELECTOR .... **OFF**

9. HDG-V/S / TRK-FPA BUTTON .... **HDG-V/S**

10. APU .... **AS REQUIRED**

The need to start the **APU** in order to supply electrical power or pneumatic air for
passenger comfort should be evaluated. The **APU** is not started until approaching
the parking area to conserve fuel and minimize **APU** service time.

11. WING ANTI-ICE SWITCH .... **OFF**

12. ENGINE ANTI-ICE SWITCH .... AS REQUIRED

It is true that the engine anti-ice should be continued during taxi-in if being operated in icing conditions; however, be aware that when we operate the engine anti-ice, *the MINIMUM IDLE IS INCREASED which could result in thrust output being increased.*

DEFINITION OF ICING
Icing conditions exist on the ground when
OUTSIDE AIR TEMPERATURE is 10° C or below, and
- visible moisture in any form is present
- the existence of surface snow, standing water, or slush
  may be ingested by the engine..

BE AWARE OF THIS

If **ANTI-ICE is ON**, perform engine runups
EVERY 10 MINUTES DURING TAXI-IN.
If icing conditions exist, leave engine anti-ice **ON** until engine shutdown.

It is a requirement that pilots report braking action to the controlling **ATC** agency and the company when they experience braking action less than good.

---

13. DIFFERENTIAL CABIN PRESS .... VERIFY ZERO

If differential pressure is **NOT** zero go to the Irregular Procedures section and it will tell you to:

1. Cabin Press mode ...... **MANUAL**

2. Manual V/S control ...... **FULL UP**

Put page number from your
Pilot Flight Manual for this irregular procedure.

WARNING:
Automatic depressurization **WILL NOT** occur upon landing when the cabin pressurization is being operating in the manual mode.
In that case,
YOU MUST ENSURE THE DIFFERENTIAL PRESSURE
IS ZERO BEFORE OPENING ANY CABIN EXIT.

---

page 386

14. BRAKE TEMPERATURE .... MONITOR

The **BRAKE TEMPERATURES** are displayed on the **ECAM WHEEL** page. If **BRAKES HOT ECAM** message is displayed on the upper **ECAM** message, then you are **REQUIRED** to advise Station Manager/Maintenance and **REQUEST THE GEAR BE CHOCKED**.

CAUTION

MAINTENANCE ACTION REQUIRED WHEN:

- Autobrakes or maximum manual braking was used to reject a take-off.

- Maximum manual braking used for landing.

- The temperature difference between two brakes on the same gear is greater than 150° C and the temperature of one of those brakes is lower or equal to 60°C.

- any brake's temperature exceeds 900°C.

Approaching the gate area, we need to make an evaluation regarding the braking action. Can we stop and turn and maneuver as will be necessary? If not, it might make sense to get a tow-in to the gate and parking position.

If the brakes are to be released for cooling

CHOCK THE WHEELS and
RELEASE THE BRAKES
CAUTION

POSITIVELY CONFIRM

Either have a flight crew member or ground personnel visually verify with the chocking personnel prior to releasing the parking brake.

THE AIRPLANE MAY MOVE IF NOT CHOCKED WHEN PARKING BRAKE IS RELEASED.

PARKING
CAPTAIN DOES 4 THINGS

ONCE AIRPLANE IS STOPPED

The ground personnel will be expecting the **RIGHT ENGINE** to be shut down first. It is encumbant on the flight crew to shut down that engine as expeditiously as possible to avoid injury to ground personnel.

---

1. [C] PARKING BRAKE SELECTOR .... ON

The parking brake is set simply by turning the handle to "**ON**". It is actually nothing more than a switch and **DOES NOT** require the Captain to hold the brake during the selection.

> The **ONLY** indication that the parking brake is set is an indication of **BRAKE PRESSURE** on the forward **BRAKES and ACCU PRESS** gauge.

Captain says, "**BRAKES SET, PRESSURE NORMAL.**"
First Officer verifies that the **BRAKE PRESS** gauge is indicating.

Unless released for cooling, the parking brake should be set even though the wheels are chocked. There is no situation where one would leave the airplane "un-chocked" for a prolonged period, even with the parking brake set since the accumulator pressure will gradually bleed off leaving the airplane unrestrained. It is assumed that the accumulator will hold adequate pressure for parking brakes up to 12 hours.

There are charts in the Limitations section for the holdover times for brake cooling.

---

2. [C] SEAT BELT SIGN .... OFF

---

3. [C] EMERGENCY EXIT LIGHT SWITCH .... OFF

---

4. [C] ENGINES SHUTDOWN .... REQUEST

WHAT CAPTAINS CAN SCREW UP !!!

DO NOT PRESS THE BRAKE PEDALS DURING ENGINE SHUTDOWN.

If you have the **TOE BRAKES** depressed (even a little teeny bit) when the engines are shut down, the **BSCU** will memorize the "last braking command". Then when the engines are started next time, then a brake problem could occur.

---

published by UNIVERSITY of TEMECULA PRESS, Inc.

ENGINE SHUT-DOWN

[FO] #2 ENG MASTER SWITCH ..... OFF, FUEL FLOW ZERO

If not already shut down and on the Captain's request, shut down the number 2 engine immediately after arrival at the gate. Verify engine shutdown by observing zero fuel flow, decreasing **EGT** and **N1**.
NOTE: *Failure of the **EGT** to decrease after turning the **ENG MASTER** switch **OFF** may indicate engine tailpipe torching.*

This is a typical Check Pilot ruse, so be ready. The procedure is in the **QUICK REFERENCE CHECKLIST**(QRC), so ask for the **QRC** checklist.

[C,FO] ESTABLISH ELECTRICAL POWER

IF USING EXTERNAL POWER:

1. [C,FO] Verify the EXT PWR AVAIL light .... ON

2. [C,FO] EXTERNAL POWER SWITCH .... ON

3. [C,FO] VERIFY "ON" LIGHT .... Illuminates.

IF USING APU POWER:

1. [C,FO] Verify the APU PWR AVAIL light .... ON

[FO] #1 ENG MASTER SWITCH ..... OFF, FUEL FLOW ZERO

Once **GROUND POWER** or **APU** available, shut down the #1 engine.
The electrical power will shift over automatically.

---

or ... Simple PROBLEM

As an awareness item, the Check Pilot may give you a sim problem to see if you are monitoring the parameters ... and this could be a real world problem also. If all the engine parameters are **NOT** decreasing after selecting the **ENGINE MASTER** switch **OFF**, then

[C,FO] PUSH ASSOCIATED ENGINE FIRE SWITCH.

This will cut off the fuel to the engine at the Low Pressure Valve. The engine will continue to run until it has burned the remaining fuel in the fuel line. This will take about **ONE L-O-N-G** minute.

NOTICE THE DIFFERENCE BETWEEN THESE TWO SITUATIONS:
1. **QRC EMERGENCY** ... All engine parameters decreasing **EXCEPT EGT**.
2. Simple problem ... When **ENG MASTER** off, engine continues to run.

FIRST OFFICER FLOWS
PARKING AT THE GATE

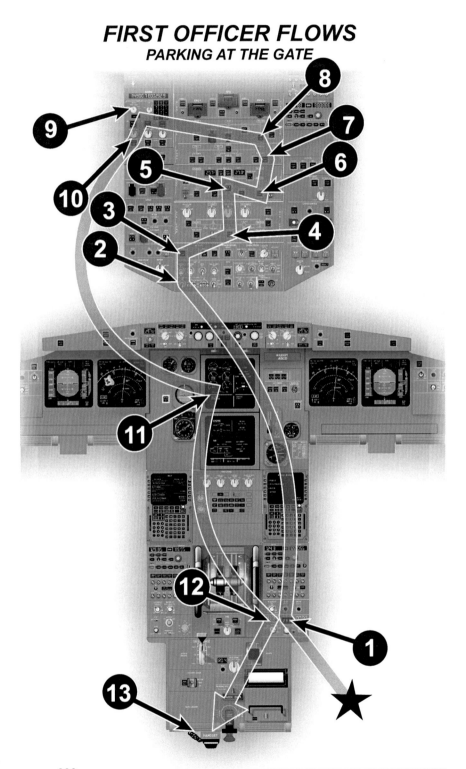

published by UNIVERSITY of TEMECULA PRESS, Inc.

FIRST OFFICER FLOWS
PARKING AT THE GATE

1. TRANSPONDER MODE SELECTOR .... OFF

2. BEACON SWITCH .... OFF

This is the signal to all the ground and servicing personnel that the engines are shut down and it is safe to approach the aircraft.

3. ENGINE ANTI-ICE SWITCHES .... OFF

4. APU BLEED SWITCH .... AS REQUIRED

If you are going to use the APU for CABIN air conditioning; wait until the engines are shut down before selecting the switch ON to prevent engine fumes from being pumped into the cabin.

5. CROSSBLEED SWITCH .... AUTO

6. #2 ENGINE GENERATOR .... ON

Required when single engine taxi procedure used.

7. FUEL PUMP SWITCHES .... OFF

There are **SIX PUMP SWITCHES** to deselect.

8. YELLOW ELECTRIC HYDRAULIC PUMP .... OFF

Required when single engine taxi procedure used.

9. AIR DATA/INERTIAL REFERENCE SYSTEM (ADIRS).

This is called the:
POSITION DEVIATION AND RESIDUAL GROUNDSPEED check.
Here is how we do it.

- Select the **POSITION MONITOR** and
Check each **IRS** position **DEVIATION**.
If position deviation greater than **5NM**
REPORT DEFECT.

-Select the **TK/GS** position and
check each IR residual groundspeed.
If greater than or equal to **15 Kts**
REPORT ANY DEFECT.

To report defects:
Send an **MRM** code 3489X, where **X** is
the **IRU** unit (such as **1, 2, or 3**) and
include the following data field:

EXAMPLE of a possible message:
> **POS DEV 1.6 NM**
> **GS 16 KTS**
> **2.8 HRS IN NAV**

Where the time in **NAV** is the trip time.

---

10. ADIRS .... ALL OFF

---

11. ECAM STATUS .... CHECK

ALL abnormal ECAM items should be cleared. Contact
MAINTENANCE personnel if a maintenance status message displays.

---

12. TRANSPONDER CODE SELECTOR .... SET ZERO

---

13. DOOR EVACUATION SLIDES .... DISARMED

THIS IS BIG!

You **MUST** ensure that **ALL DOOR SLIDES** are
disarmed. If a cabin door is opened while it is armed, the
slide will deploy and there is the potential for some serious
injury. The **FLIGHT ATTENDANTS** are the big players
here, and they will initiate a call to you using the interphone telling you
that the doors are disarmed. If you are arriving at the gate and they haven't
called ... initiate a call to the them for door disarmed confirmation.

---

published by UNIVERSITY of TEMECULA PRESS, Inc.

CAPTAIN and FIRST OFFICER FLOWS
FINAL ITEMS for PARKING AT THE GATE

14. TRANSMISSION KEYS .... OFF

Consider shutting down any radios that might be transmitting or be a potential sources of unwanted radio clutter when the flight deck is not occupied.

1. Specifically shutdown any of the **TRANSMISSIONS BUTTONS** that might be active.

2. Place the **INT/RAD** key on **INT** to preclude the **O2 MASK** from being the culprit.

15. INTERPHONE VOLUME KNOBS .... FULL UP

16. LOUDSPEAKERS .... ON

17. CRTs .... DIM

18. PARKING CHECKLIST .... COMPLETE

19. REPORTS .... COMPLETE

It is ultimately the Captain's **RESPONSIBILITY** to see that all required maintenance, company reports, defect notifications, and ATC flight plan closure and terminations are properly filed... however, it is a joint operation by both the Captain and the First Officer. It is **ALWAYS** desirable for the crews to seek out and debrief the maintenance personnel on mechanical problems in addition to the written reports in the log book.

20. FINAL ITEMS checklist .... COMPLETE

Before you remove your flight bag, slide the seat forward and leave it in the full forward position. Unless otherwise directed, it is customary to leave the cockpit door open.

CLEAN UP YOUR MESS

and generally leave the flight station in the same or better condition than you found it.

SECURE THE COCKPIT FLOWS
IF OVERNIGHT or REMOVAL OF ELECTRICAL POWER

1. [C] PARKING BRAKE .... SET, PRESSURE NORMAL

When parking for a prolonged period, keep in mind that the accumulator will bleed off pressure over time. The flight manual says that it will take "more than" 12 hours before it can no longer "set the brakes". With that in mind, if we are leaving our shiny jet at some location for awhile ...
CHECK THAT THE WHEELS ARE CHOCKED.

> The **ONLY** confirmation that the parking brakes are **SET** is an indication of pressure on the **BRAKES and ACCUMULATOR PRESSURE** indicator.

2. [C] CREW OXYGEN SWITCH .... OFF

When parking for a prolonged period, keep in mind that the OXYGEN will bleed down if left on..

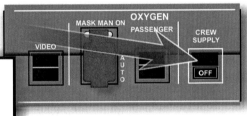

MINIMUM
**CREW OXYGEN PRESSURE
REQUIRED FOR DISPATCH:**

★ 850 PSI

Not only is it a good idea to let maintenance know if the O2 is getting low, it is essential to pass on this information.

3. [FO] NO SMOKING SIGNS .... OFF

4. [C,FO] CRTs .... OFF

WHEN APU NO LONGER NEEDED:

5. [FO] APU BLEED SWITCH .... OFF

6. [FO] APU MASTER SWITCH .... OFF

> ### CAUTION
> Wait **2 MINUTES** after the **APU AVAIL** light goes out to allow time for the closure of the **APU FLAP** before turning OFF the batteries.

6. [FO] BATTERY 1 and 2 SWITCHES .... OFF

GO TO LAYOVER HOTEL.

published by UNIVERSITY of TEMECULA PRESS, Inc.

APPENDIX

... mostly just the stuff that didn't seem to fit anywhere else.

THERE ARE
at least 10
SCREW UPS!

... any ordinary garden variety Airline pilot can experience!

This list is by no means all the ways that pilots can ruin an otherwise perfectly good afternoon. Even if I were to expand the list to include everything I could think of ... there is always some brilliant brain surgeon pretending to be a pilot out there that figures out a new way to **SCREW UP!**

For openers, here are three THRILLING
BRICK WALL
OPPORTUNITIES.

Here is the rule: **The SPEEDBRAKE lever must be in the RET position and DOWN position   prior to arming the ground spoilers**. Here is the problem. The autobrakes system can be armed with the PARK BRK selected ON, and further, autobraking is initiated by ground spoiler actuation, that is, the ground spoiler lever being moved "'*OUT OF THE DOWN DETENT*!" Should you start to taxi with the autobrake in **MAX** and pull the spoiler lever up to activate them for slowing the taxi or if the ground spoiler lever is out of the DOWN position when you select autobrakes to MAX ... the autobrakes may activate.

Look at it another way, if you have both **MAX BRAKING** selected, and the ground spoiler lever out the detent ... **WHAM**, the airplane will stop like right now! *OOOOOUCH, BRICK WALL!!!*

Along the same thread ... If during the flight control check ... and a good crew can do the check in a mere matter of seconds. Here is the problem: If the First Officer is too quick to go from **FLIGHT CONTROL CHECK** to the next item which is **ARM** the **AUTOBRAKES** ... Second opportunity to screw up the same way ... hitting a brick wall. Not pretty. Here's the rule:
Ensure that the ground spoilers are retracted
prior to arming the autobrakes.

My third "**BRICK WALL** goober involves the infamous **BSCU** ... clearly the most mis-understood system on the Airbus.

Here's the situation: released from guidance with a clearance to taxi, you push up the thrust levers and crank the steering tiller to start your turn and "**OMIGOSH**" you don't have any steering or brakes. Here's where the **BIG PROBLEM** occurs.

The Captain yells at the First Officer, "*Shut off the antiskid and nosewheel steering switch.*" All the while desperately pushing the toe brakes on the rudder pedals.

"**WHAM**"... *OOOOOPS!*" You hit the brick wall and depending on how much inertia the airplane has accumulated during the evolution, the "g" loading during the stop will make you an infamous target for derision with the flight attendants.

The rule for this: *Release the brake pedals before selecting the A/SKID & N/W STRG switch to OFF.*

published by UNIVERSITY of TEMECULA PRESS, Inc.

10 SCREWUPS continued

"KOZ" problem

The Captain decides that he will s-l-o-w-l-y and deliberately increase the thrust on take-off so as to avoid alarming the customers, or perhaps he is concerned that a potential icing situation warrants a smoother application of power than that supplied by the **FADEC**.

Here is the problem: This airplane has a designated **KOZ** (Keep Out Zone) where inlet scoop turbulence can interfere with engine spool-up and potentially result in an **ASYMMETRIC THRUST** situation.

Need I describe the panic as I imagine the nosewheel slewing to the side and the airplane looking at the approaching edge of the runway.
WHOOOPS!

TAIL STRIKE

Here is the **BIGGEST** cause for a **TAILSTRIKE** in this airplane.

DISCUSSION: The marvelous sidestick is an incredible tool. However, it has some quirks. One of which is the fact that if **BOTH** sticks are moved simultaneously, it will apply the **ALGEBRAIC SUM** of the inputs of both sticks.

If both pilots "get on the stick" the situation becomes quickly unmanageable.

THE RULE: If the transfer of the airplane is made prior to take-off, the Captain **SHOULD** make the following statements: "*You have the airplane, the parking brake is set/released*".

HERE'S AN ALTITUDE BUSTER.

Ever on the lookout for ways to "stay ahead of the airplane", when passing **QNE** ... a quick witted steely eyed airline professional may decide to "preselect" the destination altimeter setting. That way, when the descent is started, a mere flick of the switch and the **QNH** will already be there waiting to be selected.

BUT ... and here is a problem that is repeated every day in cockpits around the world ... the **STD (29.92/1013)** never gets selected and the airplane levels off at the altitude represented by the **QNH** of the destination airport.

Let's look at some numbers here. Say destination **QNH** is **28.00**. If we preset **28.00** and left it in the barometric selector window instead of selecting **STD (29.92)** at **QNE**. How would that affect our cruise altitude?

Answer, we would level off about *2,000 feet HIGH*! *WHOOPS!*

ALPHA PROTECTION AT ALTITUDE. YIPE!

The **EXPED** switch was designed to make life easy for the pilot who gets **HIGH** on descent all the time, and in the descent function, its major usefulness is doing the "**HIGH DIVE**" or **EMERGENCY DESCENT**. *Some major airlines restrict its use to the descent function only* ... and here is why.

SYSTEM REVIEW: Depressing the **EXPED** switch will result in the airplane making the most expeditious descent or climb to the altitude selected on the **FCU**. During climbs, it will retard the speed to the "**GREEN DOT**".

Here is the problem: **GREEN DOT** airspeed target numbers above about 25,000 feet do **NOT** provide enough **MACH** number ... and airplane will get too slow and trigger **A.PROT** (Alpha protection).

HERE'S THE RULE: *EXP CLB not recommended above FL 250.*

MORE SCREWUPS continued

"APPCH" button PROBLEM

Here is the situation: You are all set up for an autoland right down to **CAT III** minima. But, no sweat, you have everything all ready and working smoothly. Then, at **GLIDESLOPE** capture, the **AUTOPILOT** disengages and the **FLIGHT DIRECTORS** revert to some goofy **HDG-V/S** mode. What is happening???

The Problem: You armed the **ILS APPR** mode above 8,000 feet **AGL**. Radio signals are not available above this altitude, and with the **APPR** button armed, the autopilot disengages at glideslope capture and Flight Directors revert to

TAKE-OFF TOGA LK

Situation: You have just taken off and the tower advises, "*You have crossing traffic at twelve o'clock, maintain your present altitude*".

You depress the **VERTICAL SPEED** selector on the **FCU** and the nose comes over, the airplane levels off and since the airspeed is still in **TOGA**, the overspeed red bricks drop really quickly on the speed tape. Your immediate response is to grab the thrust levers and pull them to **IDLE**.

Tower calls, "*Continue your climb*". You push the thrust levers to the **CL** notch, look at the **ECAM** and see that it is annunciated and the engine N1 looks about right.

The next thing you notice is the "**A.FLOOR**" annunciated, followed almost immediately by "**TOGA LK**" and the thrust coming on in a powerful rush.

Before we take this to its ultimate extreme, here is the problem: when you pulled the thrust levers to **IDLE**, the **A/THR** deselected. Placing the thrust levers to the CL detent did not engage the autothrottles and you were trying to fly at some derated thrust setting. Eventually the airplane went into an **ALPHA PROT** protection mode and **TOGA LK** ensued.

To restore normal operation, you will need to do a couple of things. Here is a recommended solution.

1. **PUSH** the thrust levers to the **TOGA** detent to match the power setting.

2. Depress the **A/THR** switch "**OFF**" and then "**ON**" to deselect the **TOGA LK**.

3. Pull the thrust levers back into the **CL** detent.

NOSEWHEEL TAXI PROBLEM

There are two characteristics of the Nosewheel steering that we have to get used to:

- **THE NOSE GEAR SLANTS FORWARD.** This geometry means that as the wheel is rotated, less and less of the upper wheel is in contact with the surface and the frictional footprint is increasingly diminished. That means that the nosewheel has a greater tendency to slip the more the steering tiller is cranked over.

- **THE VARIABLE RATE FEATURE** that increases the rate that the wheel turns proportionally with the tiller displacement. This means that the more you turn the tiller, the faster the wheel turns.

Here's the problem: If you are operating in slippery or wet runway conditions, and the nosewheel starts to slip ... there is a tendency to "increase" steering tiller displacement to compensate. That is exactly the wrong response as it exacerbates the problem.

Solution: Slow down and back off instead of increasing the demand.

I have a bunch more ... and I think you can identify a few of your own ... but let's call it a day and wrap this thing up.

published by UNIVERSITY of TEMECULA PRESS, Inc.

LIMITING AIRSPEEDS and ALTITUDES

COCKPIT WINDOW OPEN

MAXIMUM	200 KIAS

DESIGN MANEUVERING SPEED CAUTION -VA

CAUTION

RAPIDLY ALTERNATING LARGE RUDDER APPLICATIONS IN COMBINATION WITH LARGE SIDESLIP ANGLES MAY RESULT IN STRUCTURAL FAILURE AT ANY SPEED, EVEN BELOW VA.

FLAPS/SLATS EXTENDED SPEEDS - VFE (KIAS)

These are the absolute MAXIMUM DO NOT EXCEED speeds. If they are exceeded, a MAINTENANCE REPORT and INSPECTION IS REQUIRED!

FLAPS	1	1 + F	2	3	FULL
VFE	230	215	200	185	177

FLAPS/SLATS EXTENDED SPEEDS - VFE-10 (KIAS)

To preclude a FLAP OVERSPEED problem, these are the OPERATING MAXIMUMS promulgated for your use. Treat these as ABSOLUTES. These are the numbers you should memorize and use.

FLAPS	1	1 + F	2	3	FULL
VFE-10 knots (KIAS)	★ 220	★ 205	★ 190	★ 175	★ 167

LANDING GEAR SPEEDS - VLO/VLE

LANDING GEAR CANNOT be extended at airspeeds greater that 260 kias. At airspeeds greater than 260 kias, a hydraulic safety valve closes to CUTOFF to the hydraulic supply to the landing gear.

RETRACTION (GEAR COMING UP)	★ 220
EXTENTION (GEAR GOING DOWN)	★ 250
EXTENDED (OPERATING WITH GEAR DOWN)	280 KIAS/.67 MACH

MAXIMUM OPERATING SPEED - VMM/VMO

ABSOLUTE MAXIMUM OPERATING SPEED	★ 350 KIAS/.82 Mach

MAXIMUM TIRE SPEED

TIRES (restricted NOT maximum)	195 Knots groundspeed

MAXIMUM ALTITUDE (Pressure)

TAKEOFF and LANDING	9,200 feet
OPERATING	★ 39,100 feet

MAXIMUM OPERATING ALTITUDE

FLAPS	★ 20,000 feet MSL
GEAR	25,000 feet MSL

QUICK and *DIRTY* CHARTS for *ESTIMATES ONLY.*

USE THIS CHART TO GUESS YOUR FLIGHT PATH ANGLE / DISTANCE .

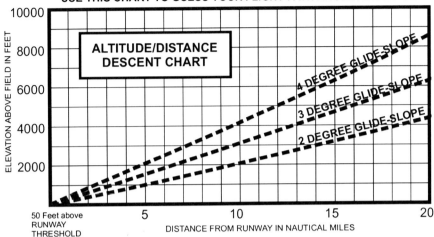

RULES OF THUMB:
Quick and "pretty close" ways to evaluate your progress along the 3 degree glideslope.

ALTITUDE = (DISTANCE TO GO) X 300.

DISTANCE TO GO = ALTITUDE divided by 300.

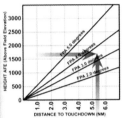

SAMPLE:
If you are 5.4 NM from touchdown, and at 1600 feet (AFE), then the FPA is about 3.5 degrees

 indicates a required memory item.

MAX WEIGHTS

MAX CERTIFIED ALTITUDE

★ 39,100 feet

	A320	**A319**
	GROSS WEIGHT (LBS X 1000 #)	
TAXI	170.6	167.3
TAKE-OFF	169.7	166.4
LANDING	★ 142.2	★ 137.7
ZERO FUEL	134.4	128.9

MAX WIND

	A320		**A319**	
WIND DIRECTION	**TAKEOFF**	**LANDING**	**TAKEOFF**	**LANDING**
Crosswind	★ 29 Kts	★ 33 Kts	★ 29 Kts	★ 33 Kts
Crosswind with GUSTS	38 Kts		38 Kts	
Tailwind	★ 15 Kts	★ 10 Kts	★ 10 Kts	

These are the maximum demonstrated crosswinds with flight controls in normal and direct law (with or without yaw damper).

AUTO-PILOT ENGAGED MIN HEIGHTs

Max **PITCH** allowed for auto-pilot *engagement* is **18° NOSE UP**

After take-off/go-around (*if SRS is indicated*)	★	100 feet AGL
Enroute	★	500 feet AGL
NON-ILS approaches	★	50 feet below DA
NON-Autoland ILS with CAT I	★	160 feet AGL
NON-Autoland ILS with CAT 2/3	★	80 feet AGL
Autoland (one or two autopilots	★	ROLLOUT/TAXI speed

NON-ILS with ENGINE OUT

On single engine **Non-ILS** approach, use of the autopilot is prohibited inside of the **FAF/FAP** when using **FINAL APP** or **NAV** modes for lateral course guidance. Use of the Flight Director is OK.

ILS WARNING
DO NOT ARM the **ILS APPR** mode
above **8,000** AGL.

OPEN DESCENT during VISUAL

During a **VISUAL APPROACH**,
the use of **OP DES** is *PROHIBITED*:
- inside the **FAF**, or
- below **1,500 Feet AGL**.

Restricted use of **TRK-FPA mode**

TRK-FPA is *NOT AUTHORIZED* for **TAKE-OFF**, and
MUST BE DESELECTED during **GO-AROUND**.

NAV note

NAV may be used between the **FAF/FAP** and the **MAP** (Missed Approach Point) ***ONLY*** when flying an **APPROACH NAV** (Line selectable non-precision) procedure . On any other type of non-precision, non-selectable instrument approach, the airplane ***MUST BE OUT OF*** NAV before crossing the **FAF/FAP**.

QUICK and DIRTY
CHARTS for ESTIMATES ONLY.

V SPEEDS guess chart

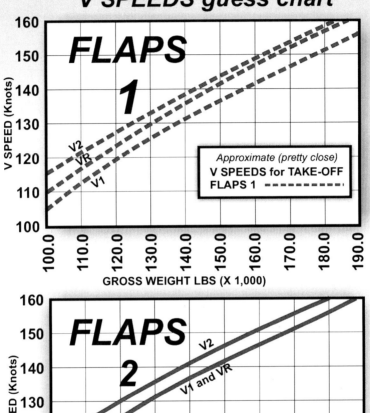

FLAPS 1

V SPEED (Knots)

V2
VR
V1

Approximate (pretty close)
V SPEEDS for TAKE-OFF
FLAPS 1 ---------------

GROSS WEIGHT LBS (X 1,000)

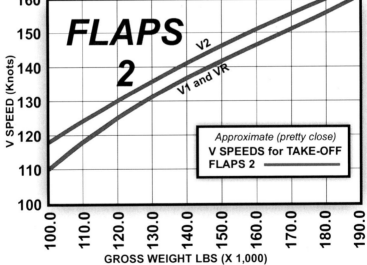

FLAPS 2

V SPEED (Knots)

V2
V1 and VR

Approximate (pretty close)
V SPEEDS for TAKE-OFF
FLAPS 2 —————

GROSS WEIGHT LBS (X 1,000)

SAMPLE:
Flaps 2
136,000 Lb takeoff weight,
V1 and VR is about 132 Kts,
V2 is about 139 Kts.

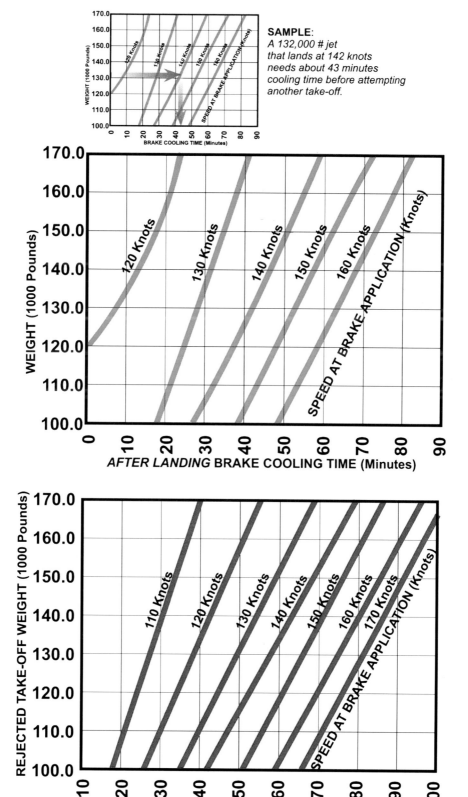

SAMPLE:
A 132,000 # jet that lands at 142 knots needs about 43 minutes cooling time before attempting another take-off.

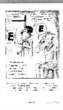

AIRPLANE PICTURES

Digital screen-shot images
created from flight simulation sources.

Presented on Mike Ray's
FINE ART AMERICA website

Check out the link on Mike Ray's website
www.UTEM.com